VB Rose™

Volume 11

Banri Hidaka

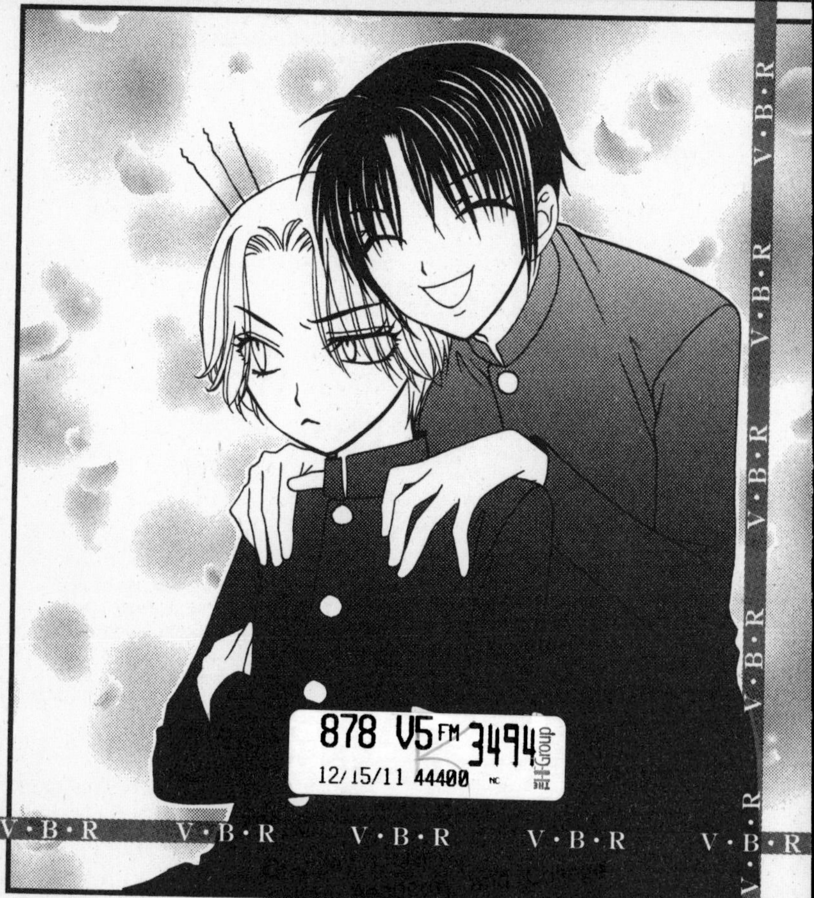
V·B·R

V.B. Rose Volume 11
Created by Banri Hidaka

Translation - Lori Riser
English Adaptation - Hope Donovan
Copy Editor - Daniella Orihuela-Gruber
Retouch and Lettering - Star Print Brokers
Production Artist - Rui Kyo
Graphic Designer - Louis Csontos

Editor - Lillian Diaz-Przybyl
Print Production Manager - Lucas Rivera
Managing Editor - Vy Nguyen
Senior Designer - Louis Csontos
Art Director - Al-Insan Lashley
Director of Sales and Manufacturing - Allyson De Simone
Associate Publisher - Marco F. Pavia
President and C.O.O. - John Parker
C.E.O. and Chief Creative Officer - Stu Levy

A 🔲 TOKYOPOP® Manga

TOKYOPOP and 🔲 are trademarks or registered trademarks of TOKYOPOP Inc.

TOKYOPOP Inc.
5900 Wilshire Blvd. Suite 2000
Los Angeles, CA 90036

E-mail: info@TOKYOPOP.com
Come visit us online at www.TOKYOPOP.com

ISBN: 978-1-4278-1289-6

First TOKYOPOP printing: January 2011
10 9 8 7 6 5 4 3 2 1
Printed in the USA

V.B. Rose

Volume 11
By Banri Hidaka

HAMBURG // LONDON // LOS ANGELES // TOKYO

Contents

.B. Rose

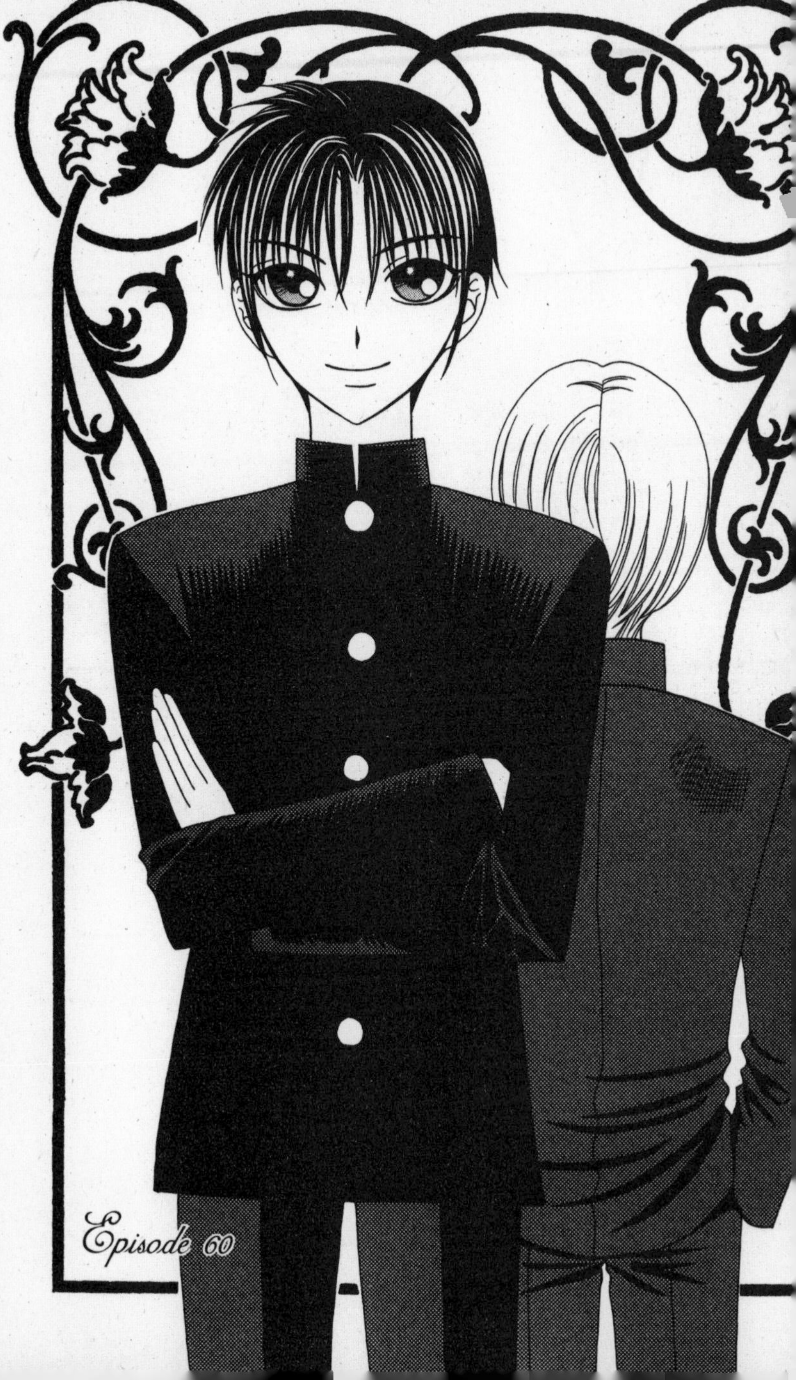
Episode 60

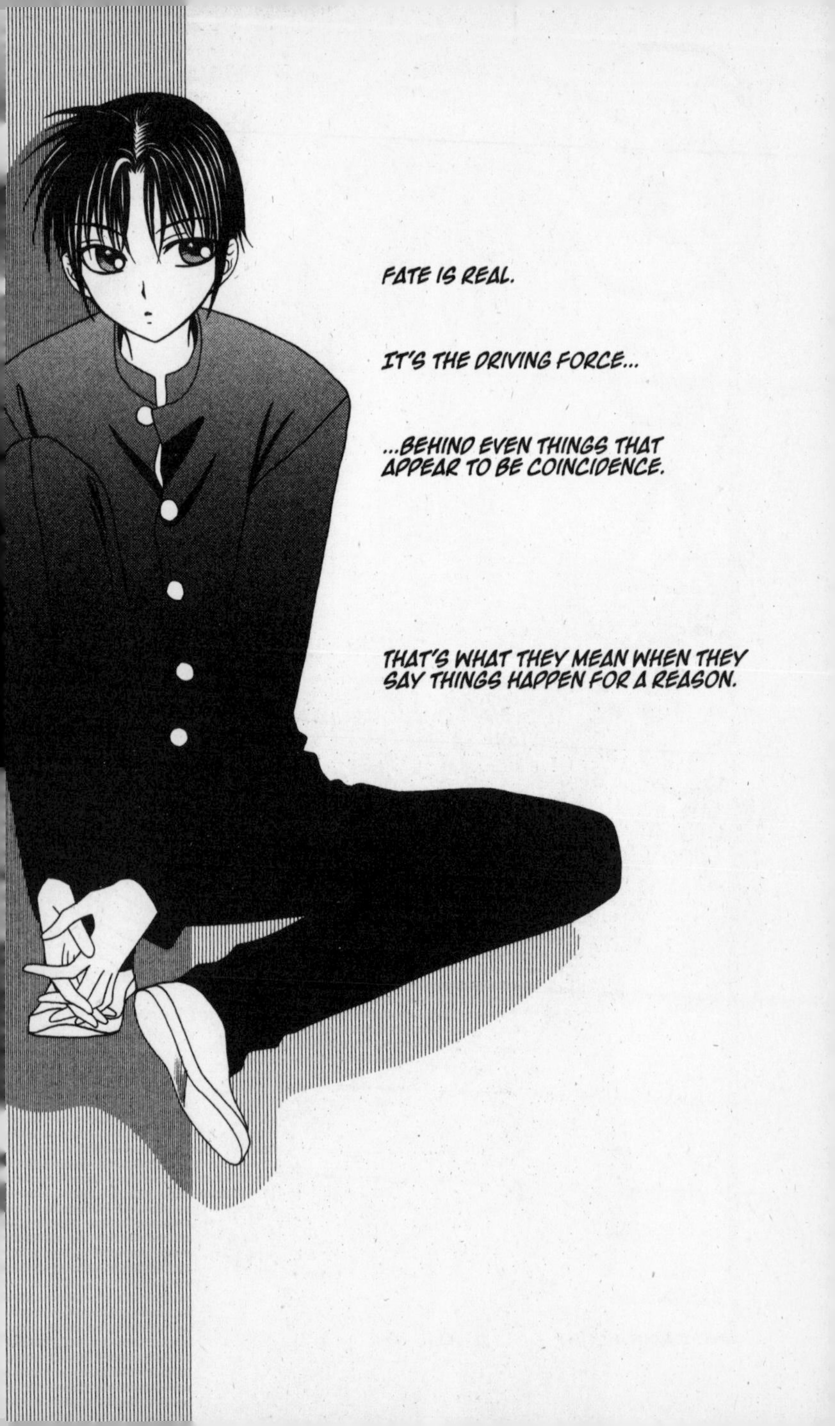
FATE IS REAL.
IT'S THE DRIVING FORCE...
...BEHIND EVEN THINGS THAT APPEAR TO BE COINCIDENCE.
THAT'S WHAT THEY MEAN WHEN THEY SAY THINGS HAPPEN FOR A REASON.

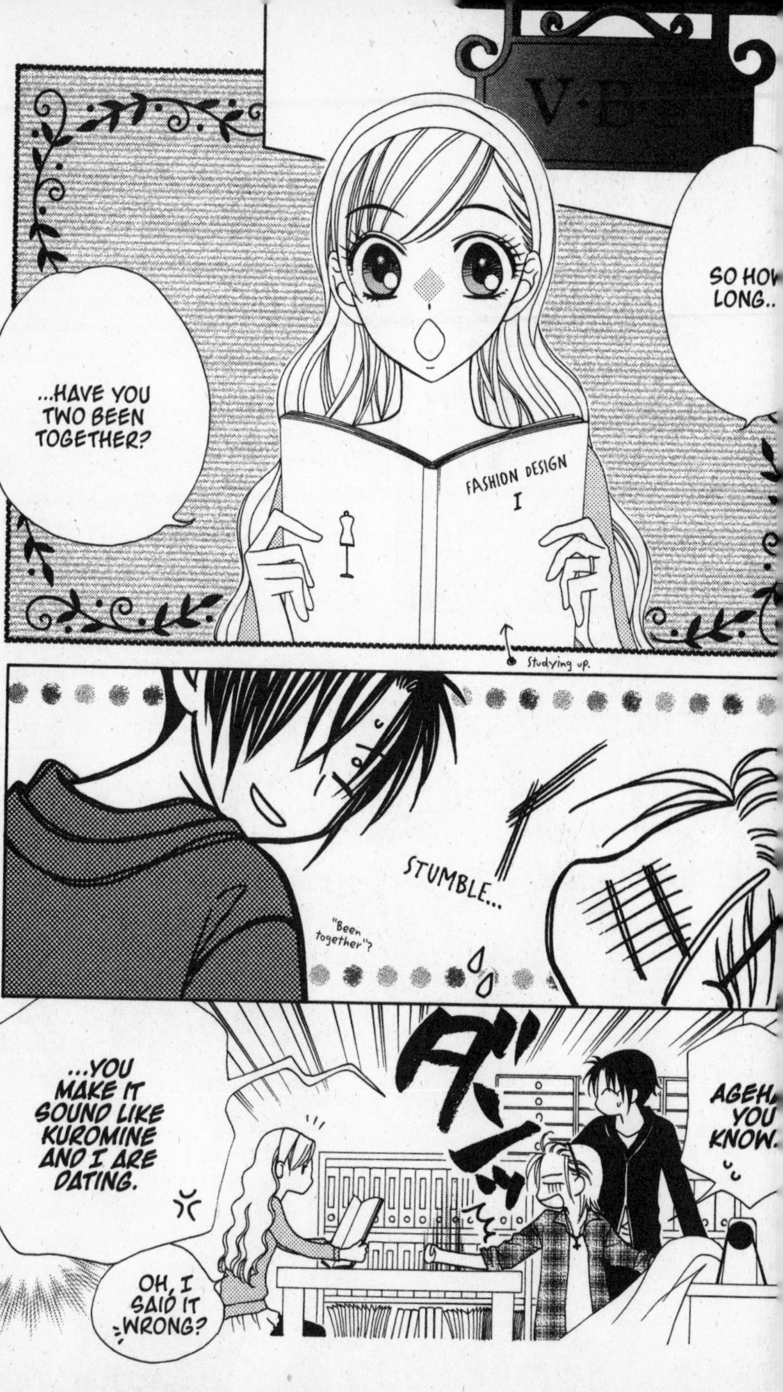
SO HOW LONG..
...HAVE YOU TWO BEEN TOGETHER?
FASHION DESIGN I
Studying up.
STUMBLE...
"Been together"?
AGEH YOU KNOW.
...YOU MAKE IT SOUND LIKE KUROMINE AND I ARE DATING.
OH, I SAID IT WRONG?

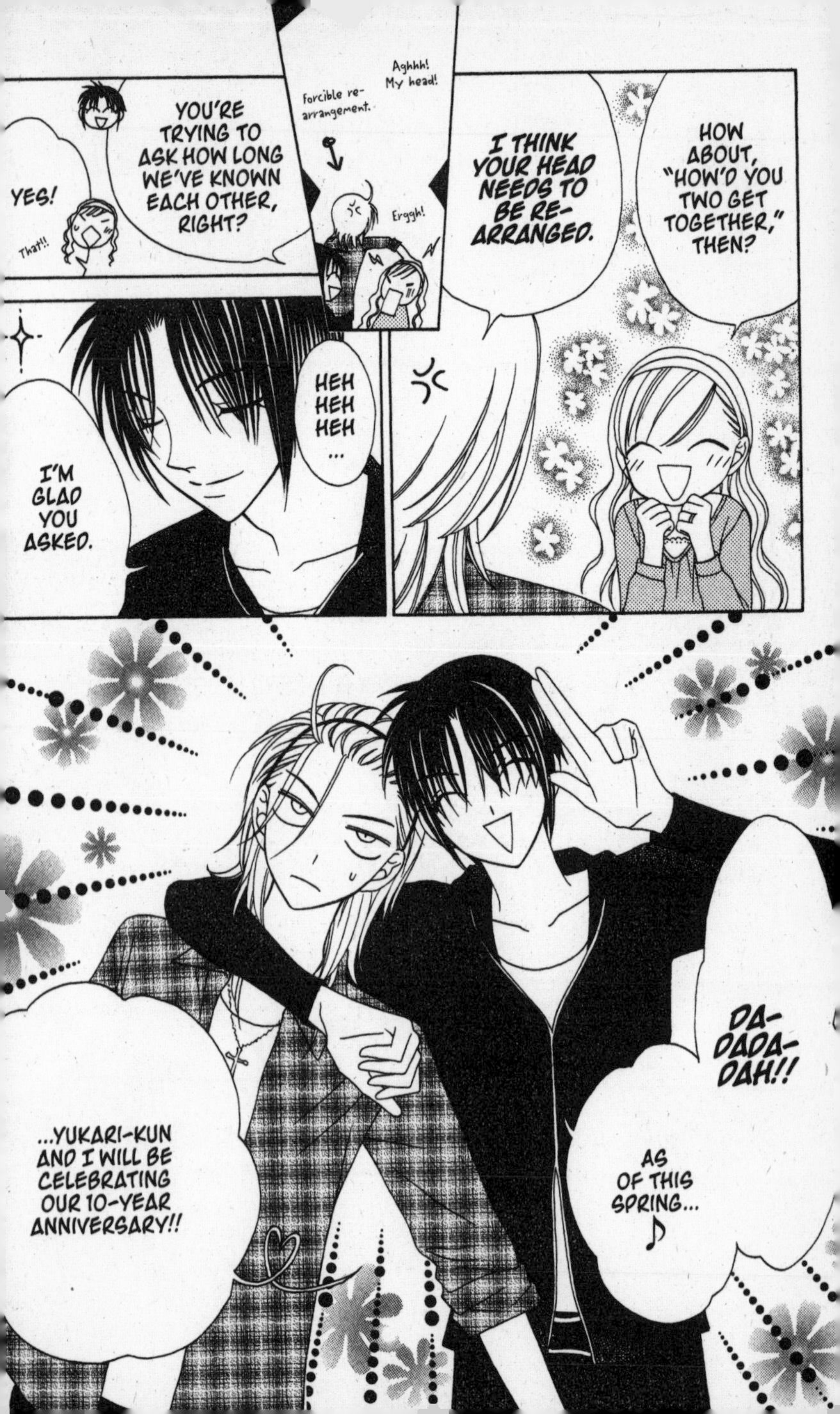

HOW ABOUT, "HOW'D YOU TWO GET TOGETHER," THEN?
I THINK YOUR HEAD NEEDS TO BE RE-ARRANGED.
Aghhh! My head!
Forcible re-arrangement.
Erggh!
YOU'RE TRYING TO ASK HOW LONG WE'VE KNOWN EACH OTHER, RIGHT?
YES!
That!!
HEH HEH HEH ...
I'M GLAD YOU ASKED.
DA-DADA-DAH!!
AS OF THIS SPRING... ♪
...YUKARI-KUN AND I WILL BE CELEBRATING OUR 10-YEAR ANNIVERSARY!!

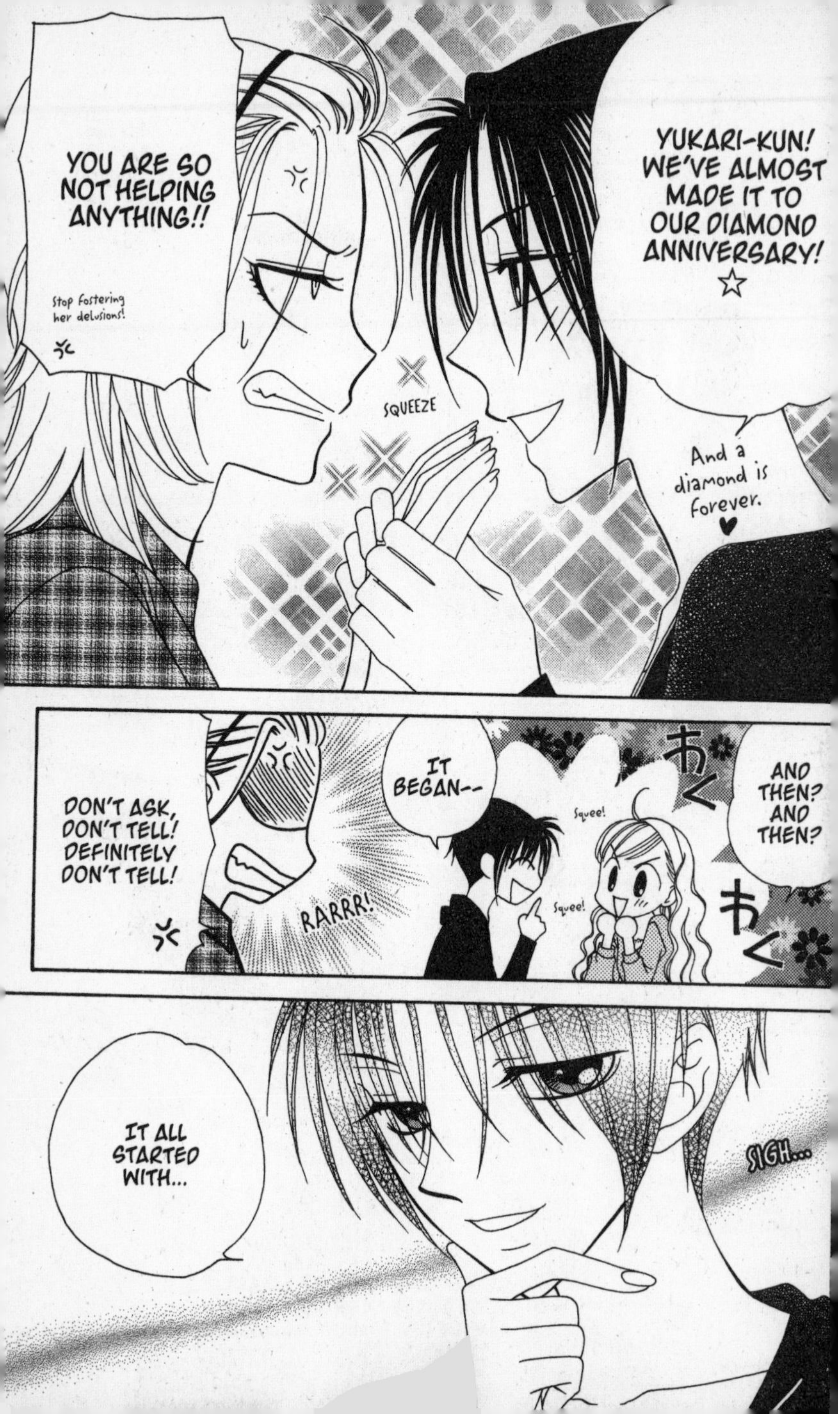
YUKARI-KUN! WE'VE ALMOST MADE IT TO OUR DIAMOND ANNIVERSARY! ☆
And a diamond is forever. ♥
SQUEEZE
YOU ARE SO NOT HELPING ANYTHING!!
Stop fostering her delusions!
AND THEN? AND THEN?
わくわく
Squee!
Squee!
IT BEGAN--
RARRR!
DON'T ASK, DON'T TELL! DEFINITELY DON'T TELL!
SIGH...
IT ALL STARTED WITH...

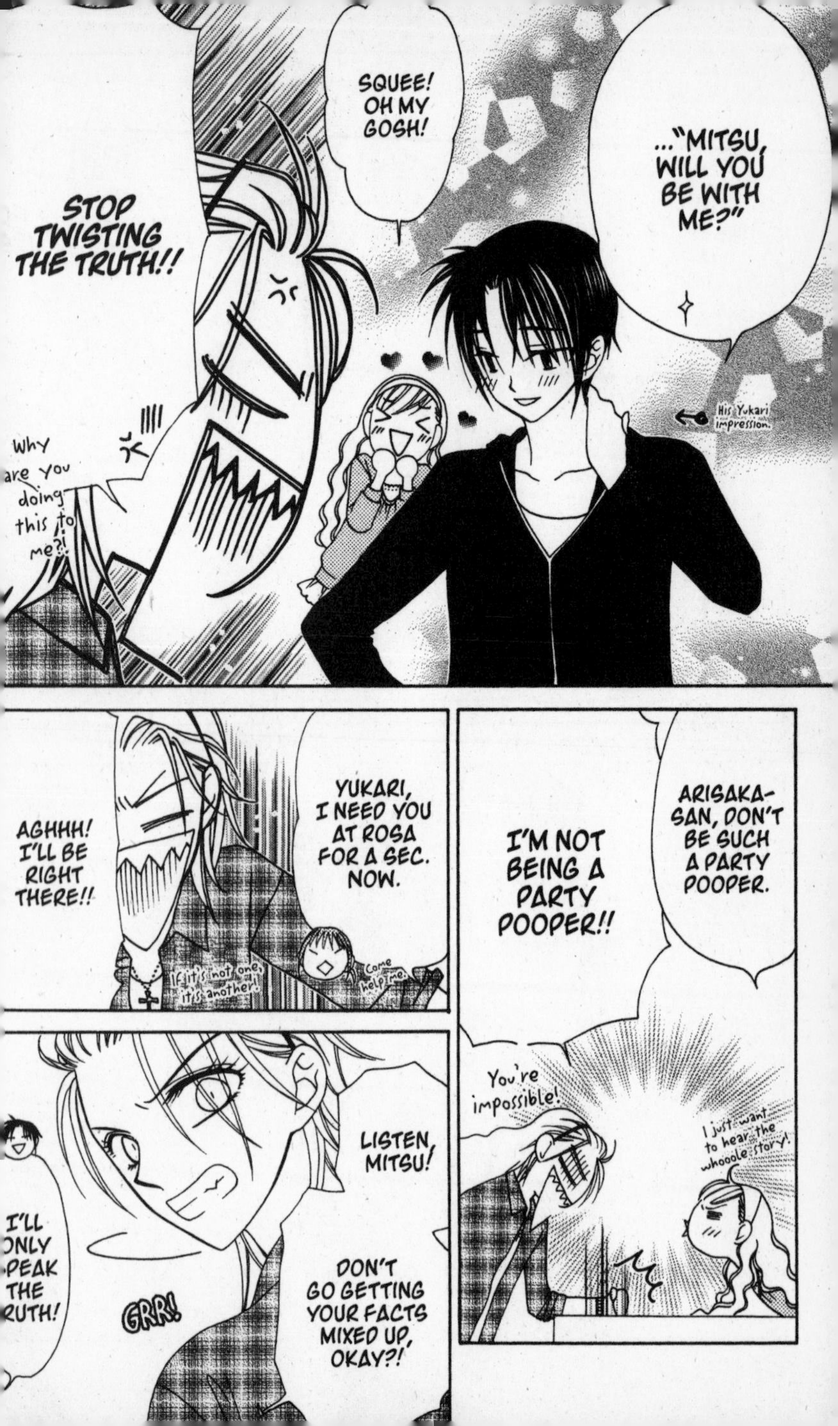
..."MITSU, WILL YOU BE WITH ME?"
His Yukari impression.
SQUEE! OH MY GOSH!
STOP TWISTING THE TRUTH!!
Why are you doing this to me?!
ARISAKA-SAN, DON'T BE SUCH A PARTY POOPER.
I'M NOT BEING A PARTY POOPER!!
You're impossible!
I just want to hear the whooole story!
YUKARI, I NEED YOU AT ROSA FOR A SEC. NOW.
Come help me.
AGHHH! I'LL BE RIGHT THERE!!
If it's not one, it's another!
LISTEN, MITSU!
DON'T GO GETTING YOUR FACTS MIXED UP, OKAY?!
GRR!
I'LL NLY PEAK THE RUTH!

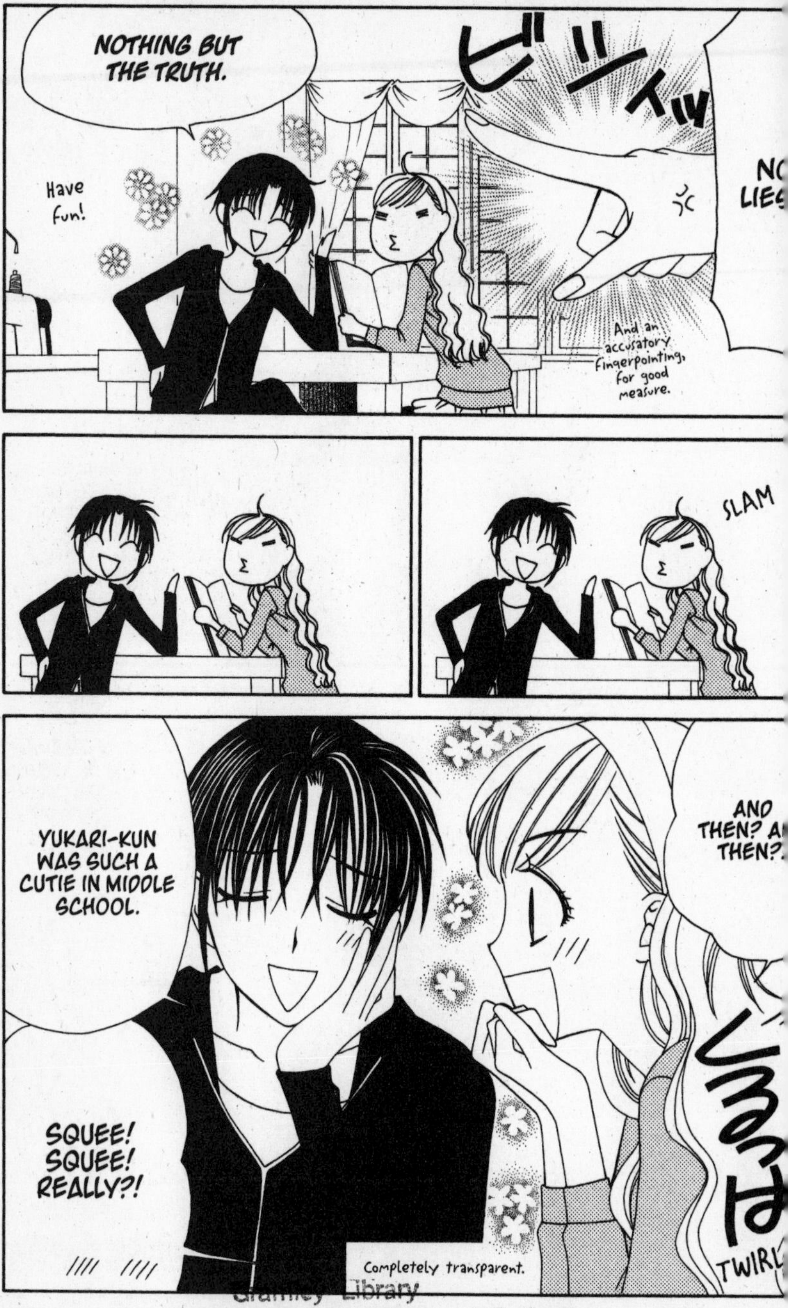
LIES
NOTHING BUT THE TRUTH.
Have fun!
And an accusatory fingerpointing, for good measure.
SLAM
AND THEN?
TWIRL
YUKARI-KUN WAS SUCH A CUTIE IN MIDDLE SCHOOL.
SQUEE! SQUEE! REALLY?!
Completely transparent.

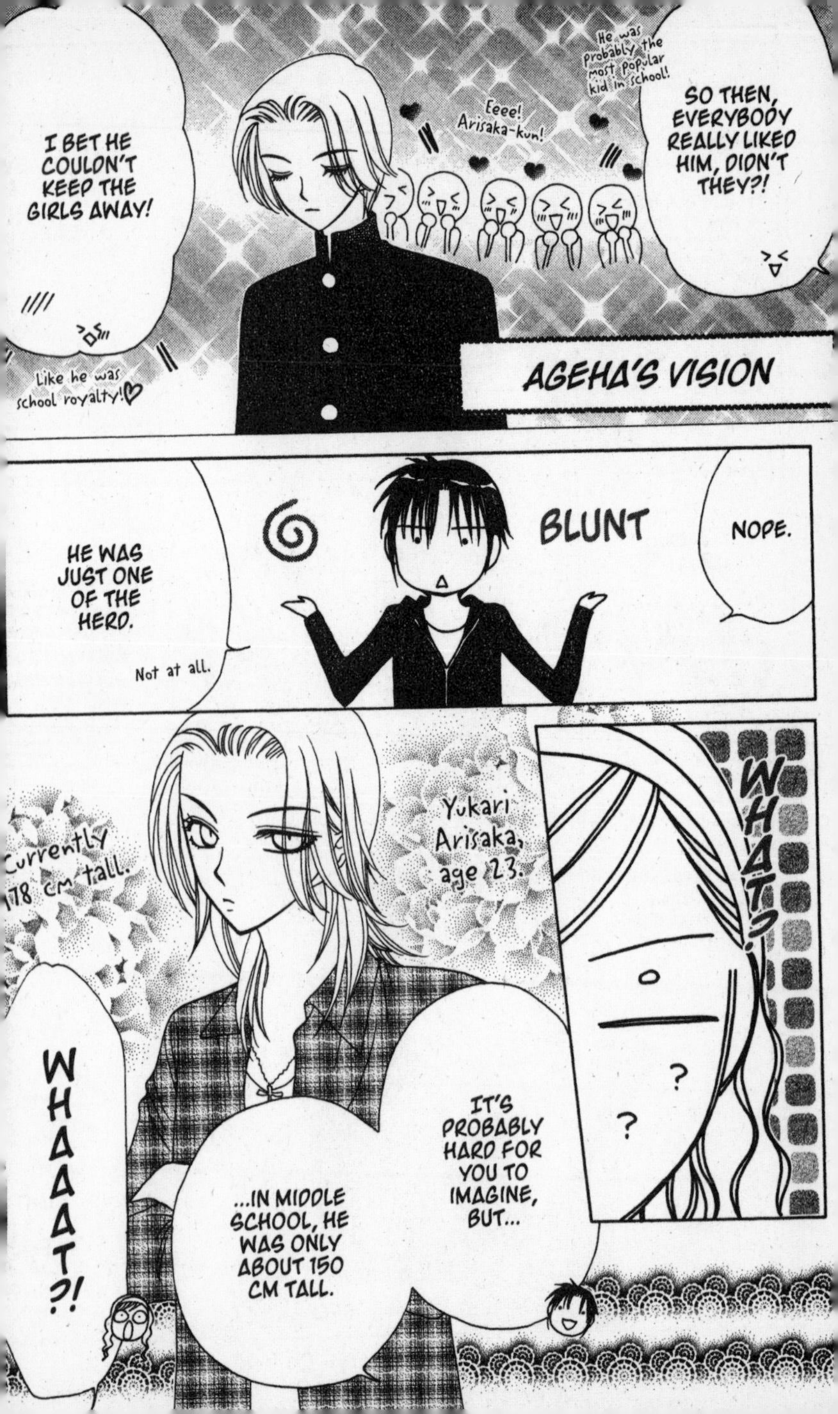
SO THEN, EVERYBODY REALLY LIKED HIM, DIDN'T THEY?!
He was probably the most popular kid in school!
Eeee! Arisaka-kun!
I BET HE COULDN'T KEEP THE GIRLS AWAY!
Like he was school royalty!
AGEHA'S VISION
NOPE.
BLUNT
HE WAS JUST ONE OF THE HERD.
Not at all.
WHAT?
?
?
Yukari Arisaka, age 23.
Currently 178 cm tall.
IT'S PROBABLY HARD FOR YOU TO IMAGINE, BUT...
...IN MIDDLE SCHOOL, HE WAS ONLY ABOUT 150 CM TALL.
WHAAAAT?!

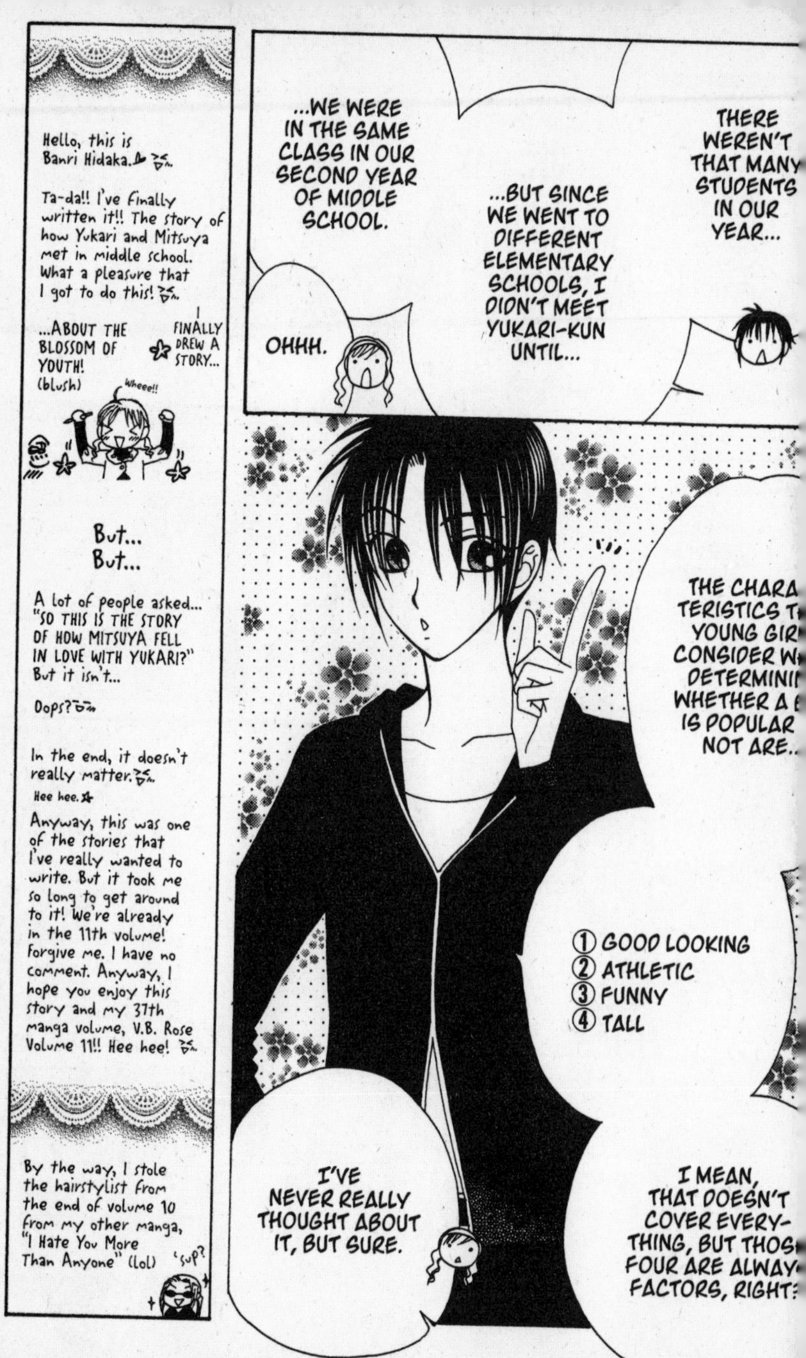
THERE WEREN'T THAT MANY STUDENTS IN OUR YEAR...
...BUT SINCE WE WENT TO DIFFERENT ELEMENTARY SCHOOLS, I DIDN'T MEET YUKARI-KUN UNTIL...
...WE WERE IN THE SAME CLASS IN OUR SECOND YEAR OF MIDDLE SCHOOL.
OHHH.
THE CHARA TERISTICS T YOUNG GIR CONSIDER W DETERMINI WHETHER A IS POPULAR NOT ARE...
① GOOD LOOKING
② ATHLETIC
③ FUNNY
④ TALL
I MEAN, THAT DOESN'T COVER EVERY-THING, BUT THOS FOUR ARE ALWAY FACTORS, RIGHT?
I'VE NEVER REALLY THOUGHT ABOUT IT, BUT SURE.

Hello, this is Banri Hidaka.

Ta-da!! I've finally written it!! The story of how Yukari and Mitsuya met in middle school. What a pleasure that I got to do this!

...ABOUT THE BLOSSOM OF YOUTH! (blush)

I FINALLY DREW A STORY...

Wheee!!

But...
But...

A lot of people asked... "SO THIS IS THE STORY OF HOW MITSUYA FELL IN LOVE WITH YUKARI?" But it isn't...

Oops?

In the end, it doesn't really matter.

Hee hee.

Anyway, this was one of the stories that I've really wanted to write. But it took me so long to get around to it! We're already in the 11th volume! Forgive me. I have no comment. Anyway, I hope you enjoy this story and my 37th manga volume, V.B. Rose Volume 11!! Hee hee!

By the way, I stole the hairstylist from the end of volume 10 from my other manga, "I Hate You More Than Anyone" (lol)

'sup?

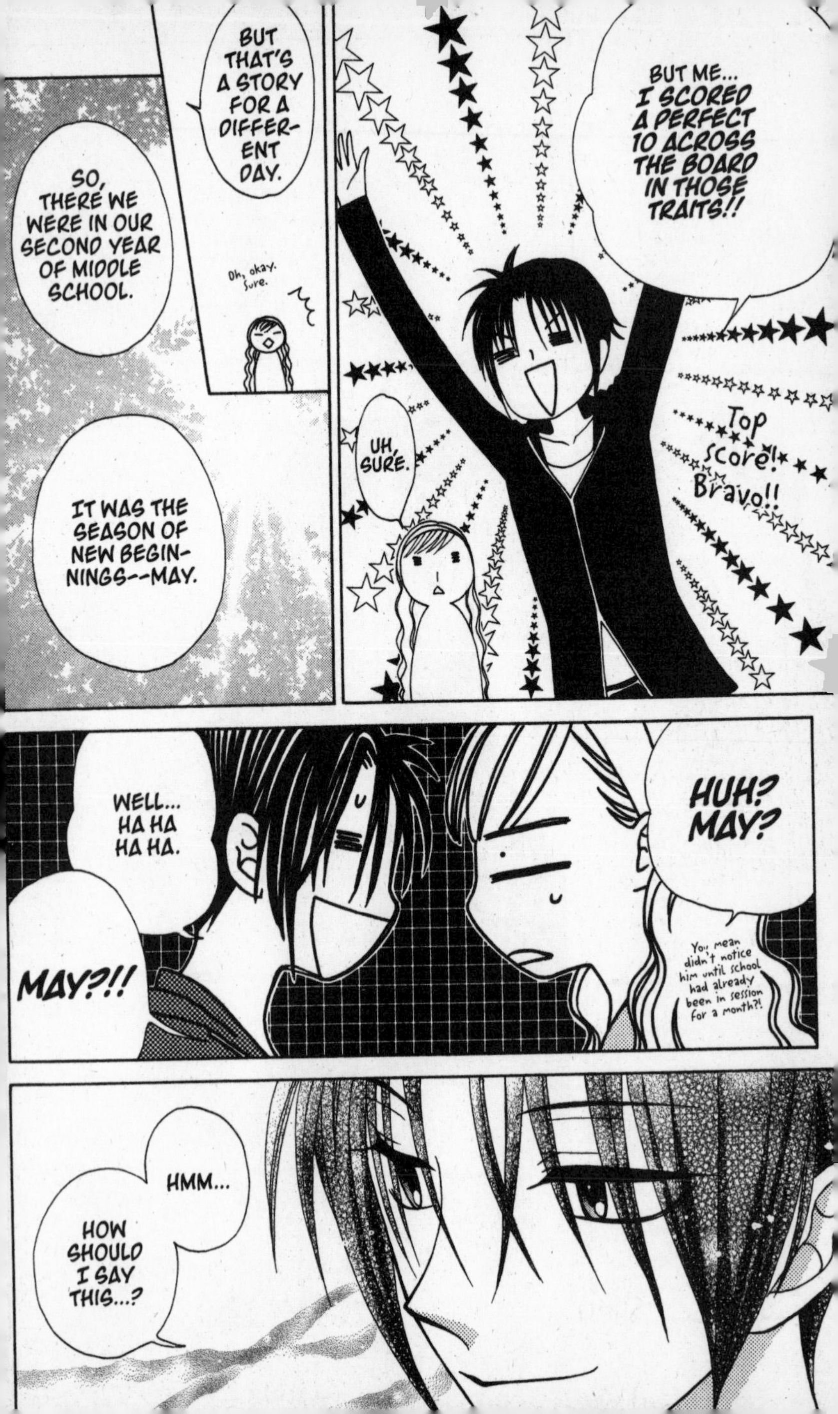
BUT ME... I SCORED A PERFECT 10 ACROSS THE BOARD IN THOSE TRAITS!!
Top score!! Bravo!!
UH, SURE.
BUT THAT'S A STORY FOR A DIFFERENT DAY.
Oh, okay. Sure.
SO, THERE WE WERE IN OUR SECOND YEAR OF MIDDLE SCHOOL.
IT WAS THE SEASON OF NEW BEGINNINGS--MAY.
HUH? MAY?
You mean didn't notice him until school had already been in session for a month?!
WELL... HA HA HA HA.
MAY?!!
HMM...
HOW SHOULD I SAY THIS...?

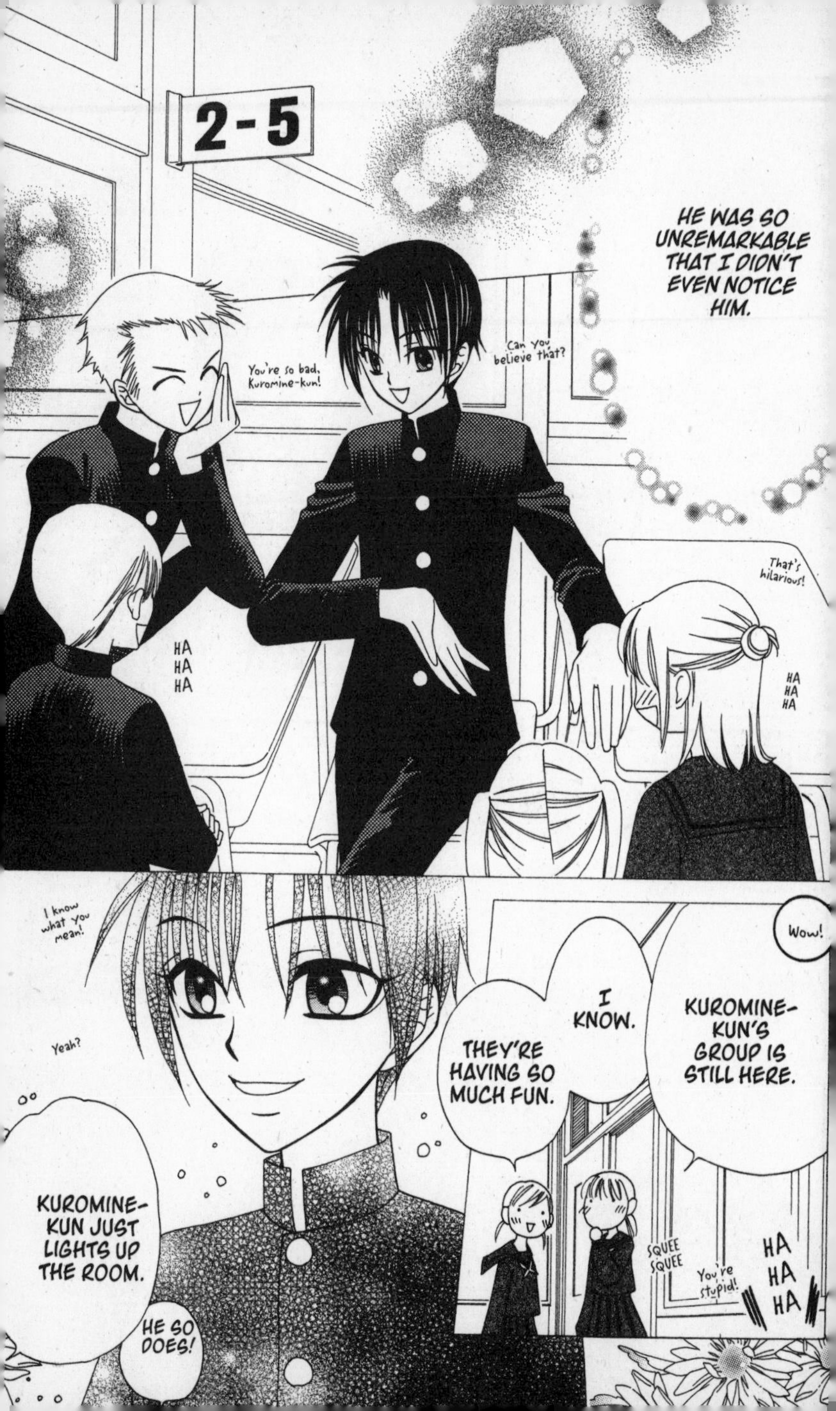

2-5
HE WAS SO UNREMARKABLE THAT I DIDN'T EVEN NOTICE HIM.
That's hilarious!
HA HA HA
Can you believe that?
You're so bad, Kuromine-kun!
HA HA HA
Wow!
KUROMINE-KUN'S GROUP IS STILL HERE.
I KNOW.
THEY'RE HAVING SO MUCH FUN.
HA HA HA
You're stupid!
SQUEE SQUEE
I know what you mean!
Yeah?
KUROMINE-KUN JUST LIGHTS UP THE ROOM.
HE SO DOES!

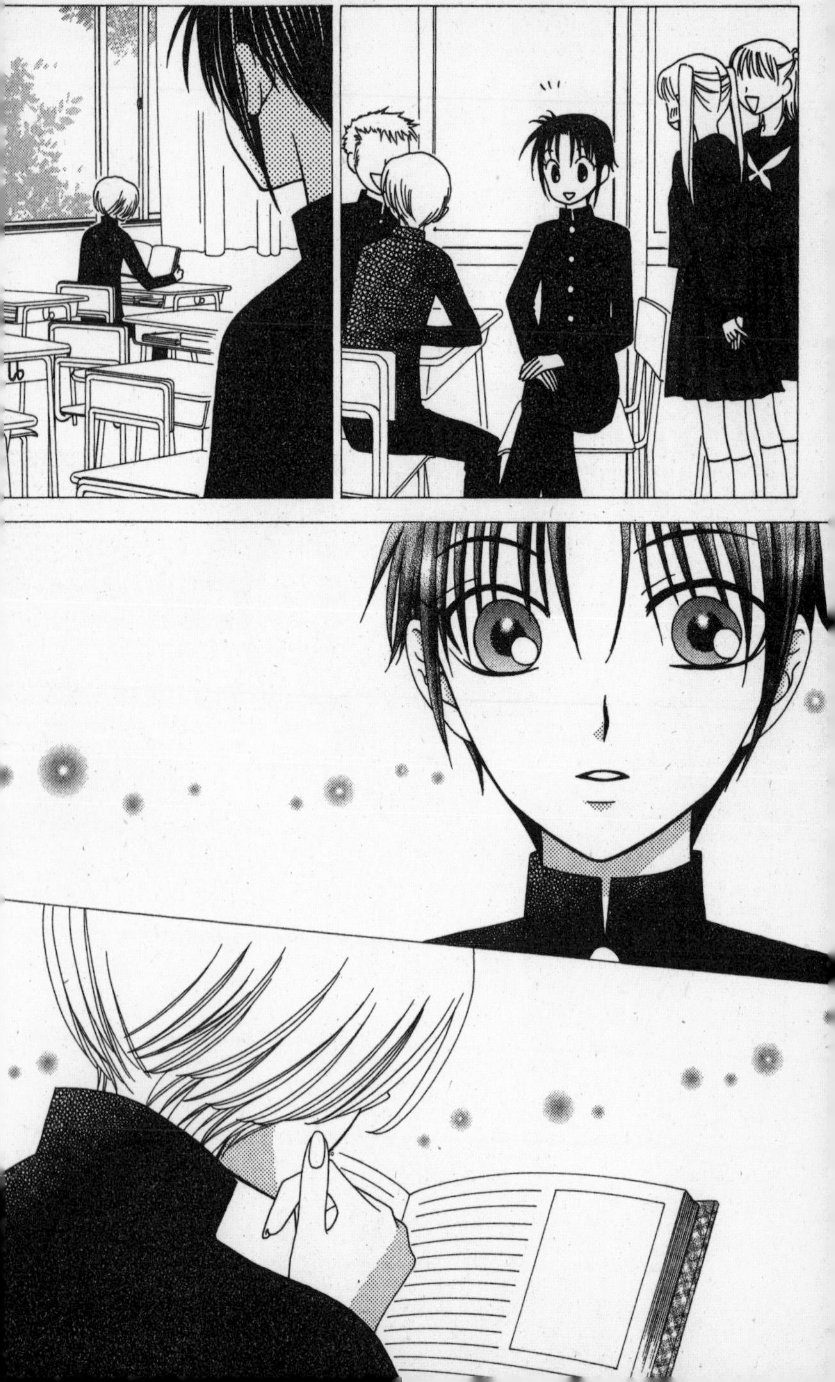

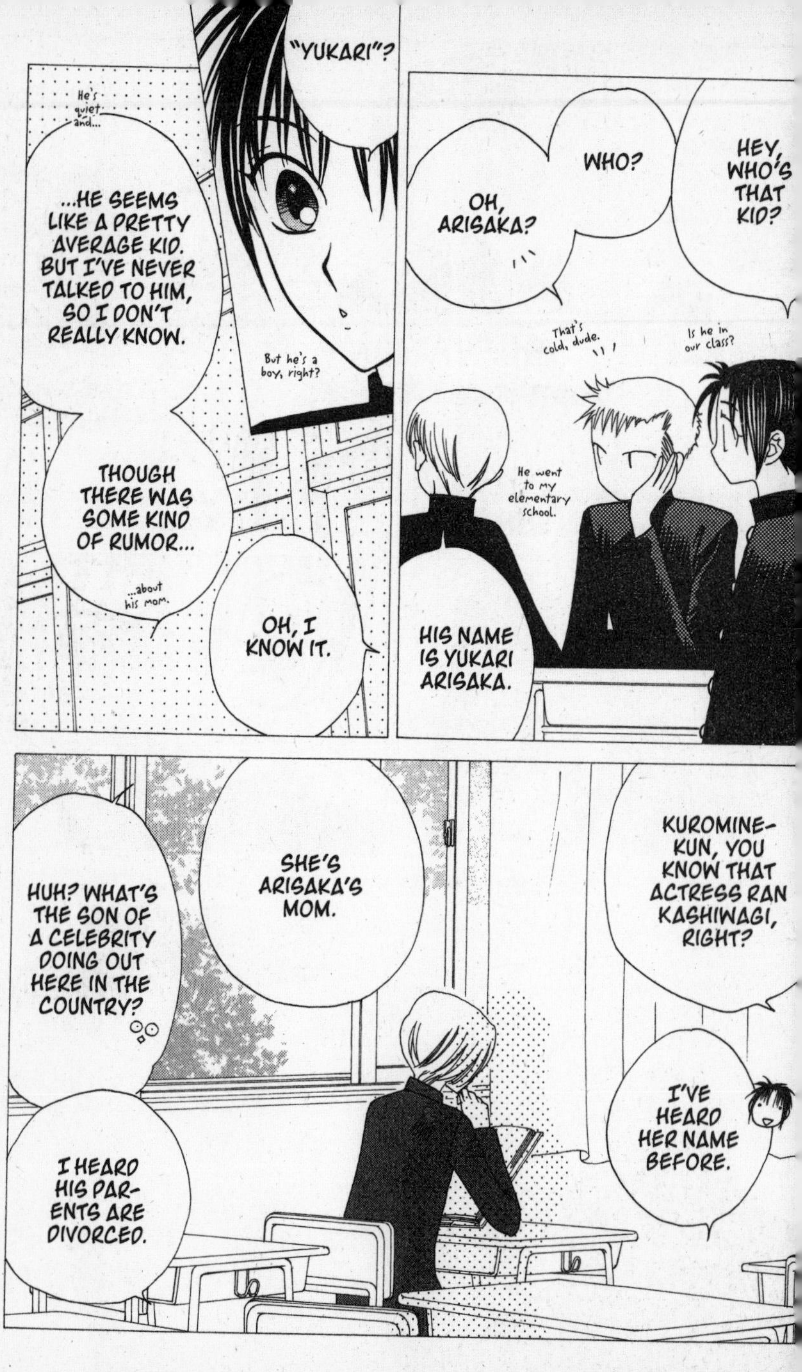
HEY, WHO'S THAT KID?
WHO?
OH, ARISAKA?
Is he in our class?
That's cold, dude.
He went to my elementary school.
HIS NAME IS YUKARI ARISAKA.
"YUKARI"?
But he's a boy, right?
He's quiet and...
...HE SEEMS LIKE A PRETTY AVERAGE KID. BUT I'VE NEVER TALKED TO HIM, SO I DON'T REALLY KNOW.
THOUGH THERE WAS SOME KIND OF RUMOR...
...about his mom.
OH, I KNOW IT.
KUROMINE-KUN, YOU KNOW THAT ACTRESS RAN KASHIWAGI, RIGHT?
I'VE HEARD HER NAME BEFORE.
SHE'S ARISAKA'S MOM.
HUH? WHAT'S THE SON OF A CELEBRITY DOING OUT HERE IN THE COUNTRY?
I HEARD HIS PARENTS ARE DIVORCED.

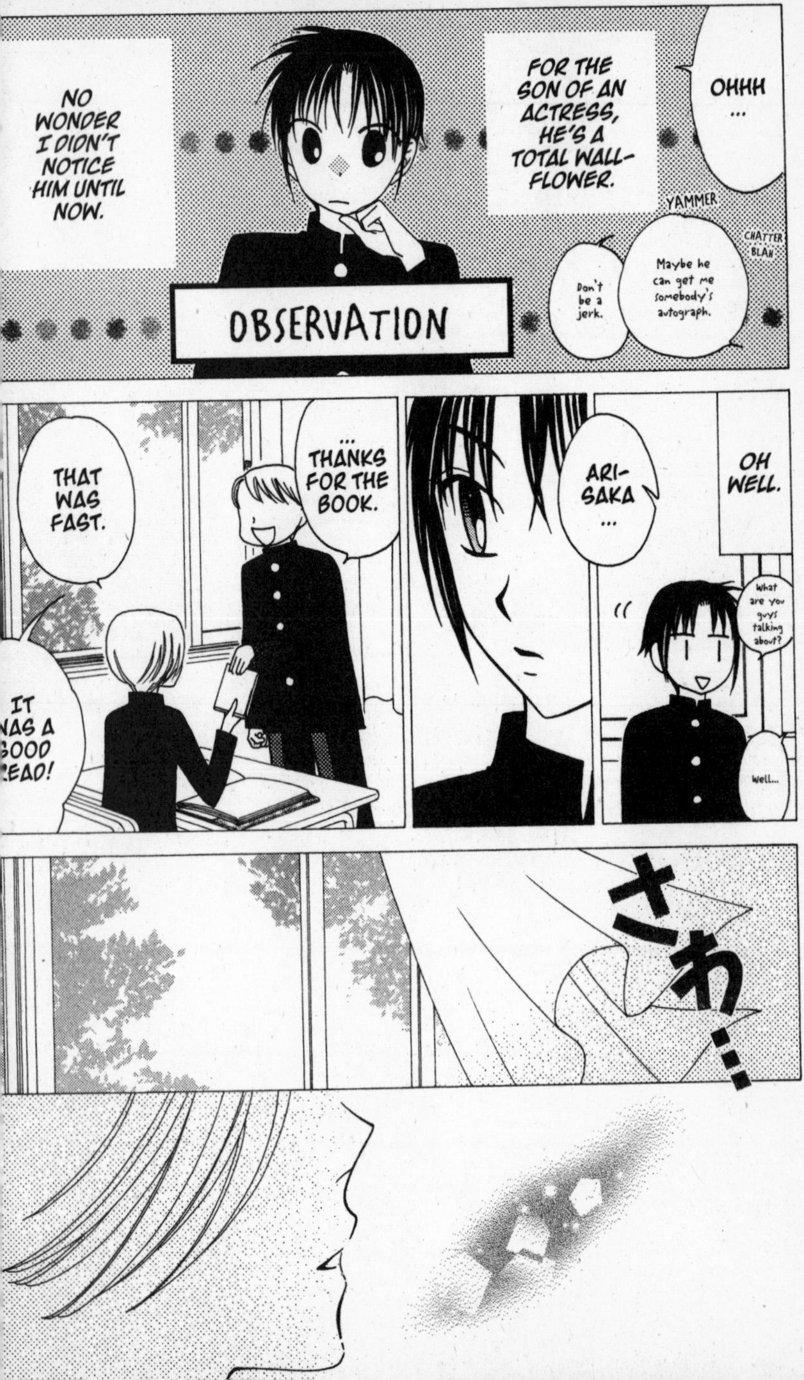
OHHH ...
FOR THE SON OF AN ACTRESS, HE'S A TOTAL WALL-FLOWER.
YAMMER
CHATTER BLAH
Maybe he can get me somebody's autograph.
Don't be a jerk.
NO WONDER I DIDN'T NOTICE HIM UNTIL NOW.
OBSERVATION
OH WELL.
What are you guys talking about?
Well...
ARI-SAKA ...
... THANKS FOR THE BOOK.
THAT WAS FAST.
IT WAS A GOOD READ!
さわ…

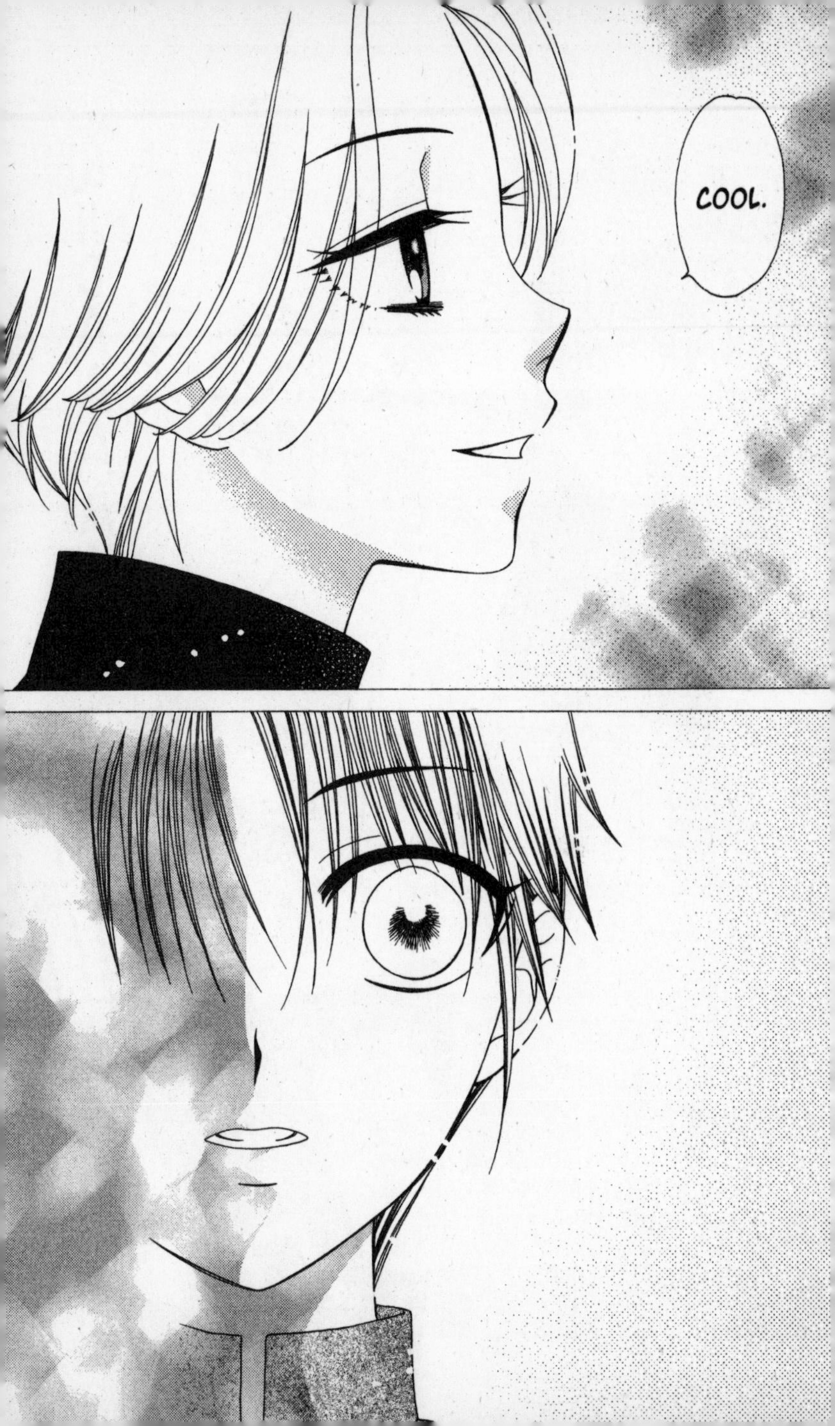
COOL.

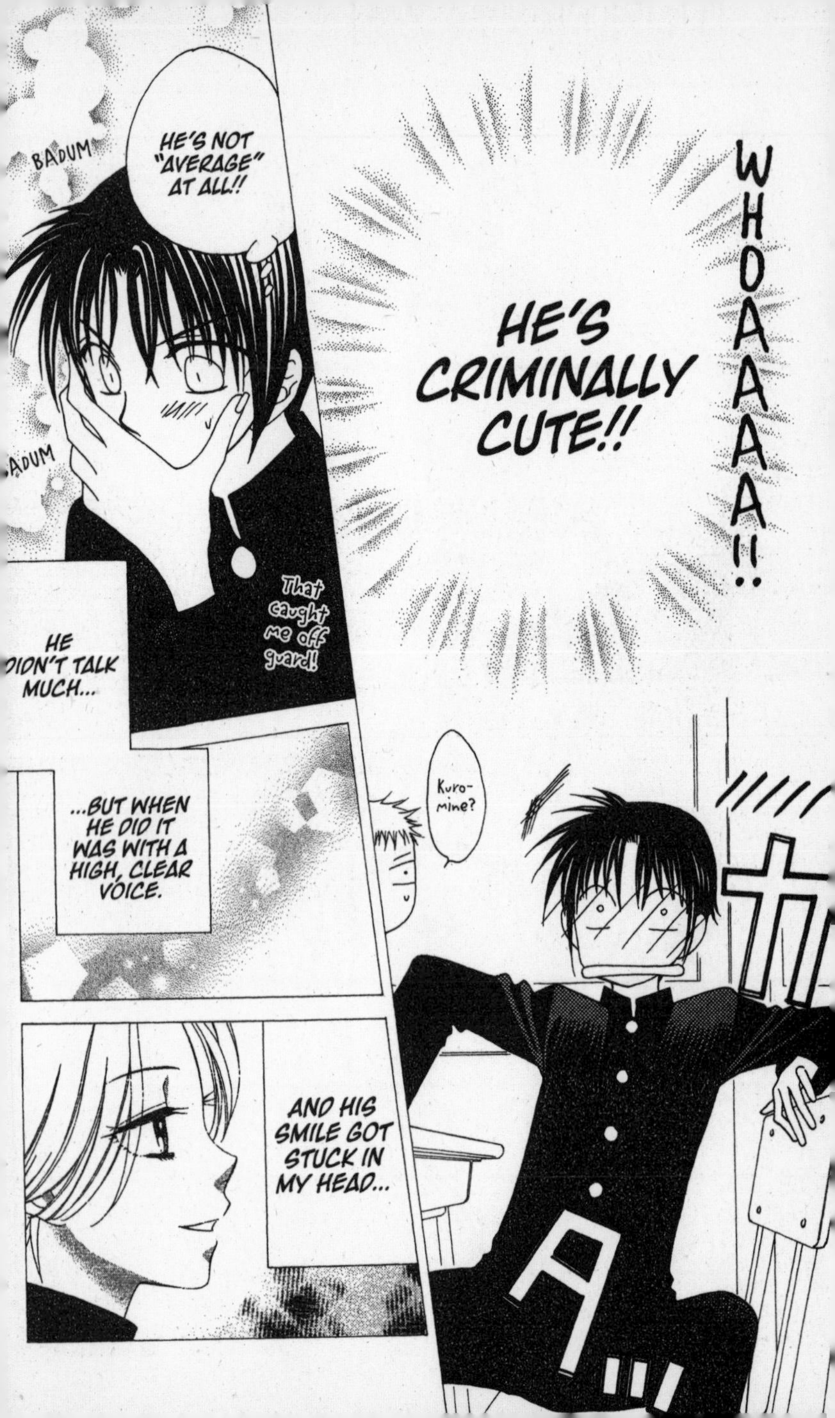
WHOAAAAA!!
HE'S CRIMINALLY CUTE!!
Kuro-mine?
HE'S NOT "AVERAGE" AT ALL!!
BADUM
BADUM
That caught me off guard!
HE DIDN'T TALK MUCH...
...BUT WHEN HE DID IT WAS WITH A HIGH, CLEAR VOICE.
AND HIS SMILE GOT STUCK IN MY HEAD...

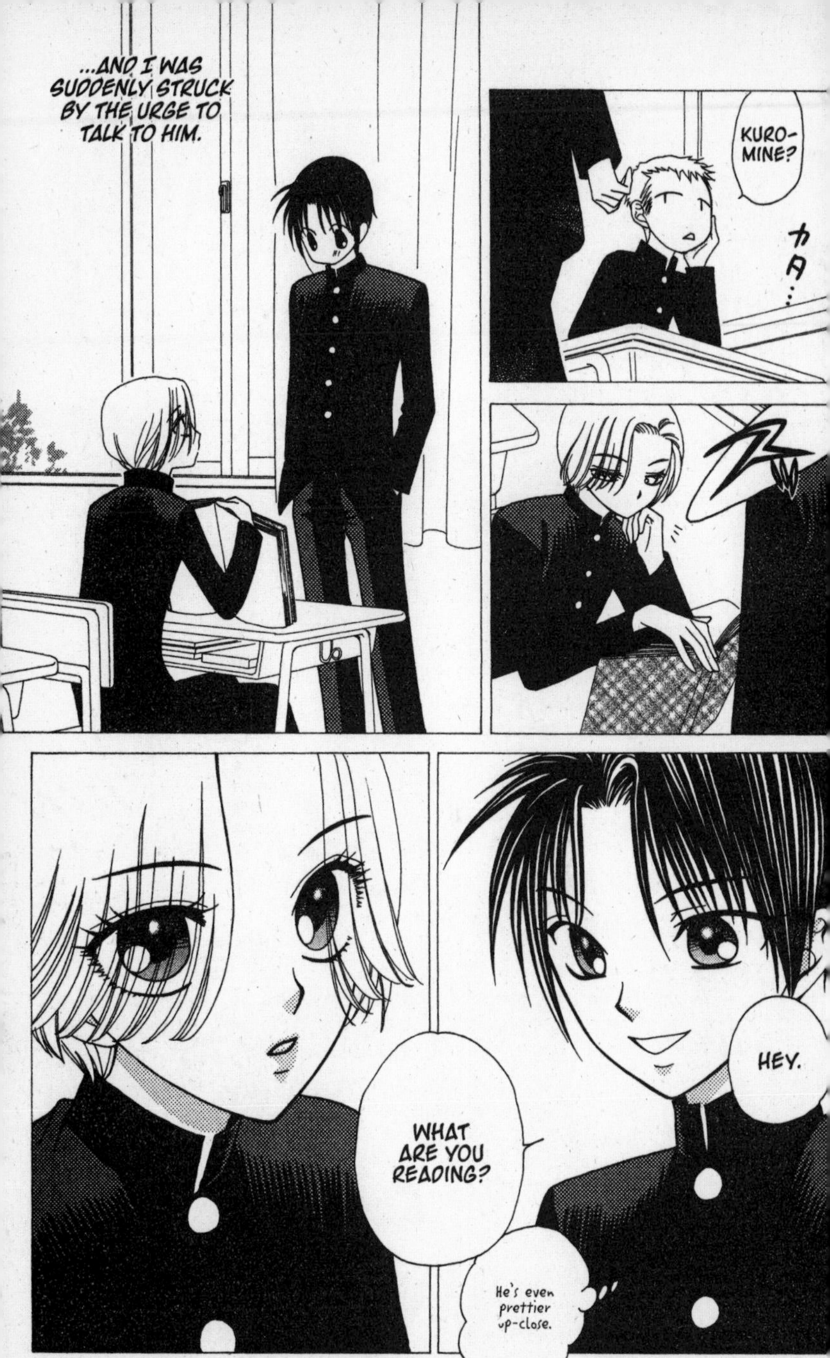
KURO-MINE?
カタ…
...AND I WAS SUDDENLY STRUCK BY THE URGE TO TALK TO HIM.
HEY.
WHAT ARE YOU READING?
He's even prettier up-close.

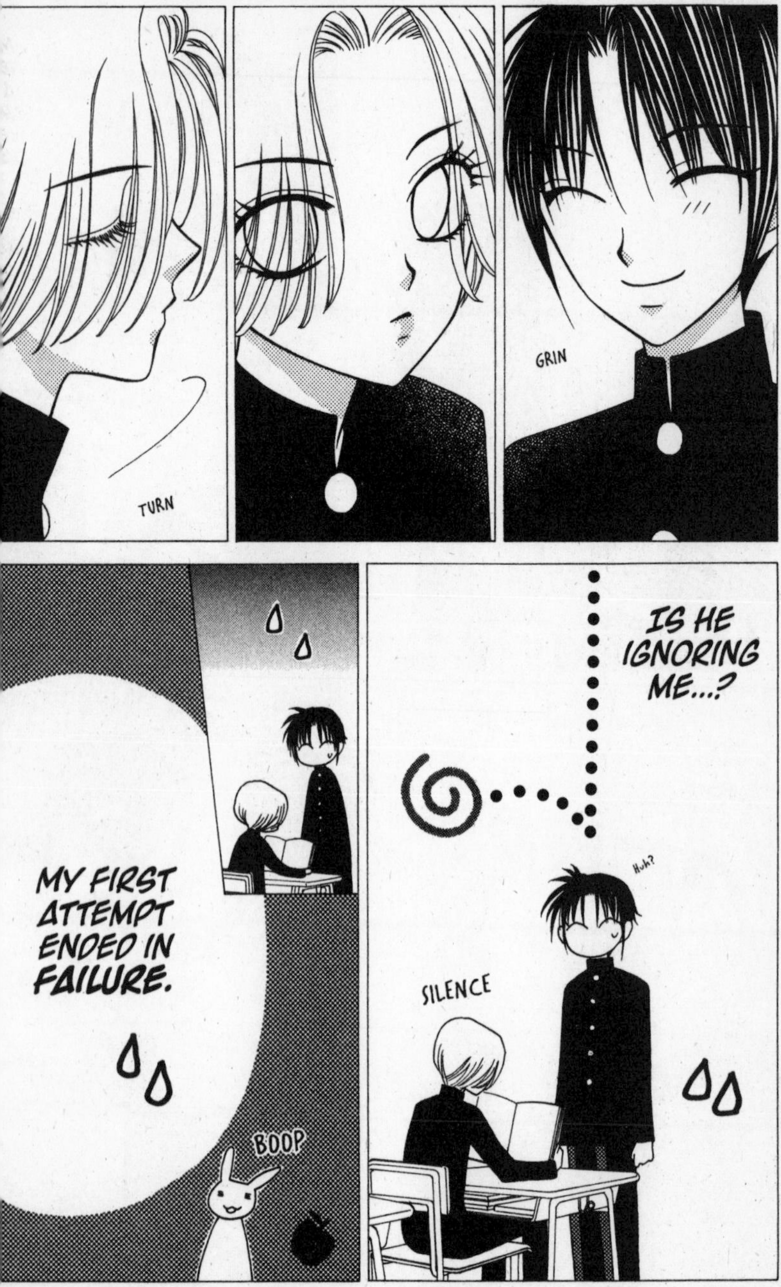
GRIN
TURN
IS HE IGNORING ME...?
Huh?
SILENCE
MY FIRST ATTEMPT ENDED IN FAILURE.
BOOP

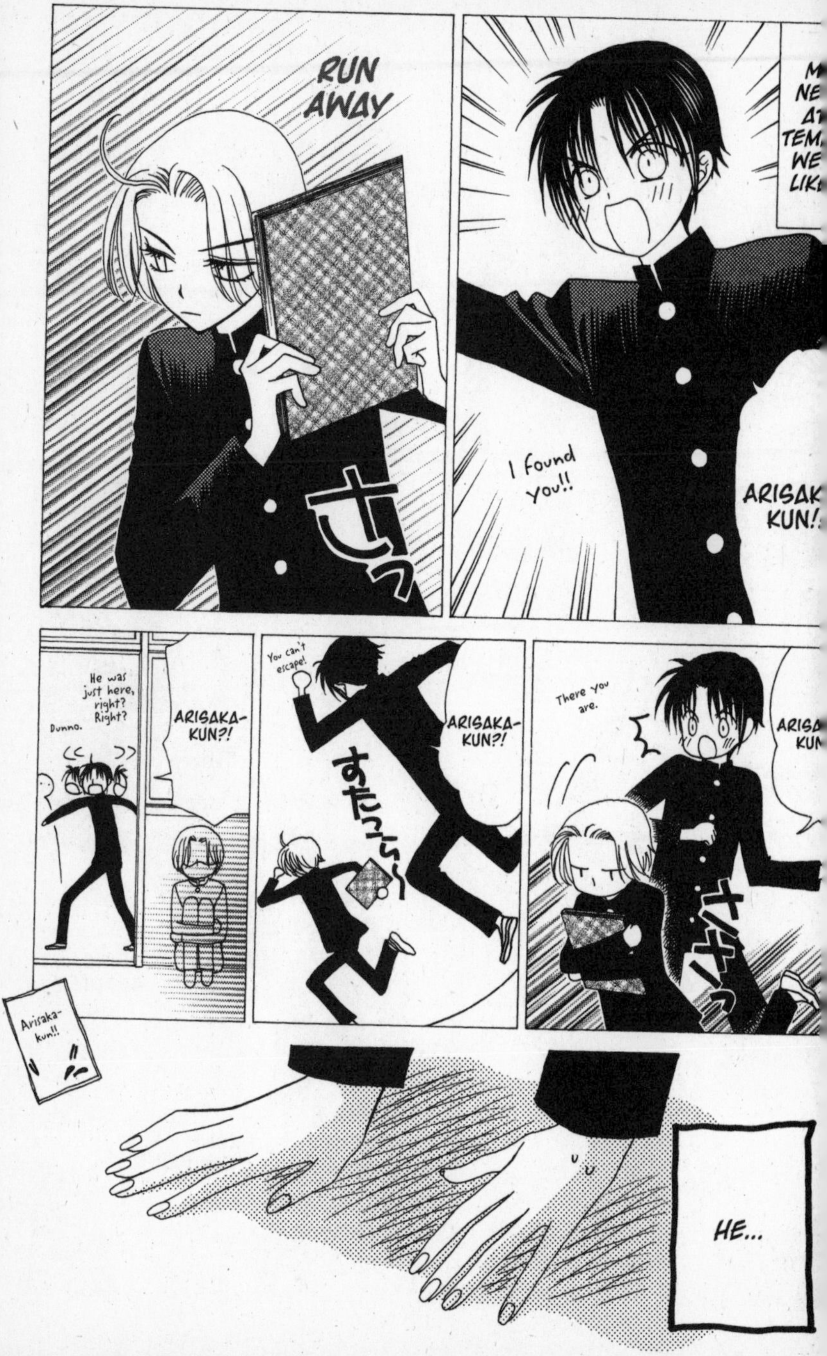
I found you!!
RUN AWAY
さっ
There you are.
ささっ
ARISAKA-KUN?!
You can't escape!
すたこら〜
ARISAKA-KUN?!
He was just here, right? Right?
Dunno.
Arisaka-kun!!
HE...

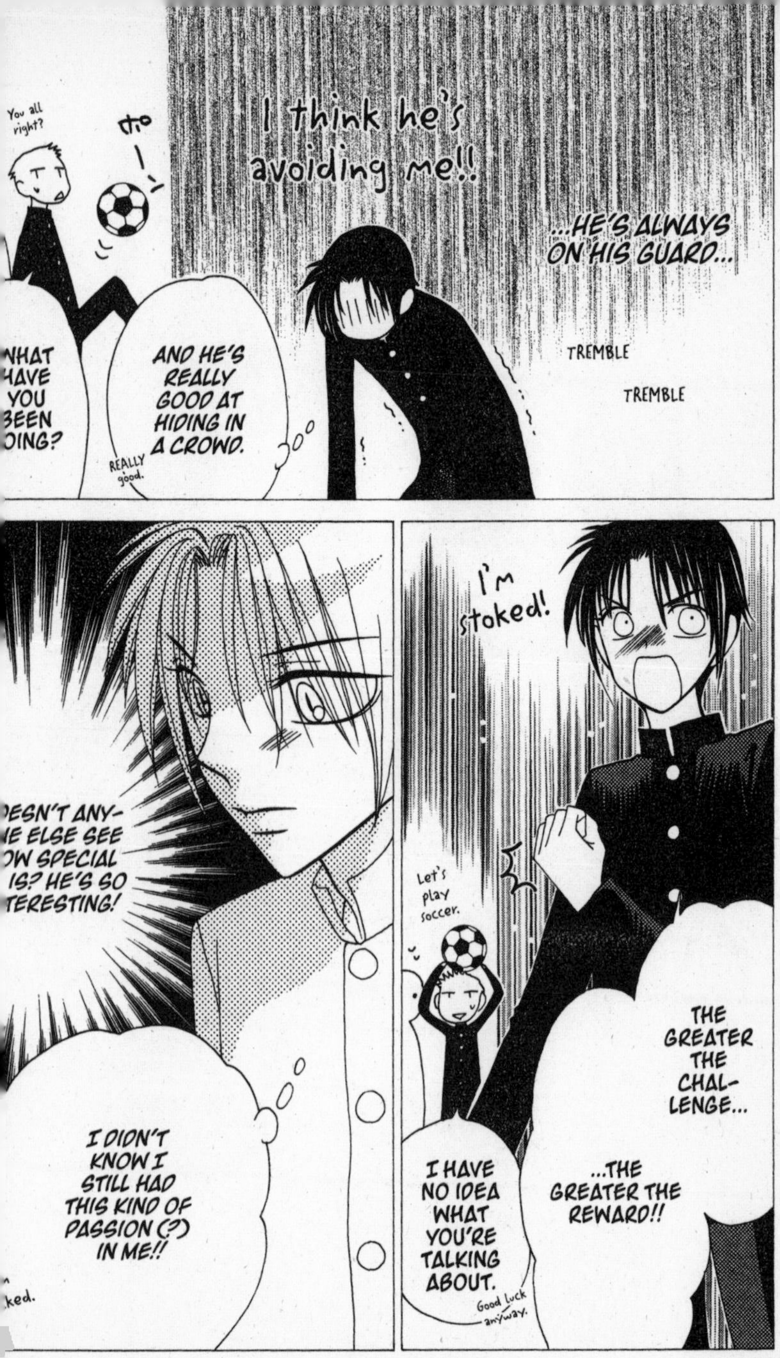
I think he's avoiding me!!
...HE'S ALWAYS ON HIS GUARD...
TREMBLE
TREMBLE
AND HE'S REALLY GOOD AT HIDING IN A CROWD.
REALLY good.
You all right?
NHAT HAVE YOU BEEN OING?
I'm stoked!
THE GREATER THE CHAL-LENGE...
...THE GREATER THE REWARD!!
Let's play soccer.
I HAVE NO IDEA WHAT YOU'RE TALKING ABOUT.
Good luck anyway.
JESN'T ANY-
IE ELSE SEE
OW SPECIAL
IS? HE'S SO
TERESTING!
I DIDN'T KNOW I STILL HAD THIS KIND OF PASSION (?) IN ME!!
ked.

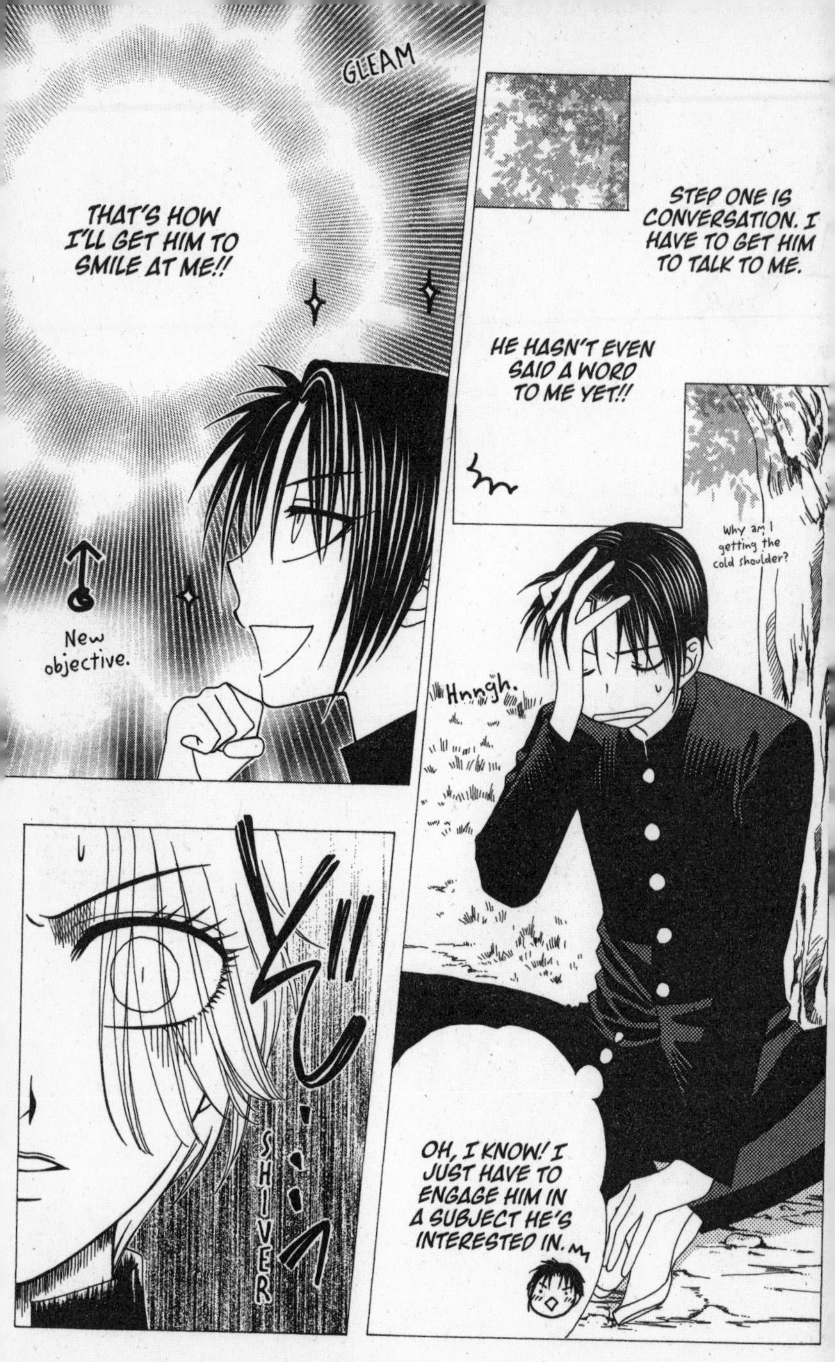
STEP ONE IS CONVERSATION. I HAVE TO GET HIM TO TALK TO ME.
HE HASN'T EVEN SAID A WORD TO ME YET!!
Why am I getting the cold shoulder?
Hnngh.
OH, I KNOW! I JUST HAVE TO ENGAGE HIM IN A SUBJECT HE'S INTERESTED IN.
GLEAM
THAT'S HOW I'LL GET HIM TO SMILE AT ME!!
New objective.
SHIVER

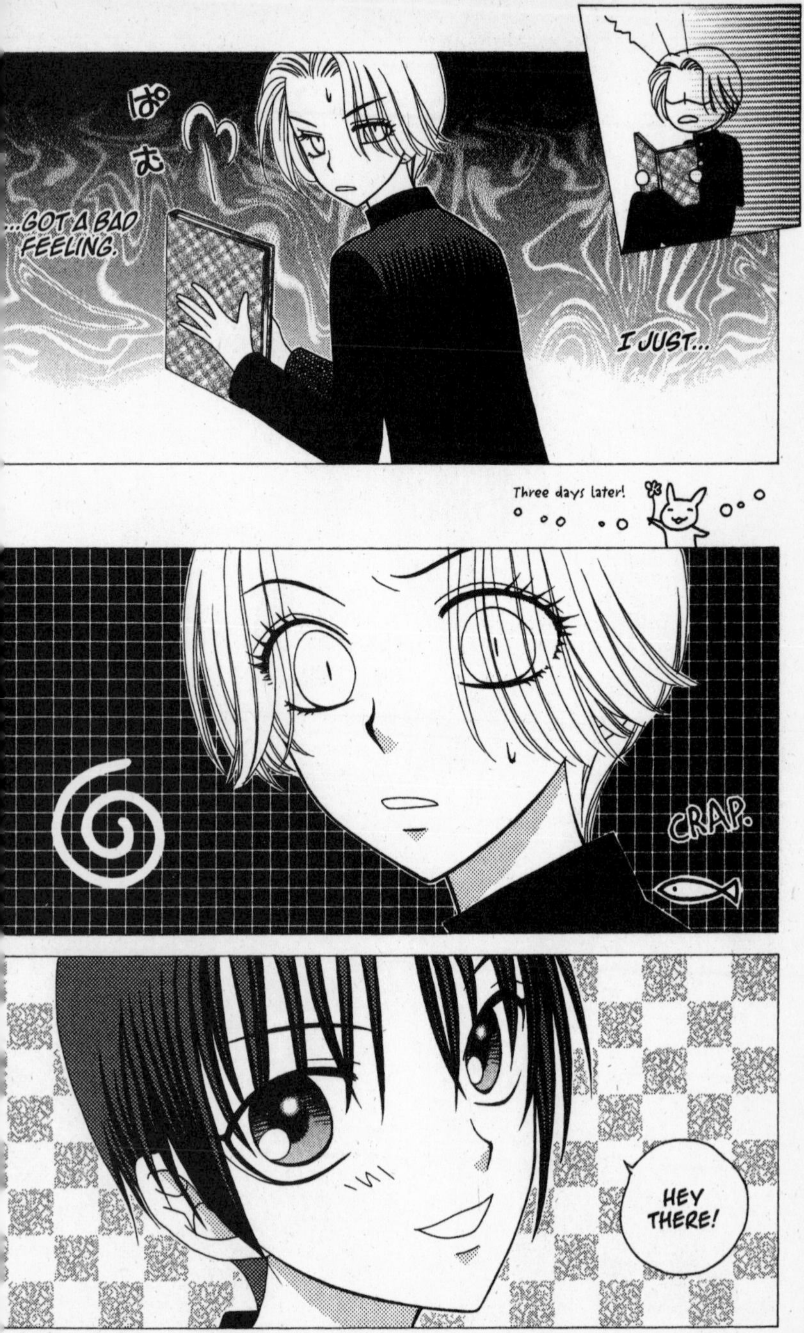
I JUST...
...GOT A BAD FEELING.
ぽむ
Three days later!
CRAP.
HEY THERE!

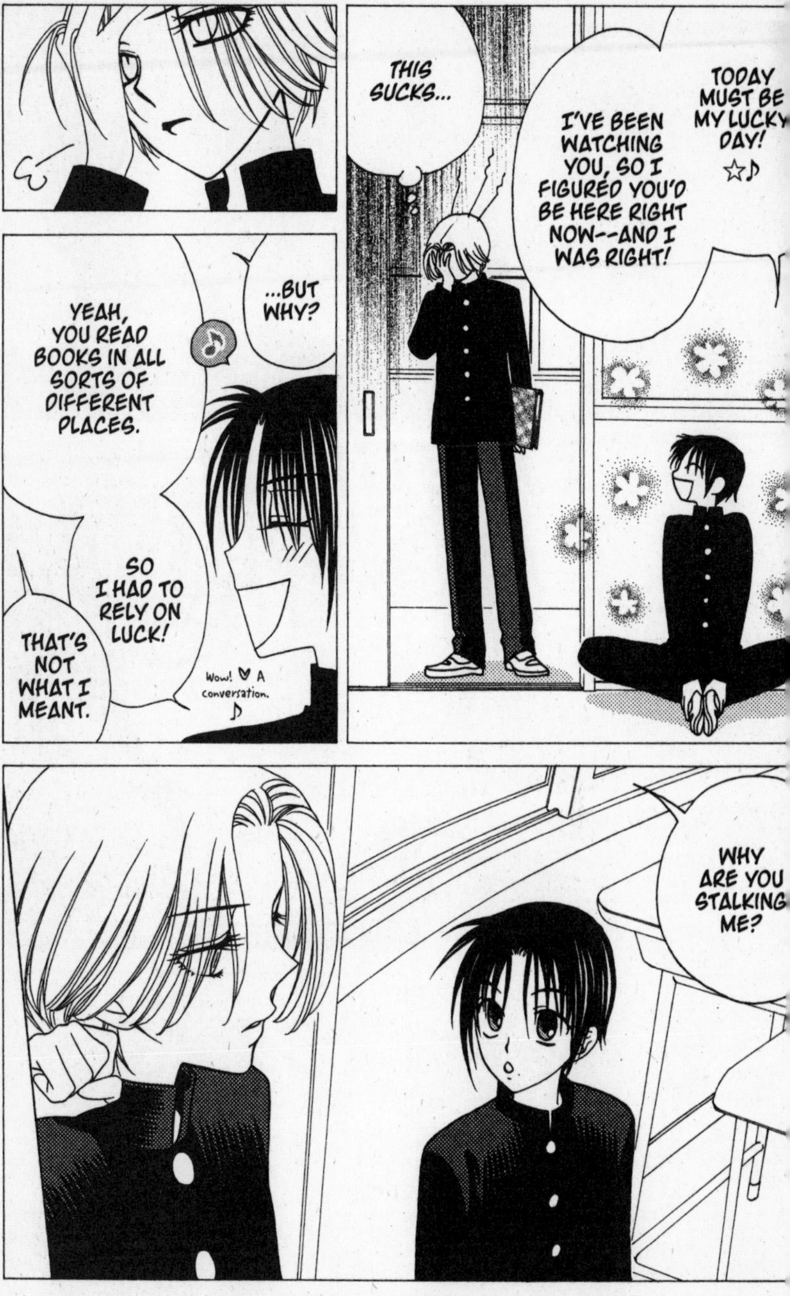
TODAY MUST BE MY LUCKY DAY! ☆♪
I'VE BEEN WATCHING YOU, SO I FIGURED YOU'D BE HERE RIGHT NOW--AND I WAS RIGHT!
THIS SUCKS...
...BUT WHY?
YEAH, YOU READ BOOKS IN ALL SORTS OF DIFFERENT PLACES.
SO I HAD TO RELY ON LUCK!
Wow! ♥ A conversation. ♪
THAT'S NOT WHAT I MEANT.
WHY ARE YOU STALKING ME?

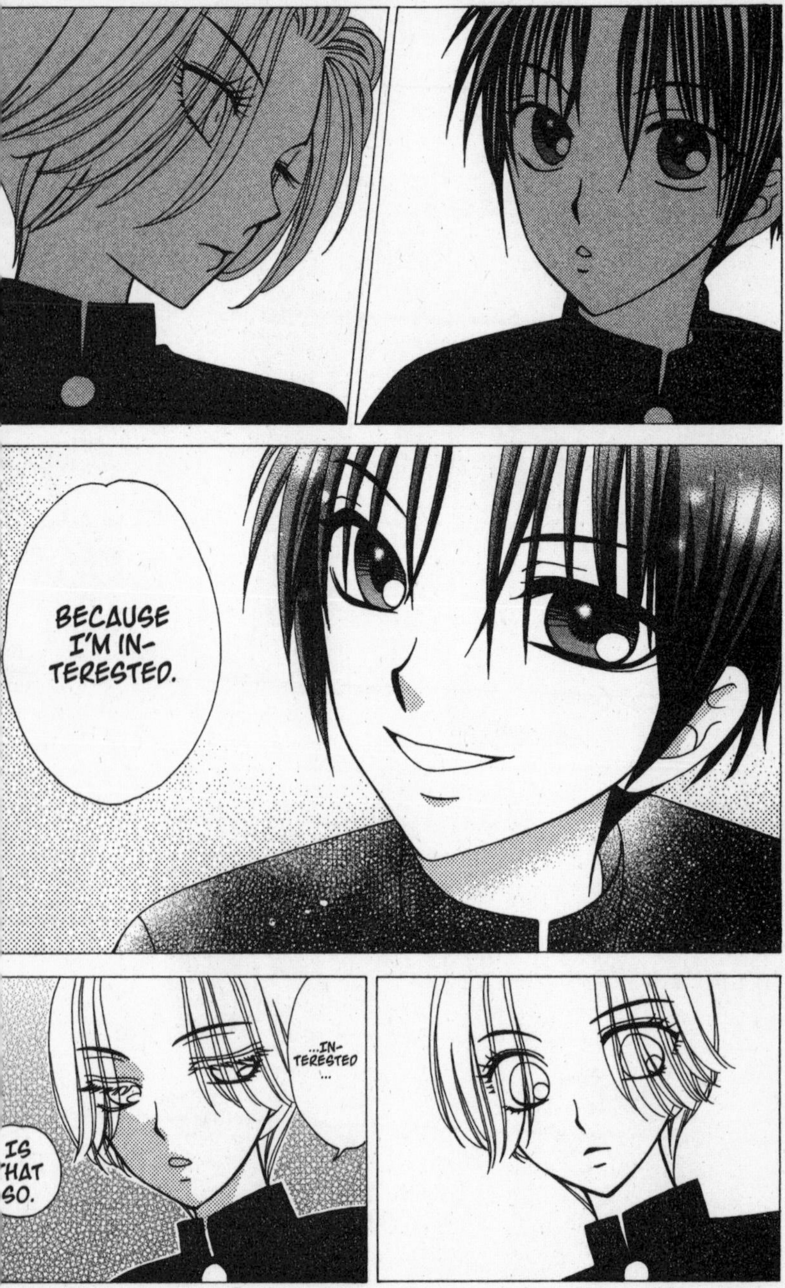
BECAUSE I'M IN-TERESTED.
...IN-TERESTED ...
IS THAT SO.

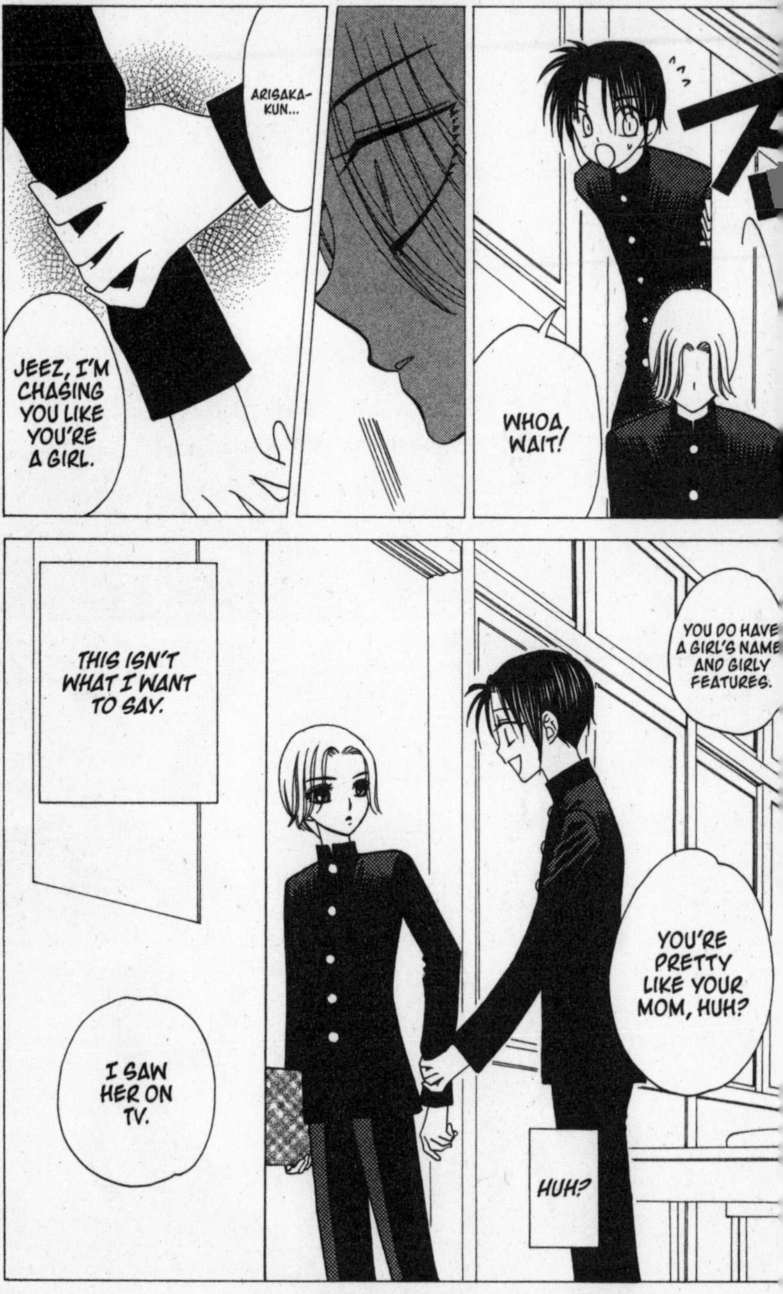
WHOA WAIT!
ARISAKA-KUN...
JEEZ, I'M CHASING YOU LIKE YOU'RE A GIRL.
YOU DO HAVE A GIRL'S NAME AND GIRLY FEATURES.
YOU'RE PRETTY LIKE YOUR MOM, HUH?
HUH?
THIS ISN'T WHAT I WANT TO SAY.
I SAW HER ON TV.

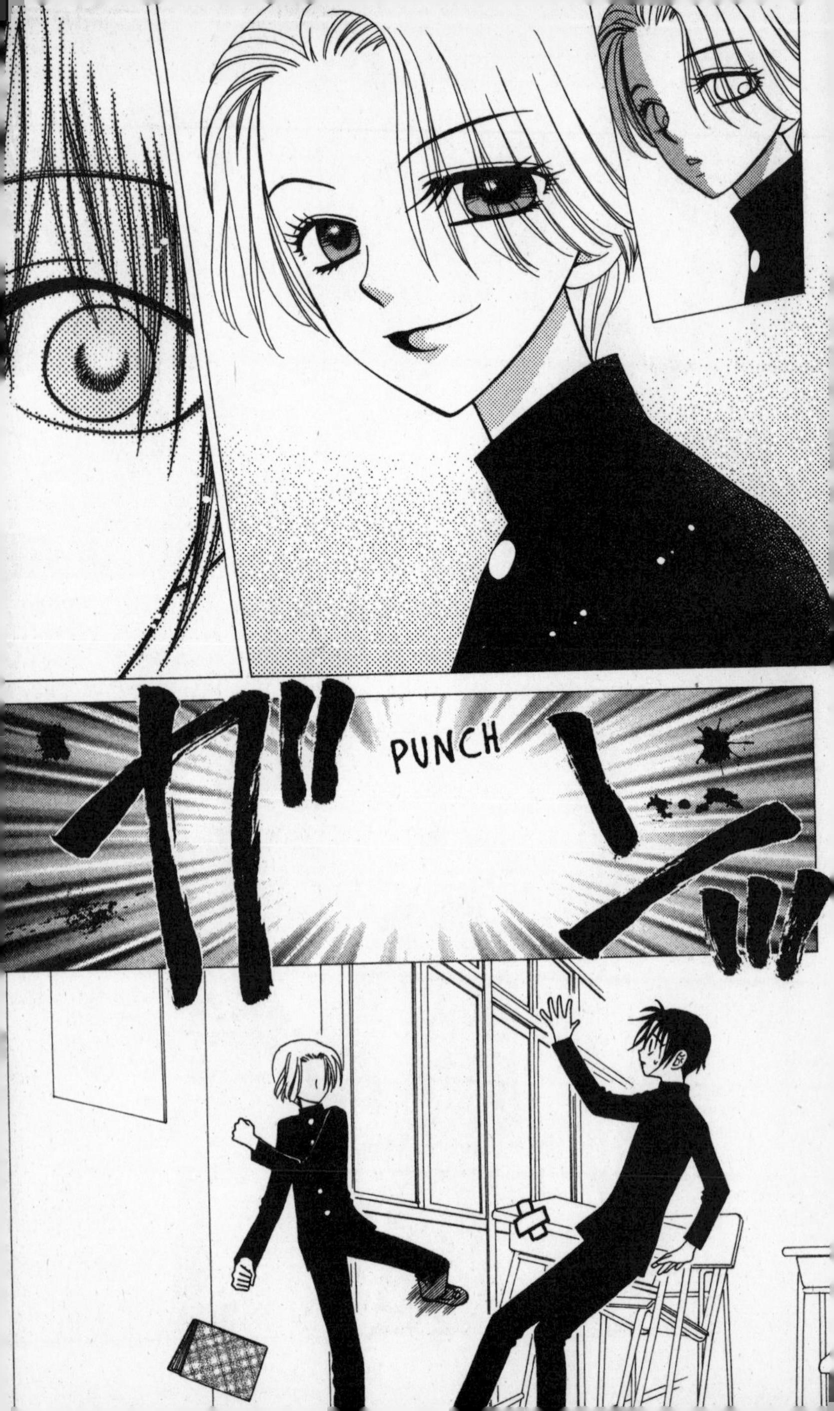
PUNCH

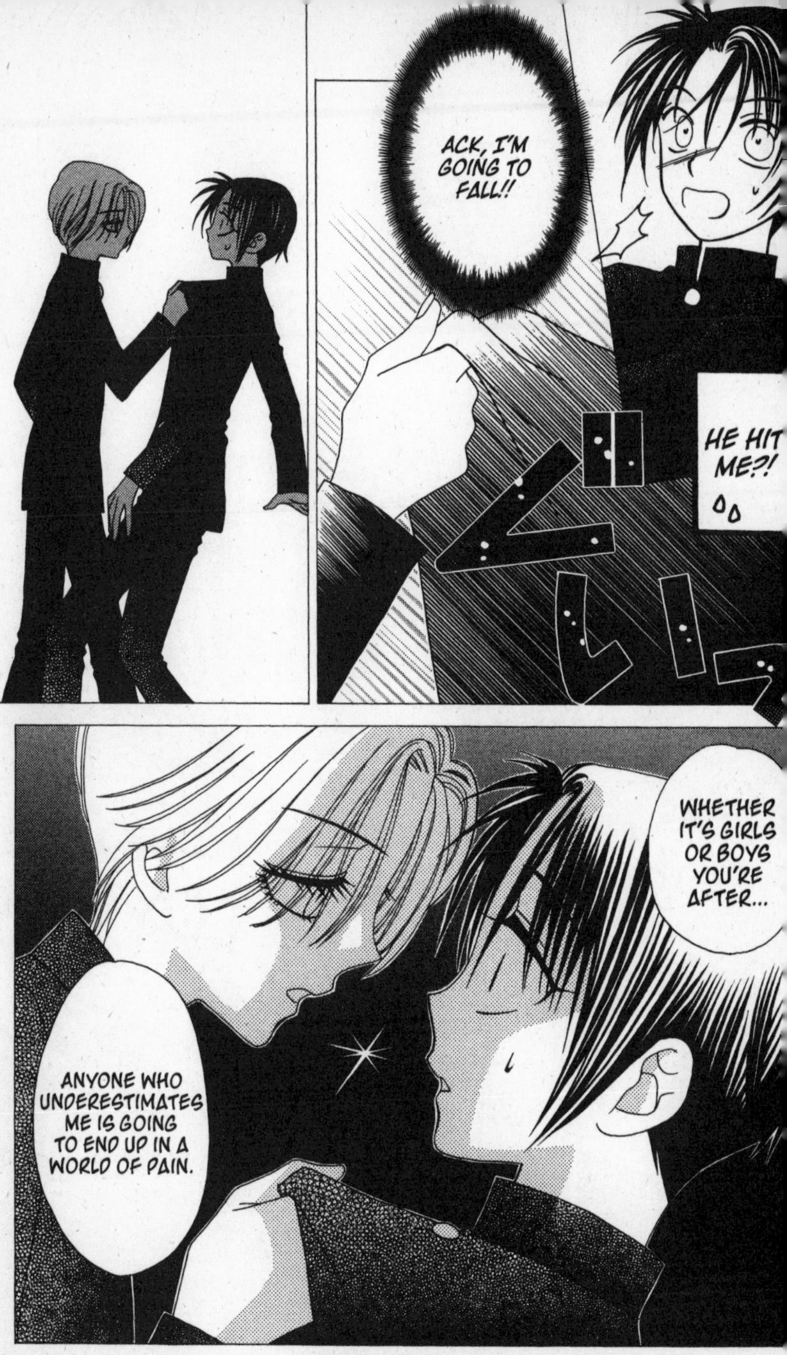
HE HIT ME?!
ACK, I'M GOING TO FALL!!
WHETHER IT'S GIRLS OR BOYS YOU'RE AFTER...
ANYONE WHO UNDERESTIMATES ME IS GOING TO END UP IN A WORLD OF PAIN.

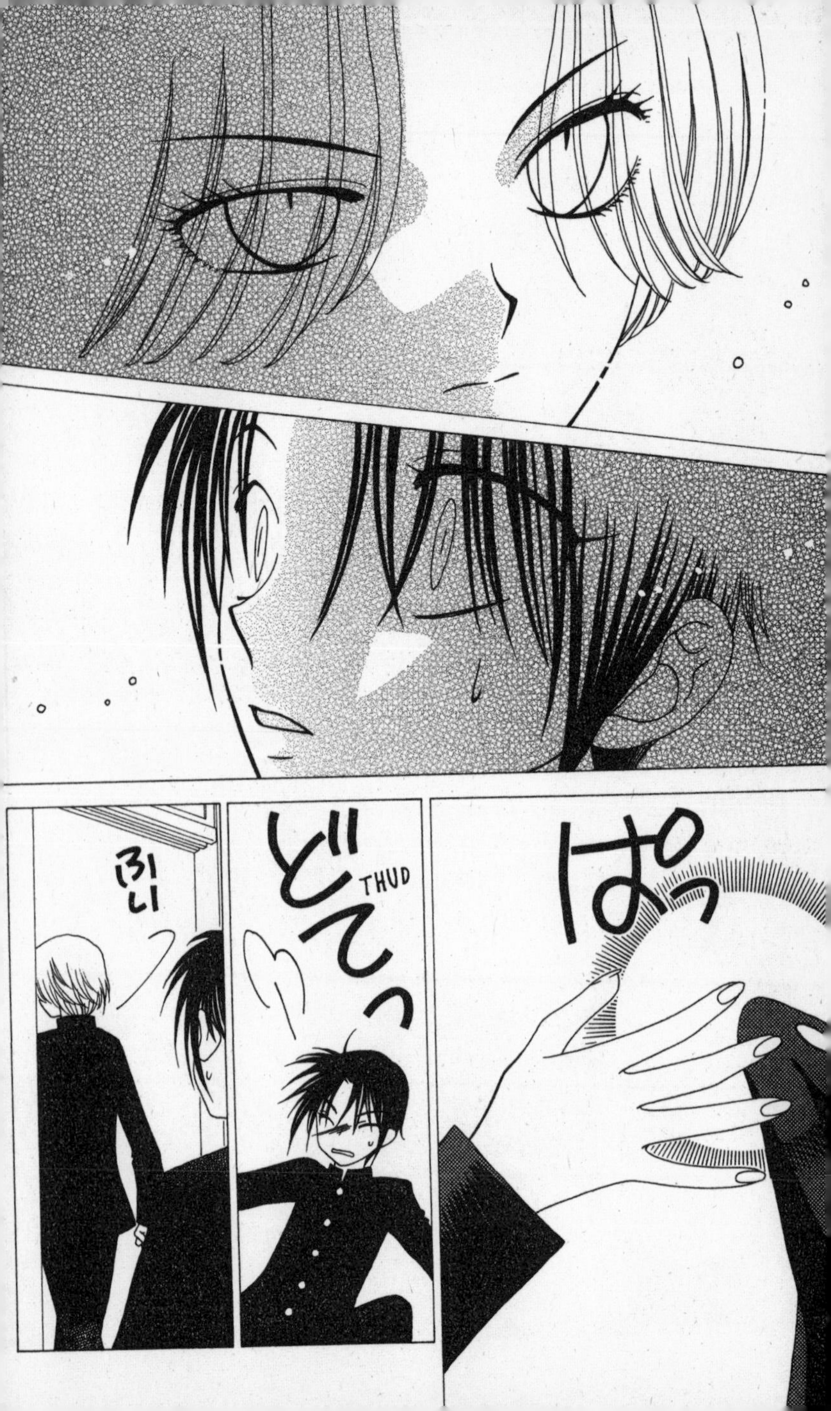
ぱっ
どてっ
THUD
ふい

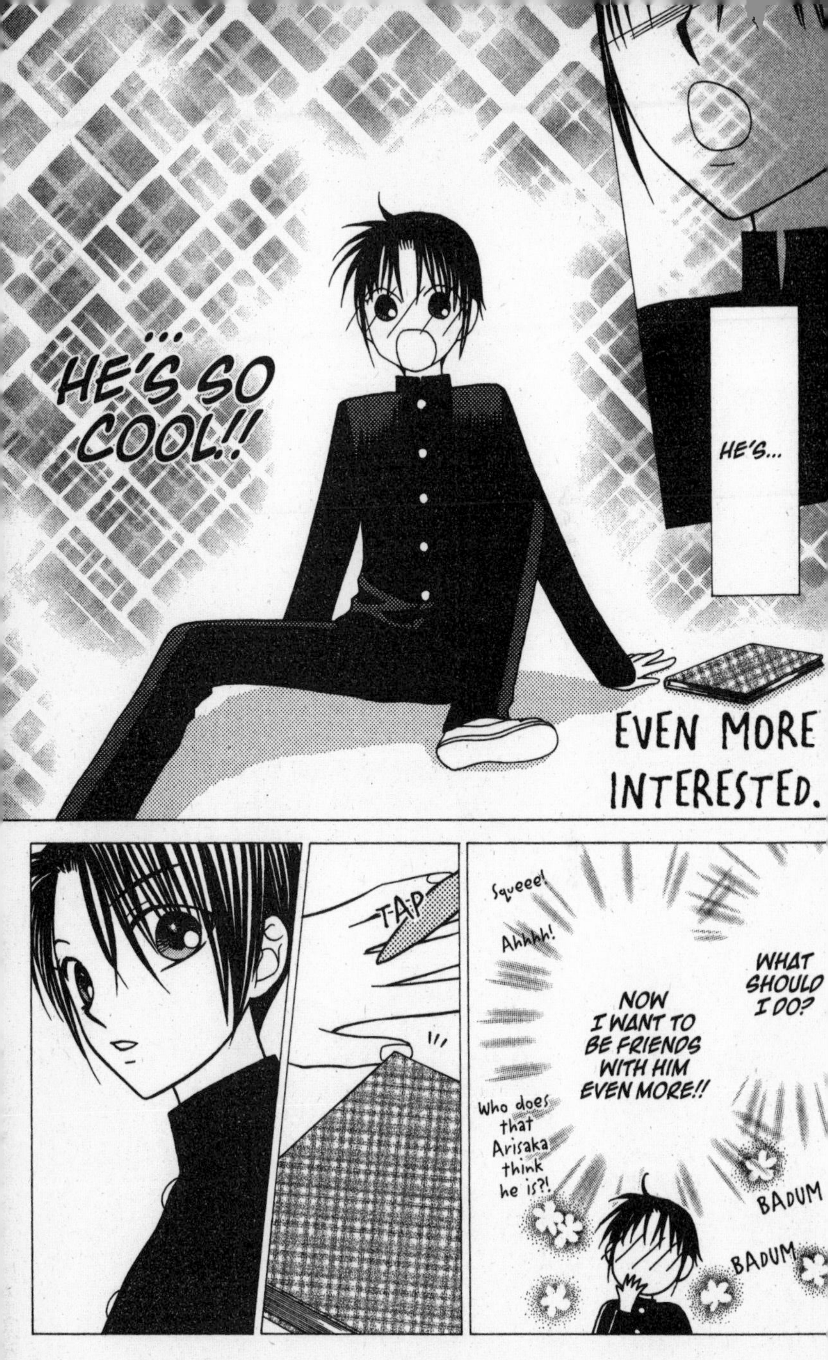
HE'S...
...HE'S SO COOL!!
EVEN MORE INTERESTED.
WHAT SHOULD I DO?
NOW I WANT TO BE FRIENDS WITH HIM EVEN MORE!!
Squeee!
Ahhhh!
Who does that Arisaka think he is?!
BADUM
BADUM
TAP

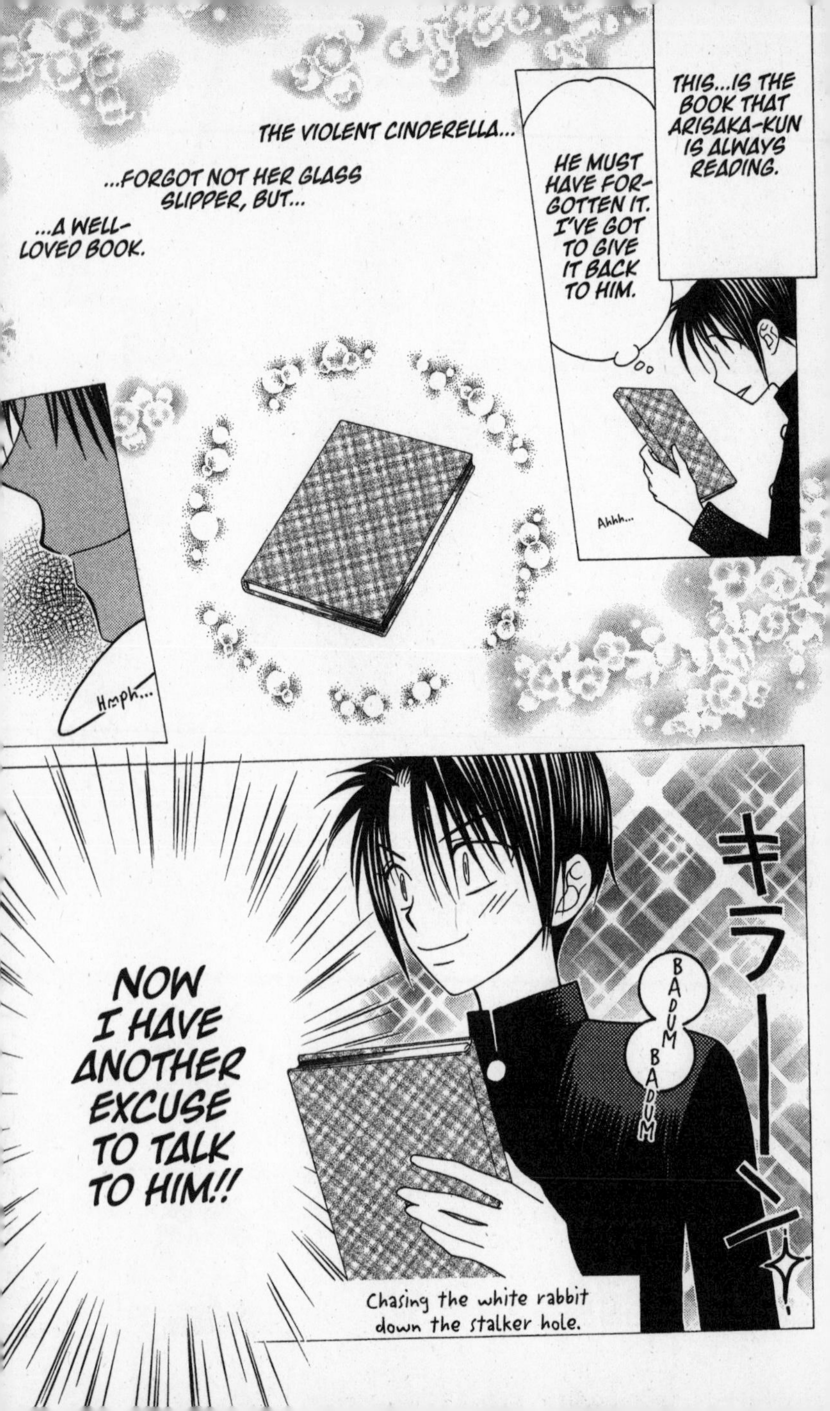
THIS...IS THE BOOK THAT ARISAKA-KUN IS ALWAYS READING.
HE MUST HAVE FOR-GOTTEN IT. I'VE GOT TO GIVE IT BACK TO HIM.
Ahhh...
THE VIOLENT CINDERELLA...
...FORGOT NOT HER GLASS SLIPPER, BUT...
...A WELL-LOVED BOOK.
Hmph...
キラーン
BADUM BADUM
NOW I HAVE ANOTHER EXCUSE TO TALK TO HIM!!
Chasing the white rabbit down the stalker hole.

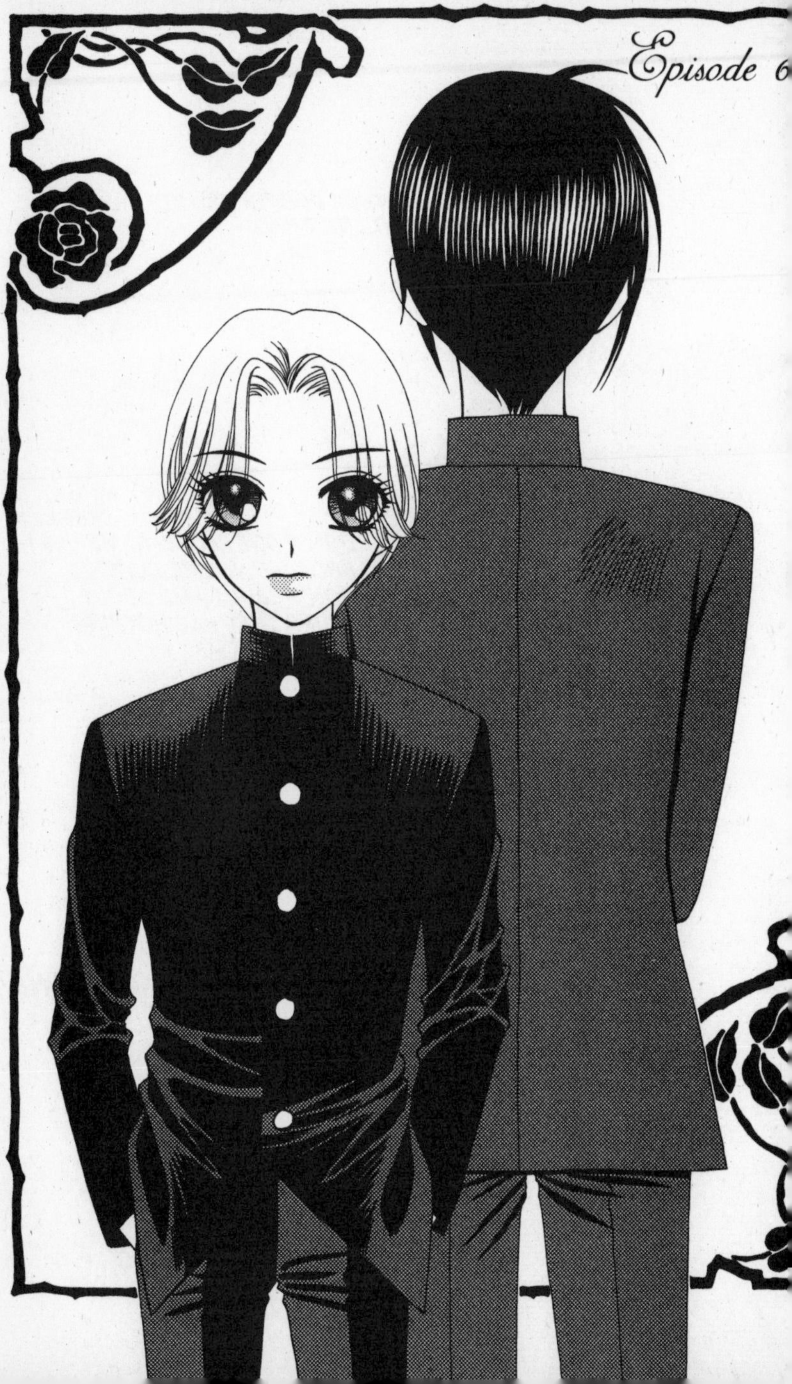
Episode 6

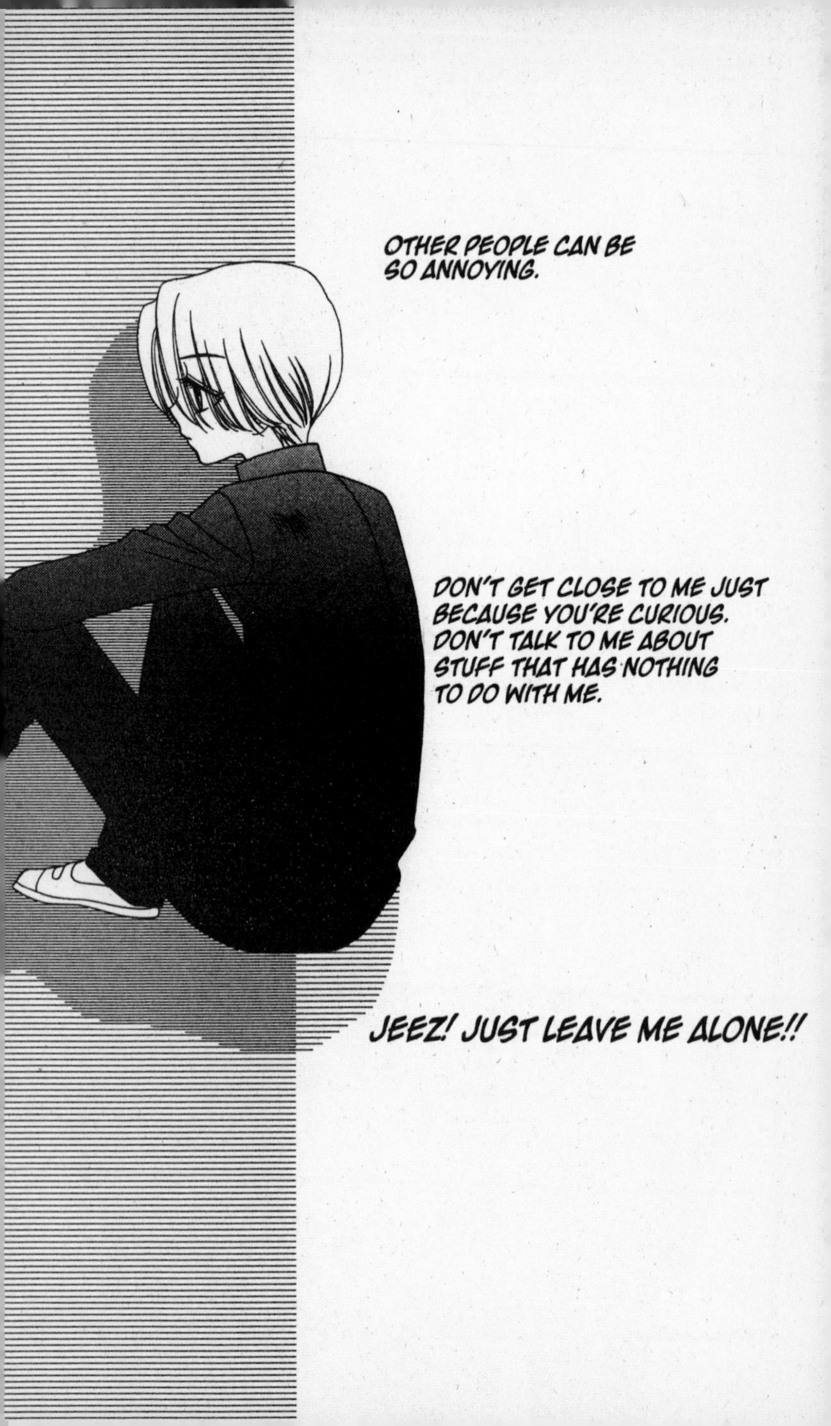
OTHER PEOPLE CAN BE SO ANNOYING.
DON'T GET CLOSE TO ME JUST BECAUSE YOU'RE CURIOUS. DON'T TALK TO ME ABOUT STUFF THAT HAS NOTHING TO DO WITH ME.
JEEZ! JUST LEAVE ME ALONE!!

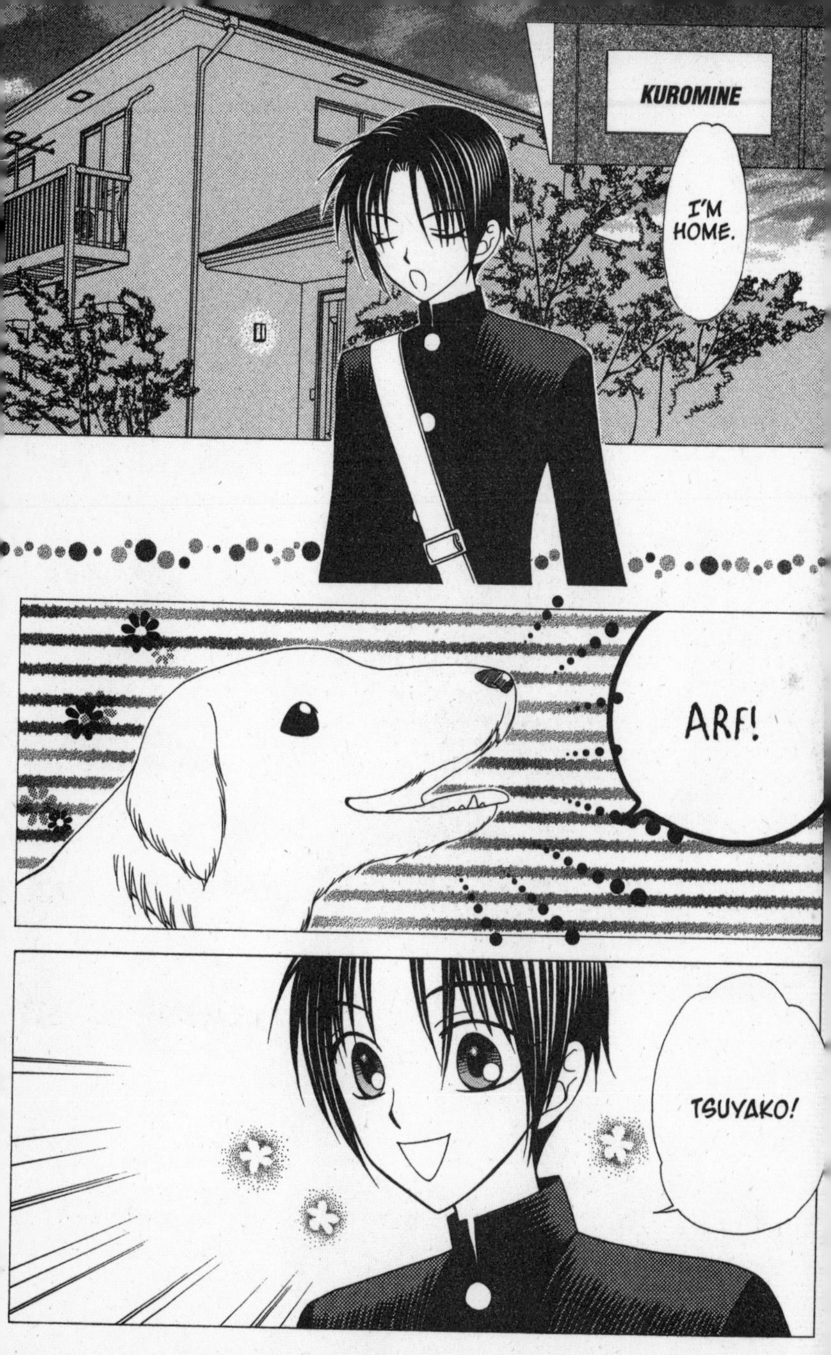
KUROMINE
I'M HOME.
ARF!
TSUYAKO!

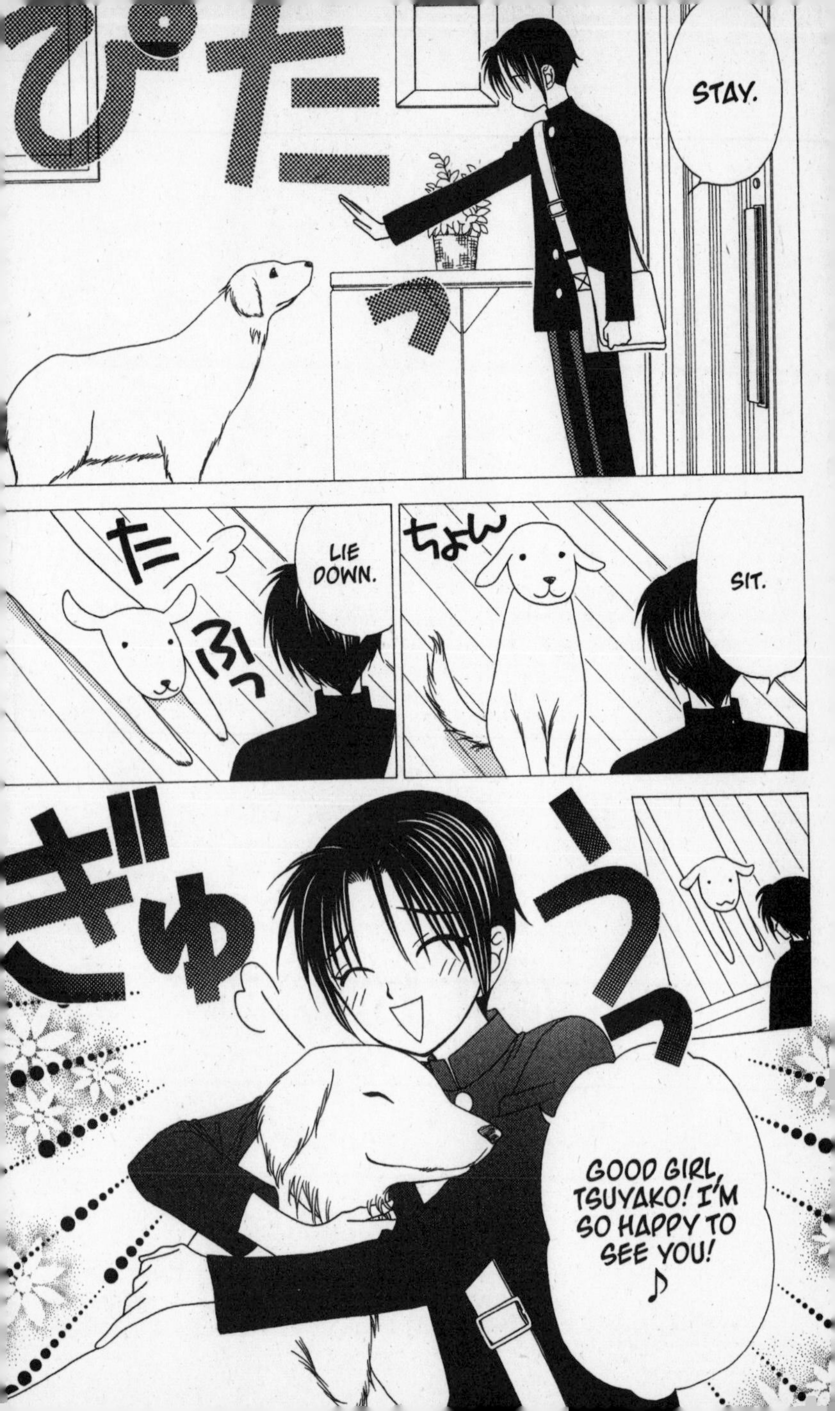
STAY.
ぴたっ
SIT.
ちょん
LIE DOWN.
たふっ
ぎゅうっ
GOOD GIRL, TSUYAKO! I'M SO HAPPY TO SEE YOU! ♪

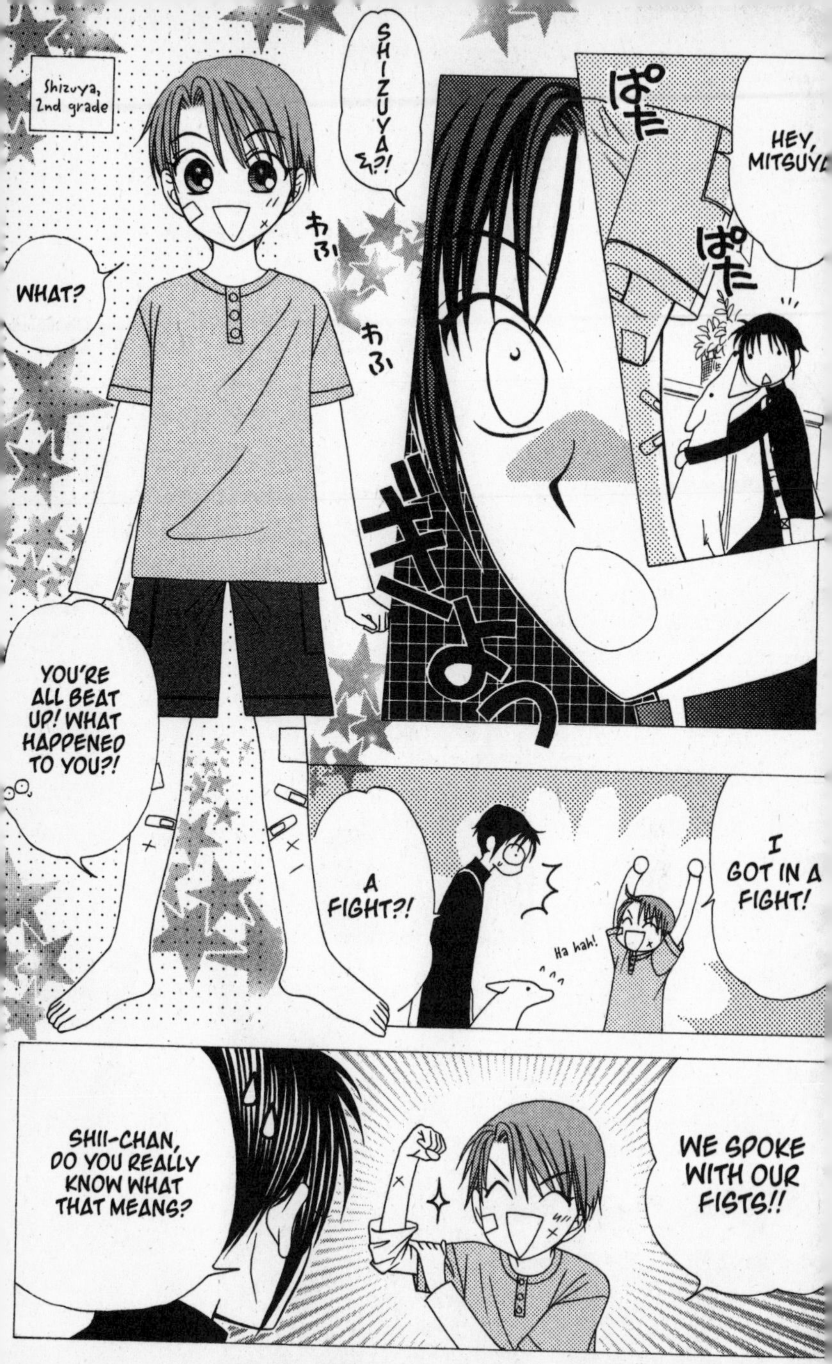

ぱた
HEY, MITSUYA
ぱた
ギょっ
I GOT IN A FIGHT!
A FIGHT?!
Ha hah!
SHIZUYA え?!
Shizuya, 2nd grade
わふ
わふ
WHAT?
YOU'RE ALL BEAT UP! WHAT HAPPENED TO YOU?!
WE SPOKE WITH OUR FISTS!!
SHII-CHAN, DO YOU REALLY KNOW WHAT THAT MEANS?

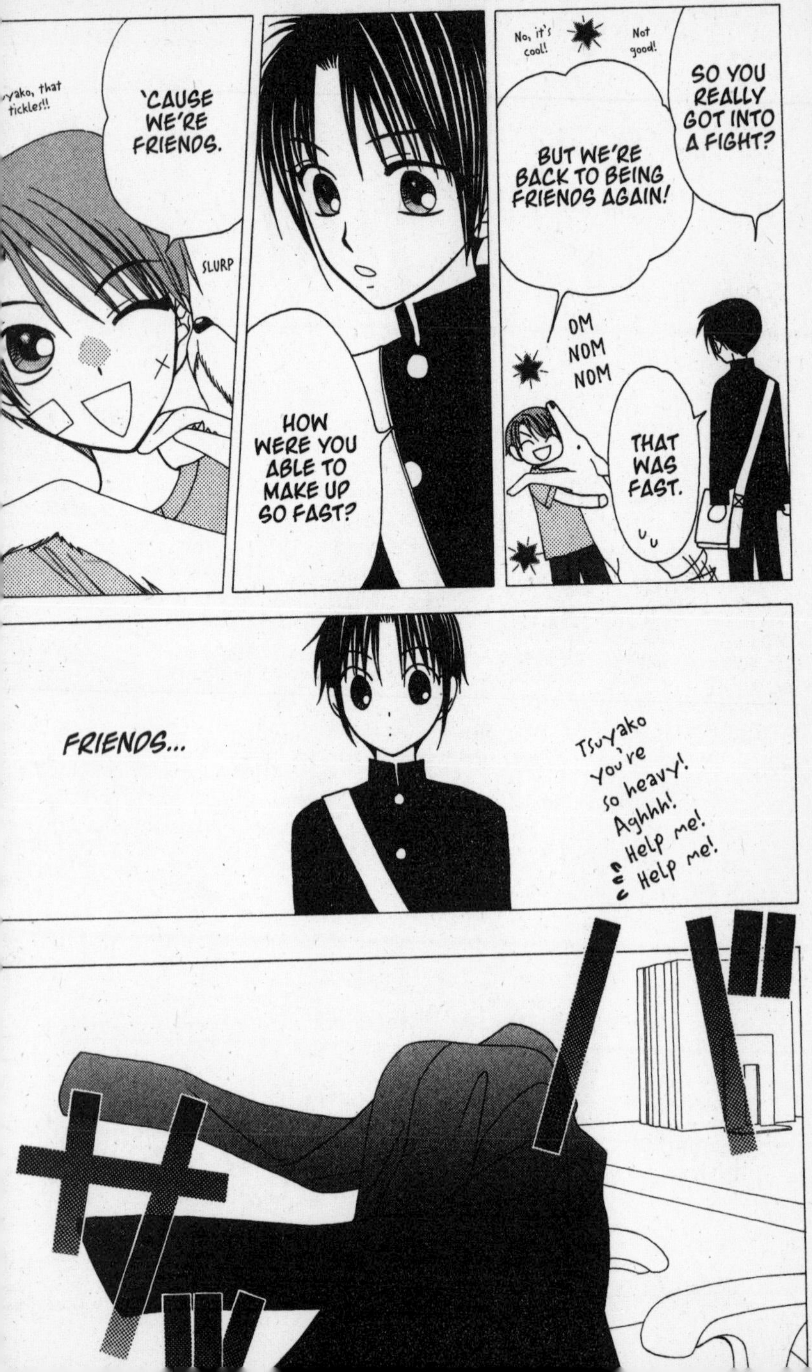
SO YOU REALLY GOT INTO A FIGHT?
Not good!
No, it's cool!
BUT WE'RE BACK TO BEING FRIENDS AGAIN!
OM NOM NOM
THAT WAS FAST.
HOW WERE YOU ABLE TO MAKE UP SO FAST?
'CAUSE WE'RE FRIENDS.
SLURP
yako, that tickles!!
Tsuyako you're so heavy! Aghhh! Help me! Help me!
FRIENDS...

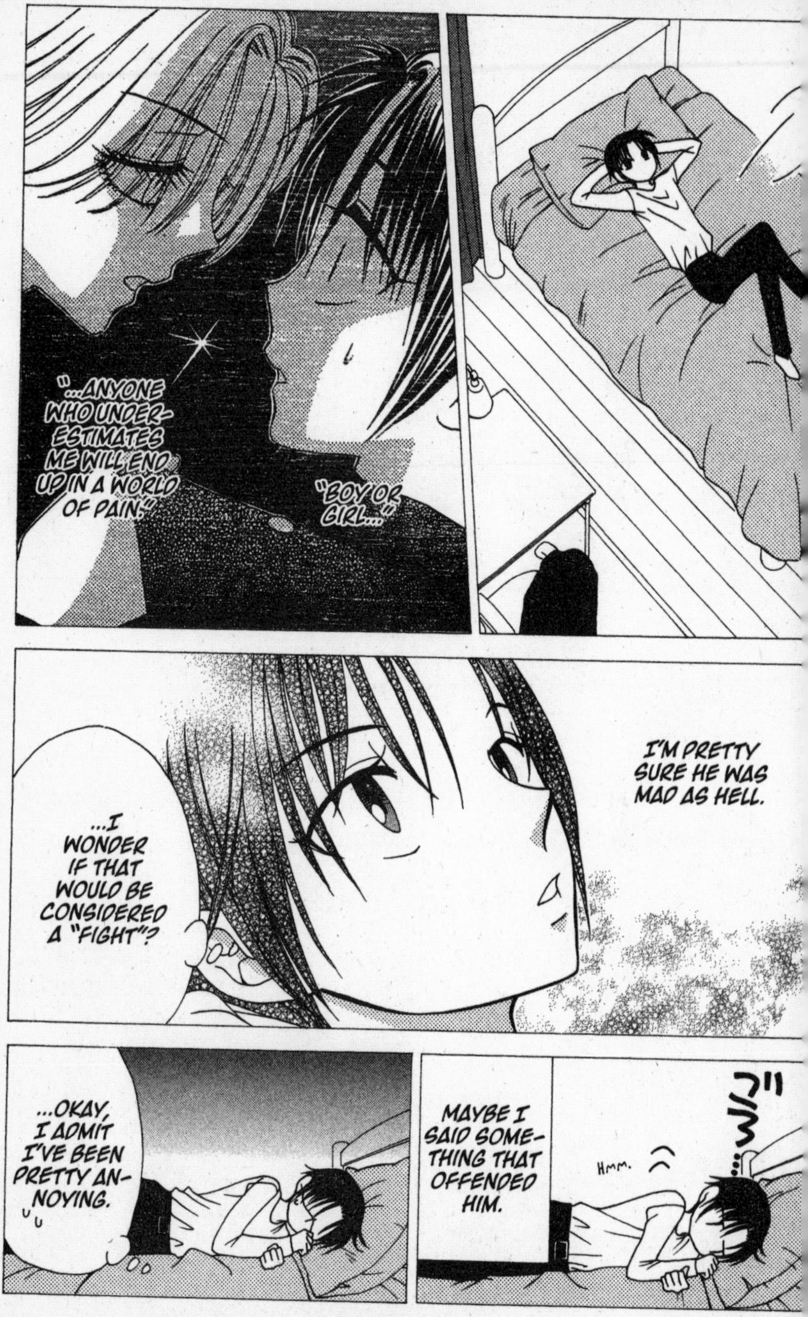
"BOY OR GIRL..."
"...ANYONE WHO UNDER-ESTIMATES ME WILL END UP IN A WORLD OF PAIN."
I'M PRETTY SURE HE WAS MAD AS HELL.
...I WONDER IF THAT WOULD BE CONSIDERED A "FIGHT"?
HMM.
MAYBE I SAID SOME-THING THAT OFFENDED HIM.
...OKAY, I ADMIT I'VE BEEN PRETTY AN-NOYING.

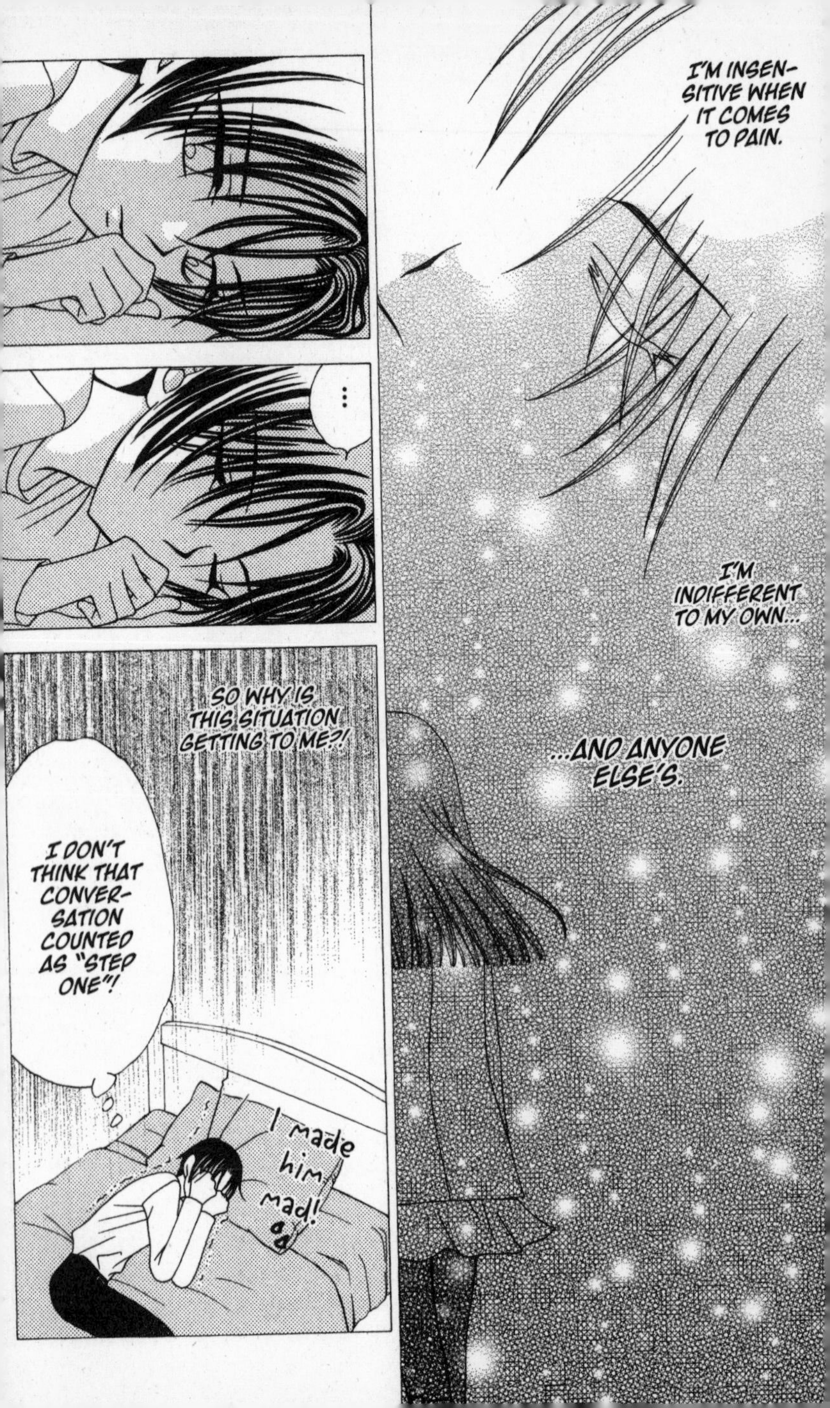
I'M INSEN-SITIVE WHEN IT COMES TO PAIN.
I'M INDIFFERENT TO MY OWN...
...AND ANYONE ELSE'S.
...
SO WHY IS THIS SITUATION GETTING TO ME?!
I DON'T THINK THAT CONVER-SATION COUNTED AS "STEP ONE"!
I made him mad!

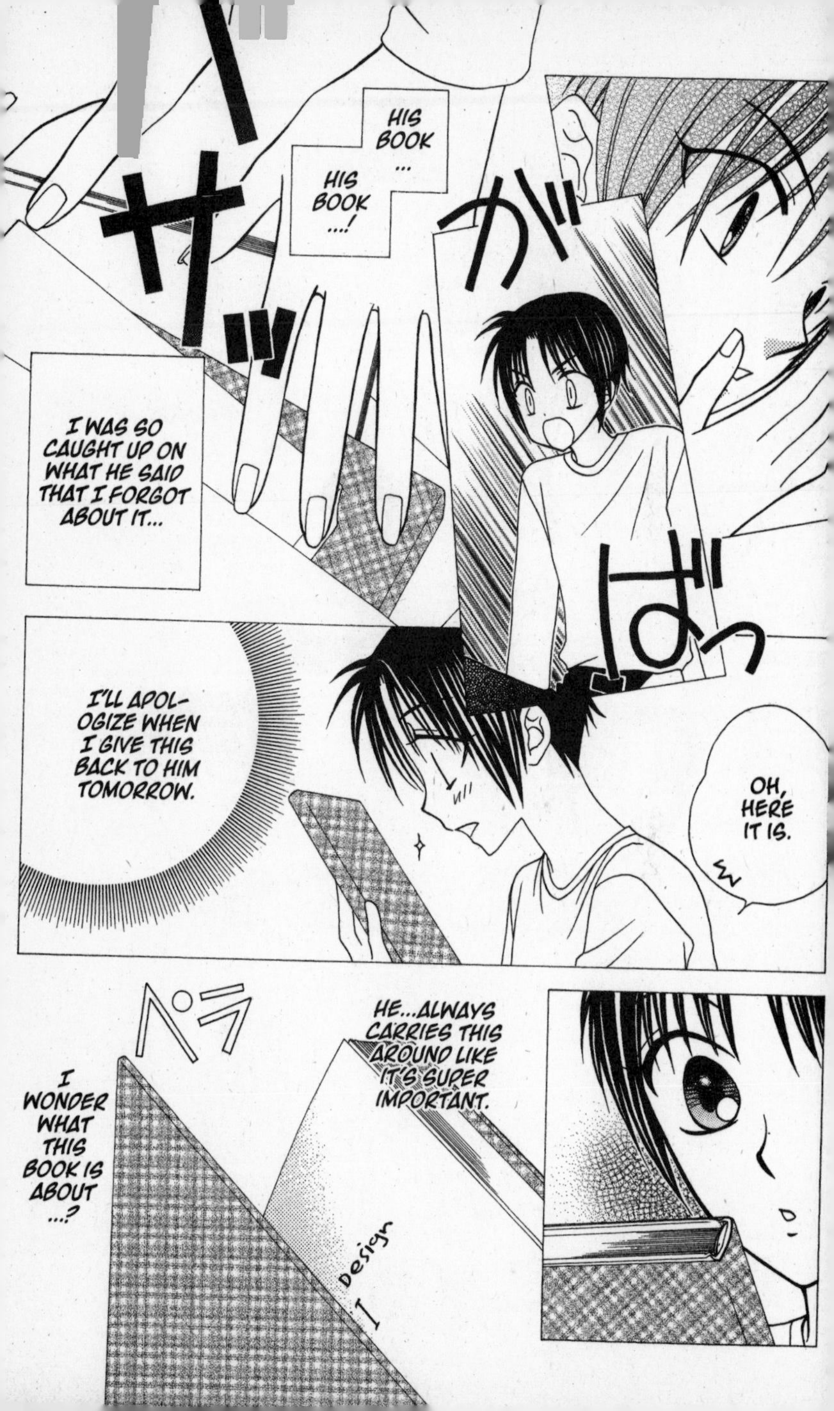
HIS BOOK ...
HIS BOOK ...!
が
ばっ
ザッ
I WAS SO CAUGHT UP ON WHAT HE SAID THAT I FORGOT ABOUT IT...
OH, HERE IT IS.
I'LL APOLOGIZE WHEN I GIVE THIS BACK TO HIM TOMORROW.
HE...ALWAYS CARRIES THIS AROUND LIKE IT'S SUPER IMPORTANT.
ペラ
I WONDER WHAT THIS BOOK IS ABOUT ...?
Design I

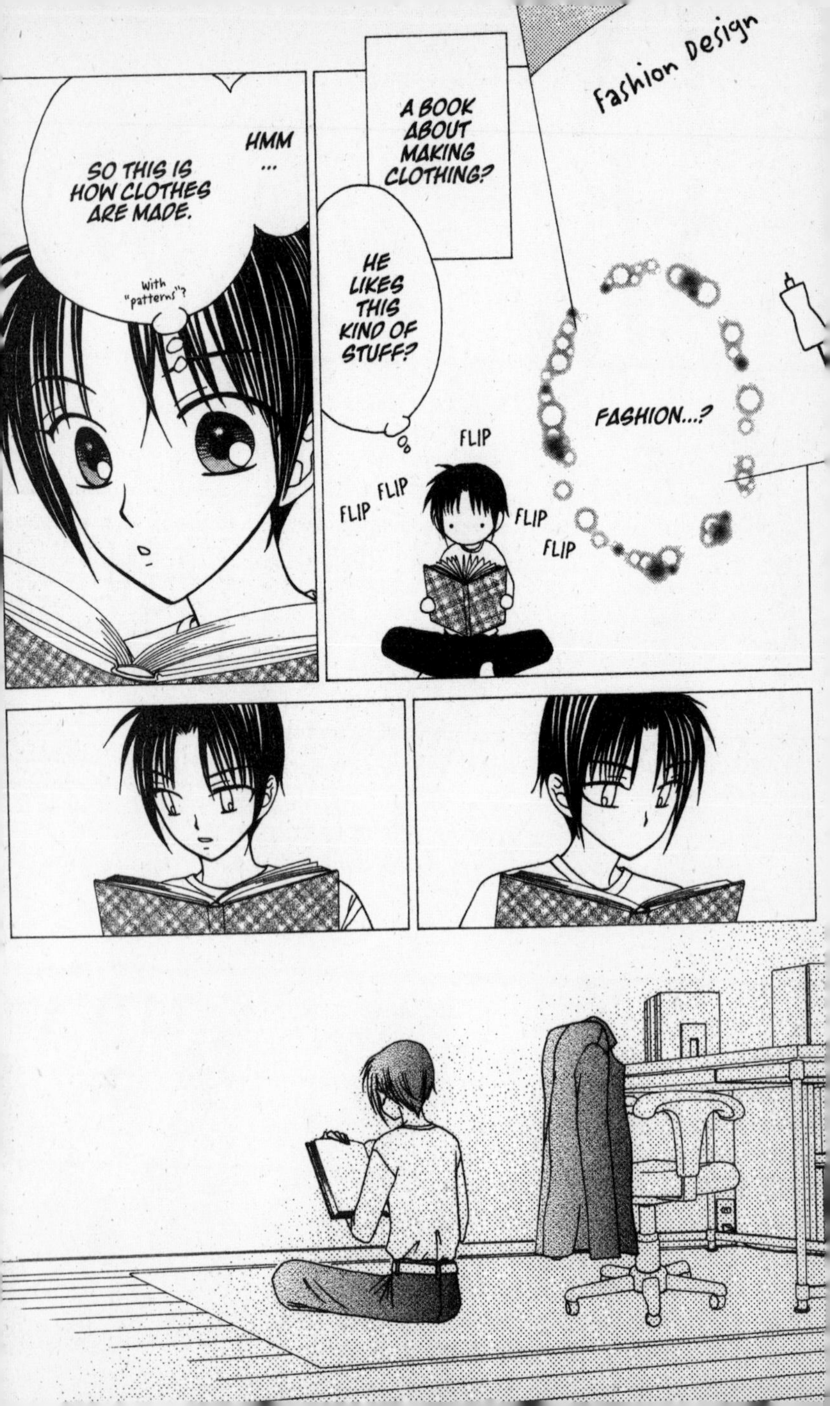
Fashion Design
A BOOK ABOUT MAKING CLOTHING?
HE LIKES THIS KIND OF STUFF?
FASHION...?
FLIP
FLIP
FLIP
FLIP
FLIP
HMM ...
SO THIS IS HOW CLOTHES ARE MADE.
with "patterns"?

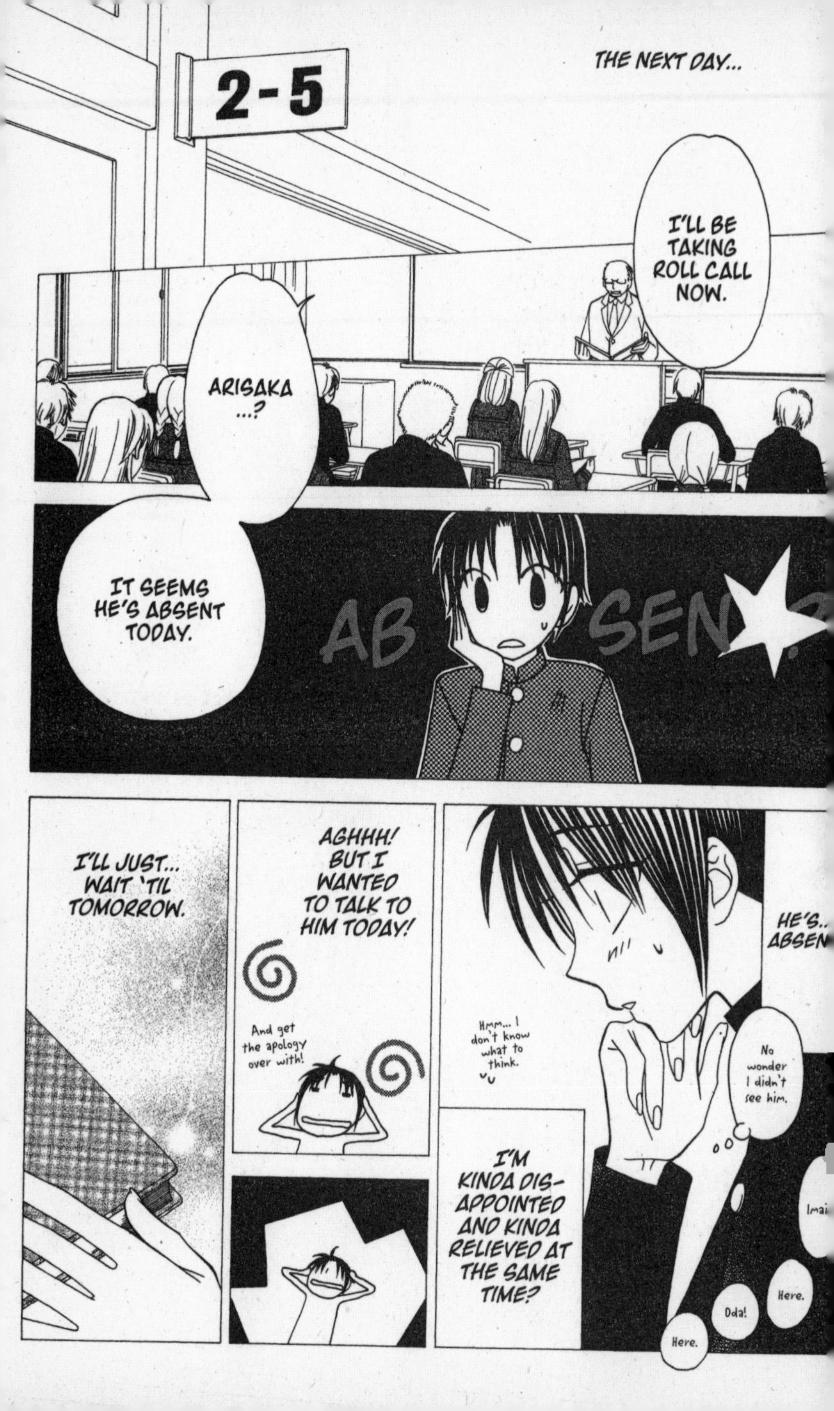

THE NEXT DAY...
2-5
I'LL BE TAKING ROLL CALL NOW.
ARISAKA ...?
IT SEEMS HE'S ABSENT TODAY.
AB SEN
HE'S.. ABSEN
Imai
Here.
Oda!
Here.
No wonder I didn't see him.
Hmm... I don't know what to think.
I'M KINDA DIS-APPOINTED AND KINDA RELIEVED AT THE SAME TIME?
AGHHH! BUT I WANTED TO TALK TO HIM TODAY!
And get the apology over with!
I'LL JUST... WAIT 'TIL TOMORROW.

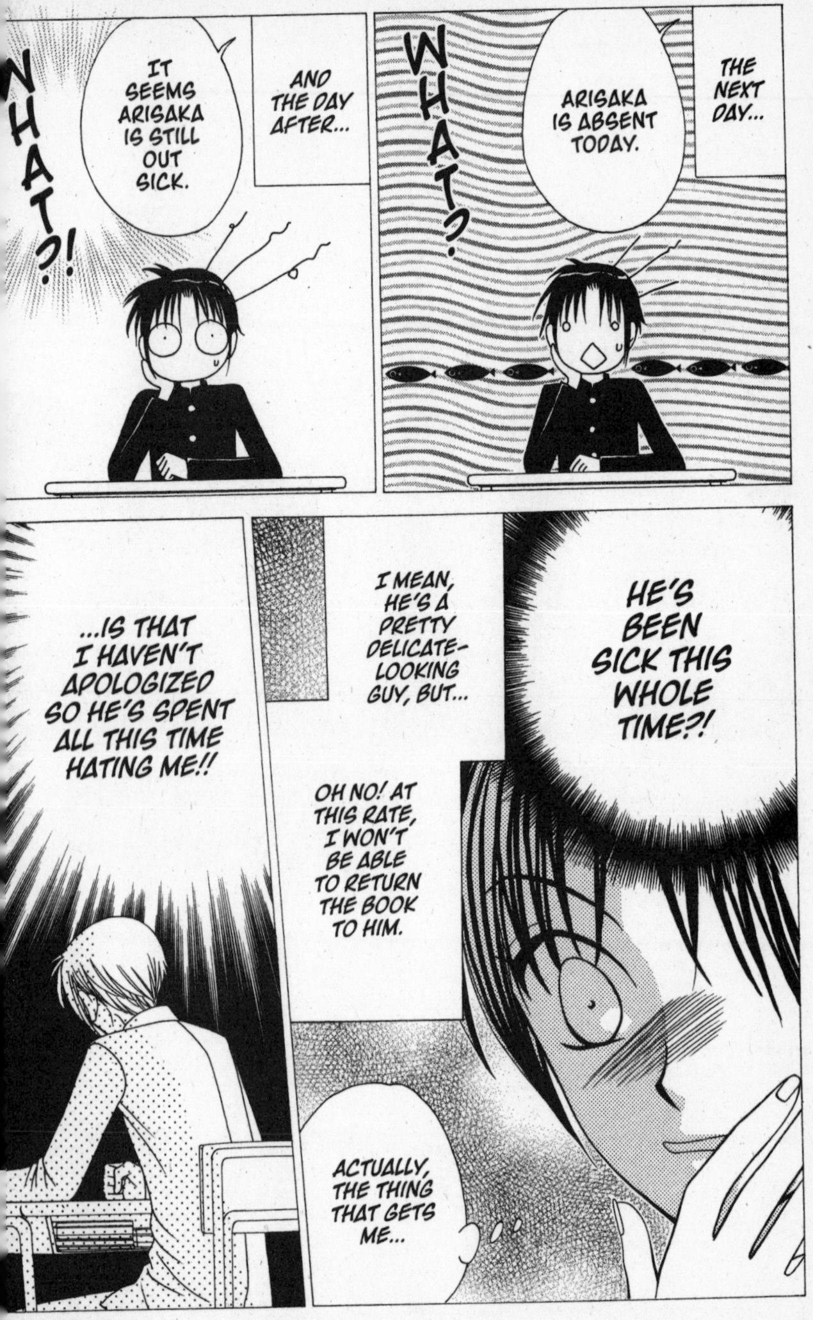
THE NEXT DAY...
ARISAKA IS ABSENT TODAY.
WHAT?
AND THE DAY AFTER...
IT SEEMS ARISAKA IS STILL OUT SICK.
WHAT?!
HE'S BEEN SICK THIS WHOLE TIME?!
I MEAN, HE'S A PRETTY DELICATE-LOOKING GUY, BUT...
OH NO! AT THIS RATE, I WON'T BE ABLE TO RETURN THE BOOK TO HIM.
ACTUALLY, THE THING THAT GETS ME...
...IS THAT I HAVEN'T APOLOGIZED SO HE'S SPENT ALL THIS TIME HATING ME!!

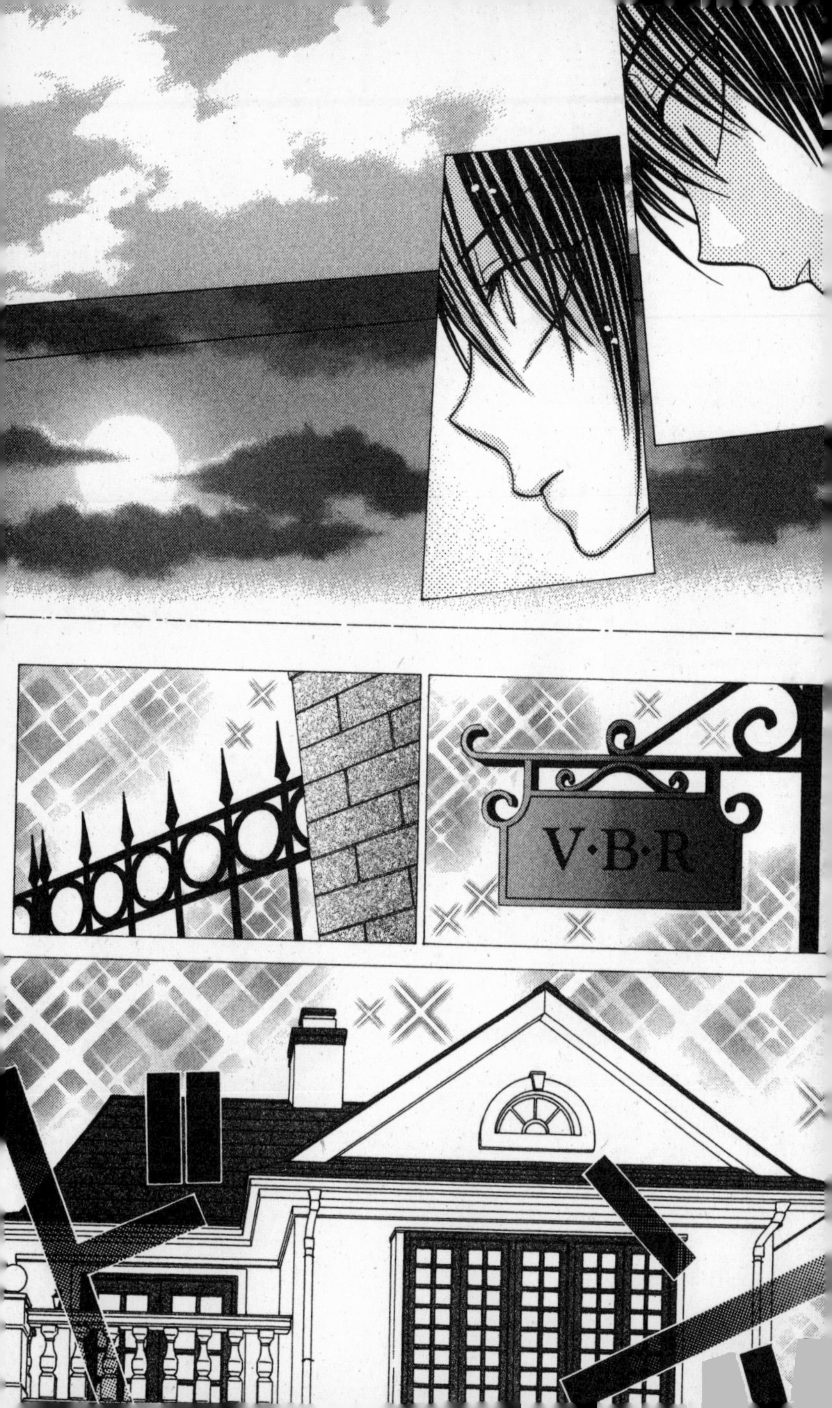
V·B·R

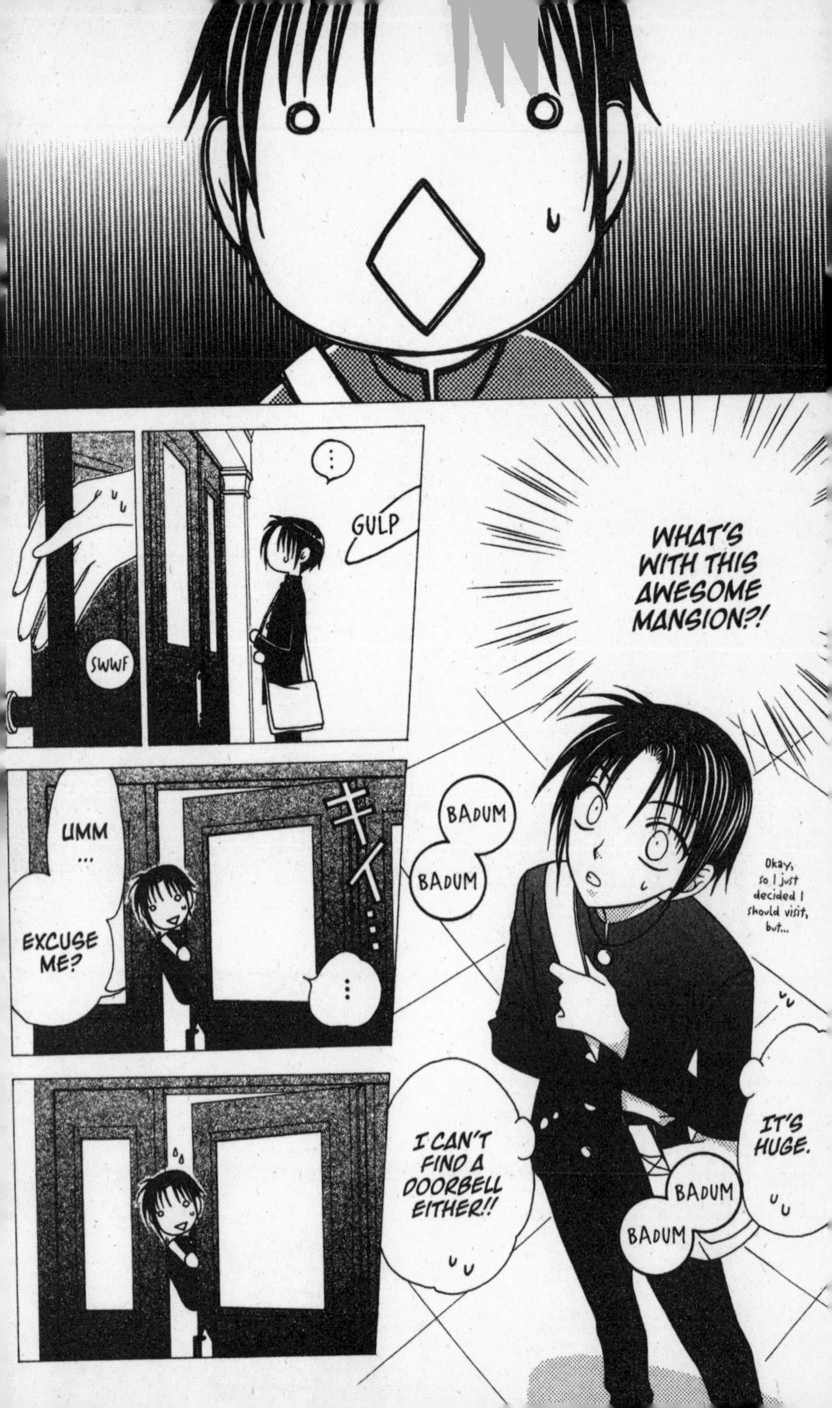
WHAT'S WITH THIS AWESOME MANSION?!
BADUM
BADUM
Okay, so I just decided I should visit, but...
IT'S HUGE.
BADUM
BADUM
I CAN'T FIND A DOORBELL EITHER!!
...
GULP
SWWF
キイ…
UMM ...
EXCUSE ME?
...

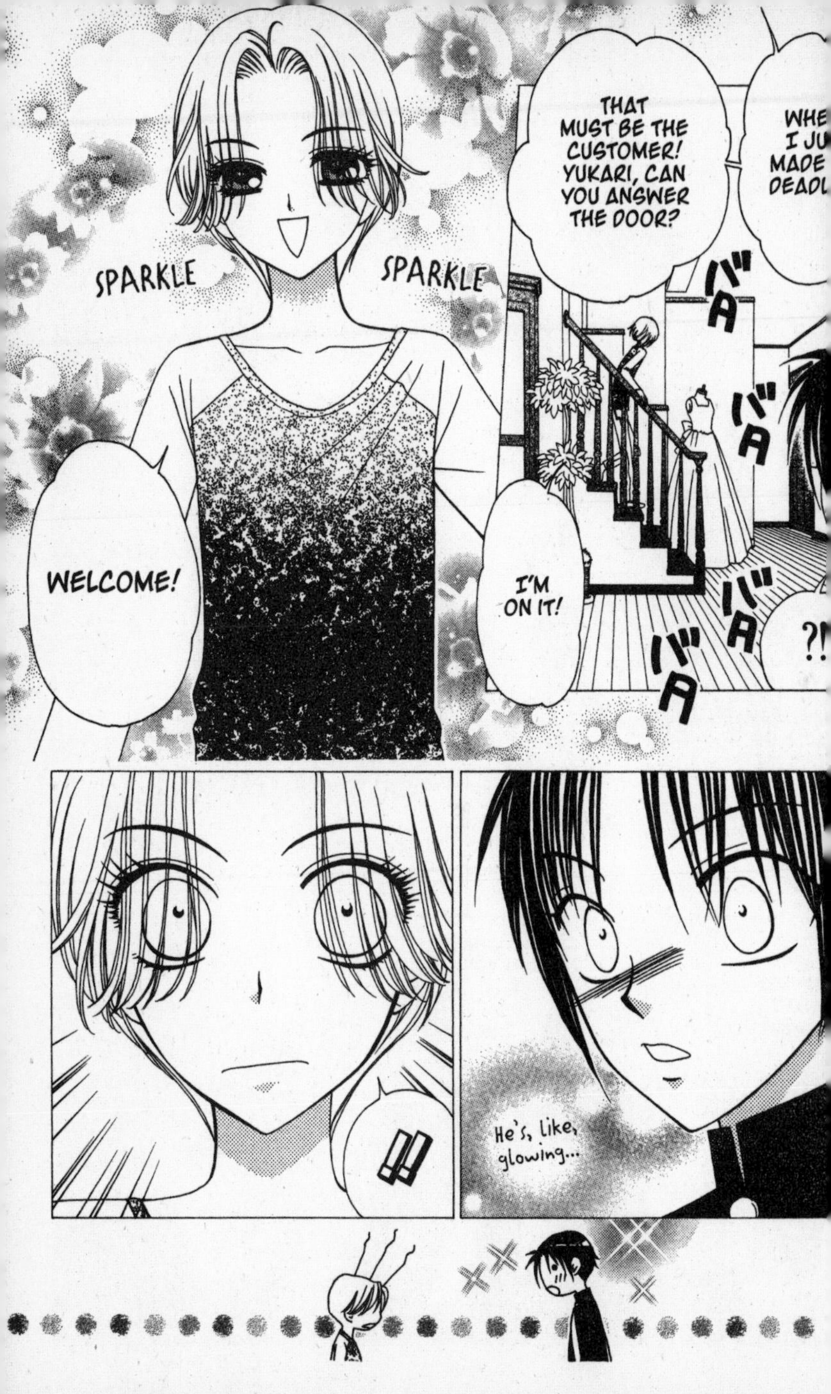
WHE I JU MADE DEADL
THAT MUST BE THE CUSTOMER! YUKARI, CAN YOU ANSWER THE DOOR?
バA バA バA バA
?!
I'M ON IT!
SPARKLE SPARKLE
WELCOME!
He's, like, glowing...
!!

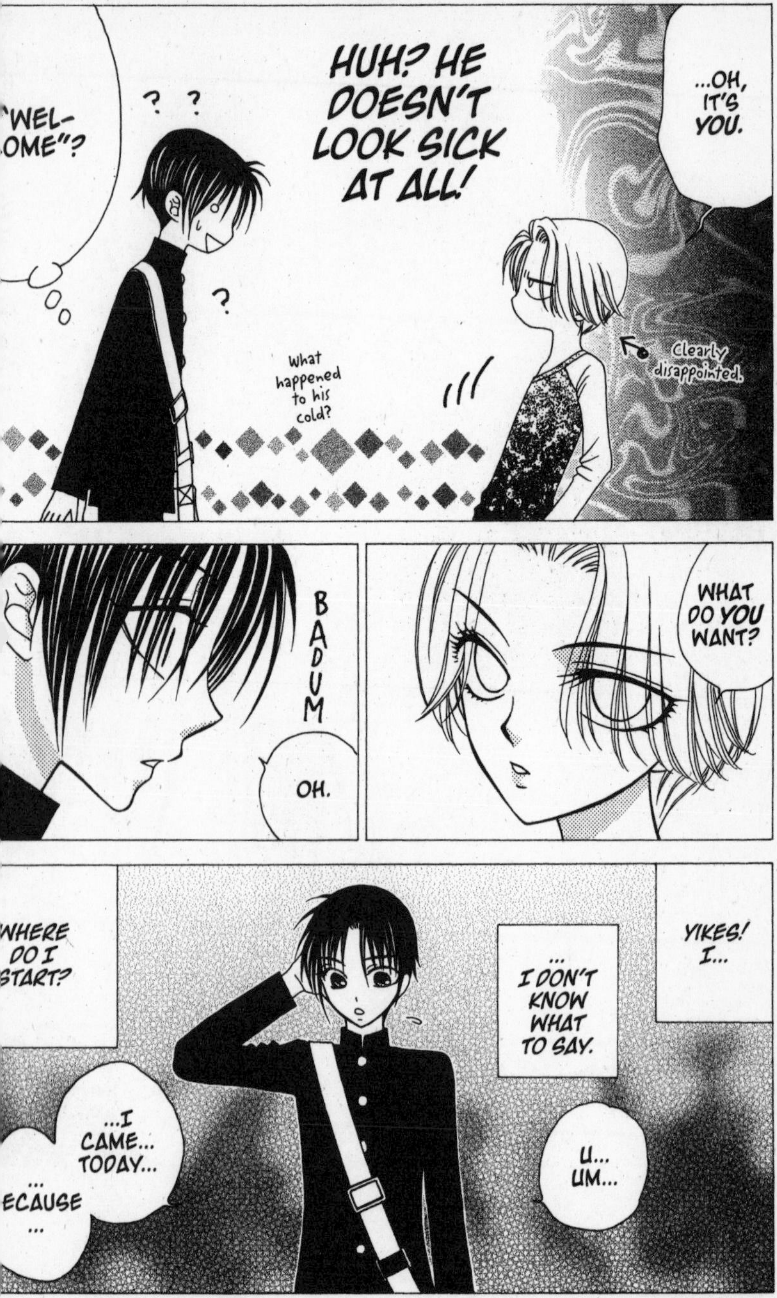
...OH, IT'S YOU.
Clearly disappointed.
HUH? HE DOESN'T LOOK SICK AT ALL!
What happened to his cold?
“WEL- OME”?
WHAT DO YOU WANT?
BADUM
OH.
YIKES! I...
... I DON'T KNOW WHAT TO SAY.
WHERE DO I START?
U... UM...
...I CAME... TODAY... ... ECAUSE ...

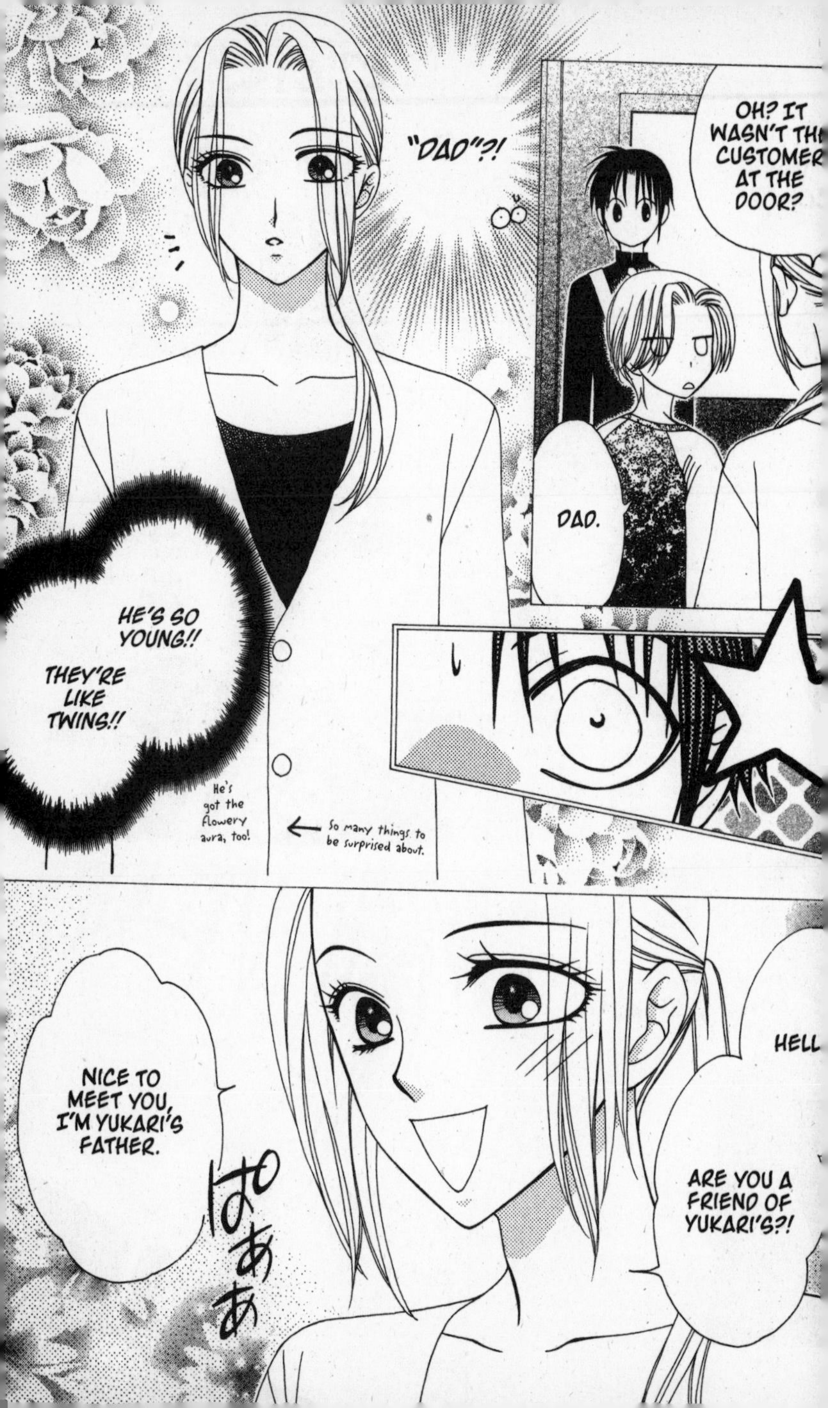
OH? IT WASN'T TH CUSTOMER AT THE DOOR?
DAD.
"DAD"?!
HE'S SO YOUNG!!
THEY'RE LIKE TWINS!!
He's got the flowery aura, too!
So many things to be surprised about.
HELL
ARE YOU A FRIEND OF YUKARI'S?!
NICE TO MEET YOU, I'M YUKARI'S FATHER.
ぱあぁ

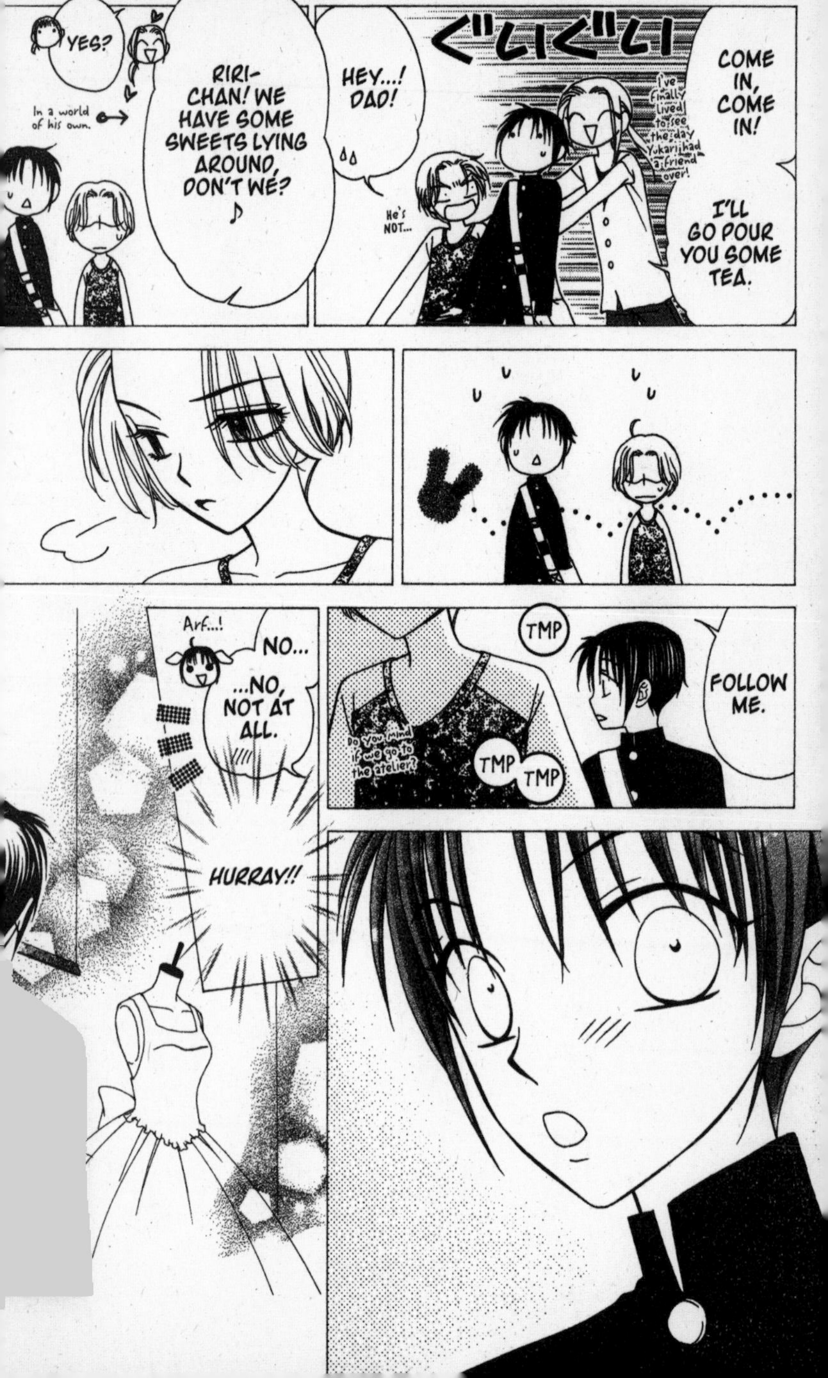
ぐいぐい
COME IN, COME IN!
I've finally lived to see the day Yukari had a friend over!
I'LL GO POUR YOU SOME TEA.
HEY...! DAD!
He's NOT...
RIRI-CHAN! WE HAVE SOME SWEETS LYING AROUND, DON'T WE? ♪
YES?
In a world of his own.
FOLLOW ME.
TMP
TMP
TMP
Do you mind if we go to the atelier?
NO...
...NO, NOT AT ALL.
Arf...!
HURRAY!!

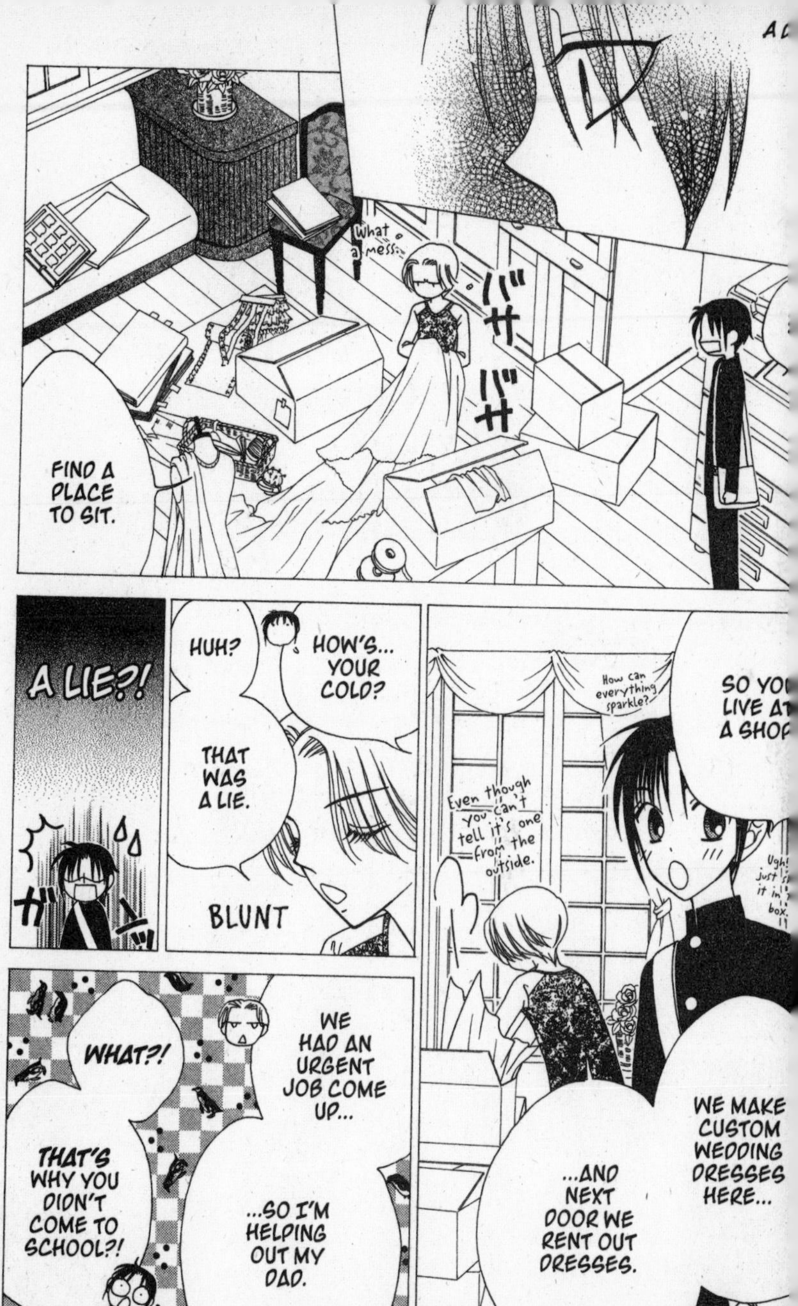
What a mess...
バサ
バサ
FIND A PLACE TO SIT.
SO YO
LIVE AT
A SHOP
How can everything sparkle?
Even though you can't tell it's one from the outside.
WE MAKE CUSTOM WEDDING DRESSES HERE...
...AND NEXT DOOR WE RENT OUT DRESSES.
HOW'S... YOUR COLD?
HUH?
THAT WAS A LIE.
BLUNT
A LIE?!
ガ
WE HAD AN URGENT JOB COME UP...
...SO I'M HELPING OUT MY DAD.
WHAT?!
THAT'S WHY YOU DIDN'T COME TO SCHOOL?!

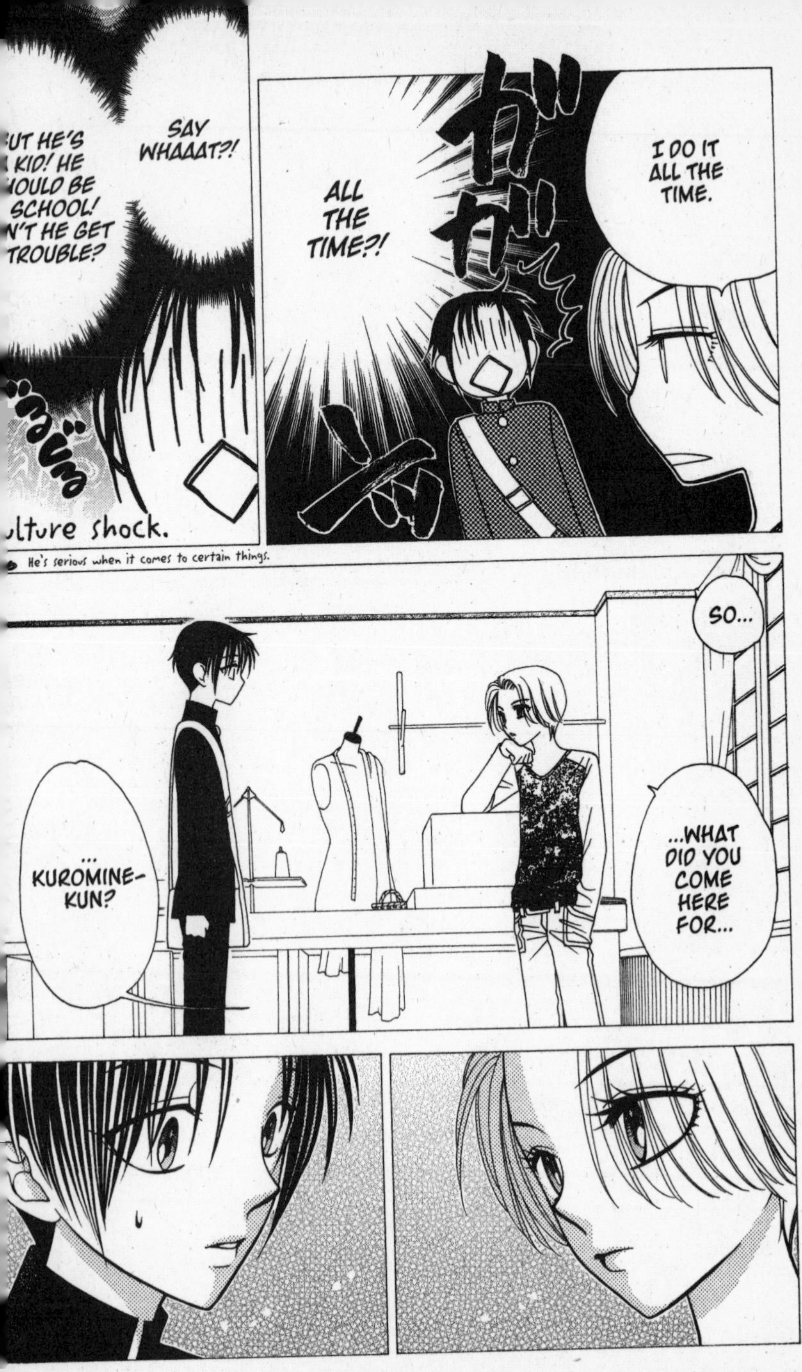
I DO IT ALL THE TIME.
ALL THE TIME?!
SAY WHAAAT?!
UT HE'S KID! HE HOULD BE SCHOOL! N'T HE GET TROUBLE?
ulture shock.
He's serious when it comes to certain things.
SO...
...WHAT DID YOU COME HERE FOR...
... KUROMINE-KUN?

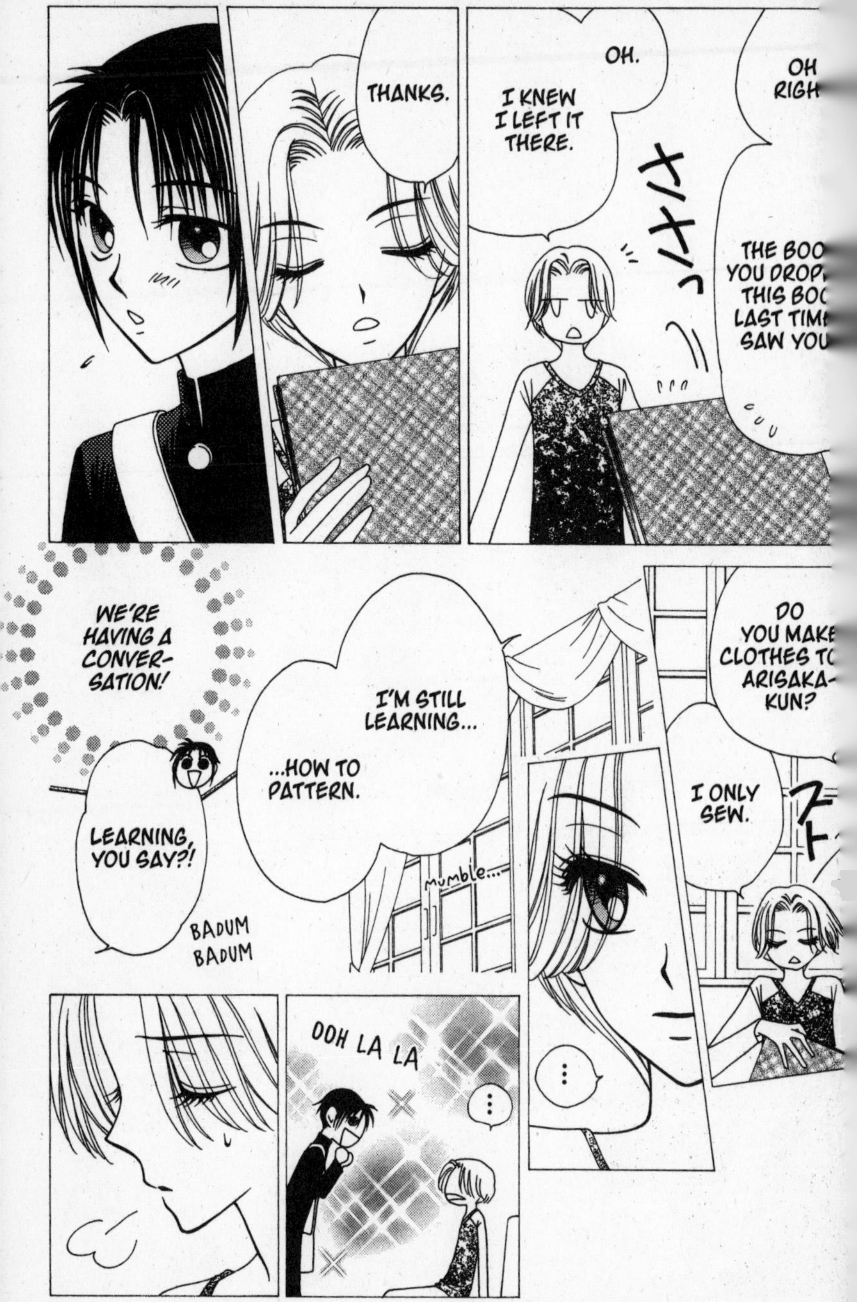
OH RIGH
THE BOO YOU DROP THIS BOO LAST TIM SAW YOU
OH.
I KNEW I LEFT IT THERE.
THANKS.
DO YOU MAKE CLOTHES TC ARISAKA-KUN?
I ONLY SEW.
...
I'M STILL LEARNING...
...HOW TO PATTERN.
mumble...
WE'RE HAVING A CONVER-SATION!
LEARNING, YOU SAY?!
BADUM BADUM
OOH LA LA
...

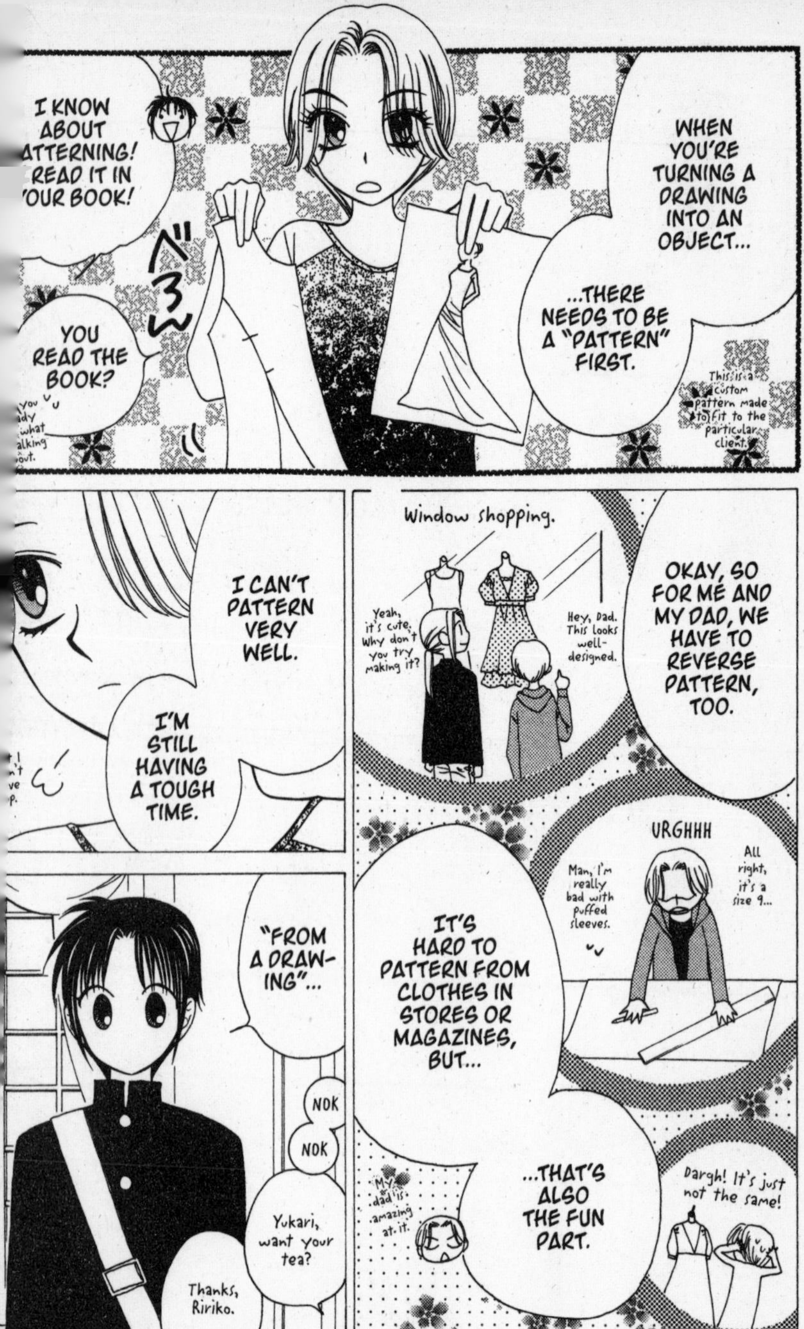
WHEN YOU'RE TURNING A DRAWING INTO AN OBJECT...
...THERE NEEDS TO BE A "PATTERN" FIRST.
This is a custom pattern made to fit to the particular client.
I KNOW ABOUT ATTERNING! READ IT IN OUR BOOK!
べろん
YOU READ THE BOOK?
Window shopping.
OKAY, SO FOR ME AND MY DAD, WE HAVE TO REVERSE PATTERN, TOO.
Hey, Dad. This looks well-designed.
Yeah, it's cute. Why don't you try making it?
URGHHH
All right, it's a size 9...
Man, I'm really bad with puffed sleeves.
IT'S HARD TO PATTERN FROM CLOTHES IN STORES OR MAGAZINES, BUT...
Dargh! It's just not the same!
...THAT'S ALSO THE FUN PART.
My dad is amazing at it.
I CAN'T PATTERN VERY WELL.
I'M STILL HAVING A TOUGH TIME.
"FROM A DRAWING"...
NOK
NOK
Yukari, want your tea?
Thanks, Ririko.

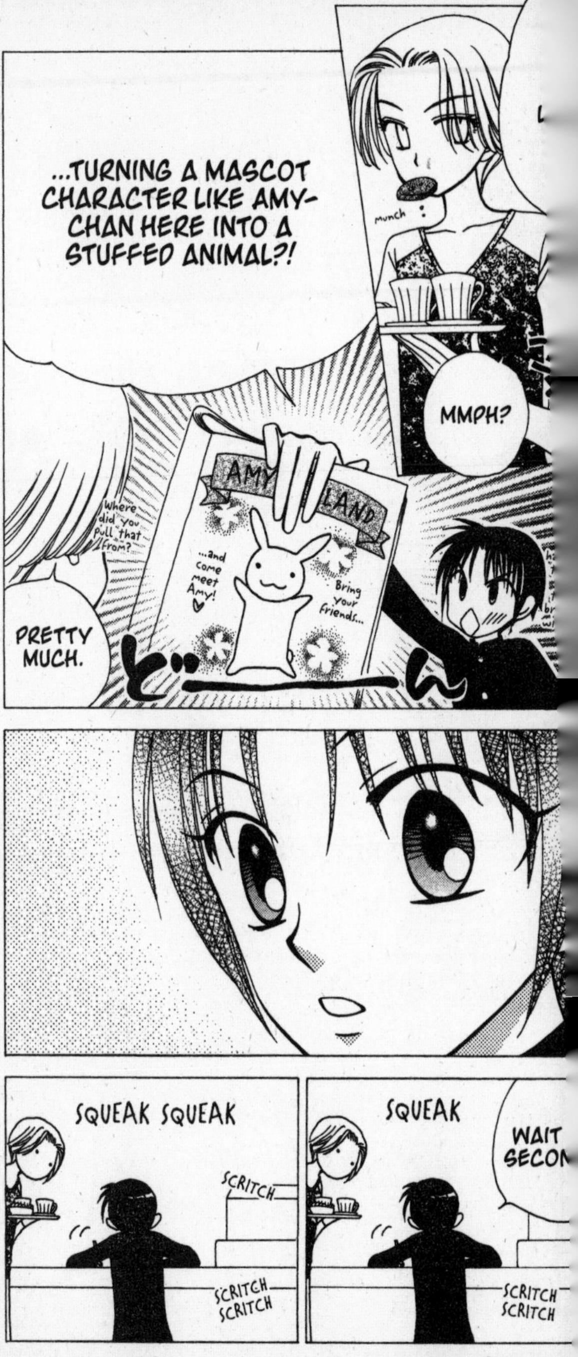
munch
MMPH?
...TURNING A MASCOT CHARACTER LIKE AMY-CHAN HERE INTO A STUFFED ANIMAL?!
AMY LAND
...and come meet Amy!
Bring your friends...
Where did you pull that from?
PRETTY MUCH.
ど———ん
SQUEAK
WAIT SECON
SCRITCH SCRITCH
SQUEAK SQUEAK
SCRITCH
SCRITCH SCRITCH

Does anyone mind if I use this space for a retrospective of 2007? The end of the year is always busy for me. Yes, busy in a lot of ways...

Let me tell you the story that is the most recent and memorable of them all, one that makes you go, "Oh my, Hidaka-san! I'm so sorry!"

It happened at the beginning of November.

MY PRECIOUS CAR BECAME SCRAP METAL.

As a result, I still have to visit the hospital off and on. Ha ha...

Should I start the story over from the beginning?

On November 2nd, I had just finished manga pages for a contest and was starting work on Episode 67 of V.B.Rose. I got in my car to pick up some reference materials from a bookstore. On the way there, as I was driving in the carpool lane, a car crashed into my right side! INTO MY RIGHT SIDE!! IT HIT THE DRIVER'S SIDE HEAD-ON!!

Eeek!

(Continued in the next column...) →

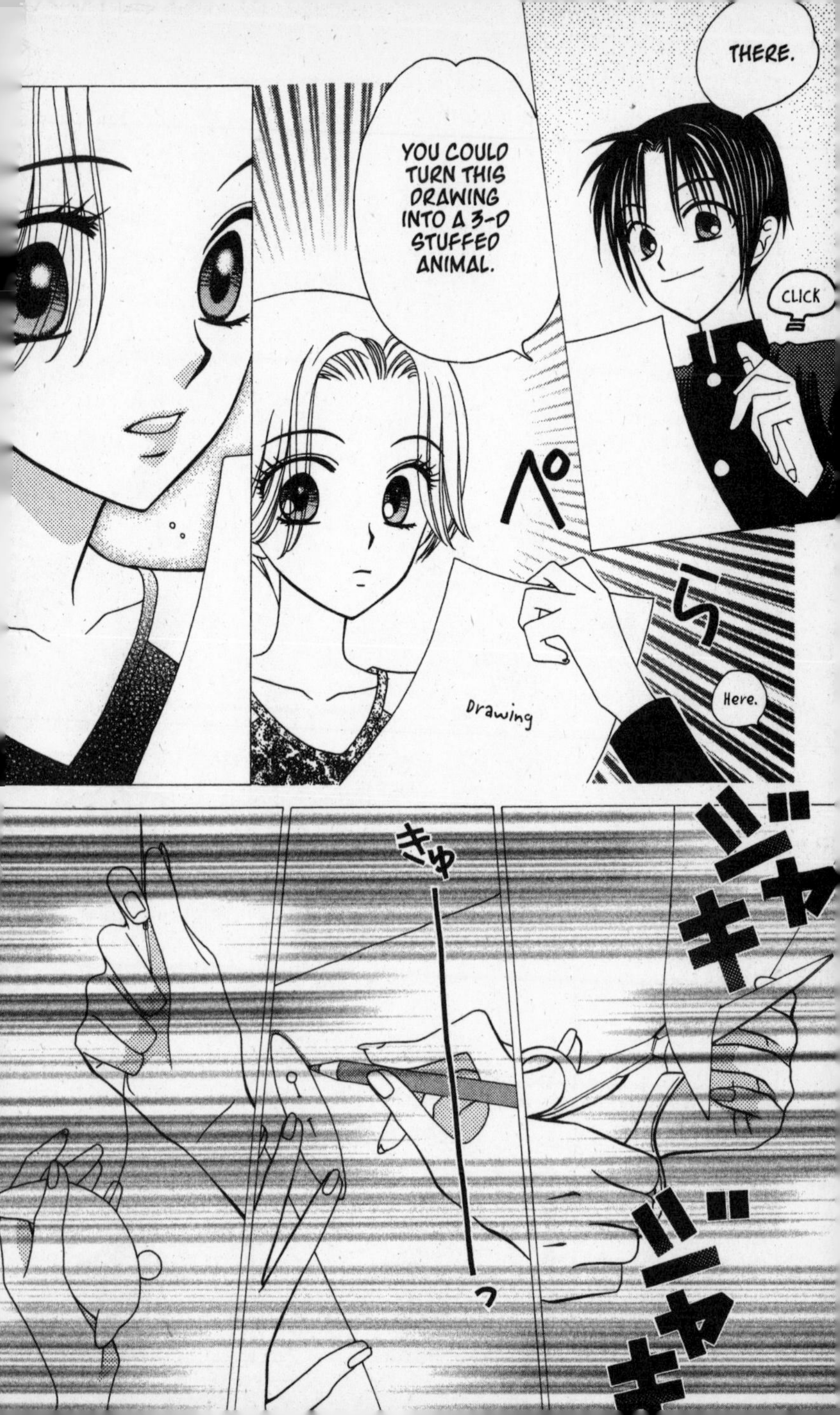
THERE.
CLICK
YOU COULD TURN THIS DRAWING INTO A 3-D STUFFED ANIMAL.
ぺ
ら
Here.
Drawing
ジャキ
ジャキ
きゅ―っ

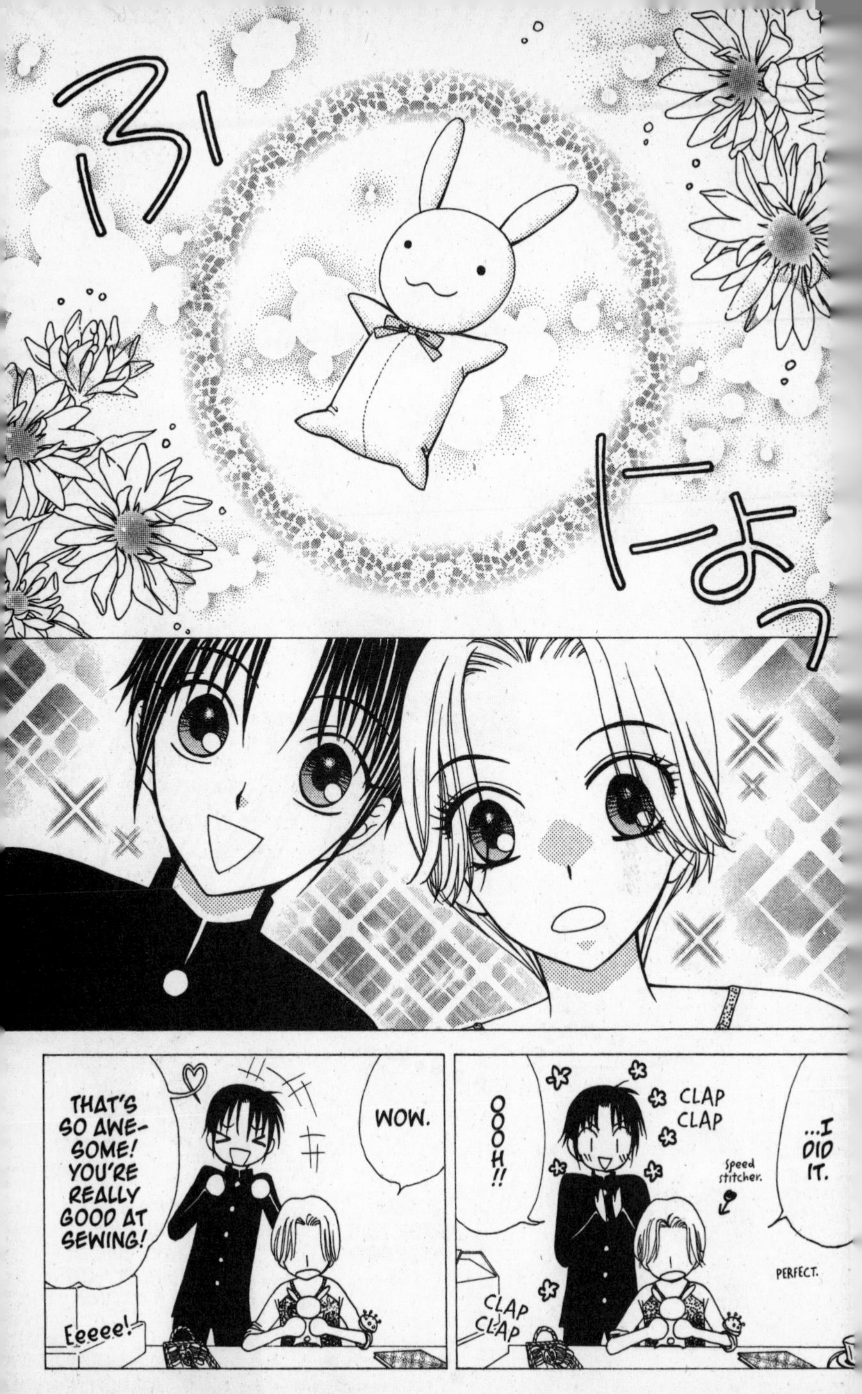

ふにょっ
...I DID IT.
PERFECT.
Speed stitcher.
CLAP CLAP
OOOH!!
CLAP CLAP
WOW.
THAT'S SO AWE-SOME! YOU'RE REALLY GOOD AT SEWING!
Eeeee!

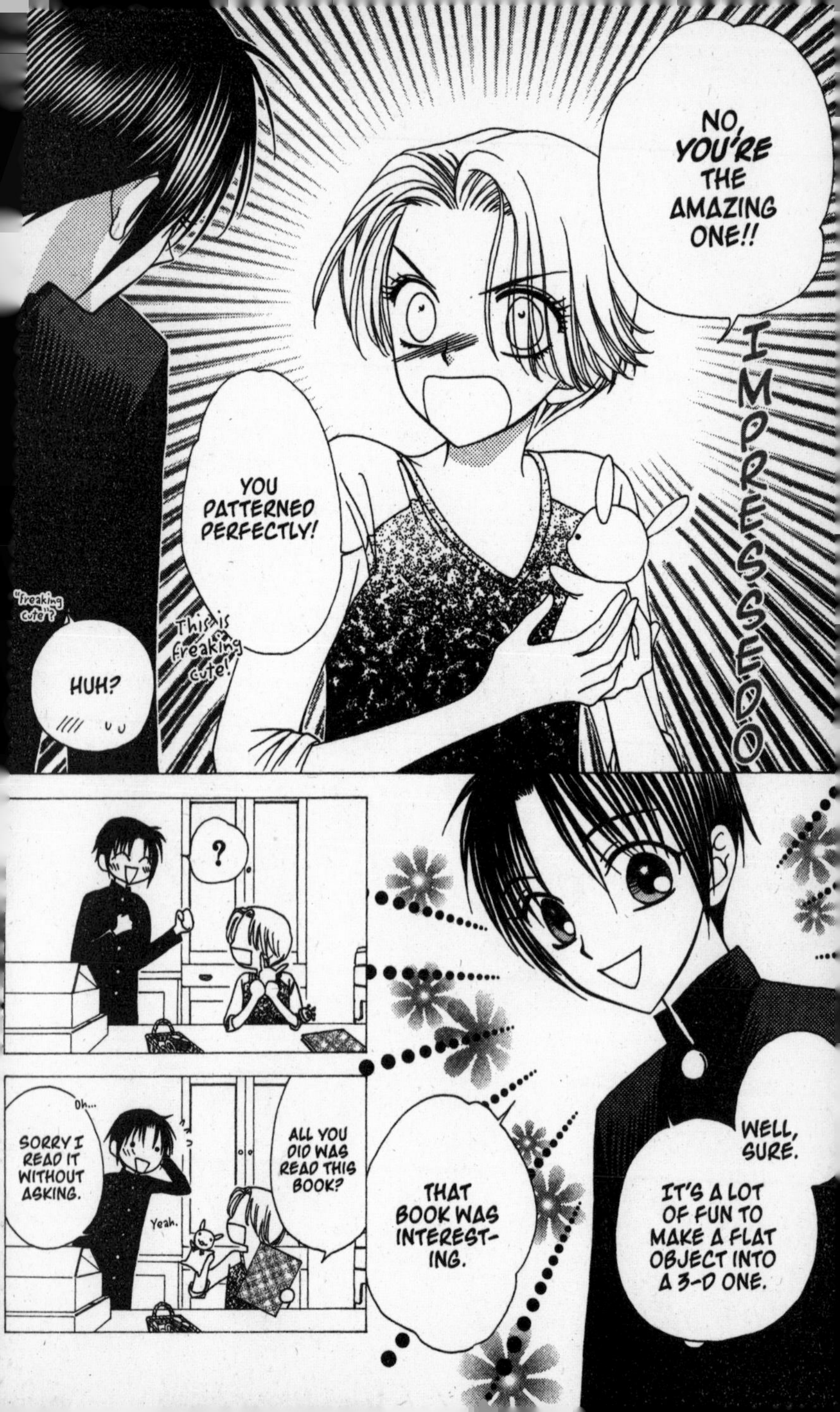
NO, YOU'RE THE AMAZING ONE!!
IMPRESSEDO
YOU PATTERNED PERFECTLY!
This is freaking cute!
HUH?
"freaking cute"?
WELL, SURE.
IT'S A LOT OF FUN TO MAKE A FLAT OBJECT INTO A 3-D ONE.
THAT BOOK WAS INTERESTING.
?
ALL YOU DID WAS READ THIS BOOK?
Oh...
SORRY I READ IT WITHOUT ASKING.
Yeah.

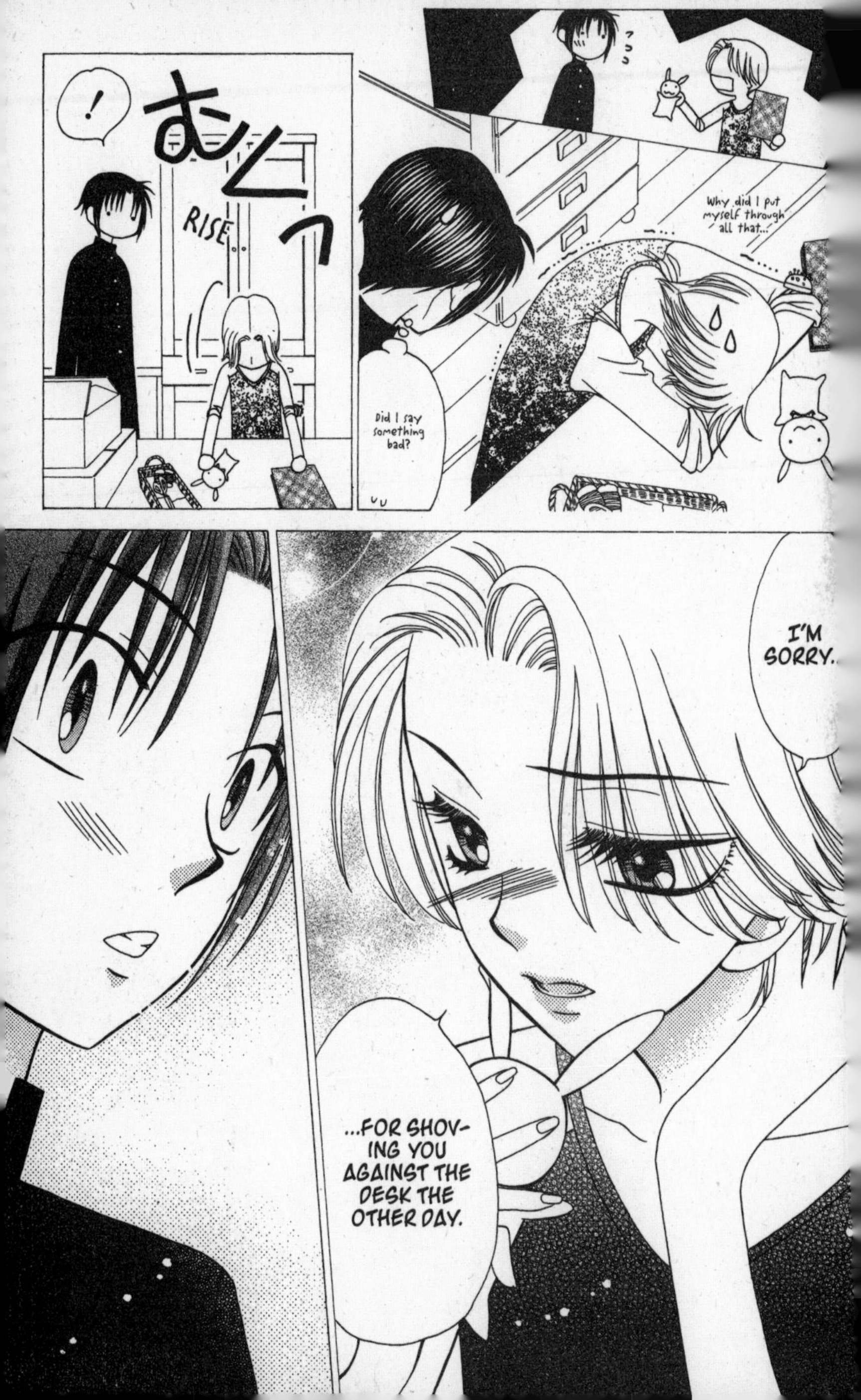
Why did I put myself through all that...
Did I say something bad?
むくっ
RISE
!
I'M SORRY...
...FOR SHOVING YOU AGAINST THE DESK THE OTHER DAY.

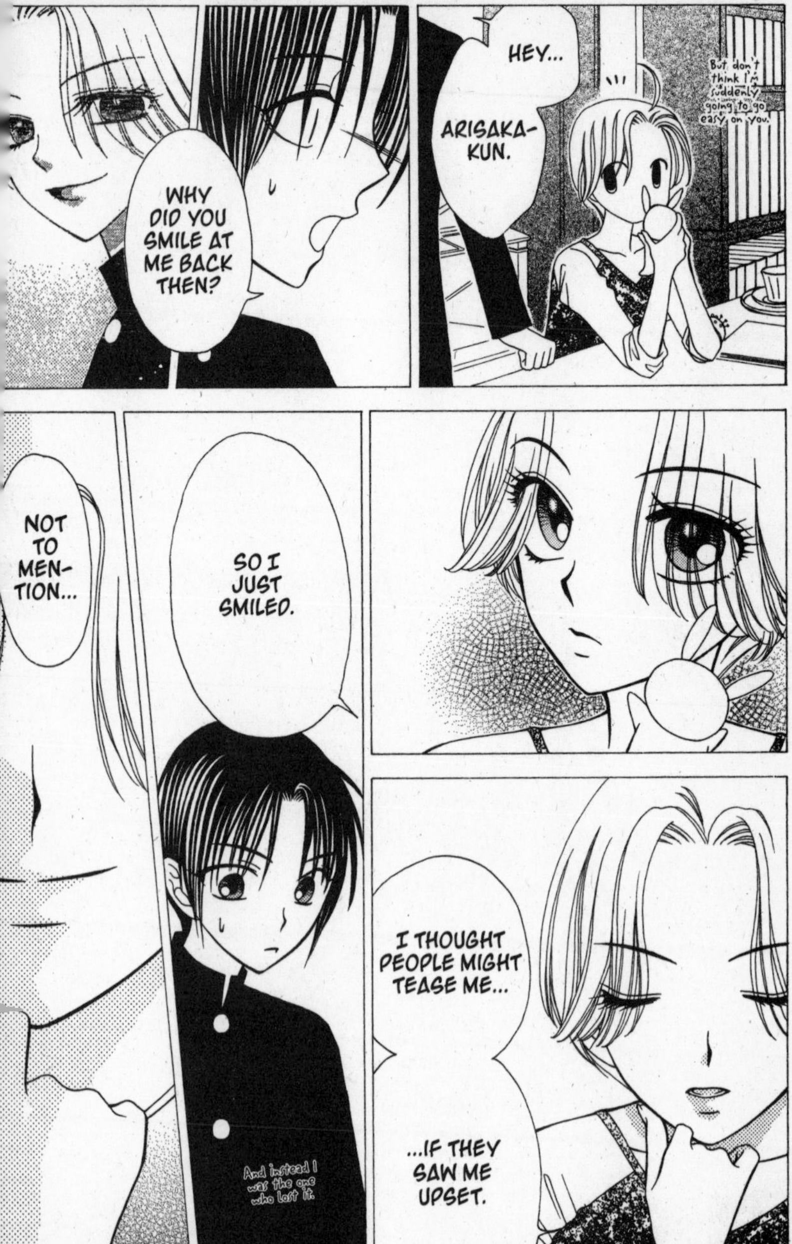
HEY...
ARISAKA-KUN.
But don't think I'm suddenly going to go easy on you.
WHY DID YOU SMILE AT ME BACK THEN?
I THOUGHT PEOPLE MIGHT TEASE ME...
...IF THEY SAW ME UPSET.
SO I JUST SMILED.
And instead I was the one who lost it.
NOT TO MEN-TION...

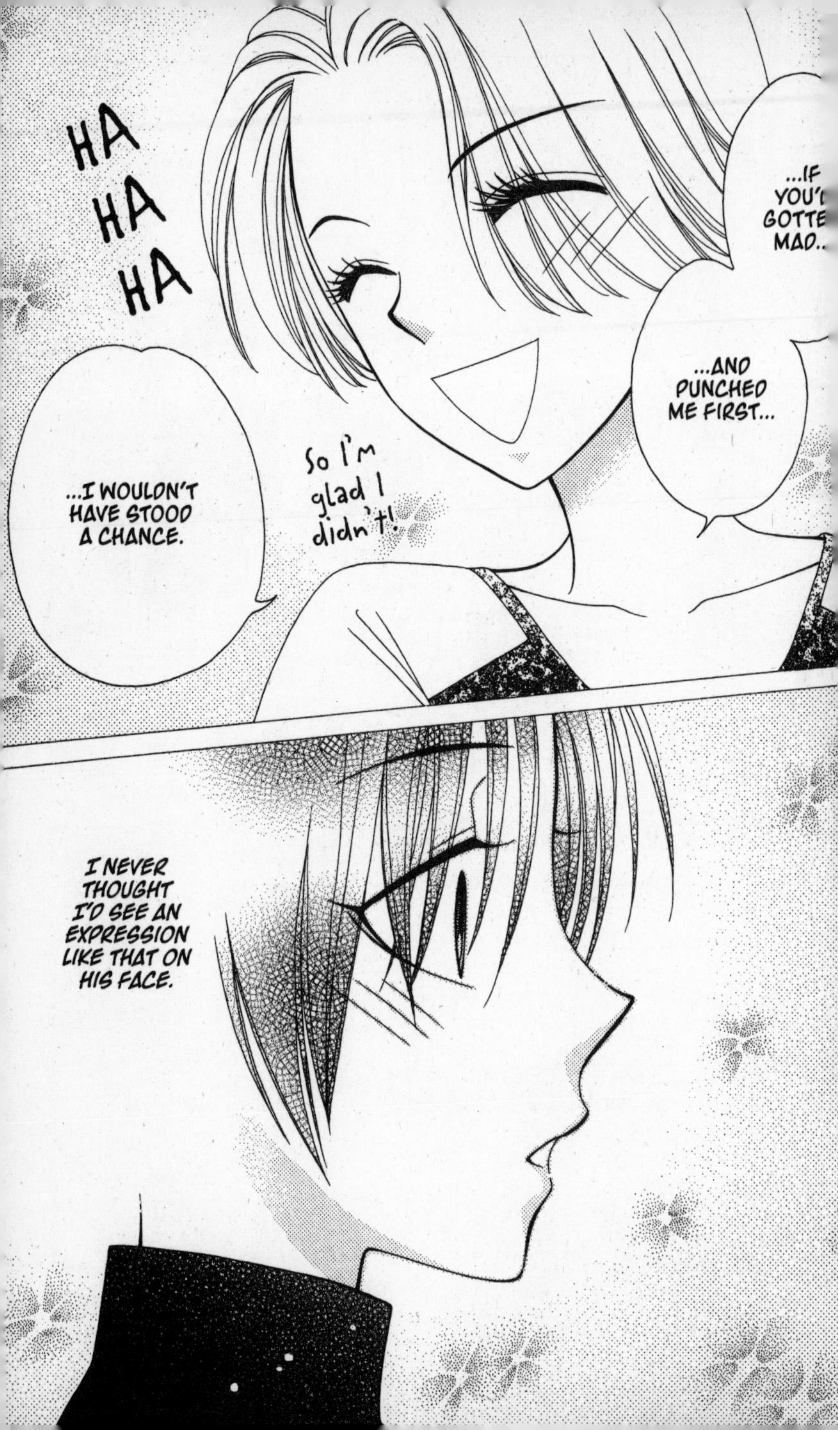
...IF YOU'D GOTTE MAD..
...AND PUNCHED ME FIRST...
HA HA HA
...I WOULDN'T HAVE STOOD A CHANCE.
So I'm glad I didn't!
I NEVER THOUGHT I'D SEE AN EXPRESSION LIKE THAT ON HIS FACE.

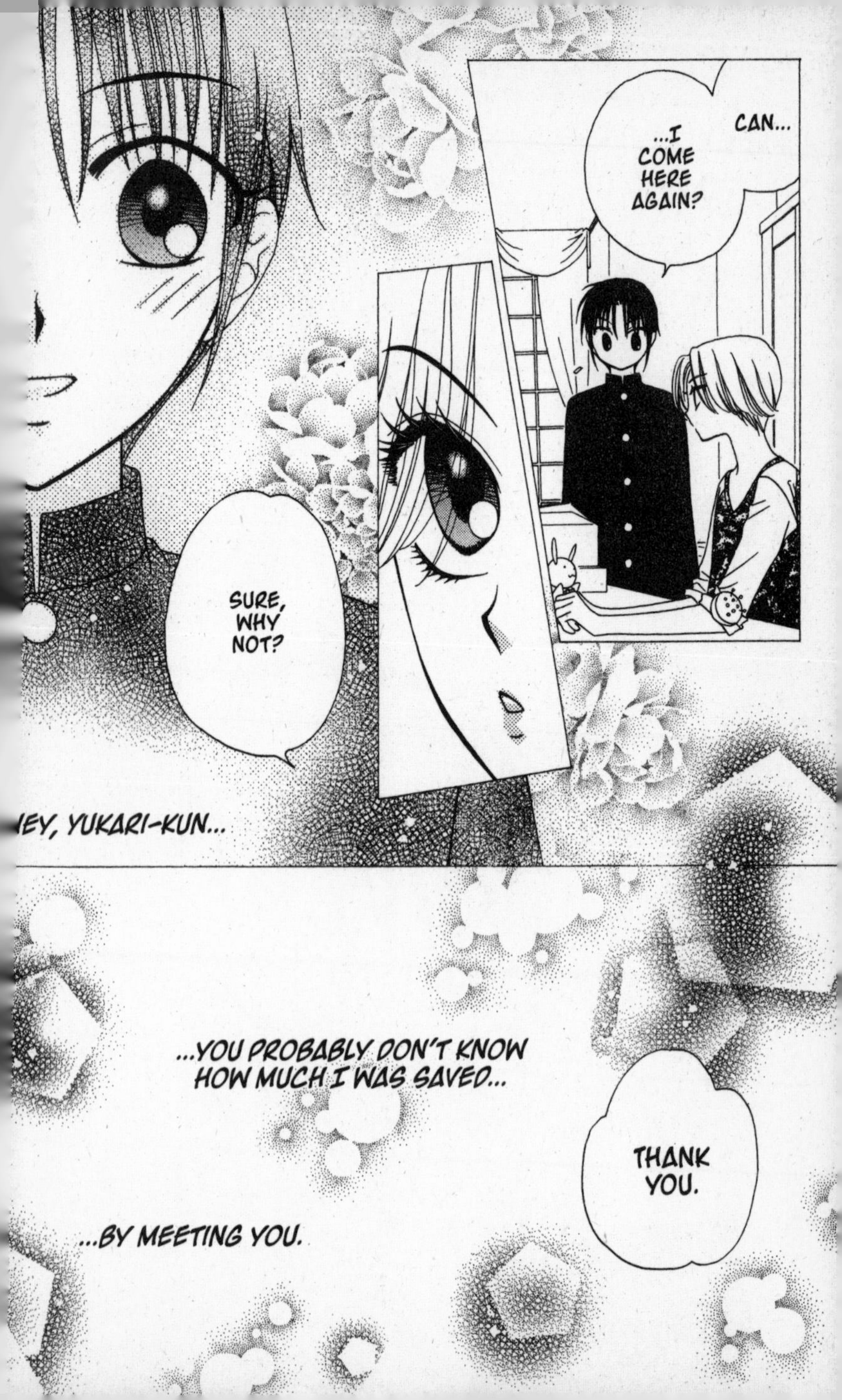
CAN...
...I COME HERE AGAIN?
SURE, WHY NOT?
HEY, YUKARI-KUN...
...YOU PROBABLY DON'T KNOW HOW MUCH I WAS SAVED...
...BY MEETING YOU.
THANK YOU.

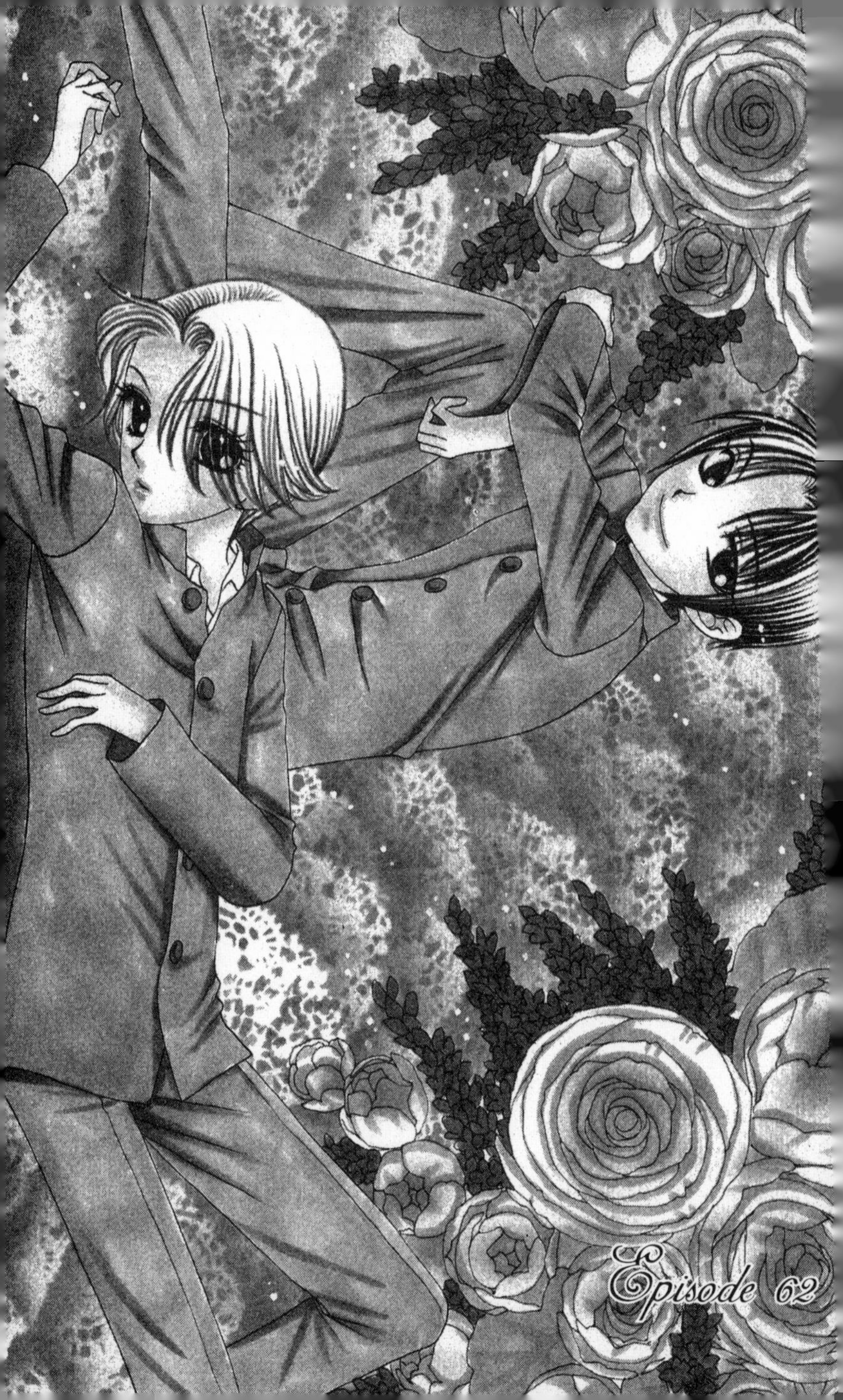
Episode 62

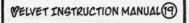

♥ELVET INSTRUCTION MANUAL ⑲

WHILE WRITING THE MIDDLE SCHOOL STORY, I DREW THE OUTSIDE OF MITSUYA'S HOUSE FOR THE FIRST TIME.
This
Hrmm.
Original
Makin' copies, makin' copies.
Maeda-san, is something wrong?
No...
Whose house is this?
It's Mitsuya's house!
Note
She inked it.
Ha ha ha!!! What a funny thing to say!

She was a little numb because V.B.R. and Ageha's house are both really nice houses.

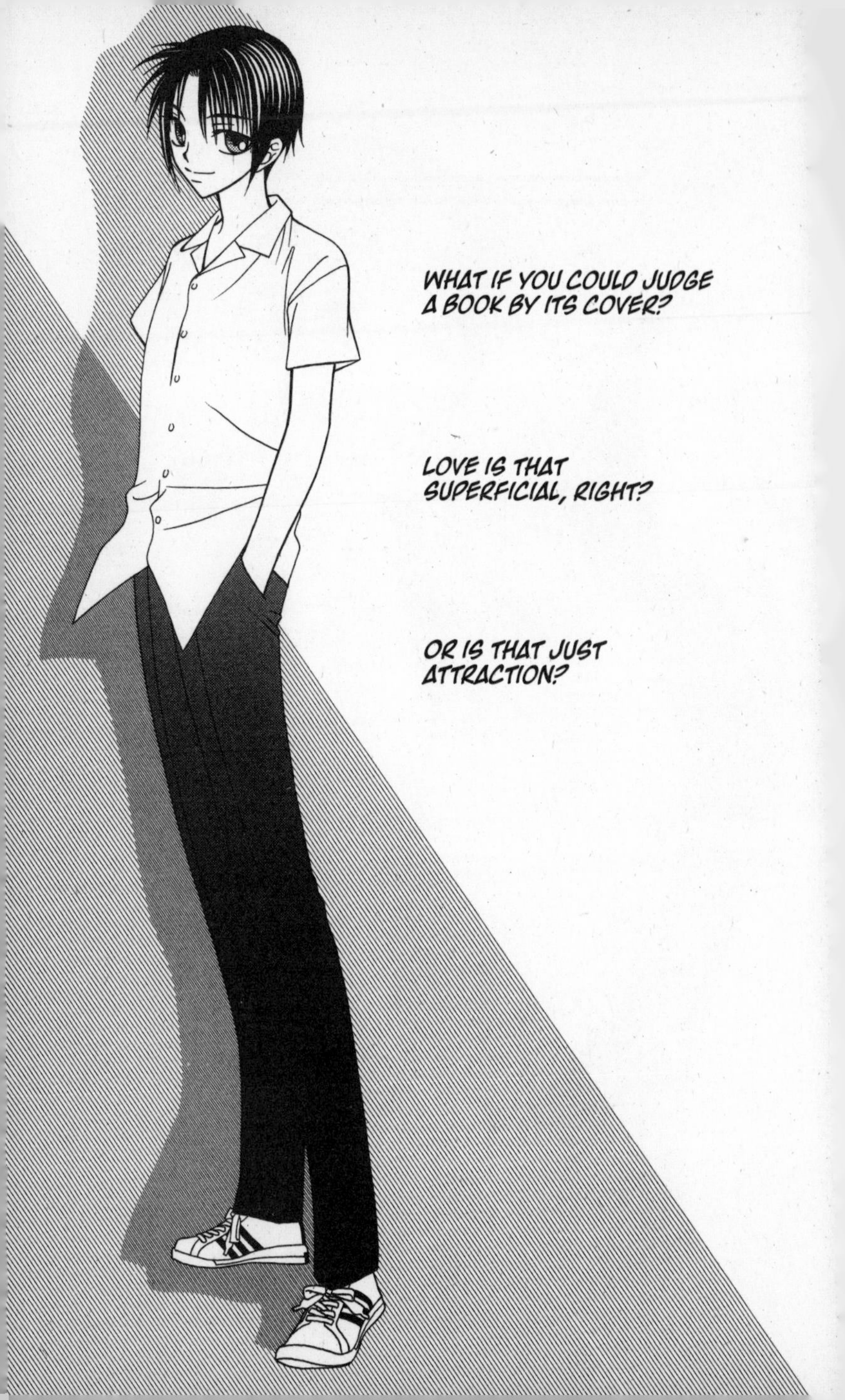
WHAT IF YOU COULD JUDGE A BOOK BY ITS COVER?
LOVE IS THAT SUPERFICIAL, RIGHT?
OR IS THAT JUST ATTRACTION?

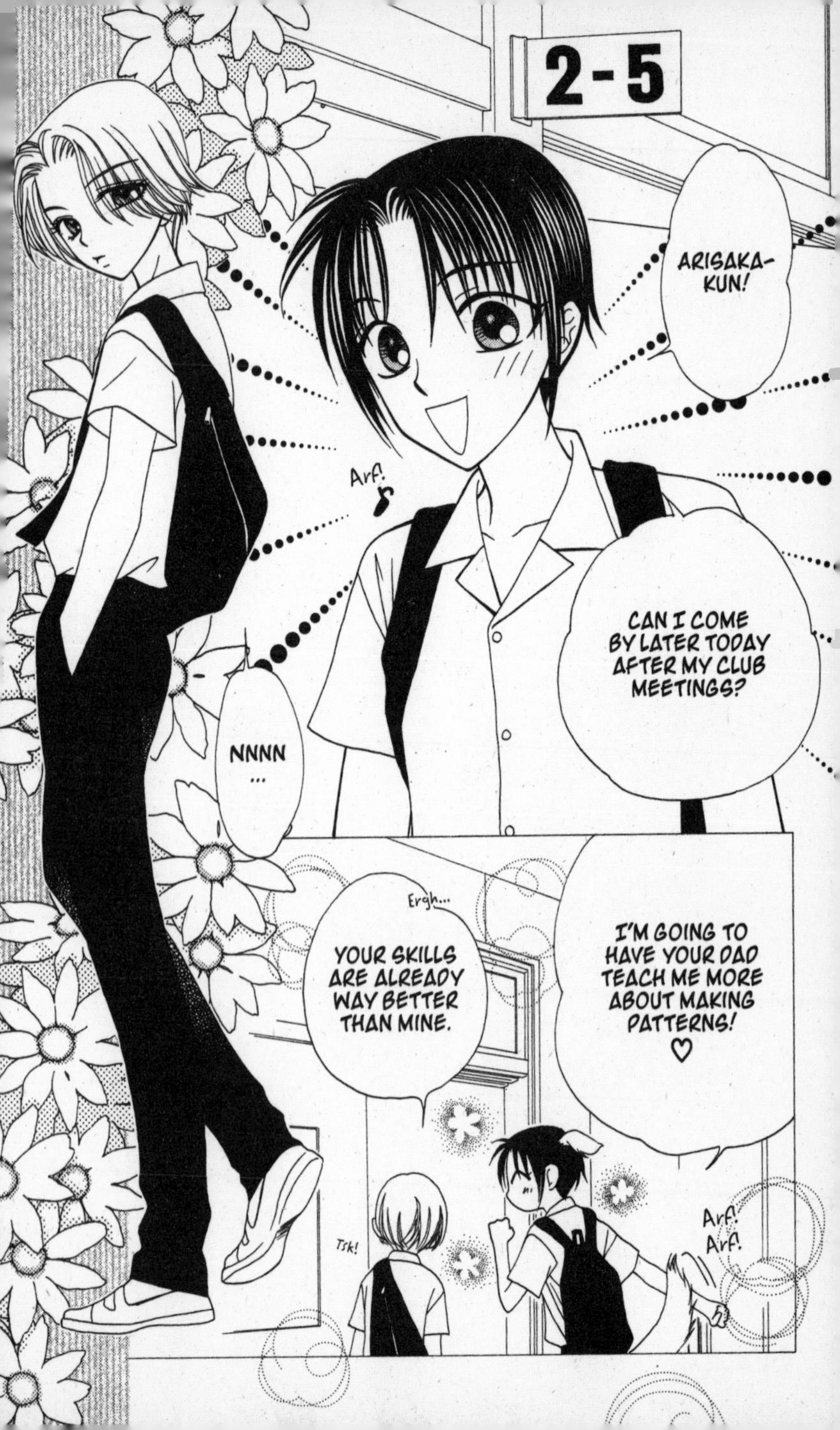
2-5
ARISAKA-KUN!
CAN I COME BY LATER TODAY AFTER MY CLUB MEETINGS?
Arf!
NNNN ...
I'M GOING TO HAVE YOUR DAD TEACH ME MORE ABOUT MAKING PATTERNS! ♡
Ergh...
YOUR SKILLS ARE ALREADY WAY BETTER THAN MINE.
Arf! Arf!
Tsk!

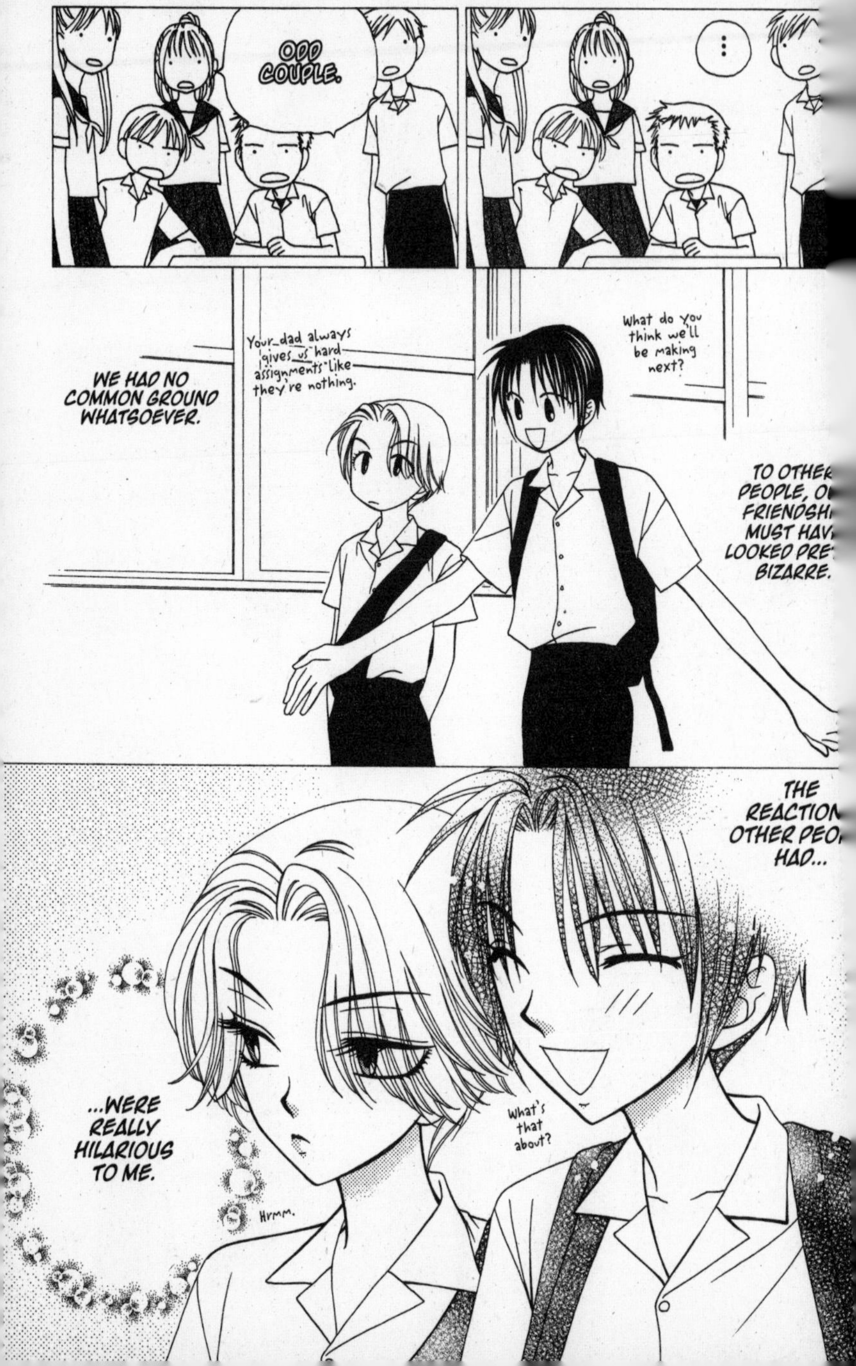
...
ODD COUPLE.
TO OTHER PEOPLE, OU FRIENDSHI MUST HAV LOOKED PRE BIZARRE.
What do you think we'll be making next?
Your dad always gives us hard assignments like they're nothing.
WE HAD NO COMMON GROUND WHATSOEVER.
THE REACTION OTHER PEO HAD...
What's that about?
Hrmm.
...WERE REALLY HILARIOUS TO ME.

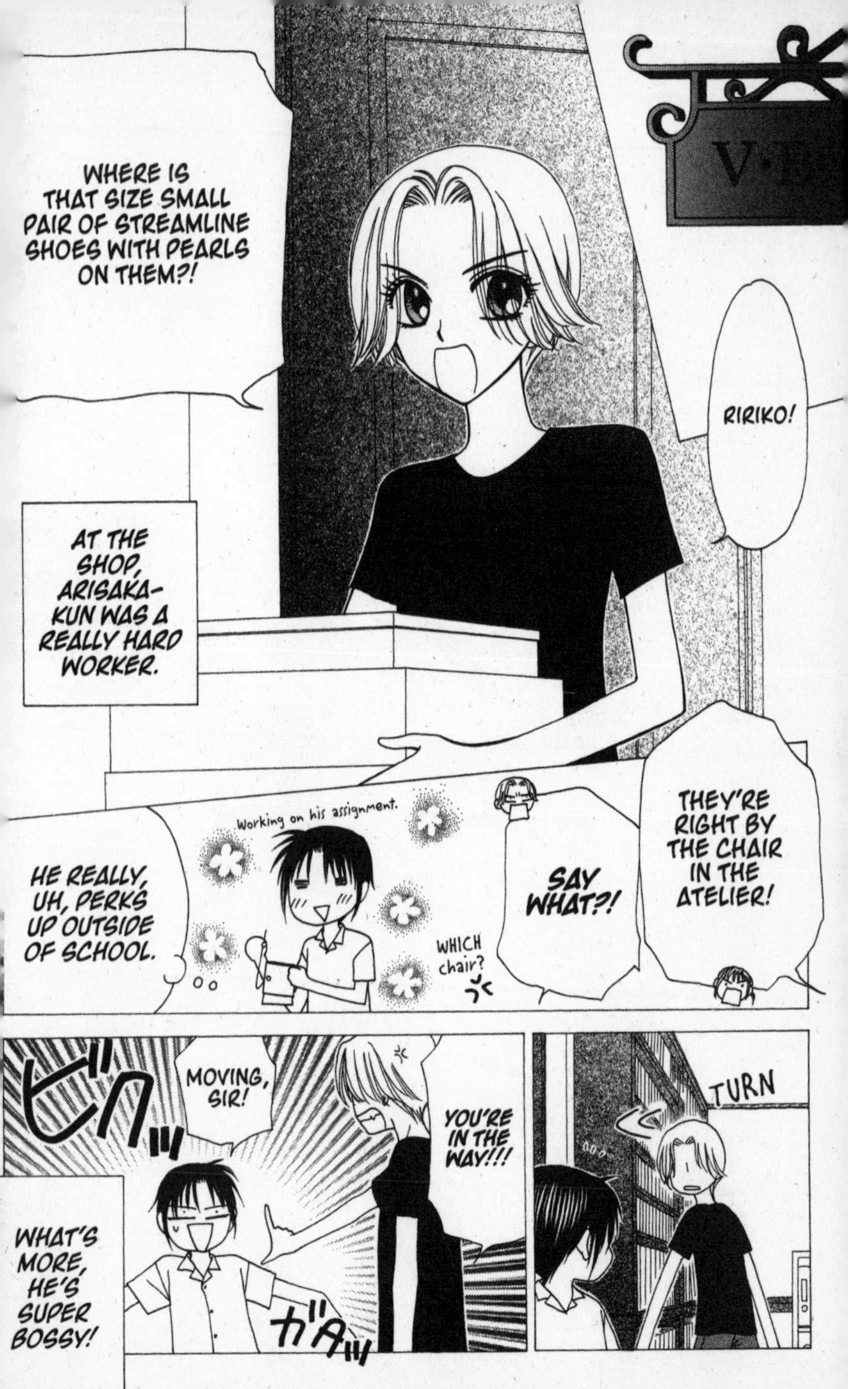
RIRIKO!
WHERE IS THAT SIZE SMALL PAIR OF STREAMLINE SHOES WITH PEARLS ON THEM?!
AT THE SHOP, ARISAKA-KUN WAS A REALLY HARD WORKER.
THEY'RE RIGHT BY THE CHAIR IN THE ATELIER!
SAY WHAT?!
WHICH chair?
Working on his assignment.
HE REALLY, UH, PERKS UP OUTSIDE OF SCHOOL.
TURN
YOU'RE IN THE WAY!!!
MOVING, SIR!
WHAT'S MORE, HE'S SUPER BOSSY!

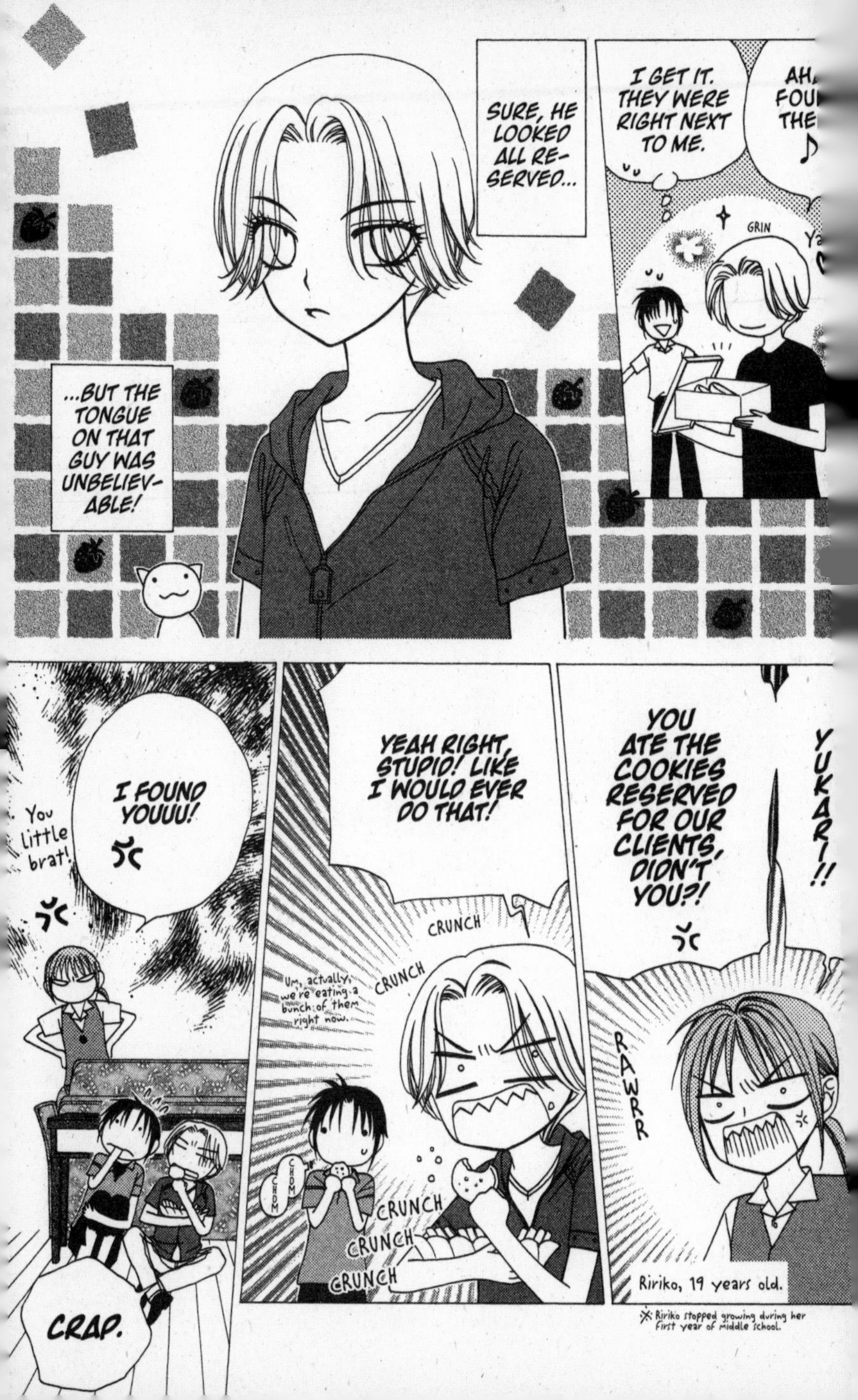
I GET IT. THEY WERE RIGHT NEXT TO ME.
GRIN
SURE, HE LOOKED ALL RE-SERVED...
...BUT THE TONGUE ON THAT GUY WAS UNBELIEV-ABLE!
YUKARI!!
YOU ATE THE COOKIES RESERVED FOR OUR CLIENTS, DIDN'T YOU?!
RAWRR
Ririko, 19 years old.
※Ririko stopped growing during her first year of middle school.
YEAH RIGHT, STUPID! LIKE I WOULD EVER DO THAT!
CRUNCH
CRUNCH
Um, actually, we're eating a bunch of them right now.
CHOM CHOM
CRUNCH
CRUNCH
CRUNCH
I FOUND YOUUU!
You little brat!
CRAP.

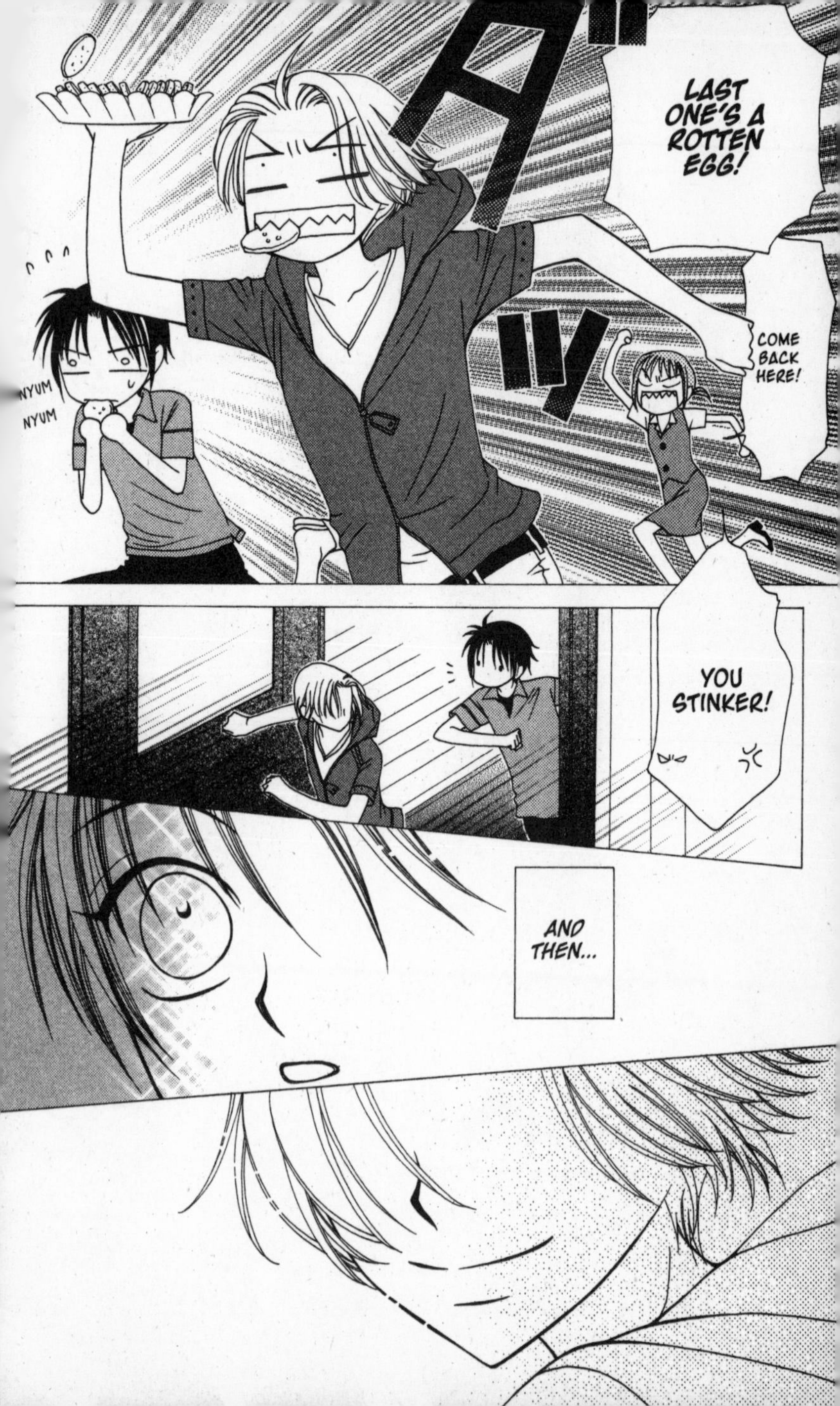
LAST ONE'S A ROTTEN EGG!
COME BACK HERE!
NYUM NYUM
YOU STINKER!
AND THEN...

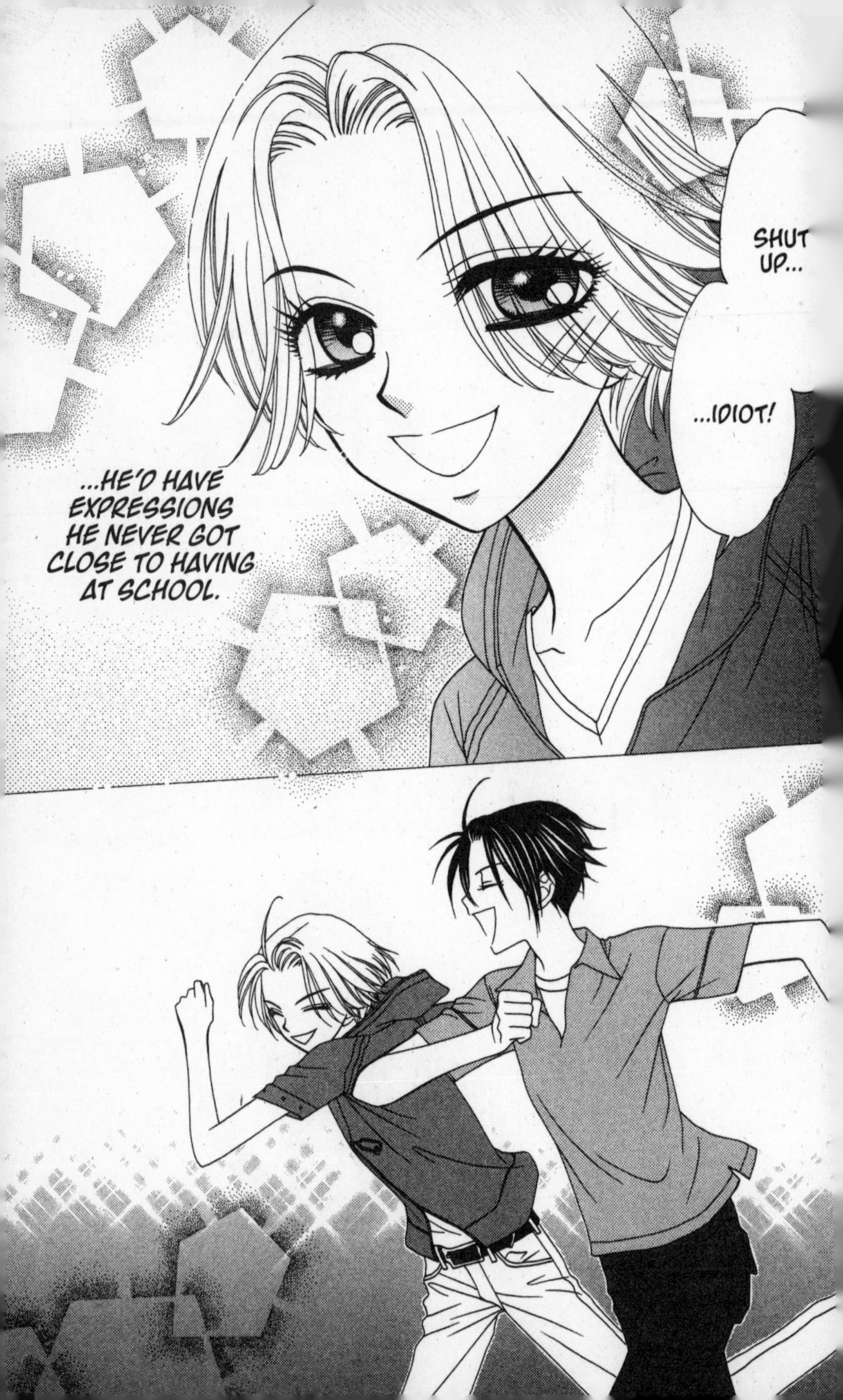
SHUT UP...
...IDIOT!
...HE'D HAVE EXPRESSIONS HE NEVER GOT CLOSE TO HAVING AT SCHOOL.

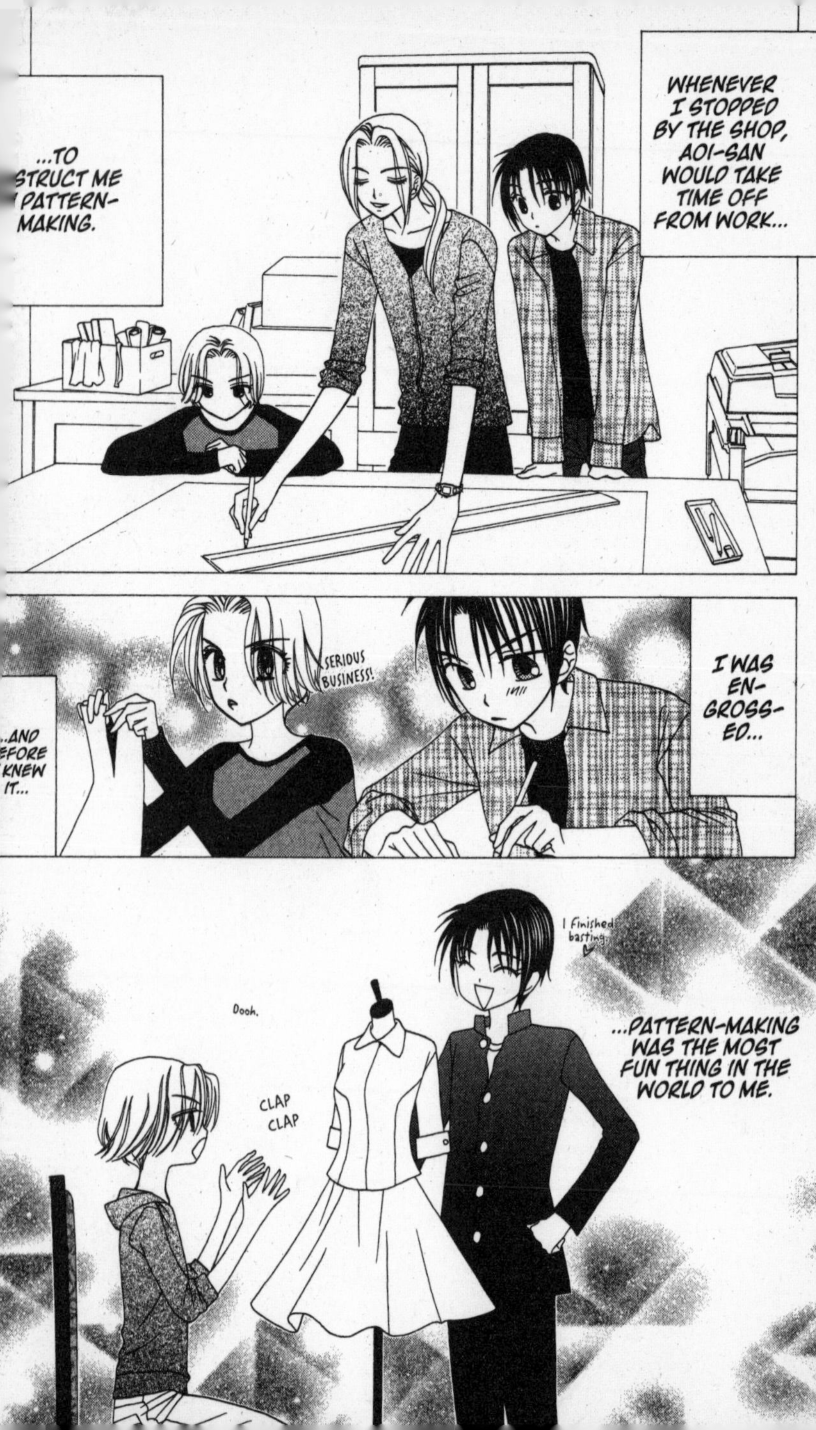
WHENEVER I STOPPED BY THE SHOP, AOI-SAN WOULD TAKE TIME OFF FROM WORK...
...TO STRUCT ME PATTERN-MAKING.
I WAS EN-GROSS-ED...
SERIOUS BUSINESS!
..AND EFORE KNEW IT...
I finished basting
...PATTERN-MAKING WAS THE MOST FUN THING IN THE WORLD TO ME.
Oooh.
CLAP CLAP

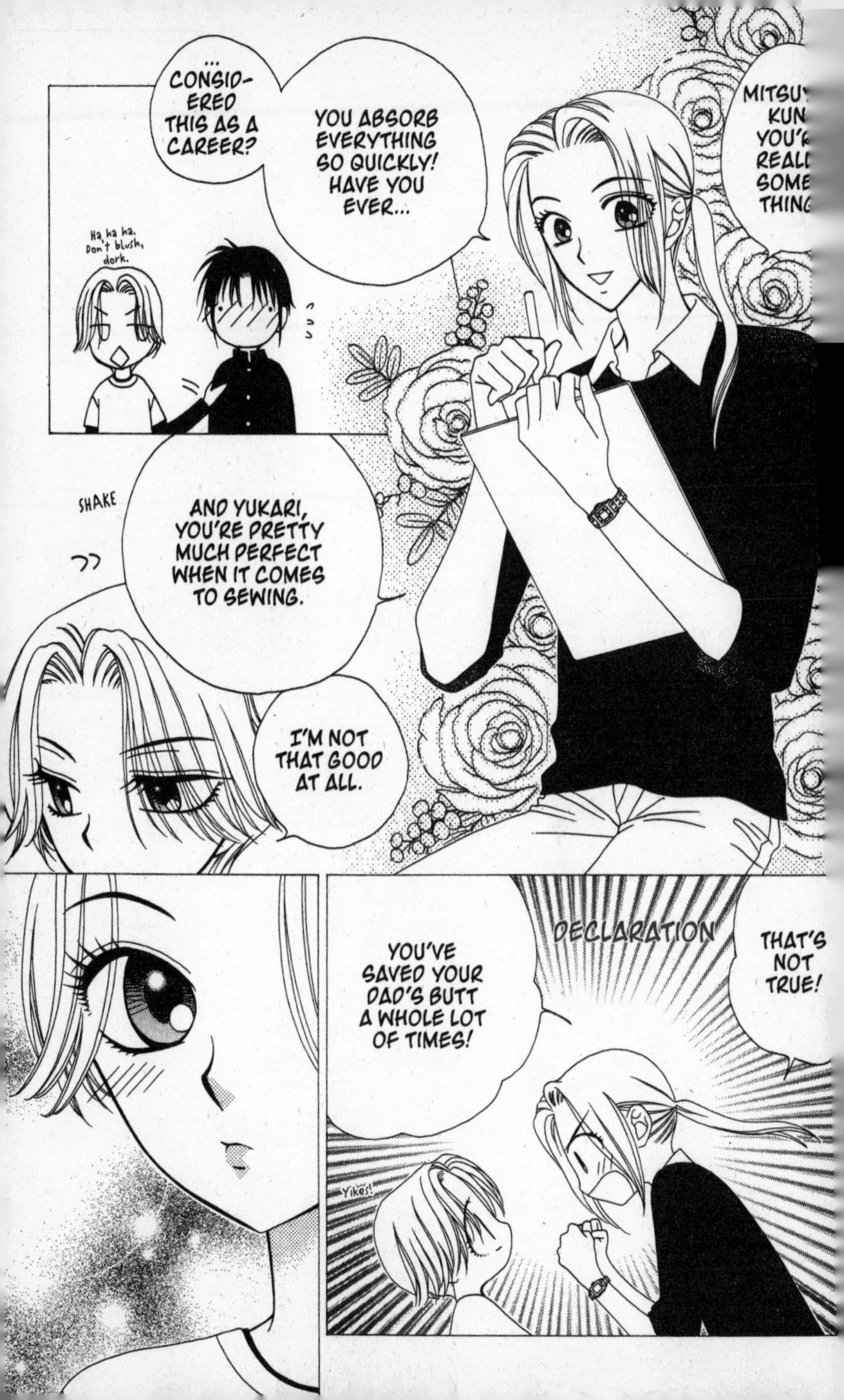

MITSU KUN YOU'R REALL SOME THING
YOU ABSORB EVERYTHING SO QUICKLY! HAVE YOU EVER...
... CONSID-ERED THIS AS A CAREER?
Ha ha ha. Don't blush, dork.
AND YUKARI, YOU'RE PRETTY MUCH PERFECT WHEN IT COMES TO SEWING.
SHAKE
I'M NOT THAT GOOD AT ALL.
THAT'S NOT TRUE!
DECLARATION
YOU'VE SAVED YOUR DAD'S BUTT A WHOLE LOT OF TIMES!
Yikes!

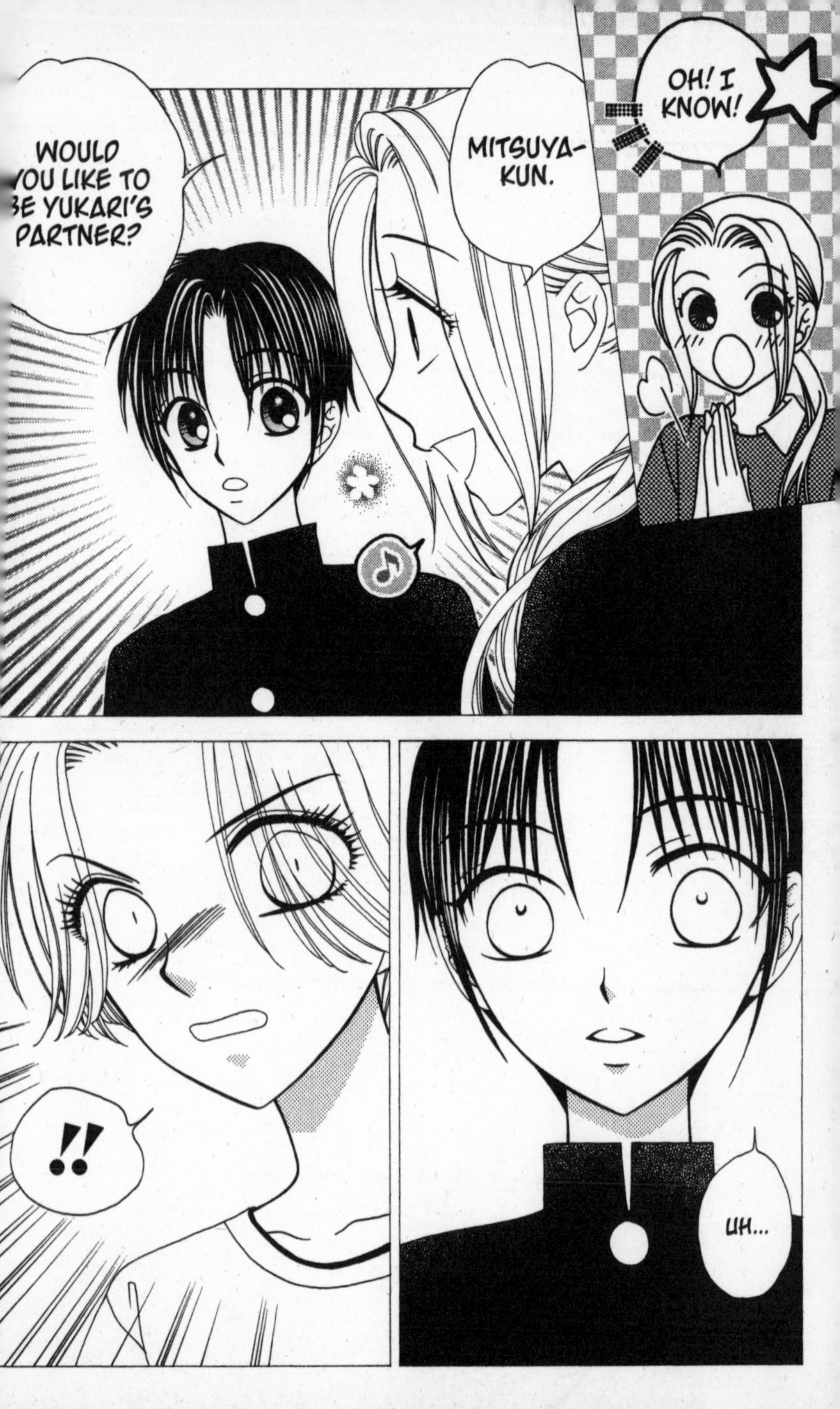
OH! I KNOW!
MITSUYA-KUN.
WOULD YOU LIKE TO BE YUKARI'S PARTNER?
UH...
!!

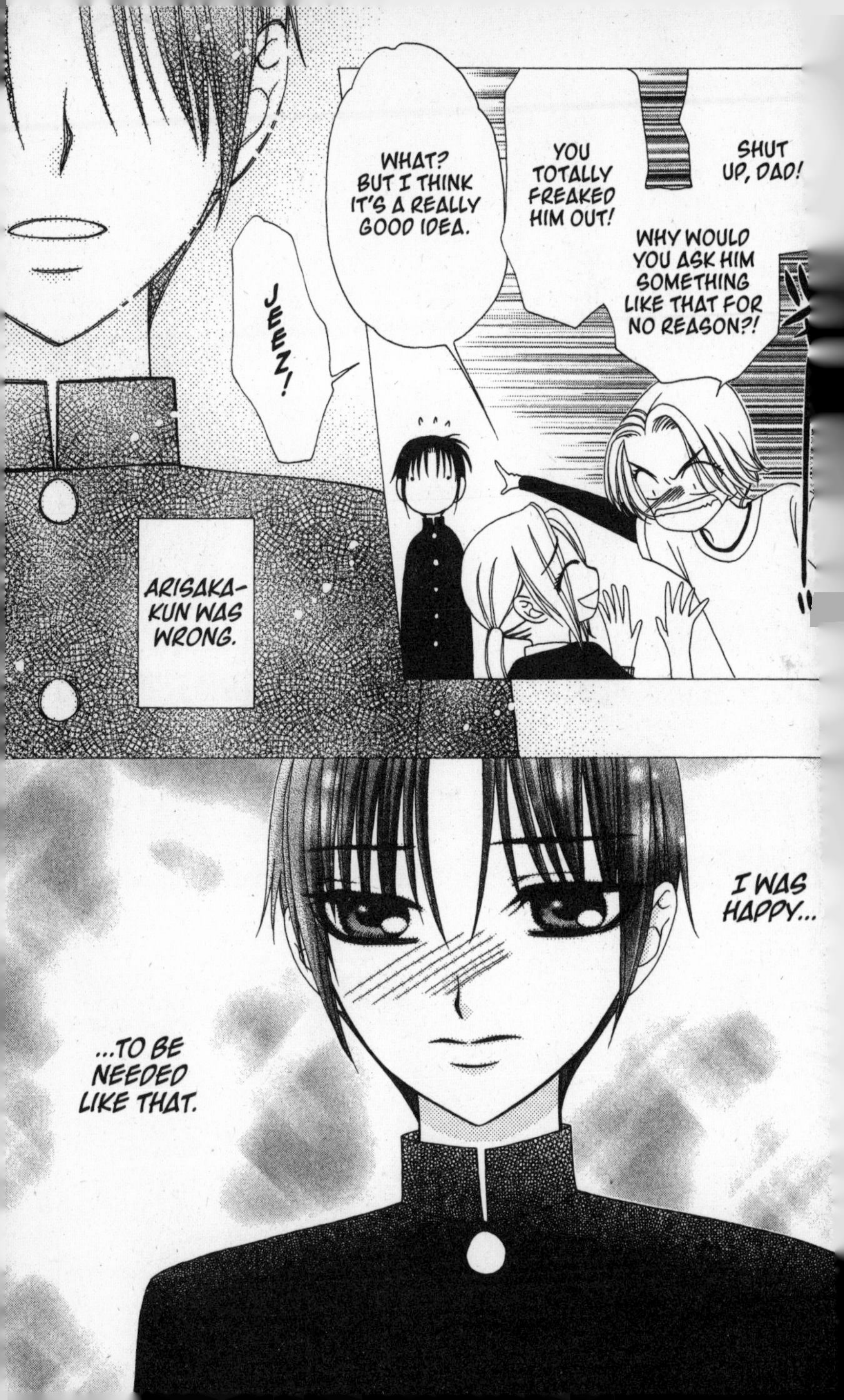
SHUT UP, DAD!
WHY WOULD YOU ASK HIM SOMETHING LIKE THAT FOR NO REASON?!
YOU TOTALLY FREAKED HIM OUT!
WHAT? BUT I THINK IT'S A REALLY GOOD IDEA.
JEEZ!
ARISAKA-KUN WAS WRONG.
I WAS HAPPY...
...TO BE NEEDED LIKE THAT.

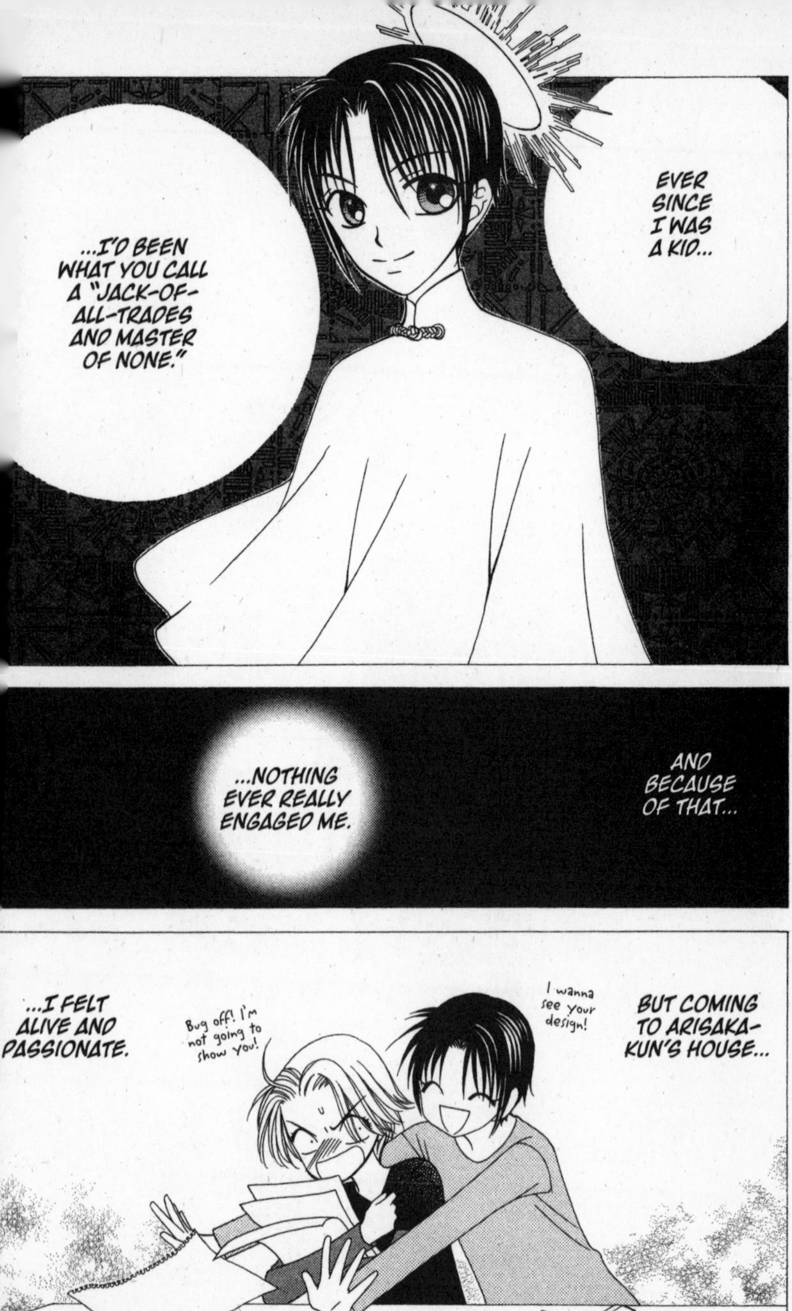
EVER SINCE I WAS A KID...
...I'D BEEN WHAT YOU CALL A "JACK-OF-ALL-TRADES AND MASTER OF NONE."
AND BECAUSE OF THAT...
...NOTHING EVER REALLY ENGAGED ME.
BUT COMING TO ARISAKA-KUN'S HOUSE...
I wanna see your design!
Bug off! I'm not going to show you!
...I FELT ALIVE AND PASSIONATE.

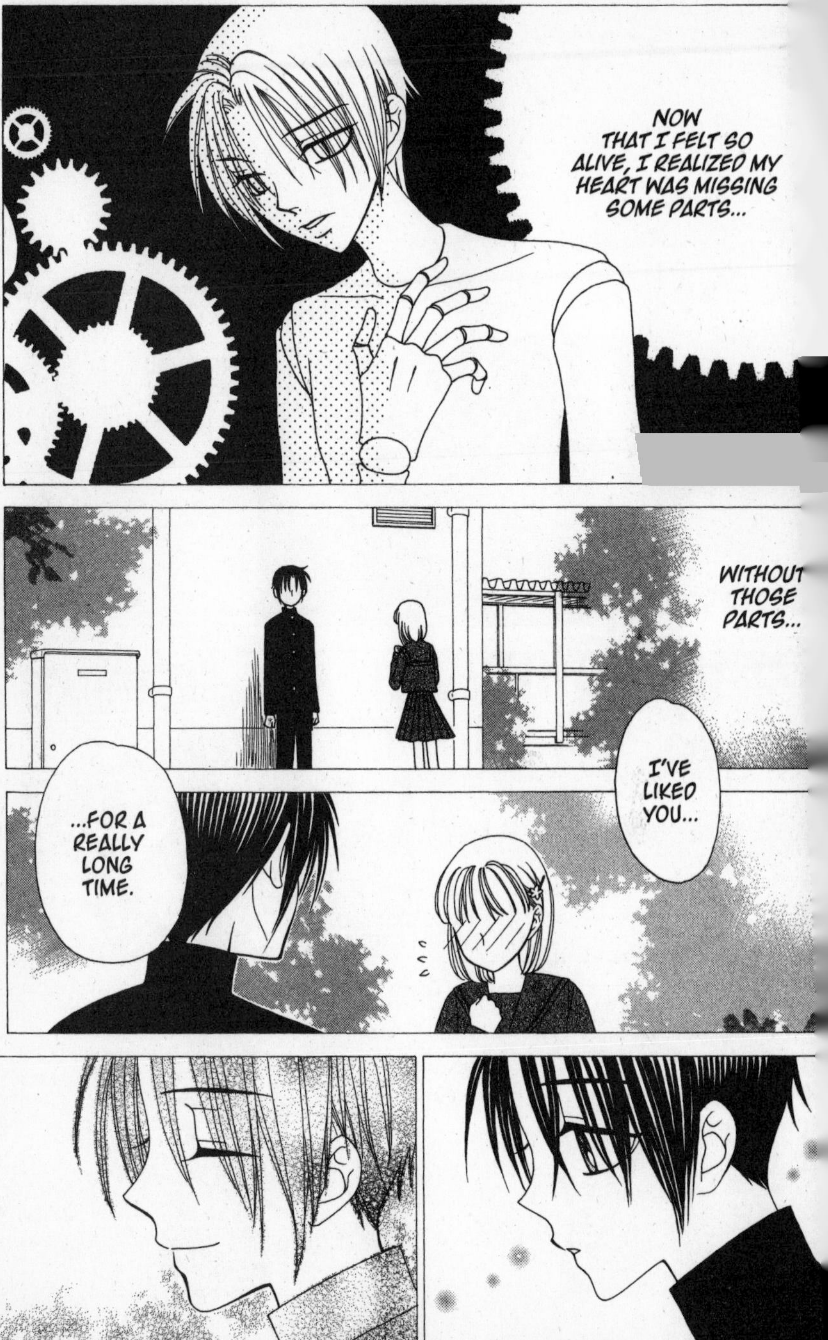
NOW THAT I FELT SO ALIVE, I REALIZED MY HEART WAS MISSING SOME PARTS...
WITHOUT THOSE PARTS...
I'VE LIKED YOU...
...FOR A REALLY LONG TIME.

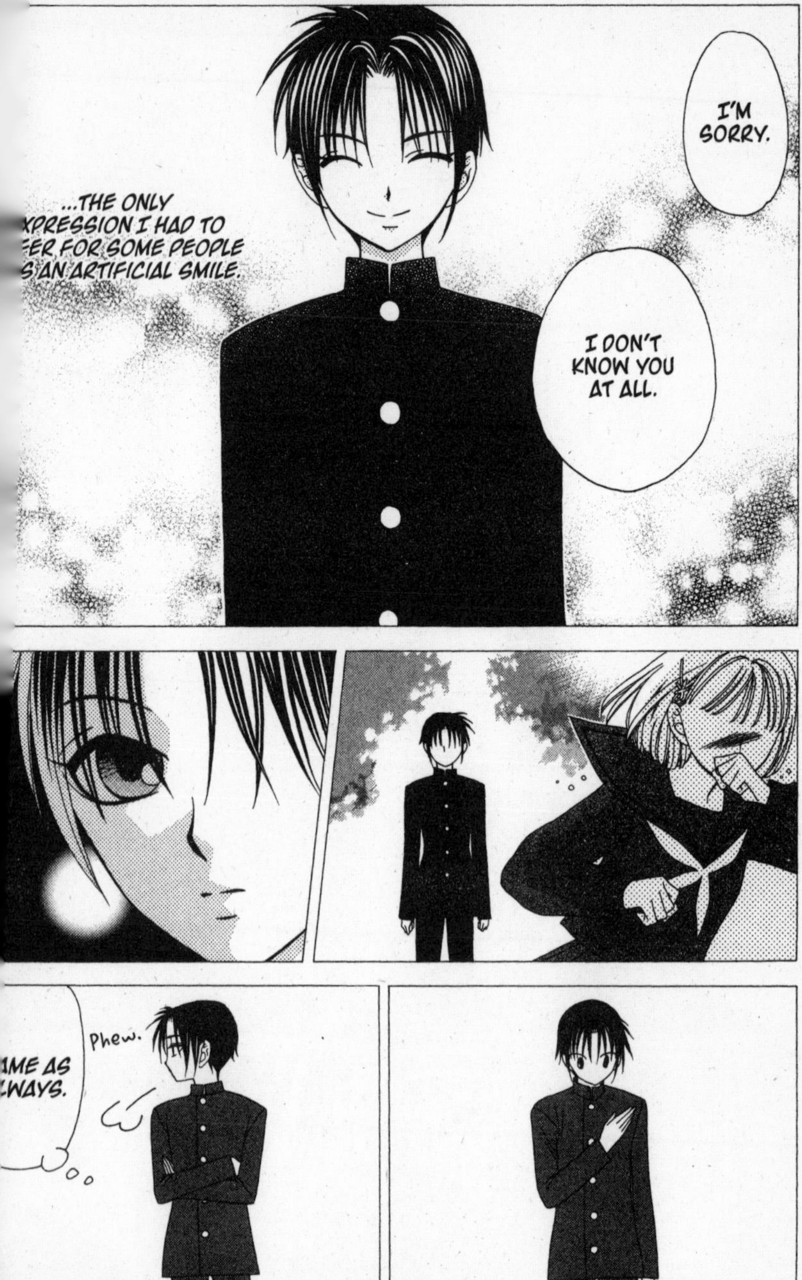
I'M SORRY.
I DON'T KNOW YOU AT ALL.
...THE ONLY XPRESSION I HAD TO FER FOR SOME PEOPLE S AN ARTIFICIAL SMILE.
Phew.
AME AS WAYS.

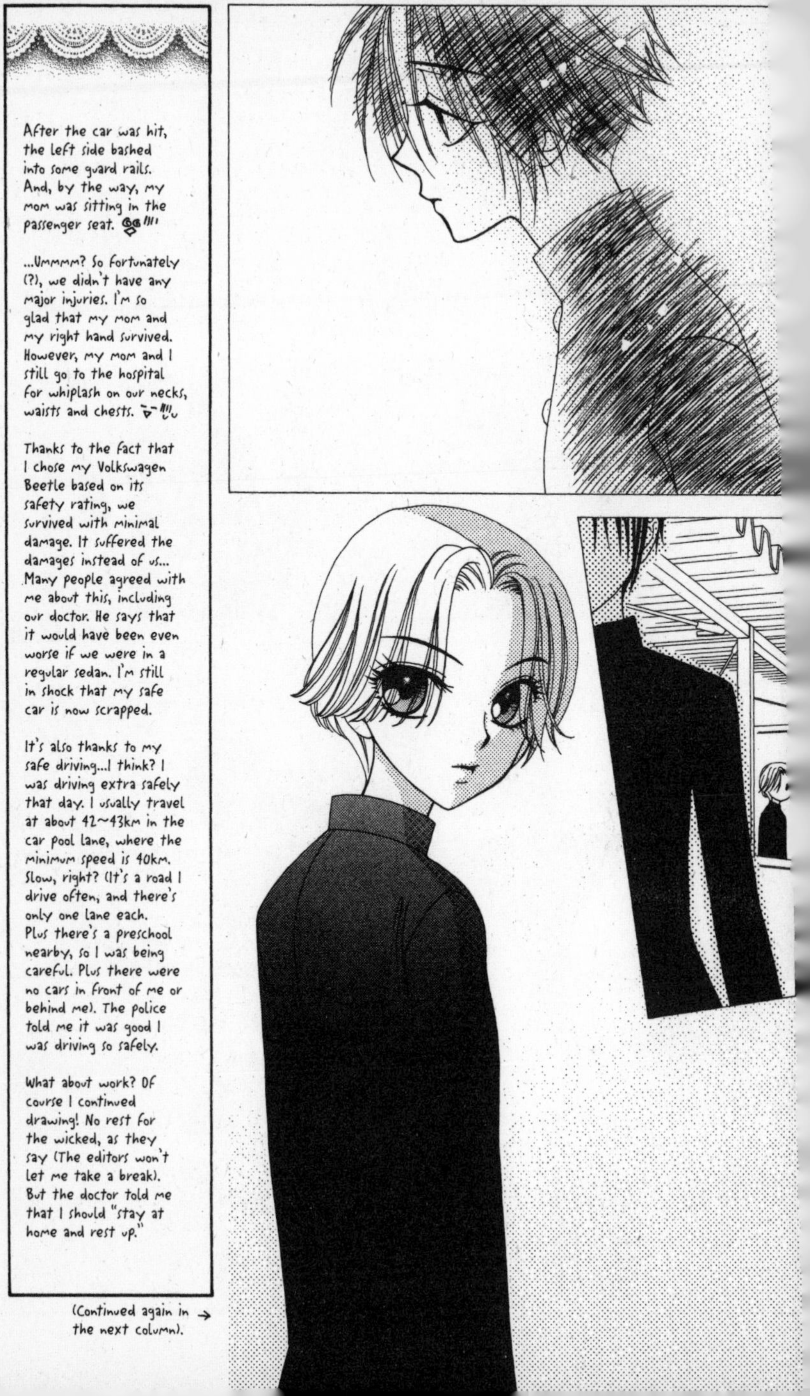

After the car was hit, the left side bashed into some guard rails. And, by the way, my mom was sitting in the passenger seat.

...Ummmm? So fortunately (?), we didn't have any major injuries. I'm so glad that my mom and my right hand survived. However, my mom and I still go to the hospital for whiplash on our necks, waists and chests.

Thanks to the fact that I chose my Volkswagen Beetle based on its safety rating, we survived with minimal damage. It suffered the damages instead of us... Many people agreed with me about this, including our doctor. He says that it would have been even worse if we were in a regular sedan. I'm still in shock that my safe car is now scrapped.

It's also thanks to my safe driving...I think? I was driving extra safely that day. I usually travel at about 42~43km in the car pool lane, where the minimum speed is 40km. Slow, right? (It's a road I drive often, and there's only one lane each. Plus there's a preschool nearby, so I was being careful. Plus there were no cars in front of me or behind me). The police told me it was good I was driving so safely.

What about work? Of course I continued drawing! No rest for the wicked, as they say (The editors won't let me take a break). But the doctor told me that I should "stay at home and rest up."

(Continued again in → the next column).

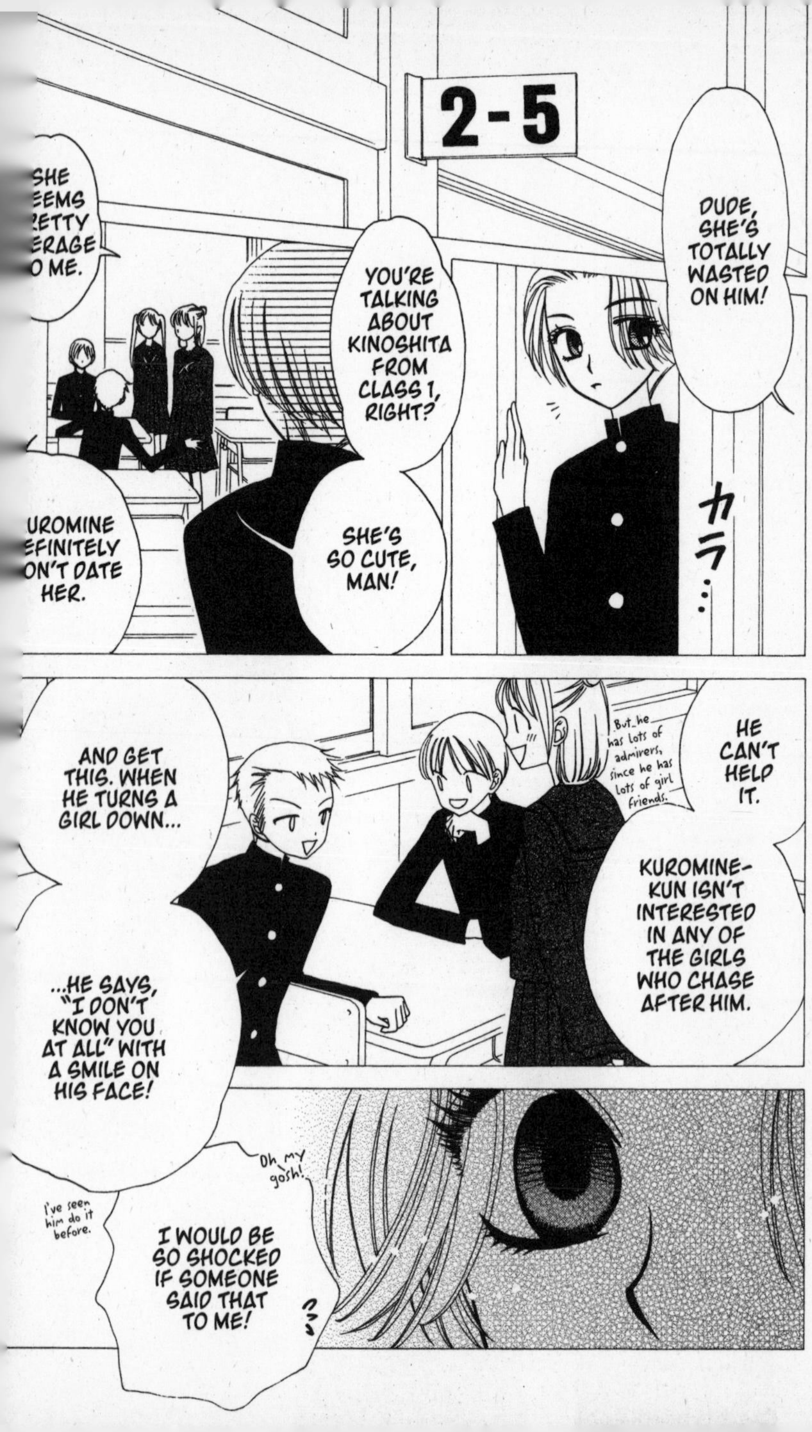
2-5
DUDE, SHE'S TOTALLY WASTED ON HIM!
カラ…
YOU'RE TALKING ABOUT KINOSHITA FROM CLASS 1, RIGHT?
SHE'S SO CUTE, MAN!
SHE EEMS RETTY ERAGE O ME.
UROMINE EFINITELY ON'T DATE HER.
HE CAN'T HELP IT.
But he has lots of admirers, since he has lots of girl friends.
KUROMINE-KUN ISN'T INTERESTED IN ANY OF THE GIRLS WHO CHASE AFTER HIM.
AND GET THIS. WHEN HE TURNS A GIRL DOWN...
...HE SAYS, "I DON'T KNOW YOU AT ALL" WITH A SMILE ON HIS FACE!
Oh my gosh!
I WOULD BE SO SHOCKED IF SOMEONE SAID THAT TO ME!
I've seen him do it before.

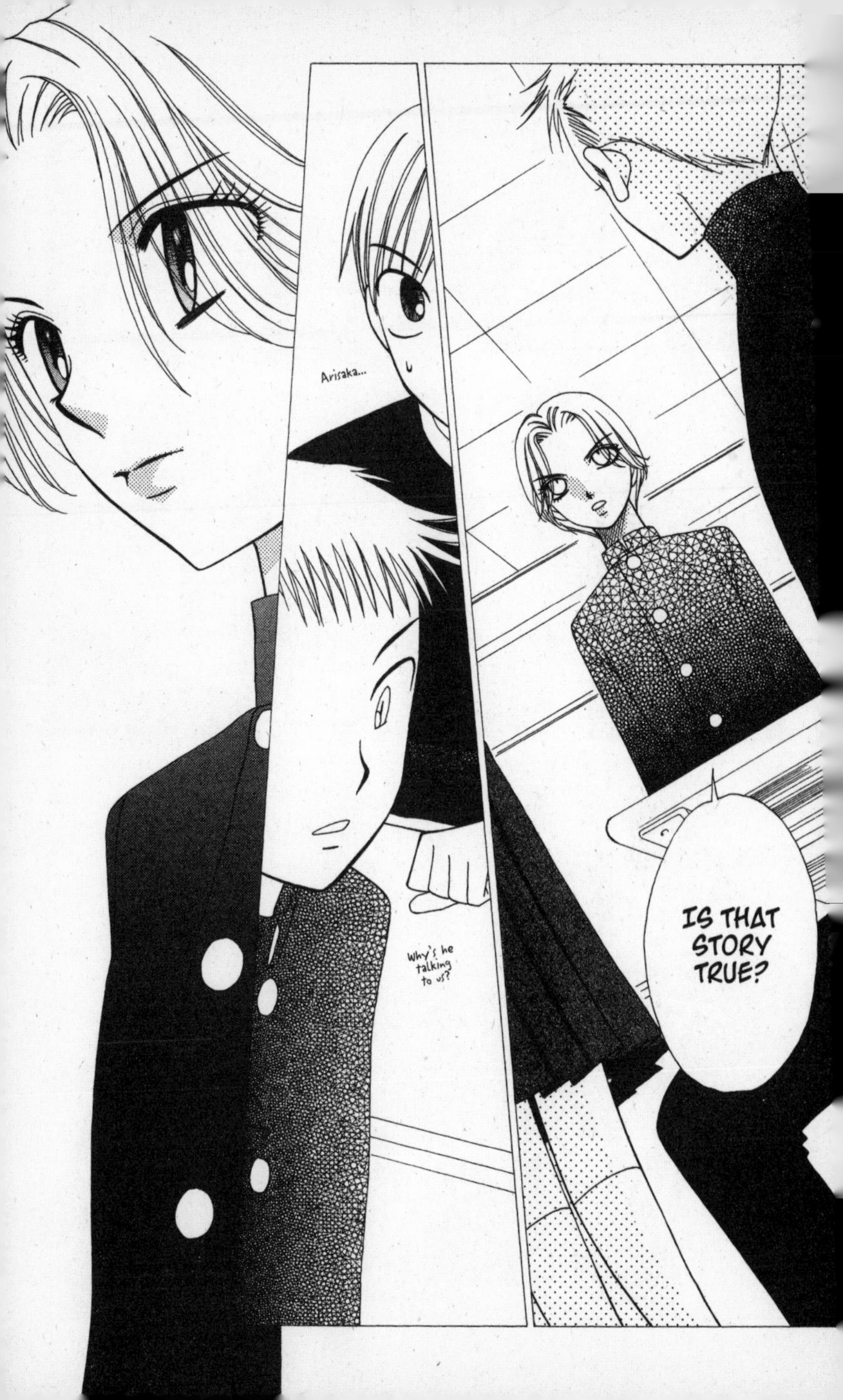
IS THAT STORY TRUE?
Arisaka...
Why's he talking to us?

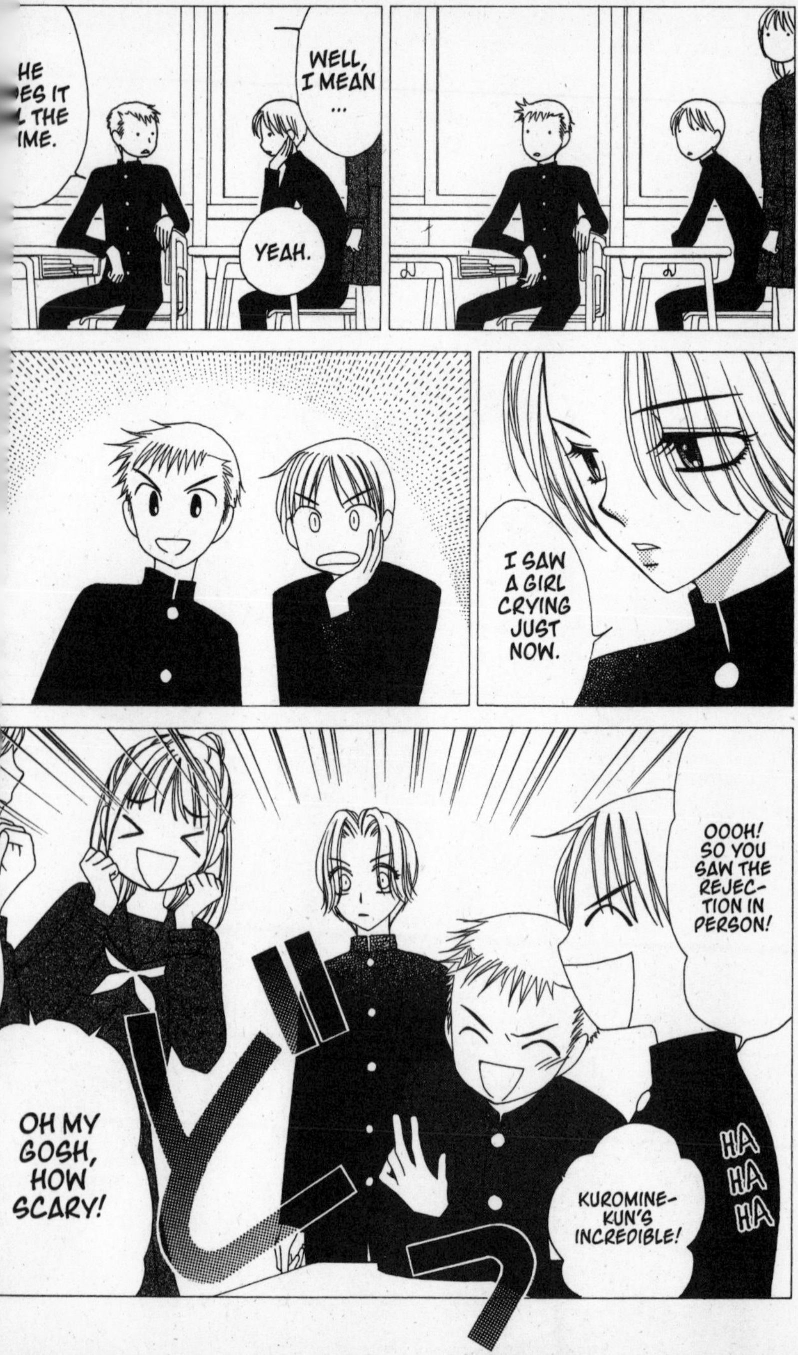
WELL, I MEAN ...
HE
ES IT
L THE
IME.
YEAH.
I SAW A GIRL CRYING JUST NOW.
OOOH! SO YOU SAW THE REJEC-TION IN PERSON!
HA HA HA
KUROMINE-KUN'S INCREDIBLE!
OH MY GOSH, HOW SCARY!

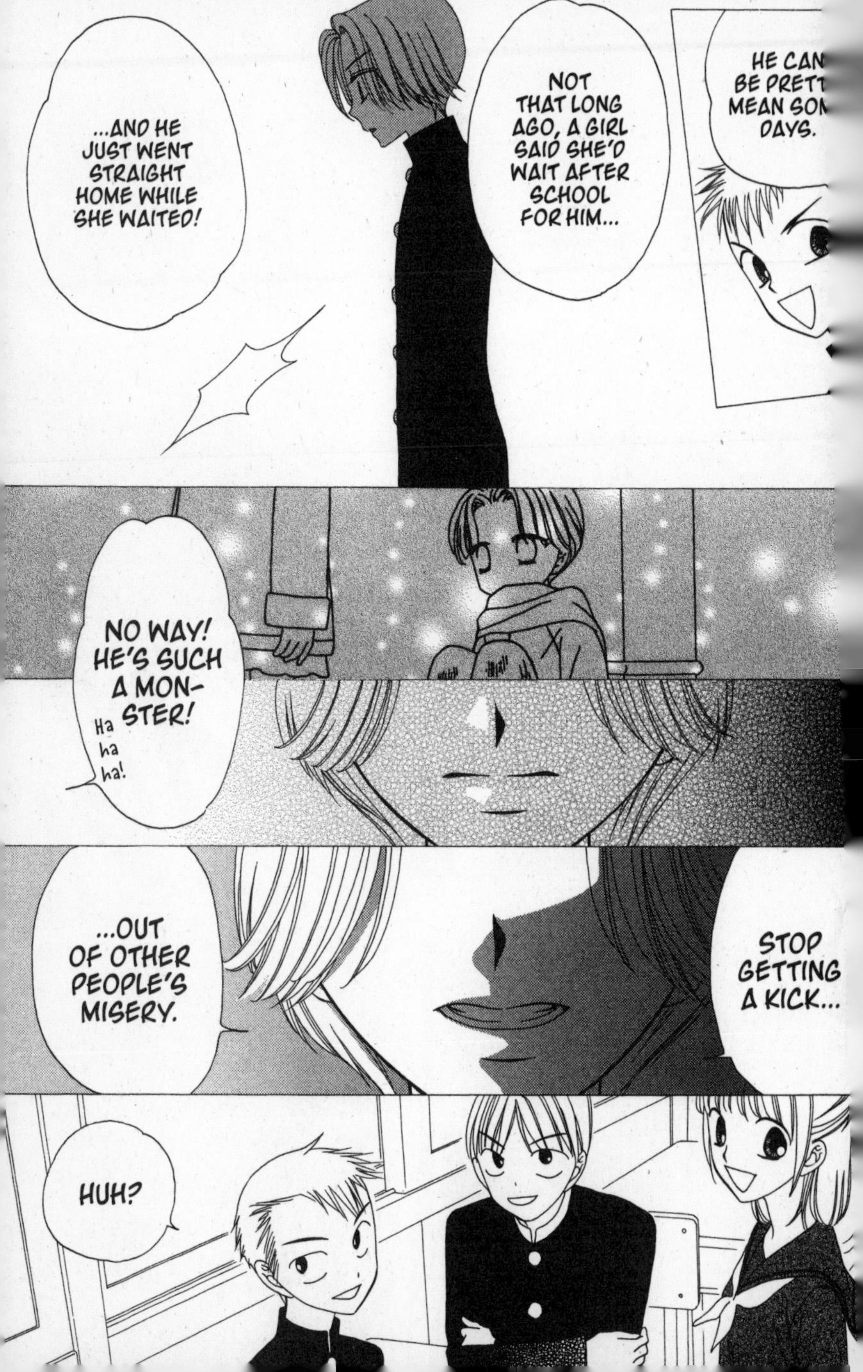
HE CAN BE PRETT MEAN SOM DAYS.
NOT THAT LONG AGO, A GIRL SAID SHE'D WAIT AFTER SCHOOL FOR HIM...
...AND HE JUST WENT STRAIGHT HOME WHILE SHE WAITED!
NO WAY! HE'S SUCH A MON-STER!
Ha ha ha!
STOP GETTING A KICK...
...OUT OF OTHER PEOPLE'S MISERY.
HUH?

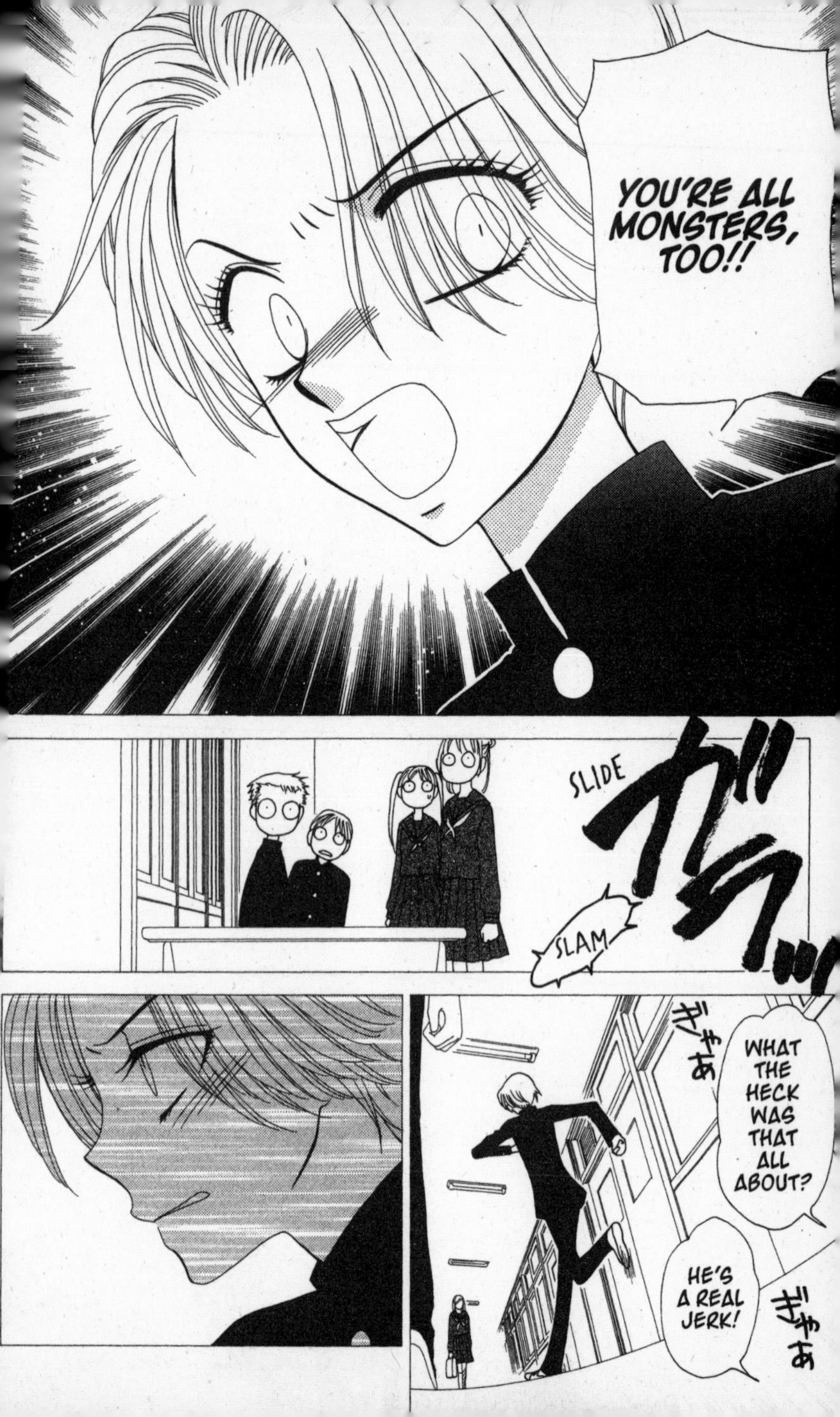
YOU'RE ALL MONSTERS, TOO!!
SLIDE
SLAM
ぎゃあ
WHAT THE HECK WAS THAT ALL ABOUT?
HE'S A REAL JERK!
ぎゃあ

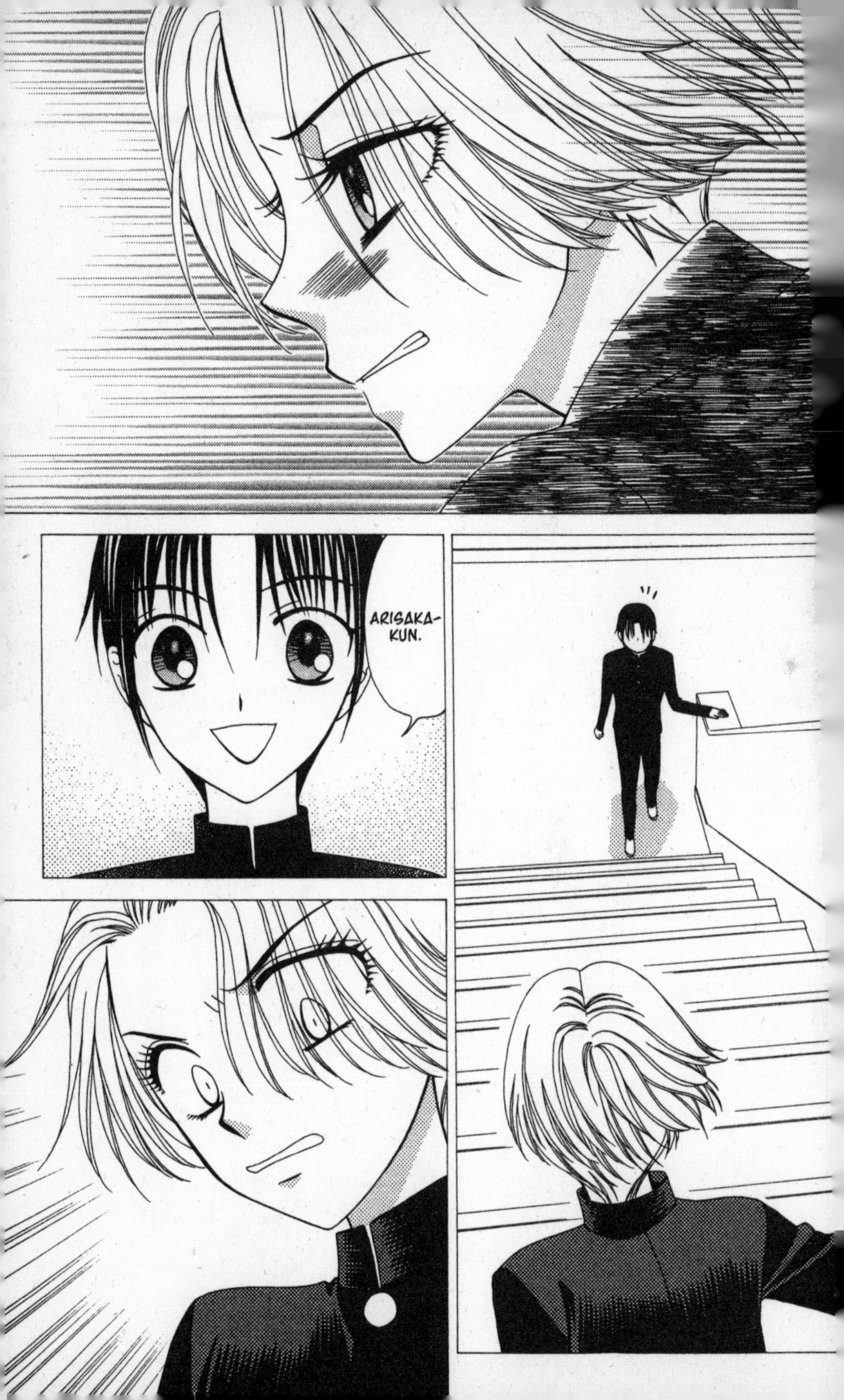
ARISAKA-KUN.

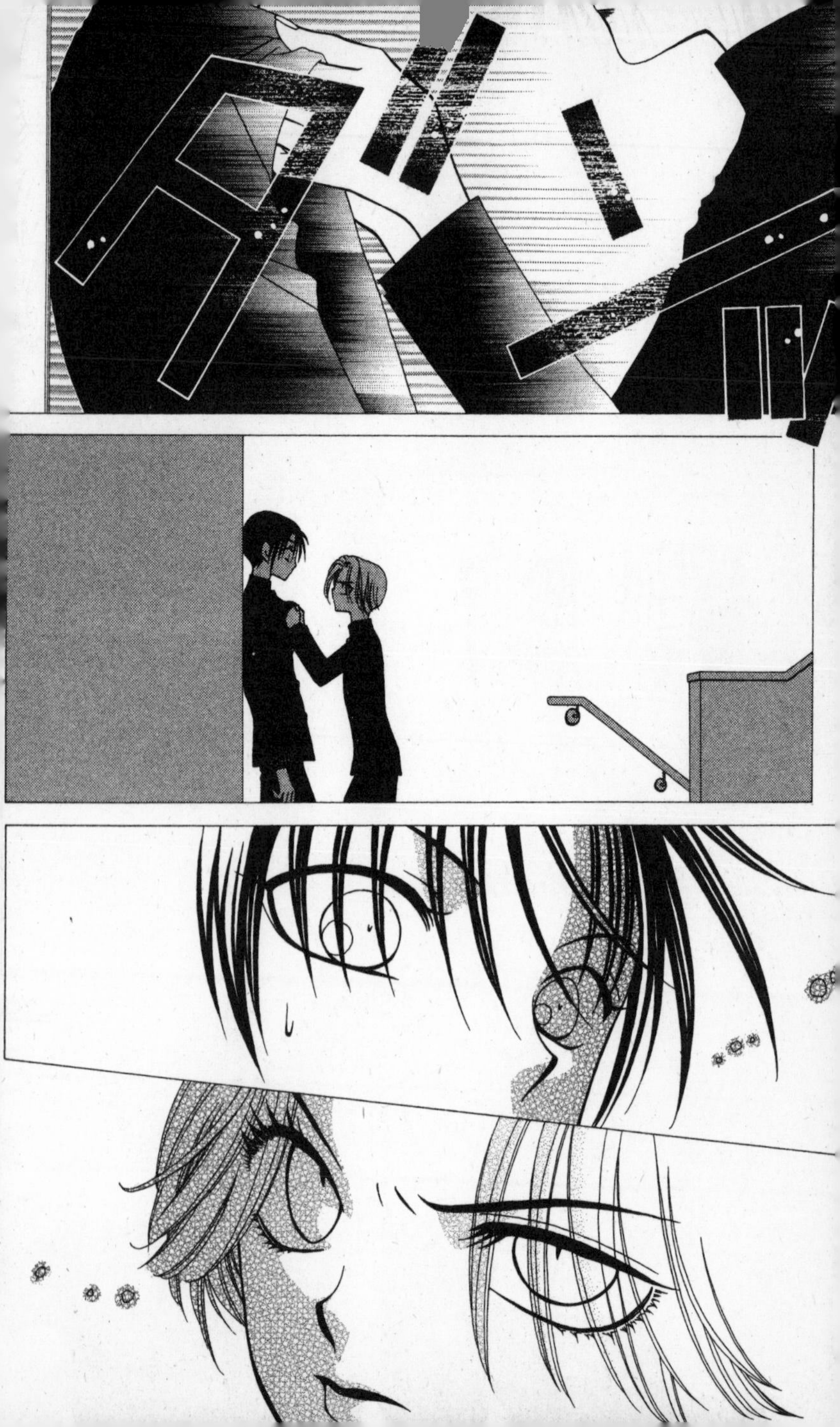

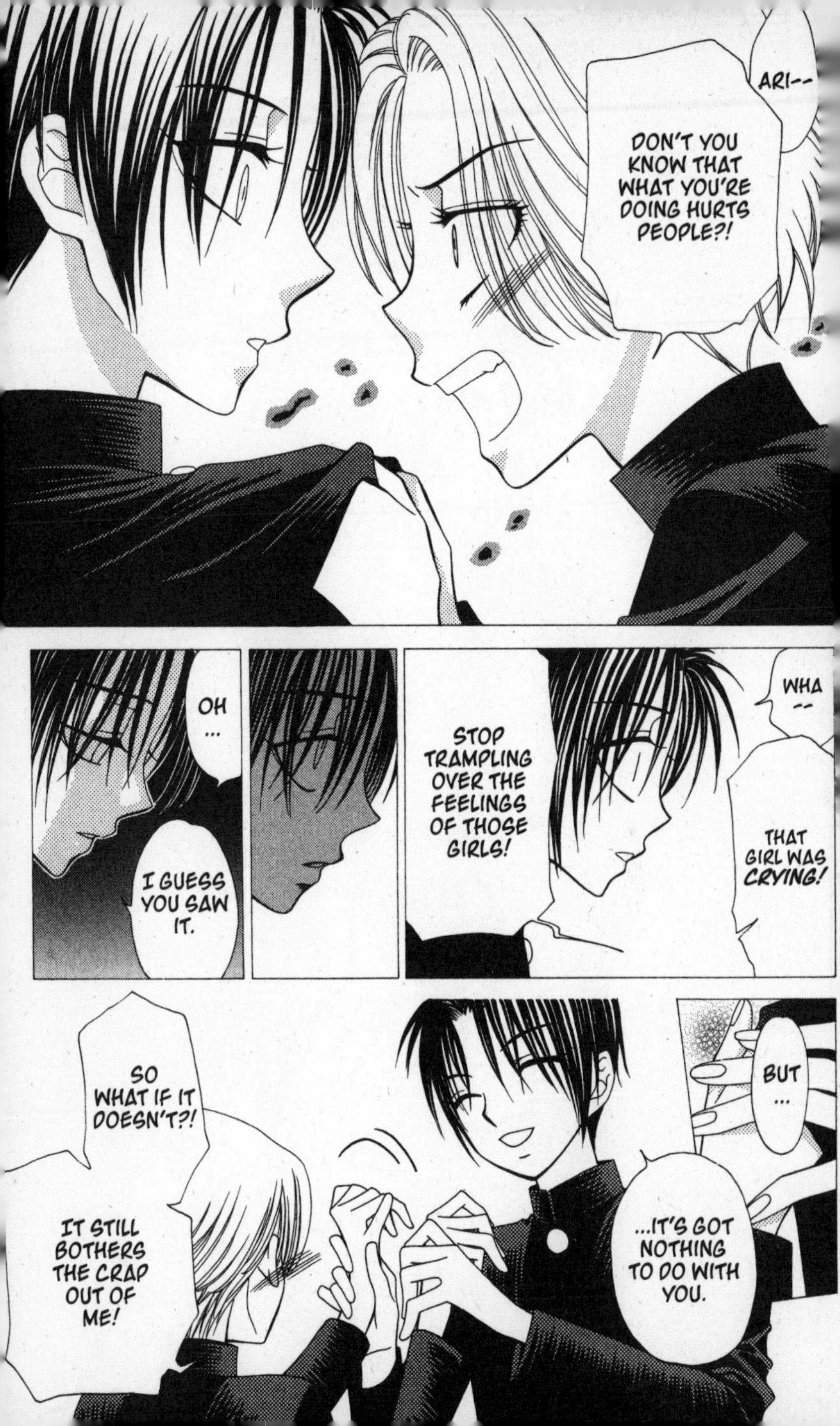

ARI--
DON'T YOU KNOW THAT WHAT YOU'RE DOING HURTS PEOPLE?!
WHA --
THAT GIRL WAS *CRYING!*
STOP TRAMPLING OVER THE FEELINGS OF THOSE GIRLS!
OH ...
I GUESS YOU SAW IT.
BUT ...
...IT'S GOT NOTHING TO DO WITH YOU.
SO WHAT IF IT DOESN'T?!
IT STILL BOTHERS THE CRAP OUT OF ME!

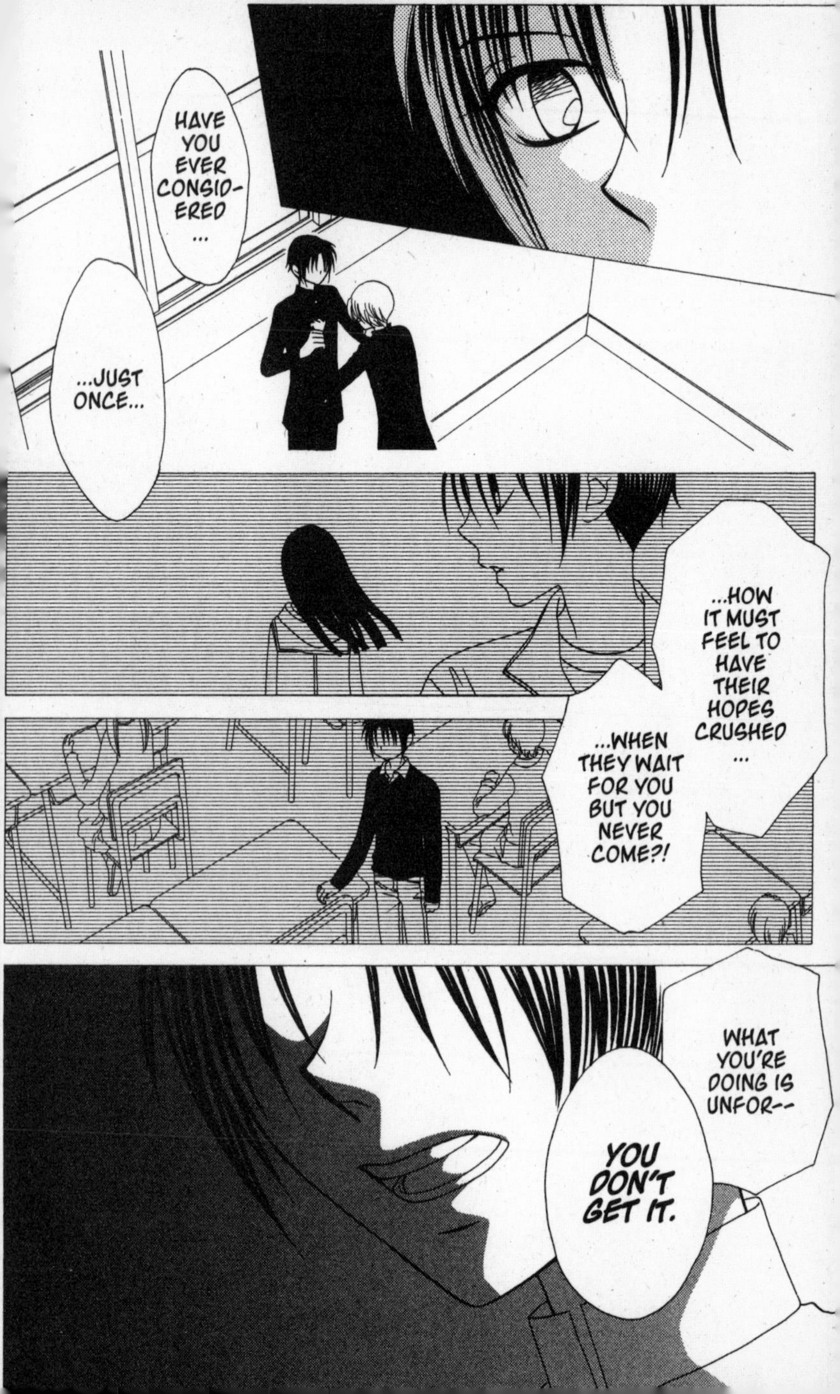
HAVE YOU EVER CONSID-ERED ...
...JUST ONCE...
...HOW IT MUST FEEL TO HAVE THEIR HOPES CRUSHED ...
...WHEN THEY WAIT FOR YOU BUT YOU NEVER COME?!
WHAT YOU'RE DOING IS UNFOR--
YOU DON'T GET IT.

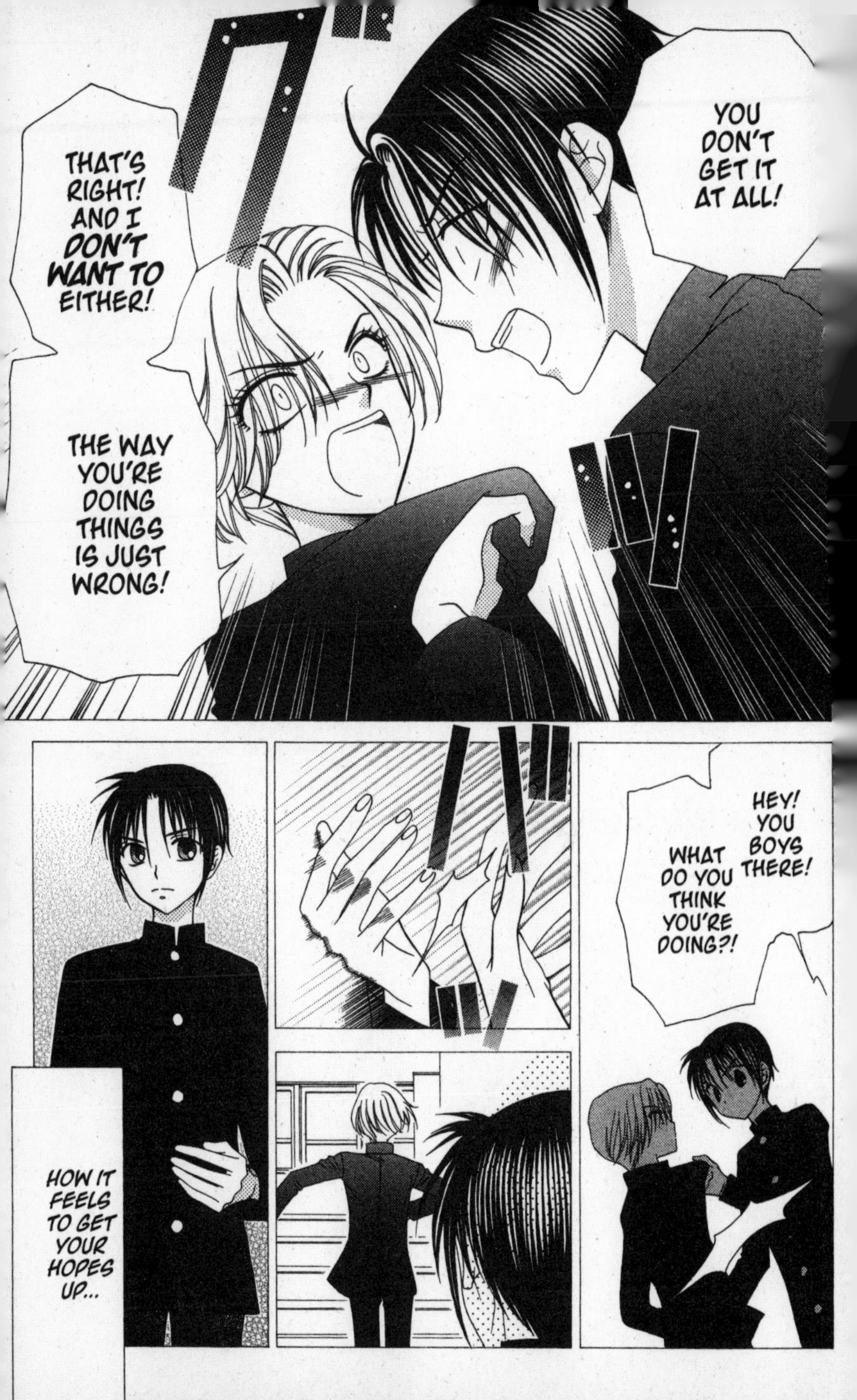
YOU DON'T GET IT AT ALL!
THAT'S RIGHT! AND I DON'T WANT TO EITHER!
THE WAY YOU'RE DOING THINGS IS JUST WRONG!
HEY! YOU BOYS THERE!
WHAT DO YOU THINK YOU'RE DOING?!
HOW IT FEELS TO GET YOUR HOPES UP...

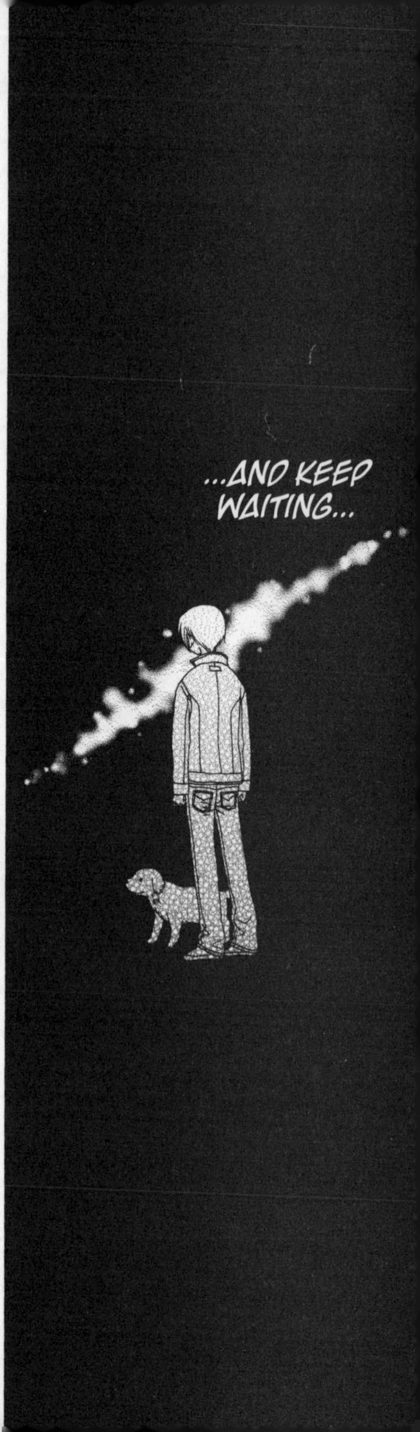
...AND KEEP WAITING...

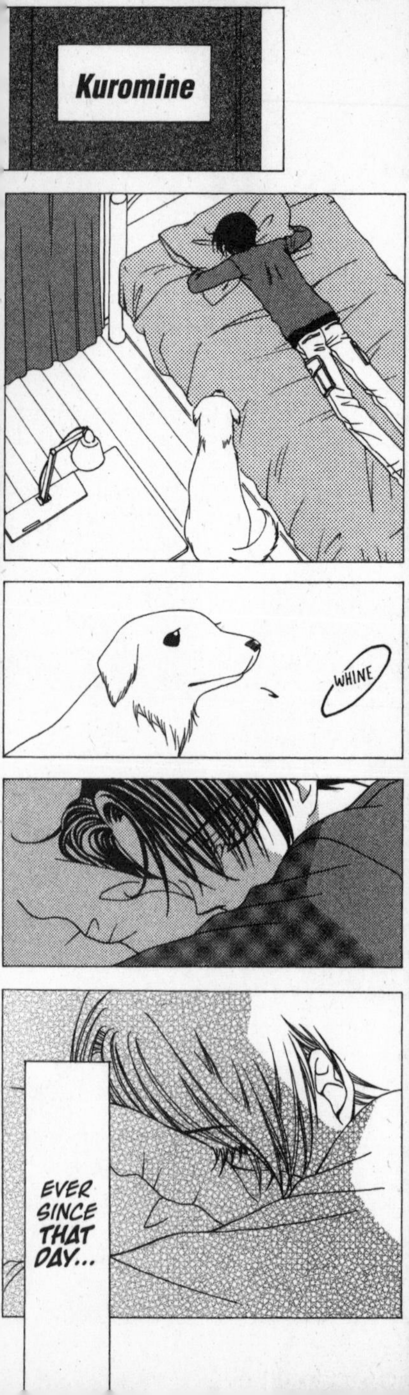
Kuromine
WHINE
EVER SINCE THAT DAY...

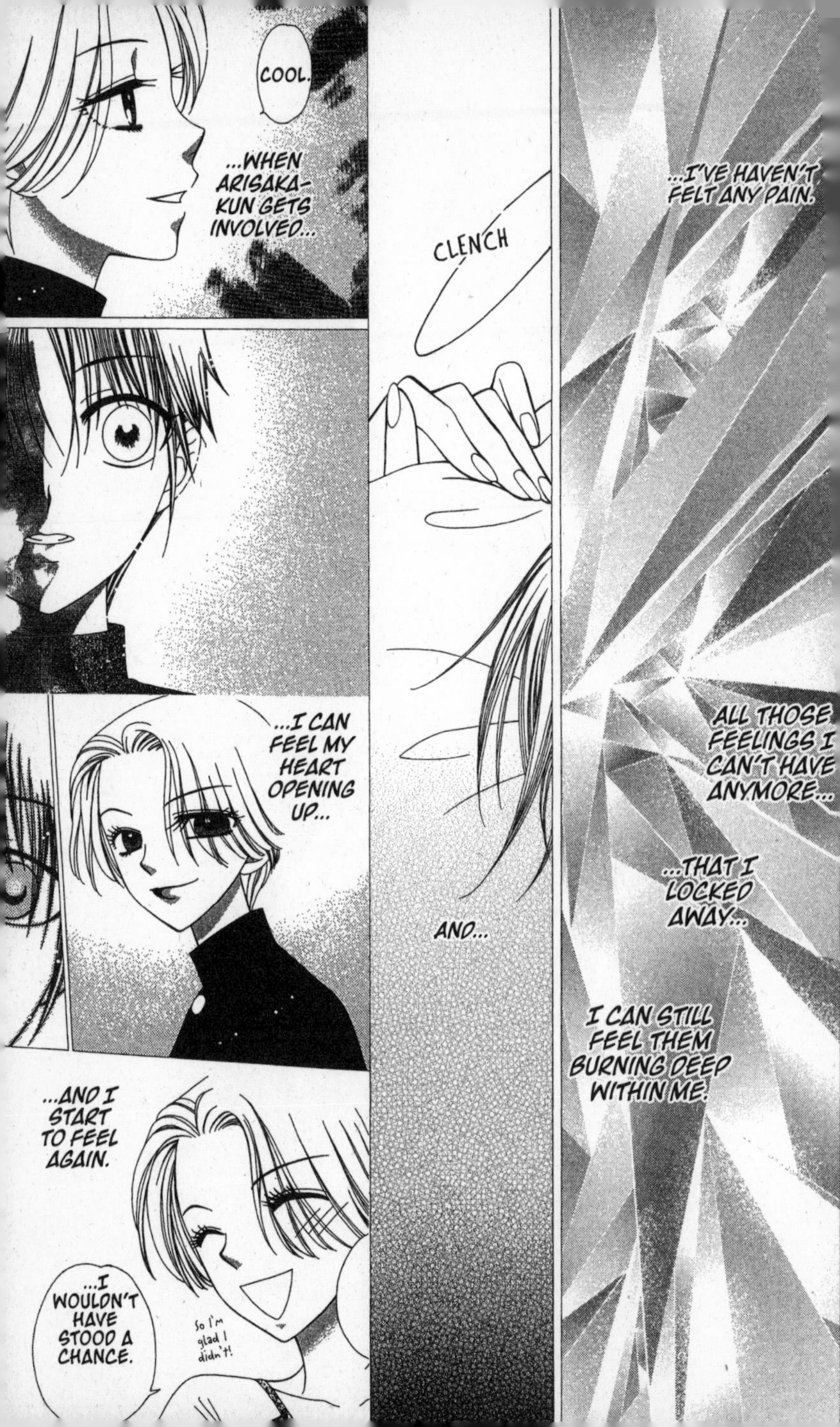
COOL.
...WHEN ARISAKA-KUN GETS INVOLVED...
...I CAN FEEL MY HEART OPENING UP...
...AND I START TO FEEL AGAIN.
...I WOULDN'T HAVE STOOD A CHANCE.
So I'm glad I didn't!
CLENCH
AND...
...I'VE HAVEN'T FELT ANY PAIN.
ALL THOSE FEELINGS I CAN'T HAVE ANYMORE...
...THAT I LOCKED AWAY...
I CAN STILL FEEL THEM BURNING DEEP WITHIN ME.

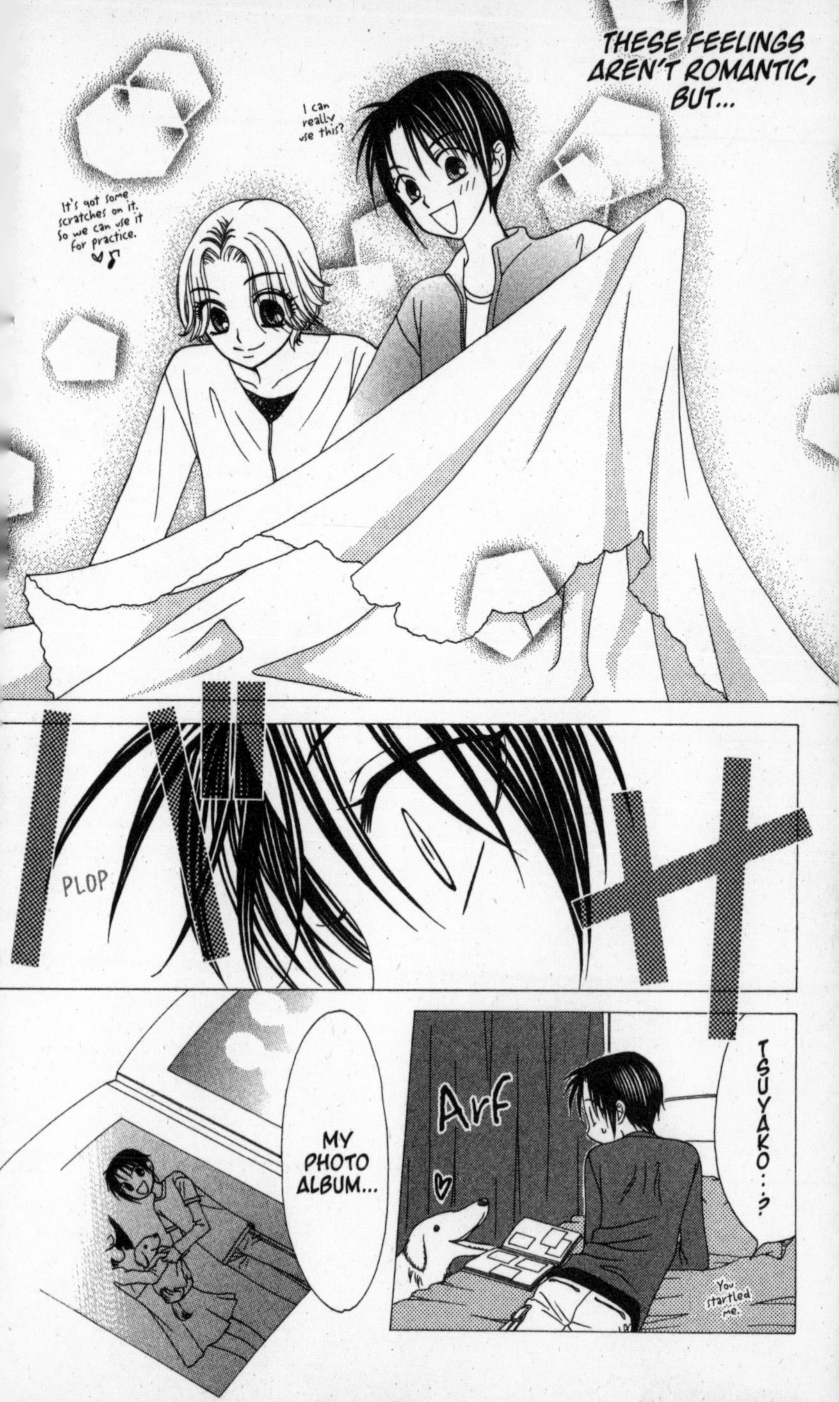
THESE FEELINGS AREN'T ROMANTIC, BUT...
I can really use this?
It's got some scratches on it. So we can use it for practice. ♥♪
PLOP
TSUYAKO...?
Arf
♥
You startled me.
MY PHOTO ALBUM...

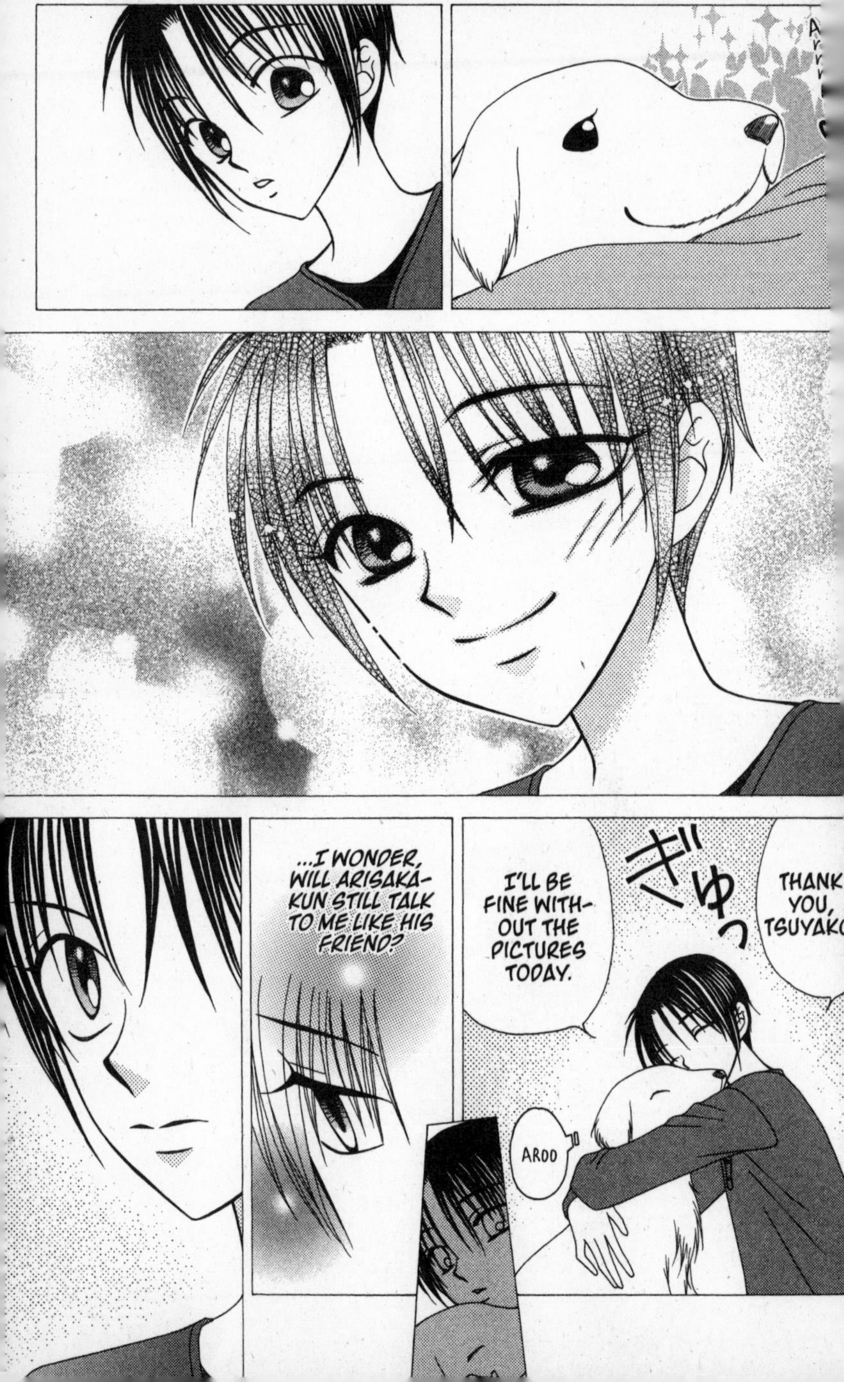
THANK YOU, TSUYAKO
ぎゅっ
I'LL BE FINE WITHOUT THE PICTURES TODAY.
AROO
...I WONDER, WILL ARISAKA-KUN STILL TALK TO ME LIKE HIS FRIEND?

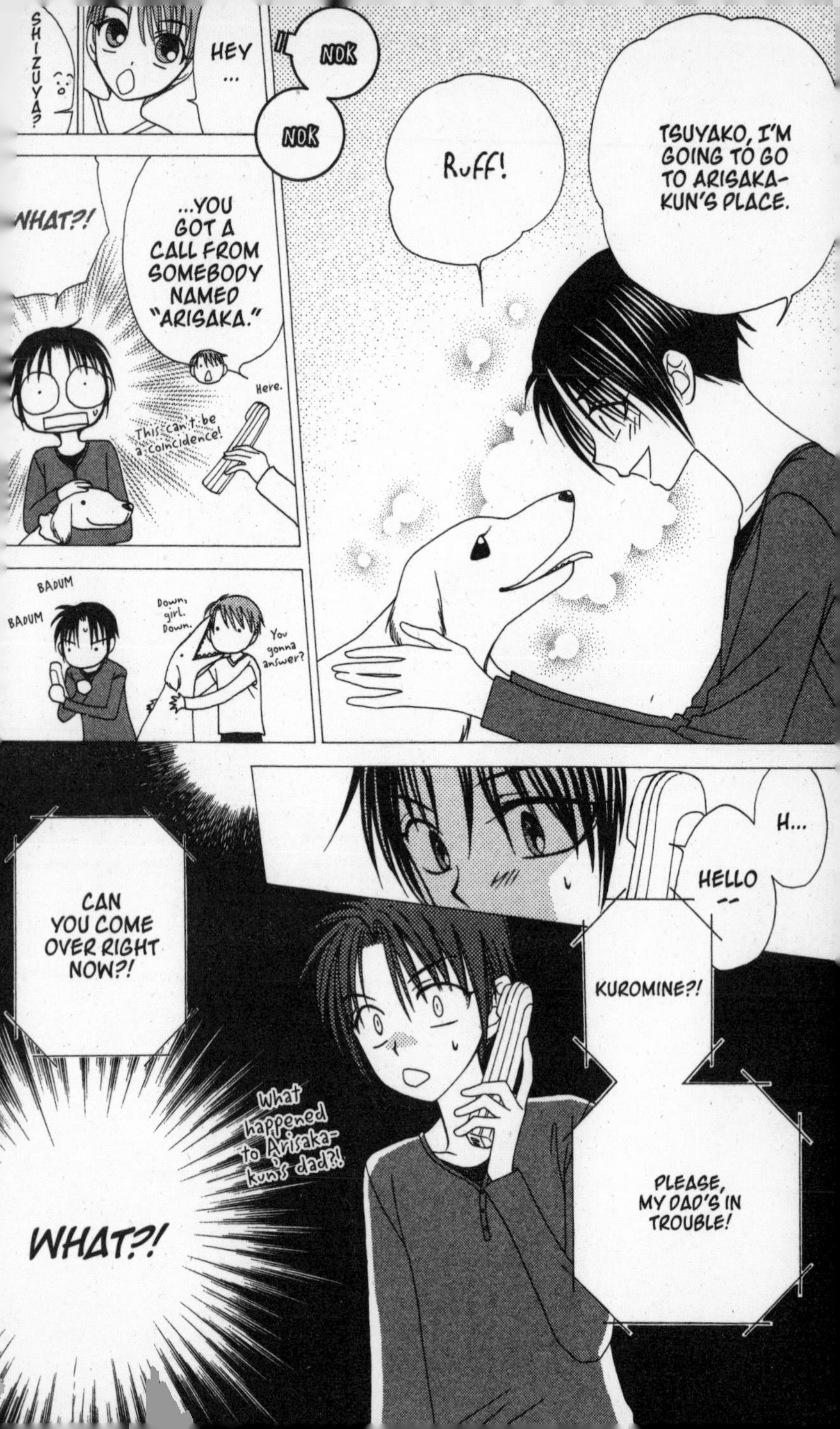
TSUYAKO, I'M GOING TO GO TO ARISAKA-KUN'S PLACE.
Ruff!
NOK
NOK
HEY ...
SHIZUYA?
...YOU GOT A CALL FROM SOMEBODY NAMED "ARISAKA."
WHAT?!
Here.
This can't be a coincidence!
You gonna answer?
Down, girl. Down.
BADUM
BADUM
H...
HELLO --
KUROMINE?!
PLEASE, MY DAD'S IN TROUBLE!
CAN YOU COME OVER RIGHT NOW?!
What happened to Arisaka-kun's dad?!
WHAT?!

♥ELVET INSTRUCTION MANUAL 20

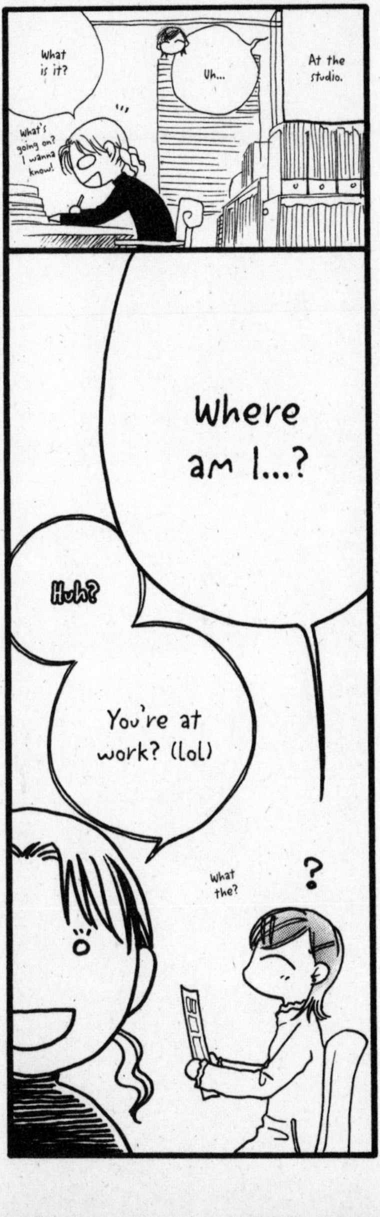
At the studio.
Uh...
What is it?
What's going on? I wanna know!
Where am I...?
Huh?
You're at work? (lol)
?
What the?

I laughed so hard... (hysterically)

Apparently her mind went completely blank.

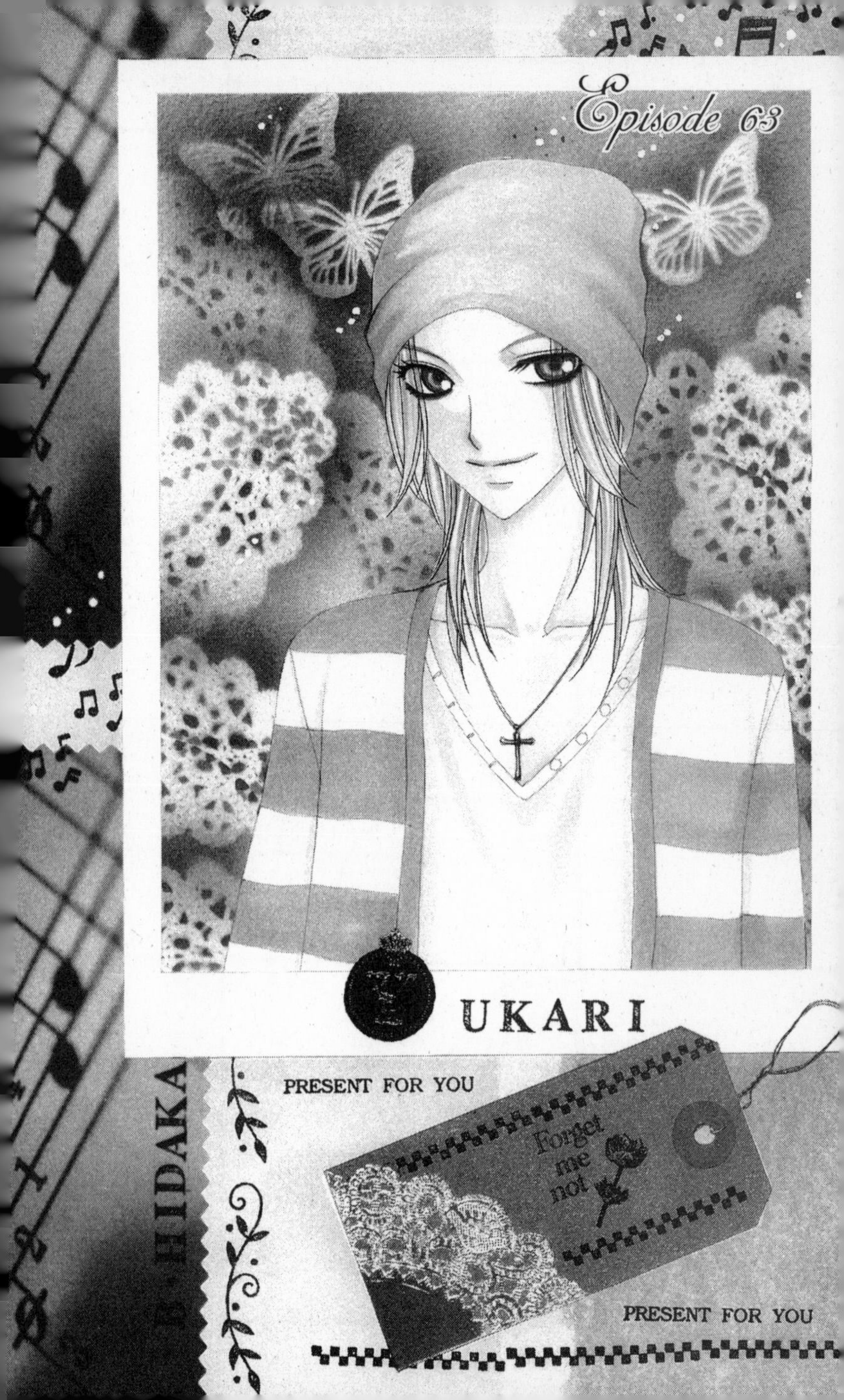
Episode 63
UKARI
HIDAKA
PRESENT FOR YOU
Forget me not
PRESENT FOR YOU

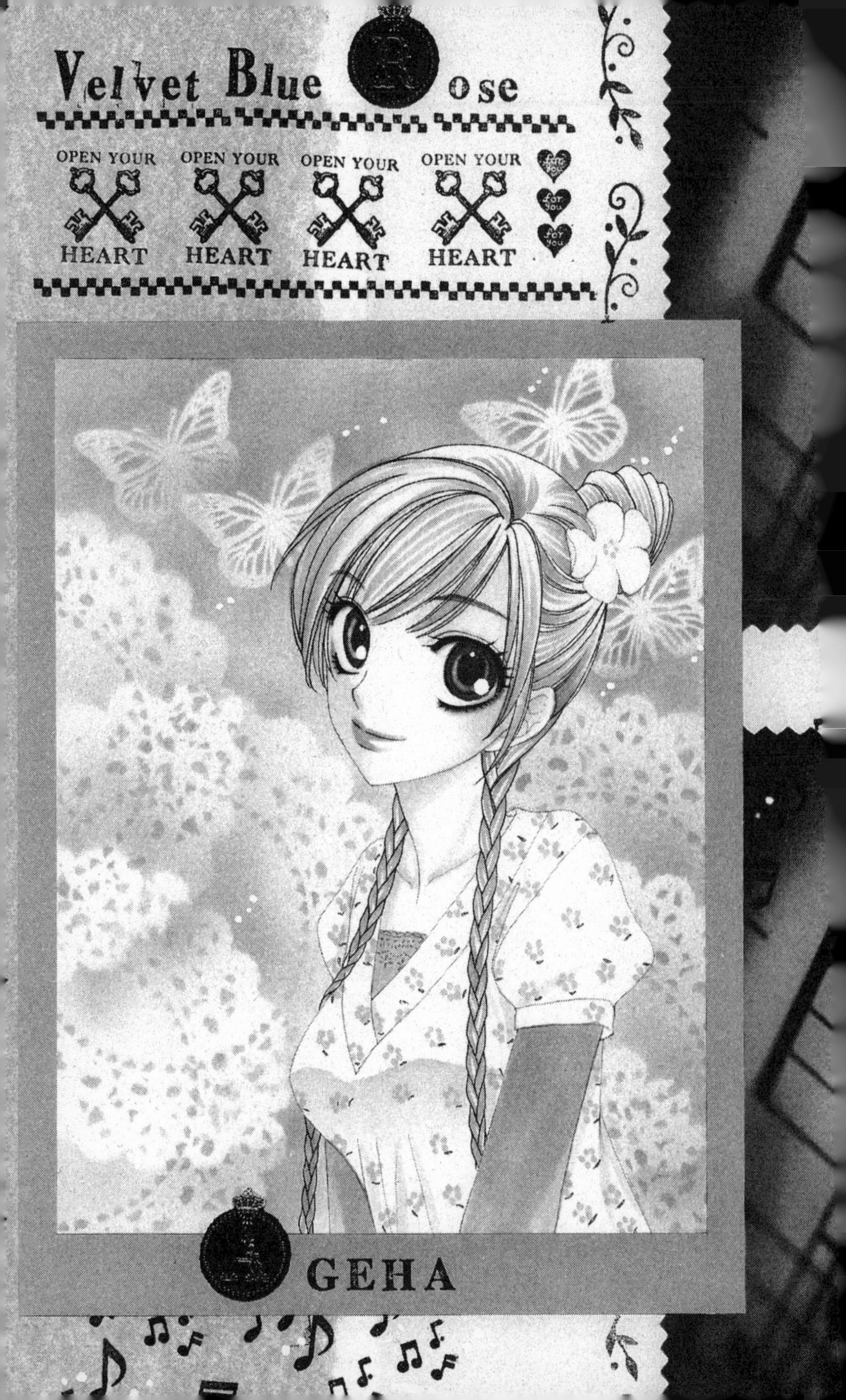
Velvet Blue Rose
OPEN YOUR HEART
OPEN YOUR HEART
OPEN YOUR HEART
OPEN YOUR HEART
for you
for you
for you
GEHA

VELVET INSTRUCTION MANUAL 21

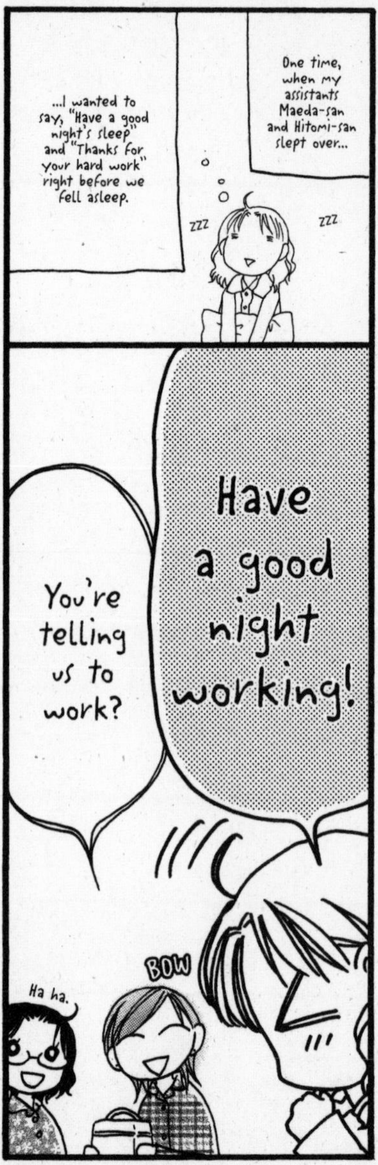
One time, when my assistants Maeda-san and Hitomi-san slept over...
...I wanted to say, "Have a good night's sleep" and "Thanks for your hard work" right before we fell asleep.
ZZZ
ZZZ
Have a good night working!
You're telling us to work?
BOW
Ha ha.

I mixed the two together.

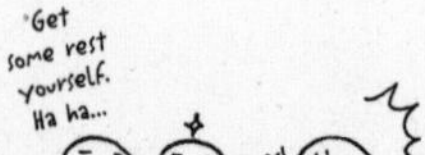
Get some rest yourself. Ha ha...
Oops!

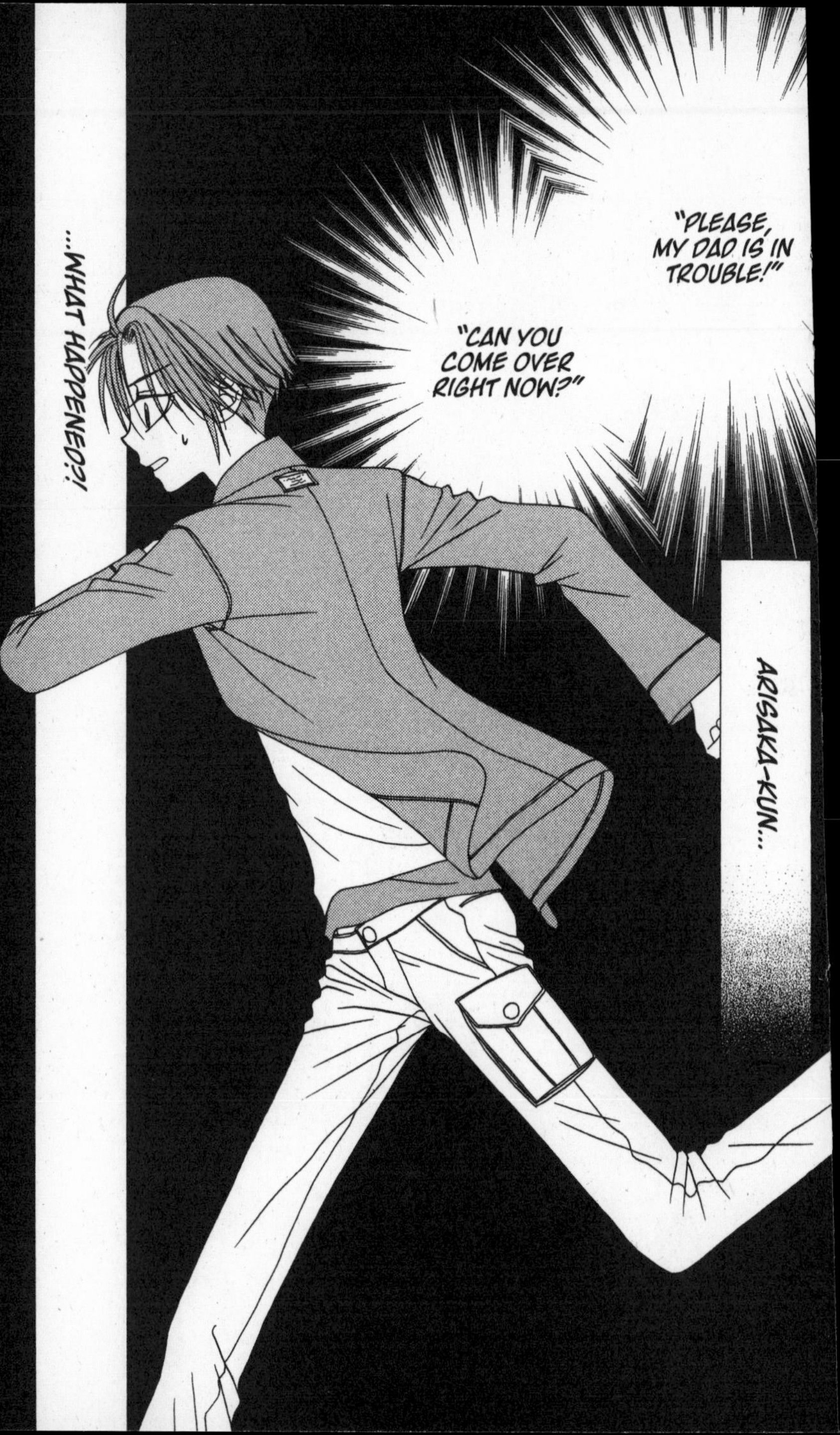
"PLEASE, MY DAD IS IN TROUBLE!"
"CAN YOU COME OVER RIGHT NOW?"
ARISAKA-KUN...
...WHAT HAPPENED?!

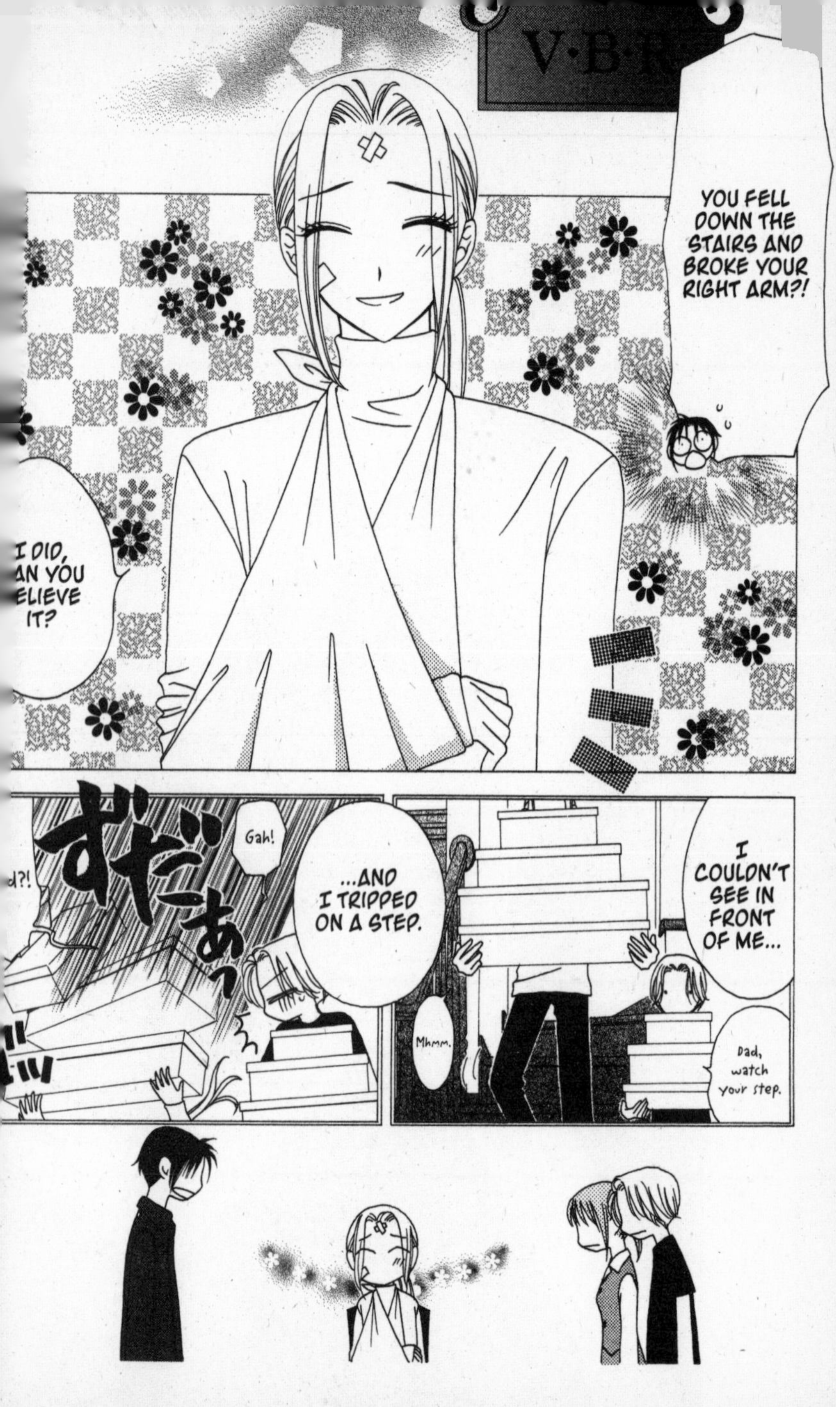
V·B·R
YOU FELL DOWN THE STAIRS AND BROKE YOUR RIGHT ARM?!
I DID, AN YOU ELIEVE IT?
I COULDN'T SEE IN FRONT OF ME...
Dad, watch your step.
Mhmm.
...AND I TRIPPED ON A STEP.
Gah!
ずだぁっ
d?!

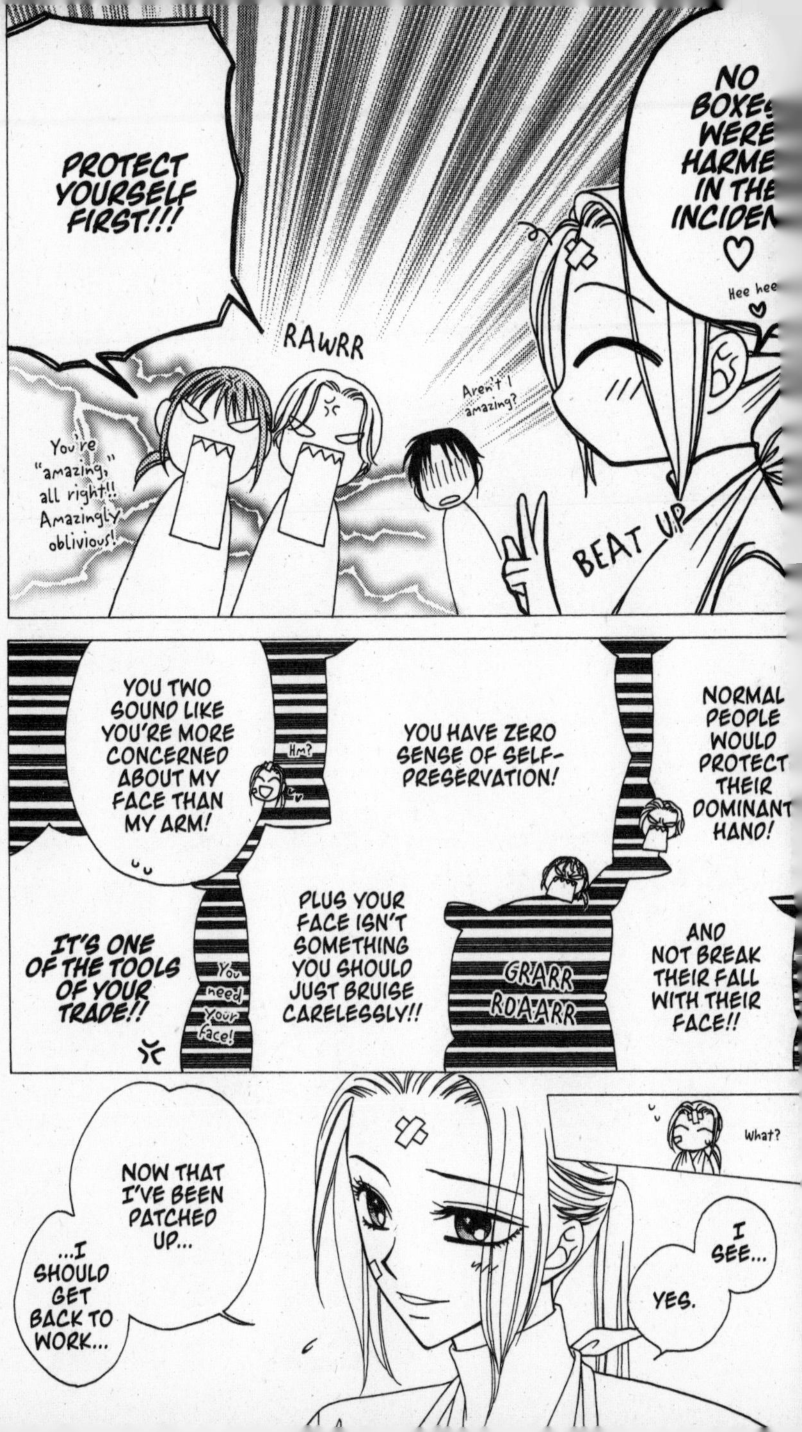
NO BOXES WERE HARME IN THE INCIDEN ♥
Hee hee ♥
BEAT UP
Aren't I amazing?
RAWRR
PROTECT YOURSELF FIRST!!!
You're "amazing," all right!! Amazingly oblivious!
NORMAL PEOPLE WOULD PROTECT THEIR DOMINANT HAND!
AND NOT BREAK THEIR FALL WITH THEIR FACE!!
GRARR ROAARR
YOU HAVE ZERO SENSE OF SELF-PRESERVATION!
PLUS YOUR FACE ISN'T SOMETHING YOU SHOULD JUST BRUISE CARELESSLY!!
Hm?
YOU TWO SOUND LIKE YOU'RE MORE CONCERNED ABOUT MY FACE THAN MY ARM!
IT'S ONE OF THE TOOLS OF YOUR TRADE!!
You need your face!
What?
I SEE...
YES.
NOW THAT I'VE BEEN PATCHED UP...
...I SHOULD GET BACK TO WORK...

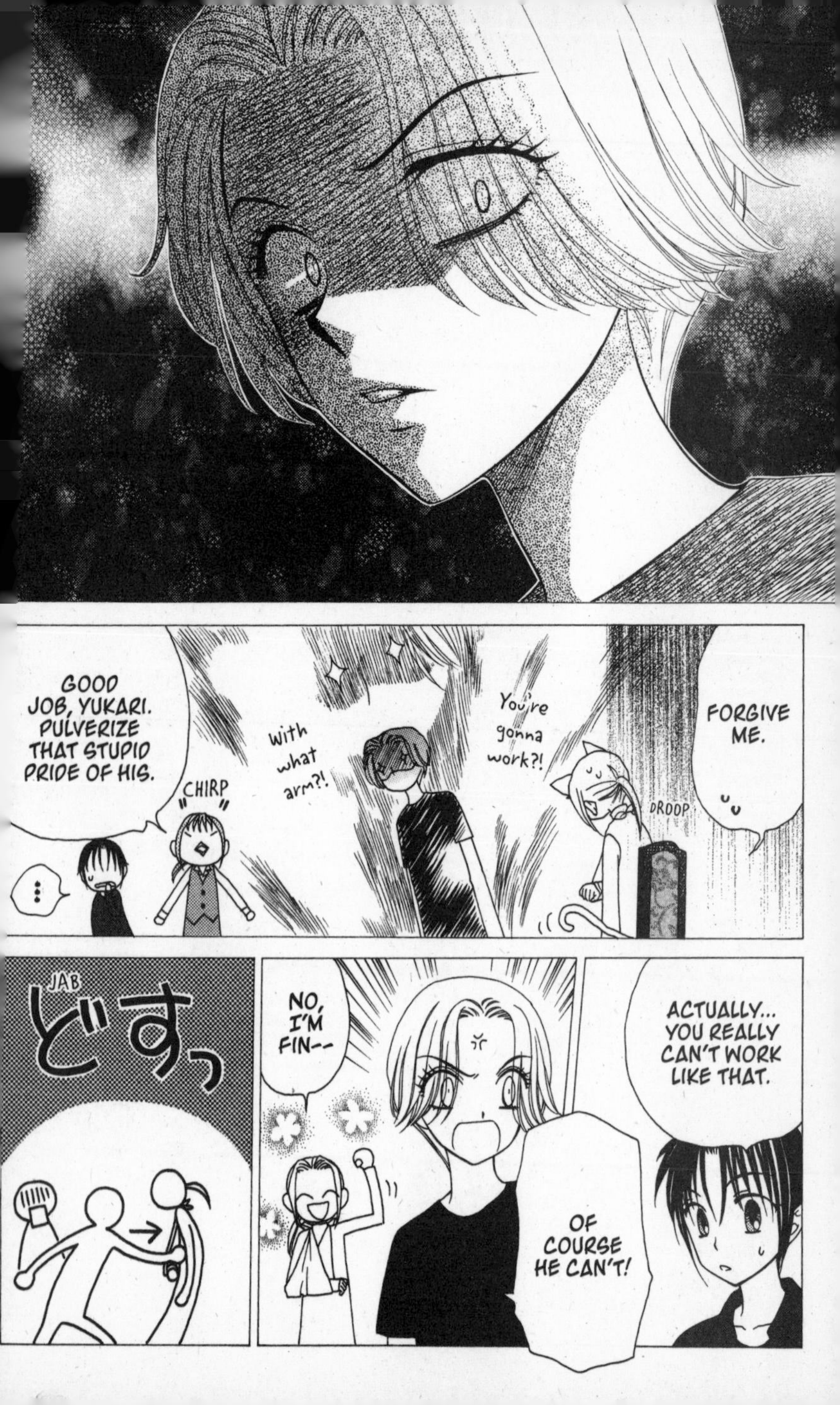
FORGIVE ME.
DROOP
You're gonna work?!
with what arm?!
CHIRP
GOOD JOB, YUKARI. PULVERIZE THAT STUPID PRIDE OF HIS.
...
ACTUALLY... YOU REALLY CAN'T WORK LIKE THAT.
NO, I'M FIN--
OF COURSE HE CAN'T!
JAB
どすっ

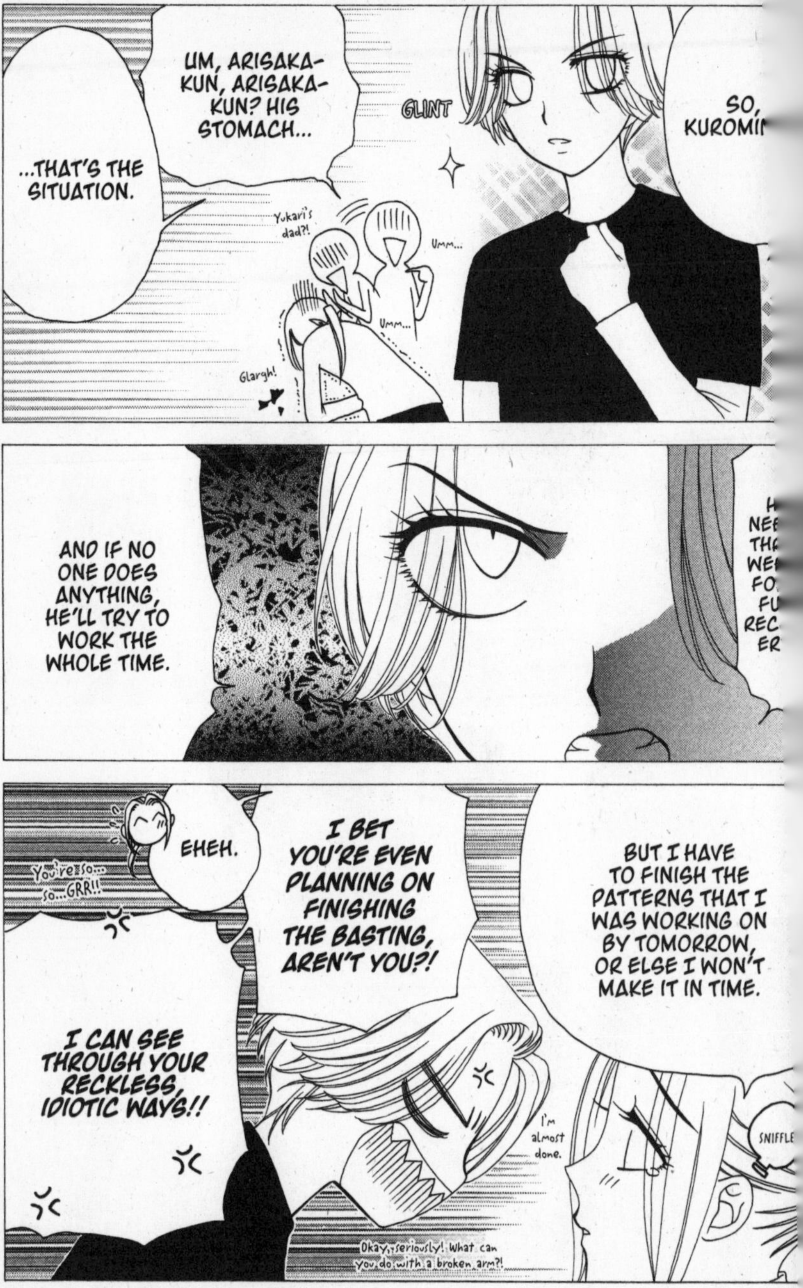
SO, KUROMI
GLINT
UM, ARISAKA-KUN, ARISAKA-KUN? HIS STOMACH...
Umm...
Umm...
Yukari's dad?!
Glargh!
...THAT'S THE SITUATION.
AND IF NO ONE DOES ANYTHING, HE'LL TRY TO WORK THE WHOLE TIME.
BUT I HAVE TO FINISH THE PATTERNS THAT I WAS WORKING ON BY TOMORROW, OR ELSE I WON'T MAKE IT IN TIME.
SNIFFLE
I'm almost done.
I BET YOU'RE EVEN PLANNING ON FINISHING THE BASTING, AREN'T YOU?!
EHEH.
You're so... so...GRR!!
I CAN SEE THROUGH YOUR RECKLESS, IDIOTIC WAYS!!
Okay, seriously! What can you do with a broken arm?!

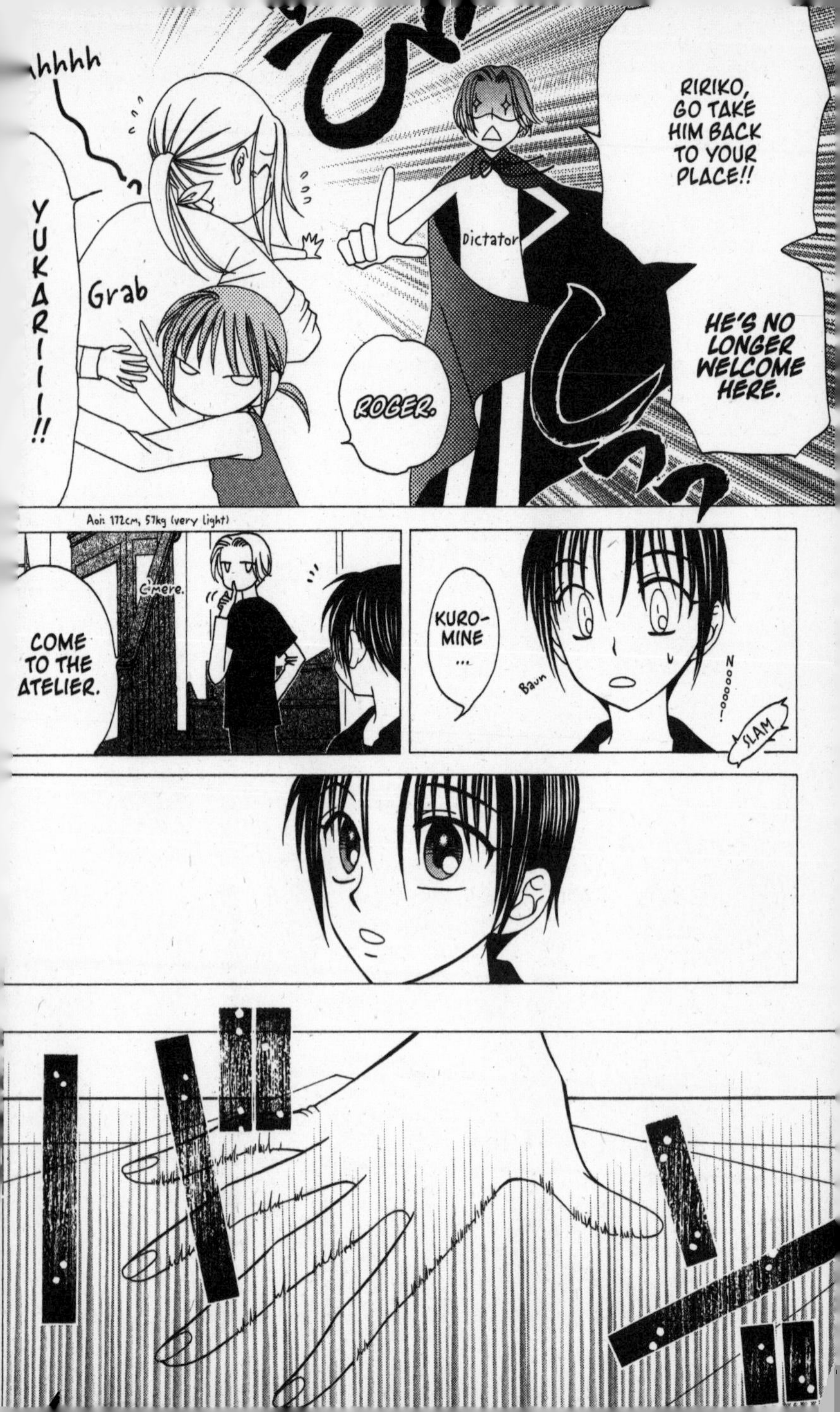
RIRIKO, GO TAKE HIM BACK TO YOUR PLACE!!
HE'S NO LONGER WELCOME HERE.
Dictator
ROGER.
Grab
hhhh
YUKARIIIII!!
Aoi: 172cm, 57kg (very light)
KURO-MINE ...
Baun
Noooooo!
SLAM
C'mere.
COME TO THE ATELIER.

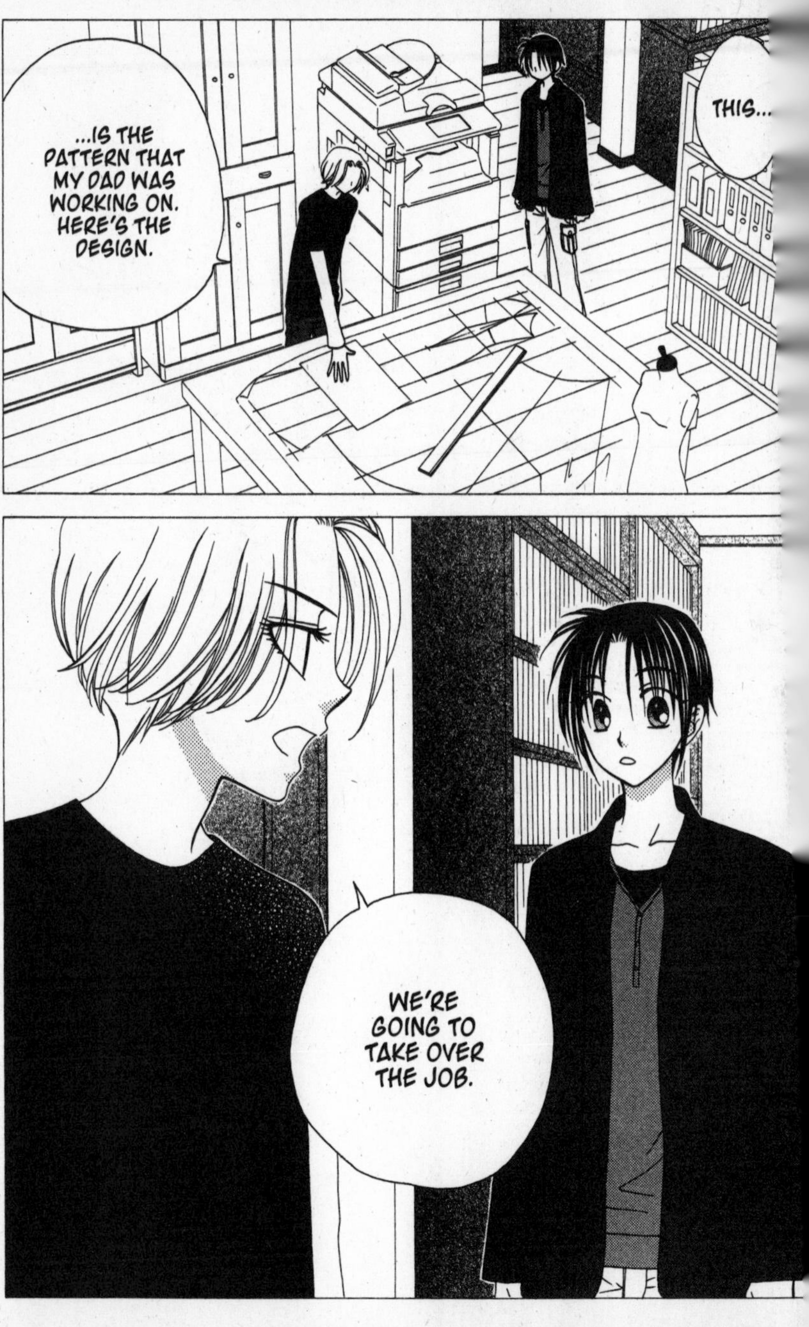
THIS...
...IS THE PATTERN THAT MY DAD WAS WORKING ON. HERE'S THE DESIGN.
WE'RE GOING TO TAKE OVER THE JOB.

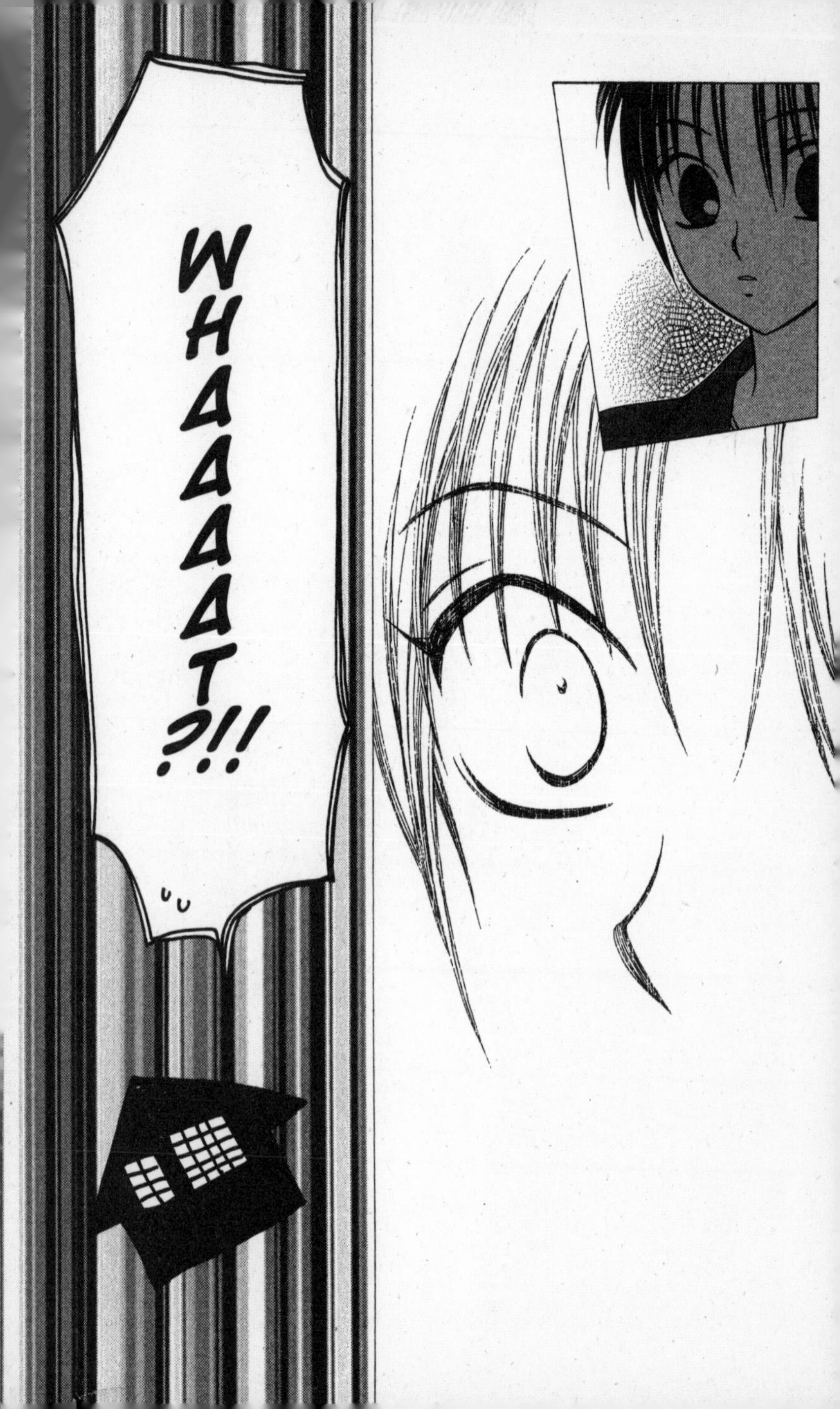
WHAAAAT?!!

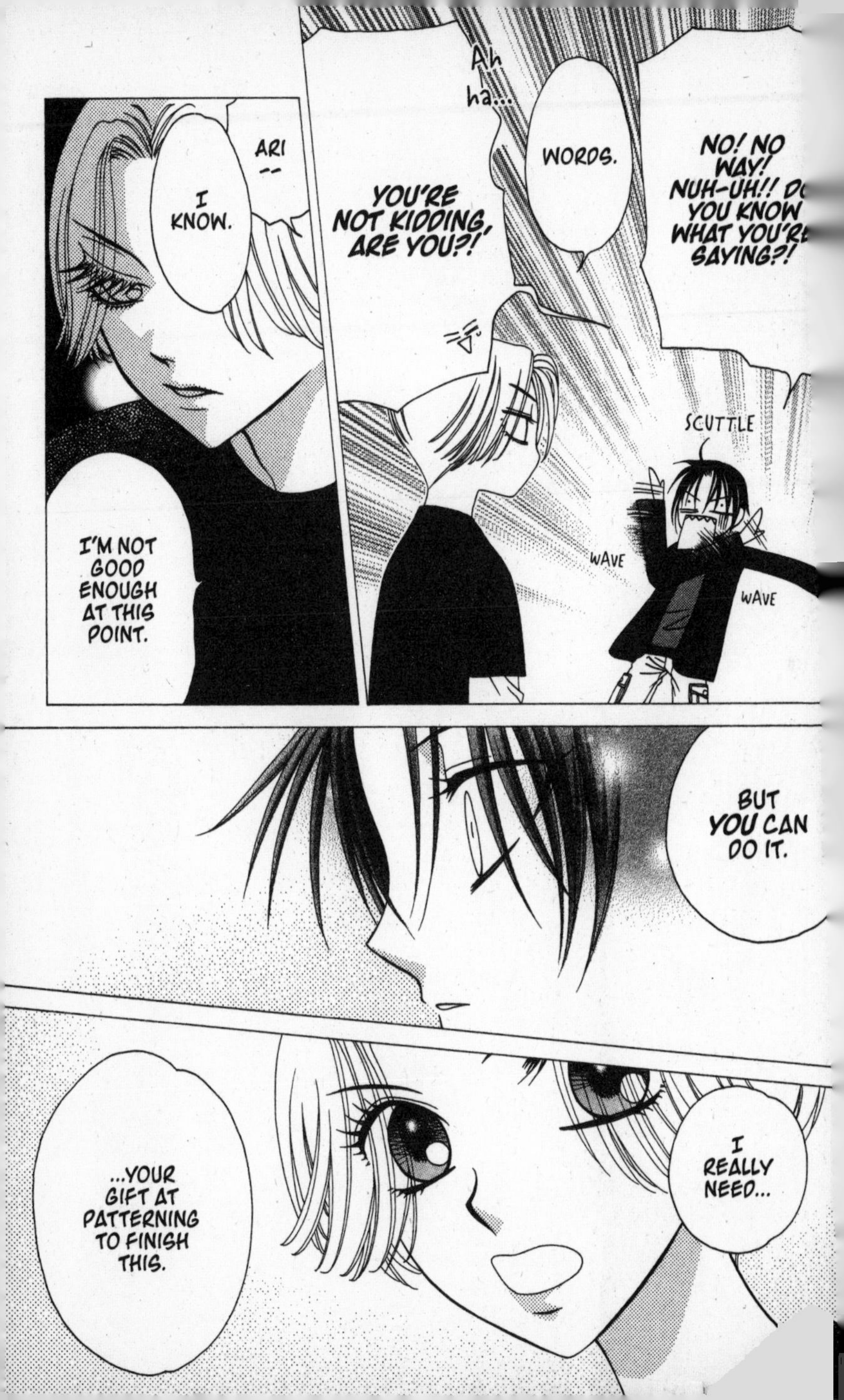
WORDS.
NO! NO WAY! NUH-UH!! DO YOU KNOW WHAT YOU'RE SAYING?!
Ah ha...
YOU'RE NOT KIDDING, ARE YOU?!
SCUTTLE
WAVE
WAVE
ARI --
I KNOW.
I'M NOT GOOD ENOUGH AT THIS POINT.
BUT YOU CAN DO IT.
I REALLY NEED...
...YOUR GIFT AT PATTERNING TO FINISH THIS.

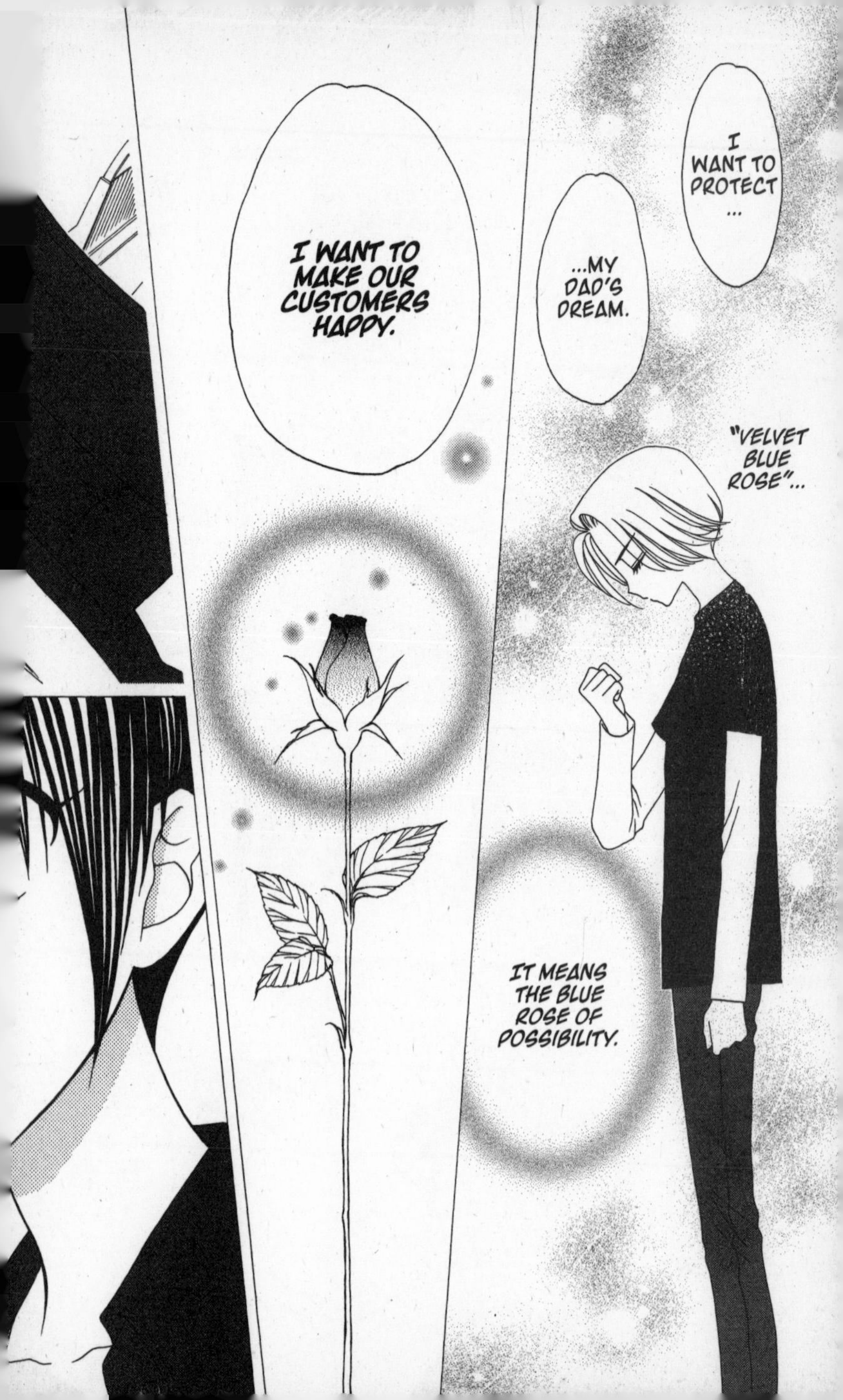
I WANT TO PROTECT ...
...MY DAD'S DREAM.
"VELVET BLUE ROSE"...
IT MEANS THE BLUE ROSE OF POSSIBILITY.
I WANT TO MAKE OUR CUSTOMERS HAPPY.

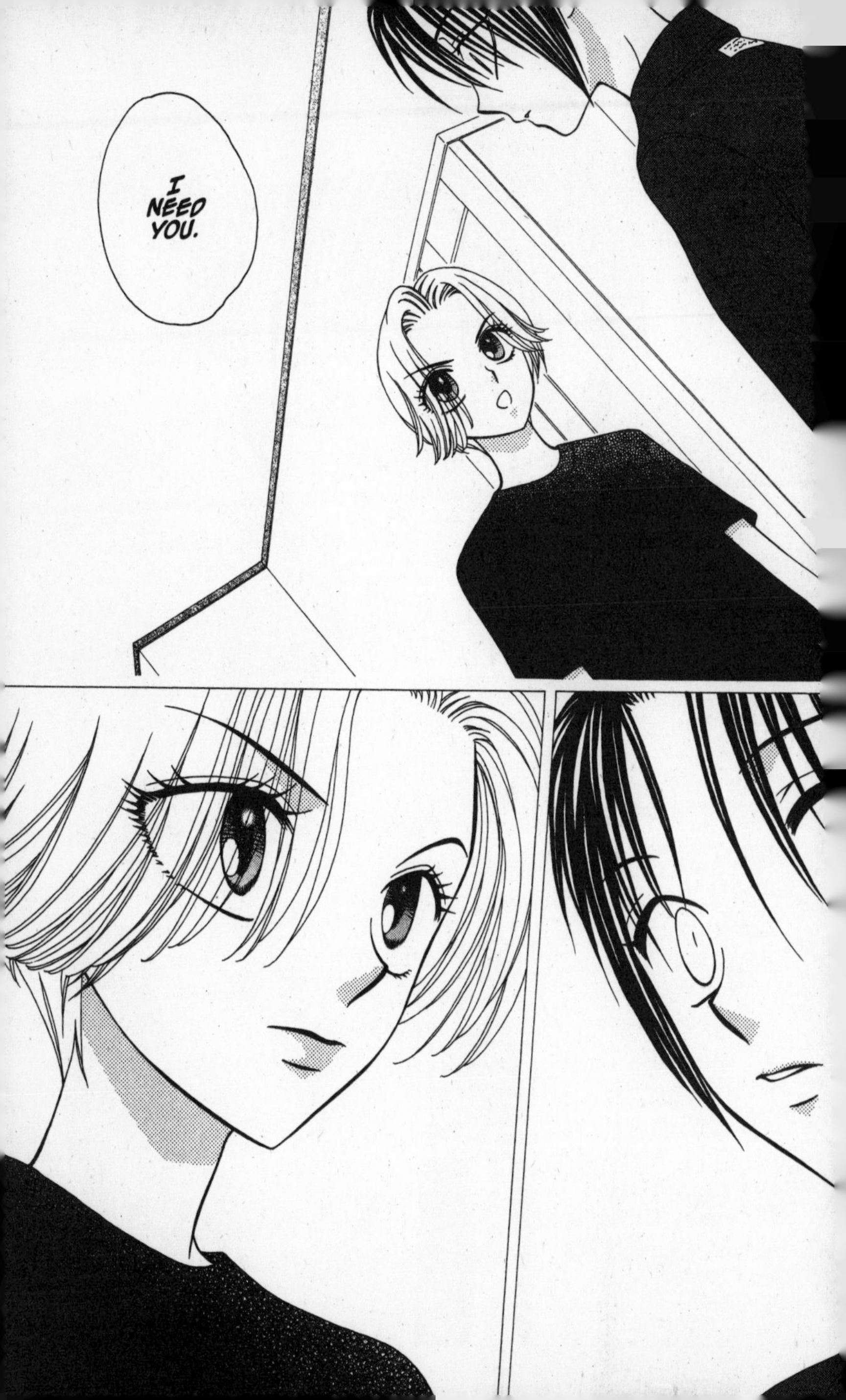
I NEED YOU.

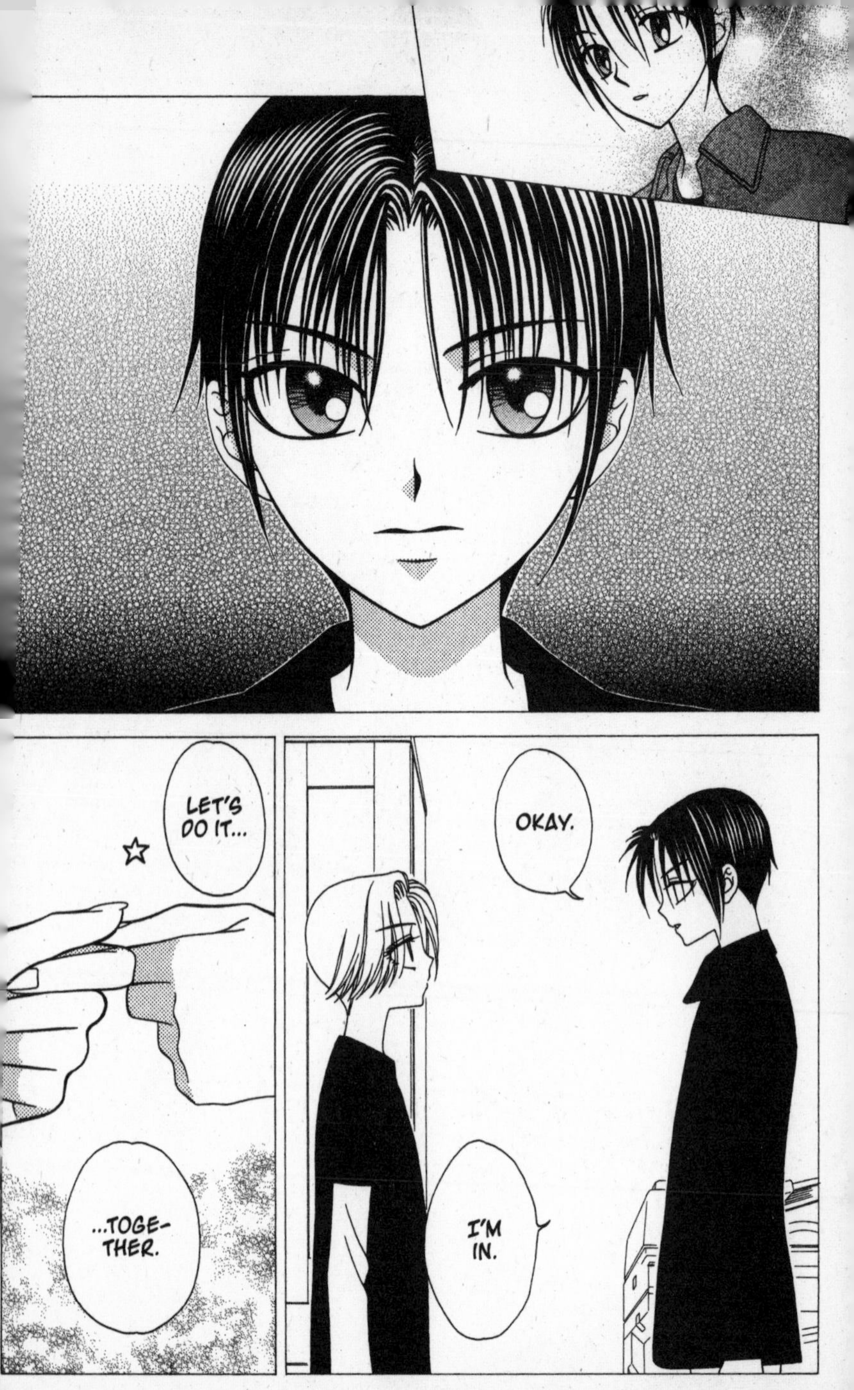
OKAY.
I'M IN.
LET'S DO IT...
...TOGE-THER.

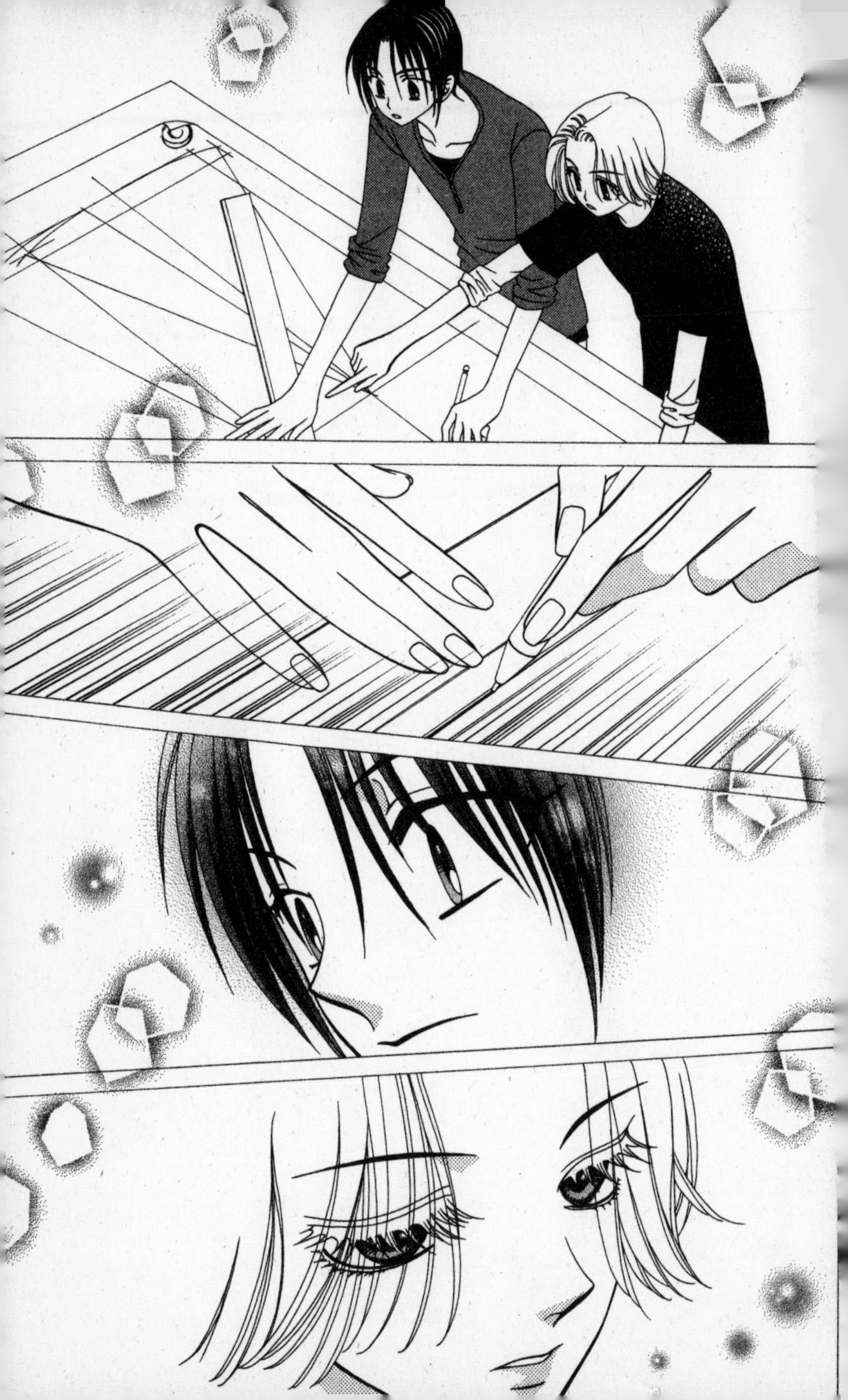

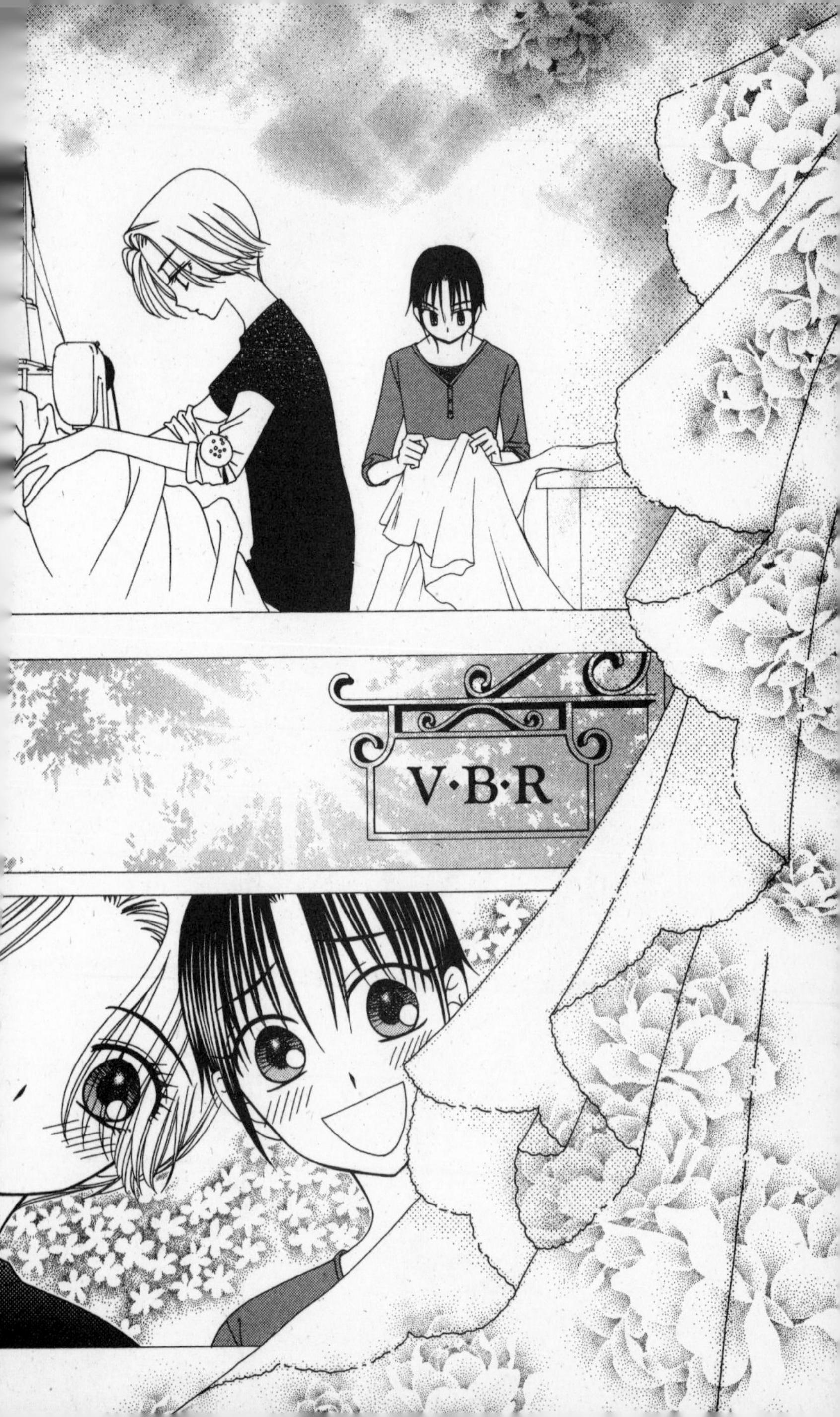
V·B·R

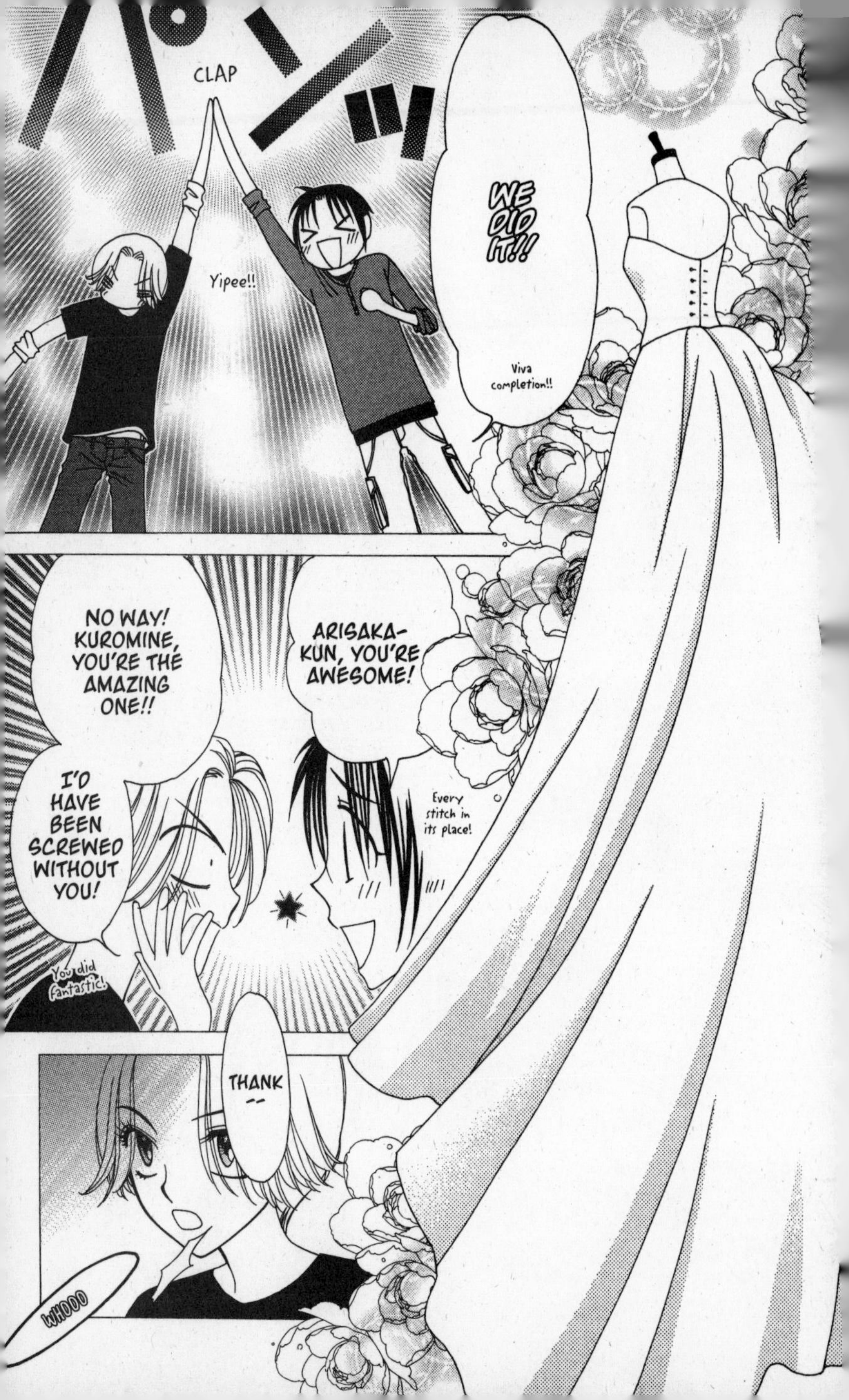
WE DID IT!!
Viva completion!!
CLAP
Yipee!!
ARISAKA-KUN, YOU'RE AWESOME!
Every stitch in its place!
NO WAY! KUROMINE, YOU'RE THE AMAZING ONE!!
I'D HAVE BEEN SCREWED WITHOUT YOU!
You did fantastic!
THANK --
WHOOO

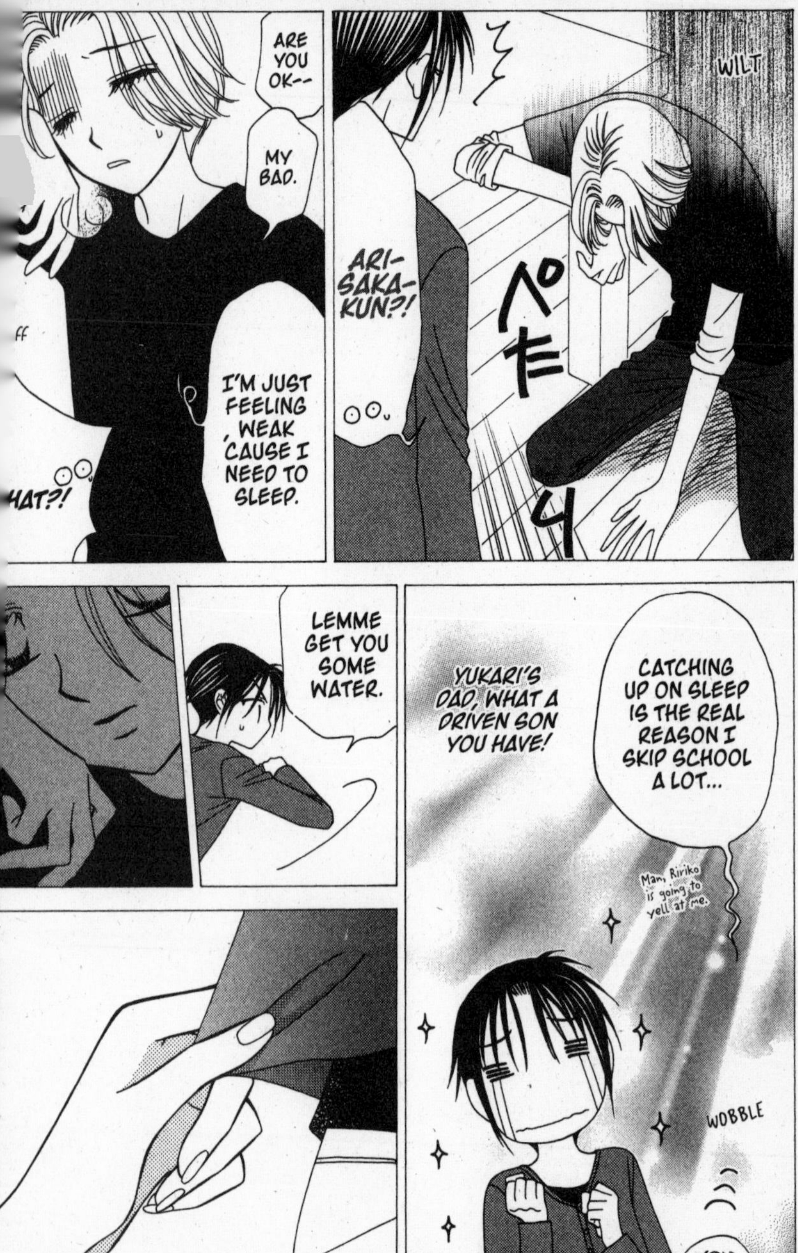
WILT
ぺたん
ARI-SAKA-KUN?!
ARE YOU OK--
MY BAD.
I'M JUST FEELING WEAK 'CAUSE I NEED TO SLEEP.
HAT?!
CATCHING UP ON SLEEP IS THE REAL REASON I SKIP SCHOOL A LOT...
YUKARI'S DAD, WHAT A DRIVEN SON YOU HAVE!
Man, Ririko is going to yell at me.
WOBBLE
LEMME GET YOU SOME WATER.

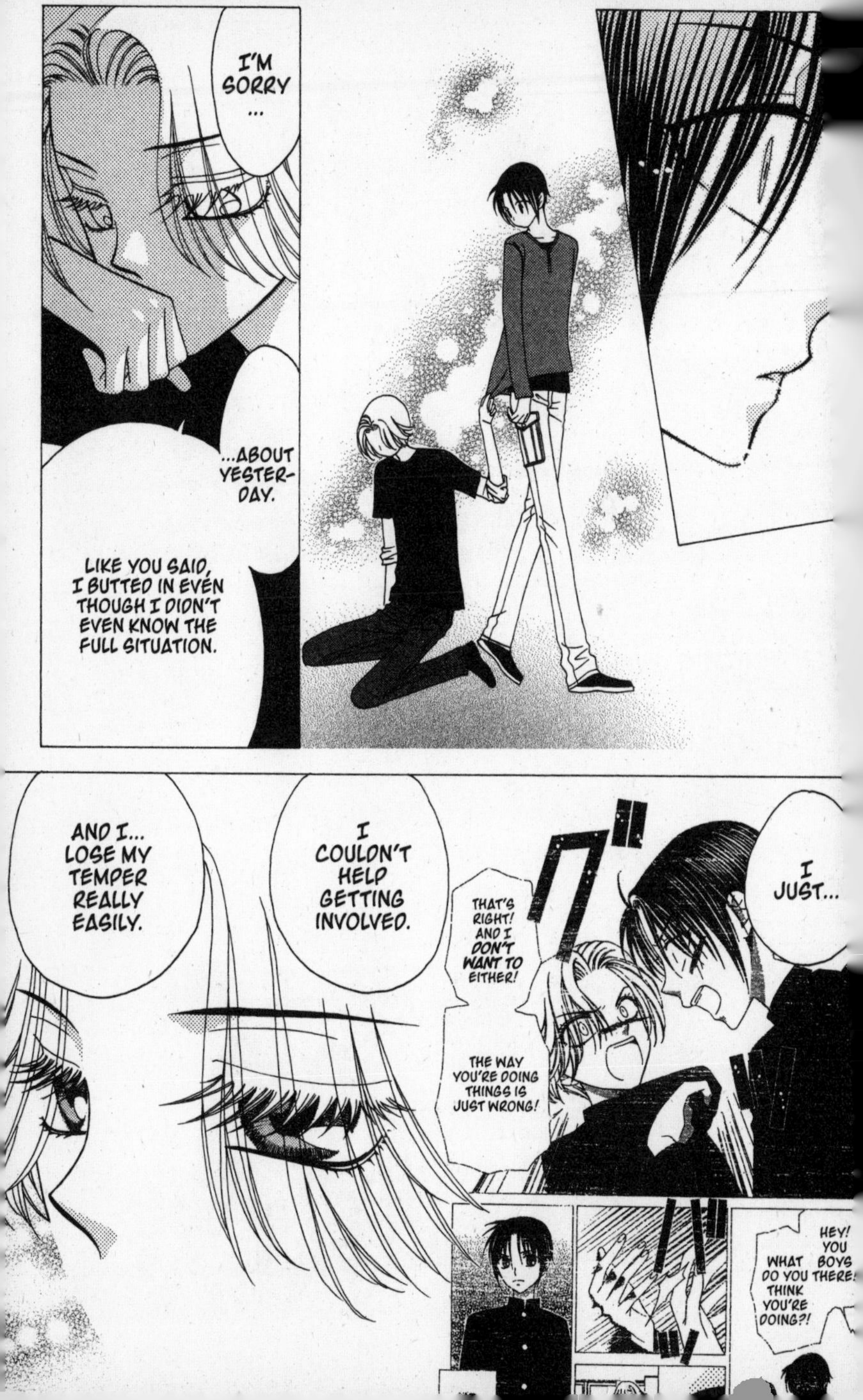
I'M SORRY...
...ABOUT YESTERDAY.
LIKE YOU SAID, I BUTTED IN EVEN THOUGH I DIDN'T EVEN KNOW THE FULL SITUATION.
I JUST...
THAT'S RIGHT! AND I DON'T WANT TO EITHER!
THE WAY YOU'RE DOING THINGS IS JUST WRONG!
I COULDN'T HELP GETTING INVOLVED.
AND I... LOSE MY TEMPER REALLY EASILY.
HEY! YOU BOYS THERE! WHAT DO YOU THINK YOU'RE DOING?!

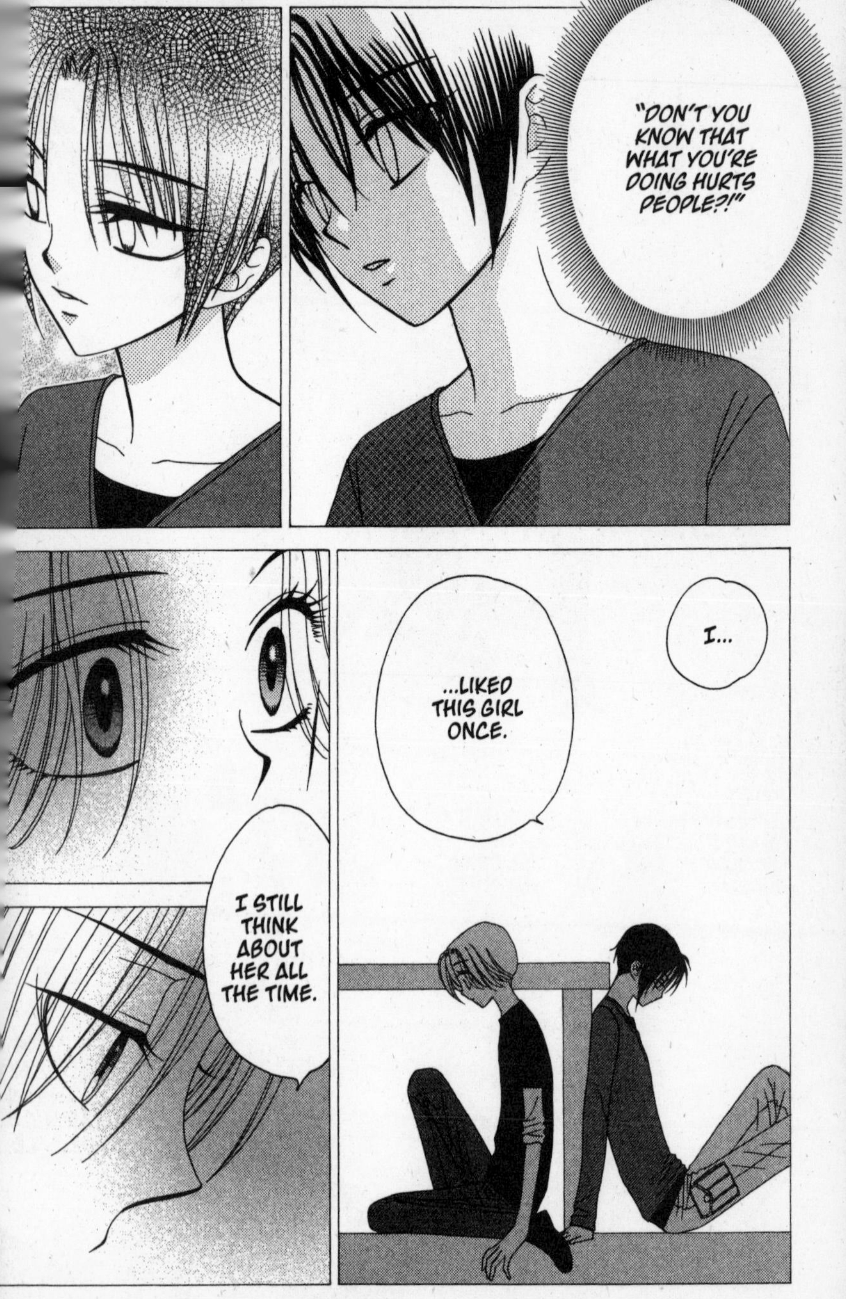
"DON'T YOU KNOW THAT WHAT YOU'RE DOING HURTS PEOPLE?!"
I...
...LIKED THIS GIRL ONCE.
I STILL THINK ABOUT HER ALL THE TIME.

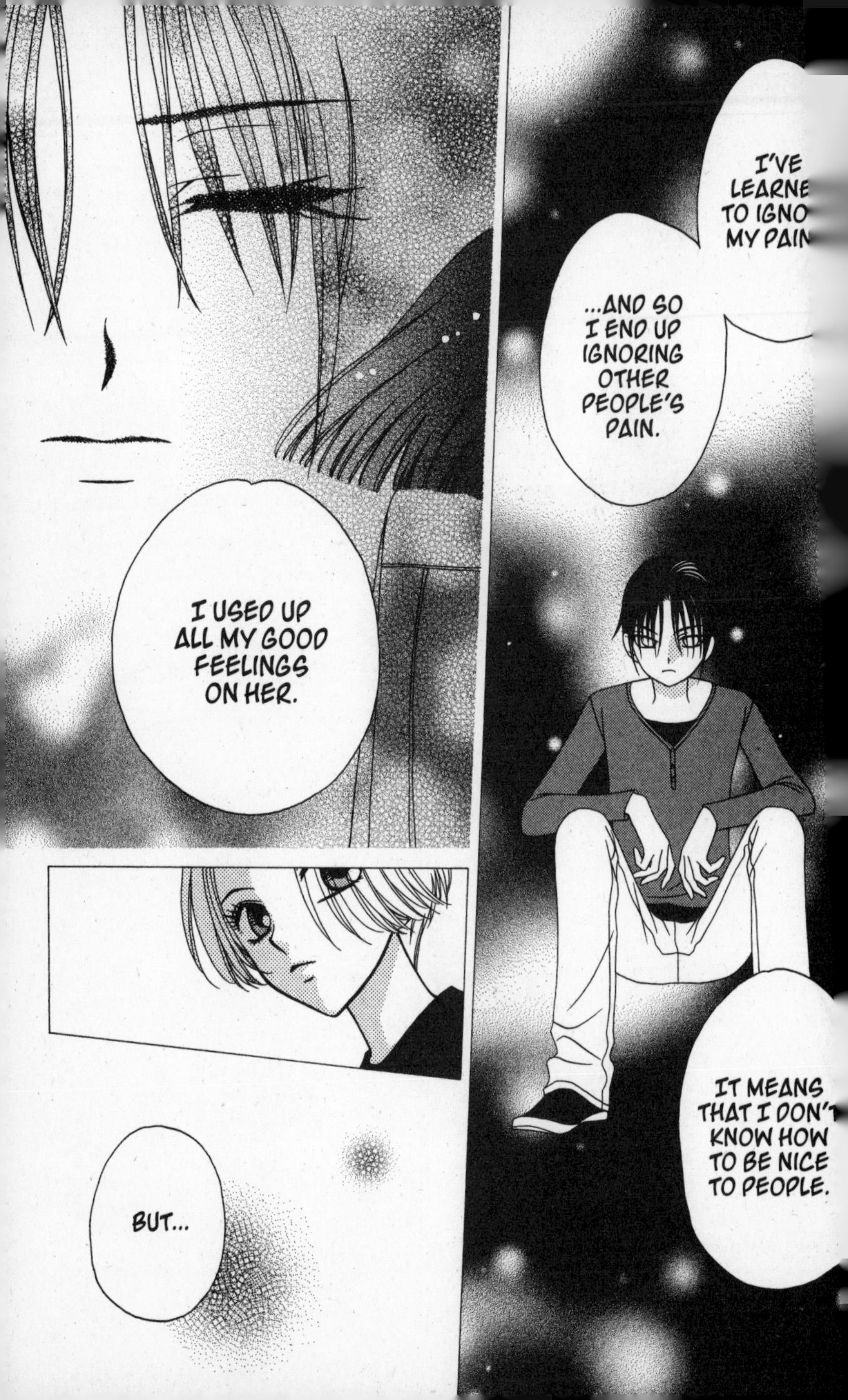
I'VE LEARNE TO IGNO MY PAIN
...AND SO I END UP IGNORING OTHER PEOPLE'S PAIN.
IT MEANS THAT I DON'T KNOW HOW TO BE NICE TO PEOPLE.
I USED UP ALL MY GOOD FEELINGS ON HER.
BUT...

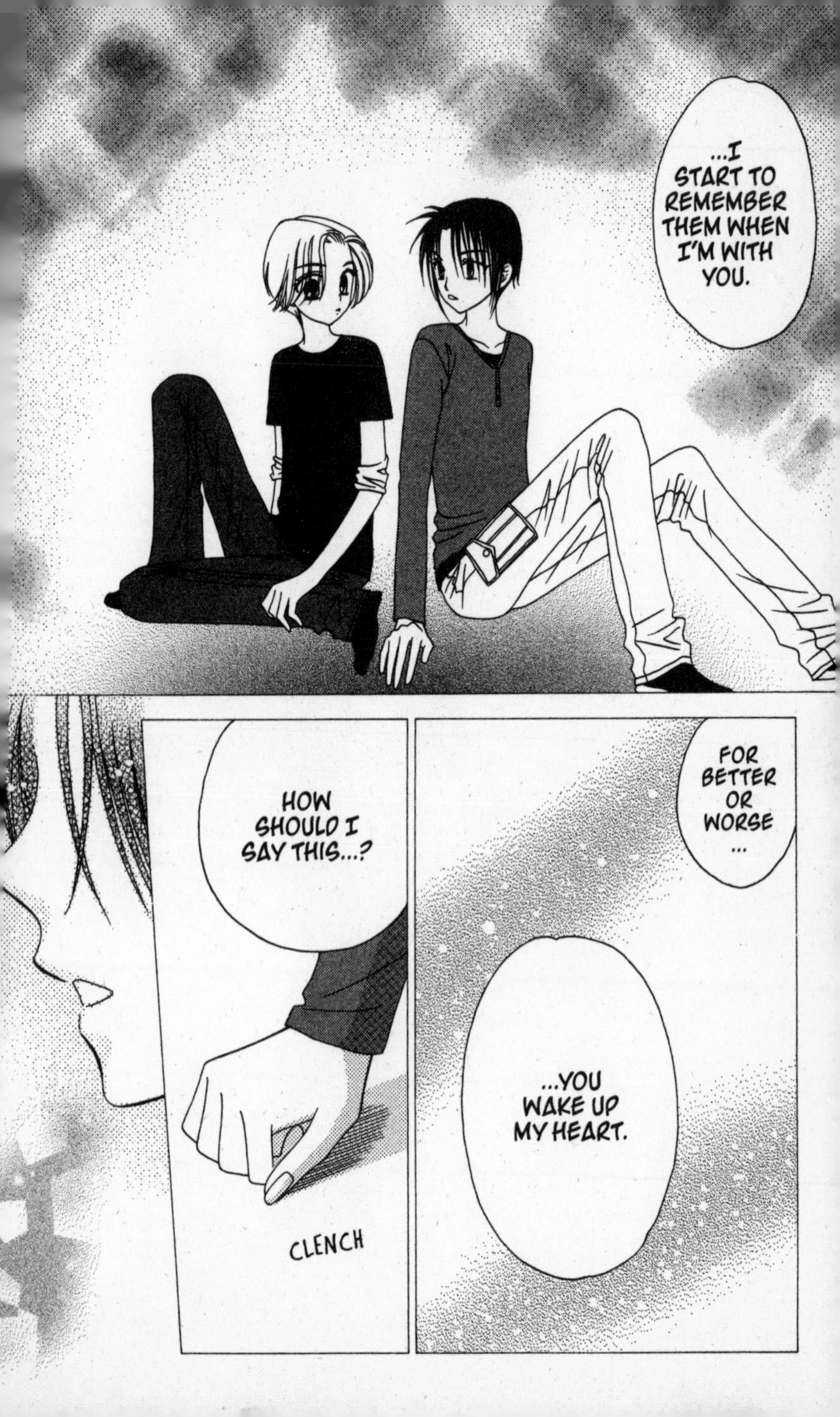
...I START TO REMEMBER THEM WHEN I'M WITH YOU.
FOR BETTER OR WORSE ...
...YOU WAKE UP MY HEART.
HOW SHOULD I SAY THIS...?
CLENCH

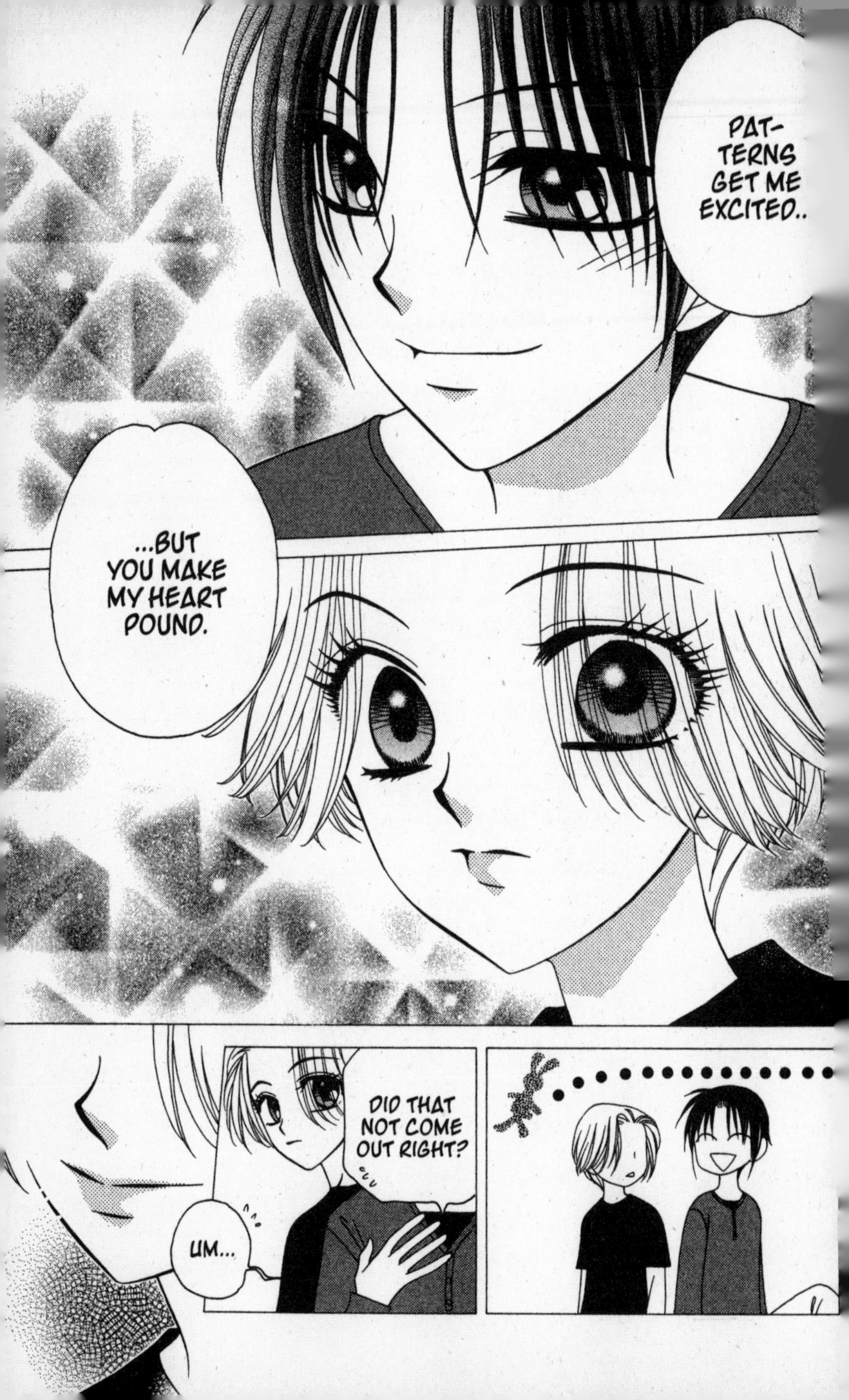
PAT-TERNS GET ME EXCITED..
...BUT YOU MAKE MY HEART POUND.
DID THAT NOT COME OUT RIGHT?
UM...

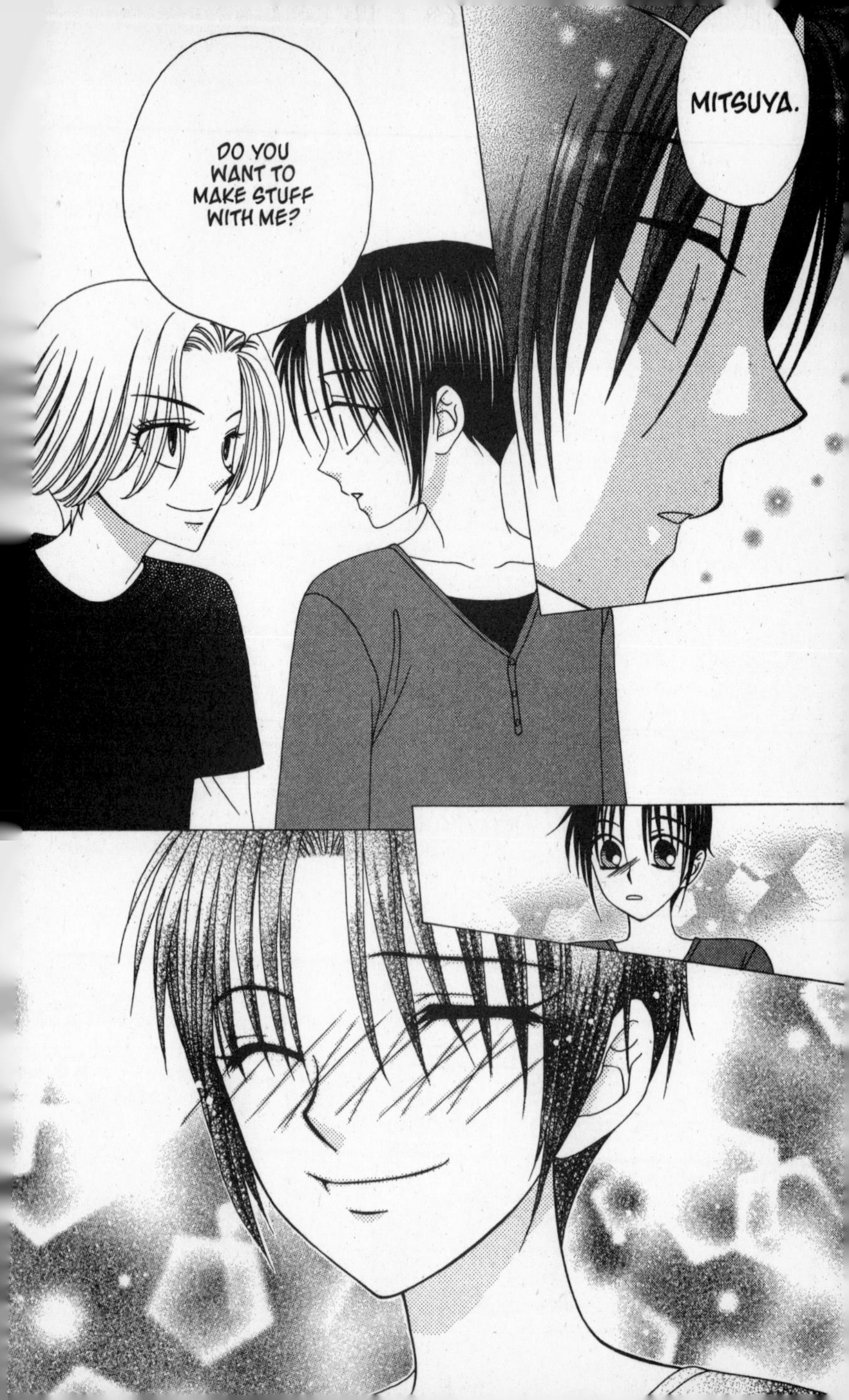
MITSUYA.
DO YOU WANT TO MAKE STUFF WITH ME?

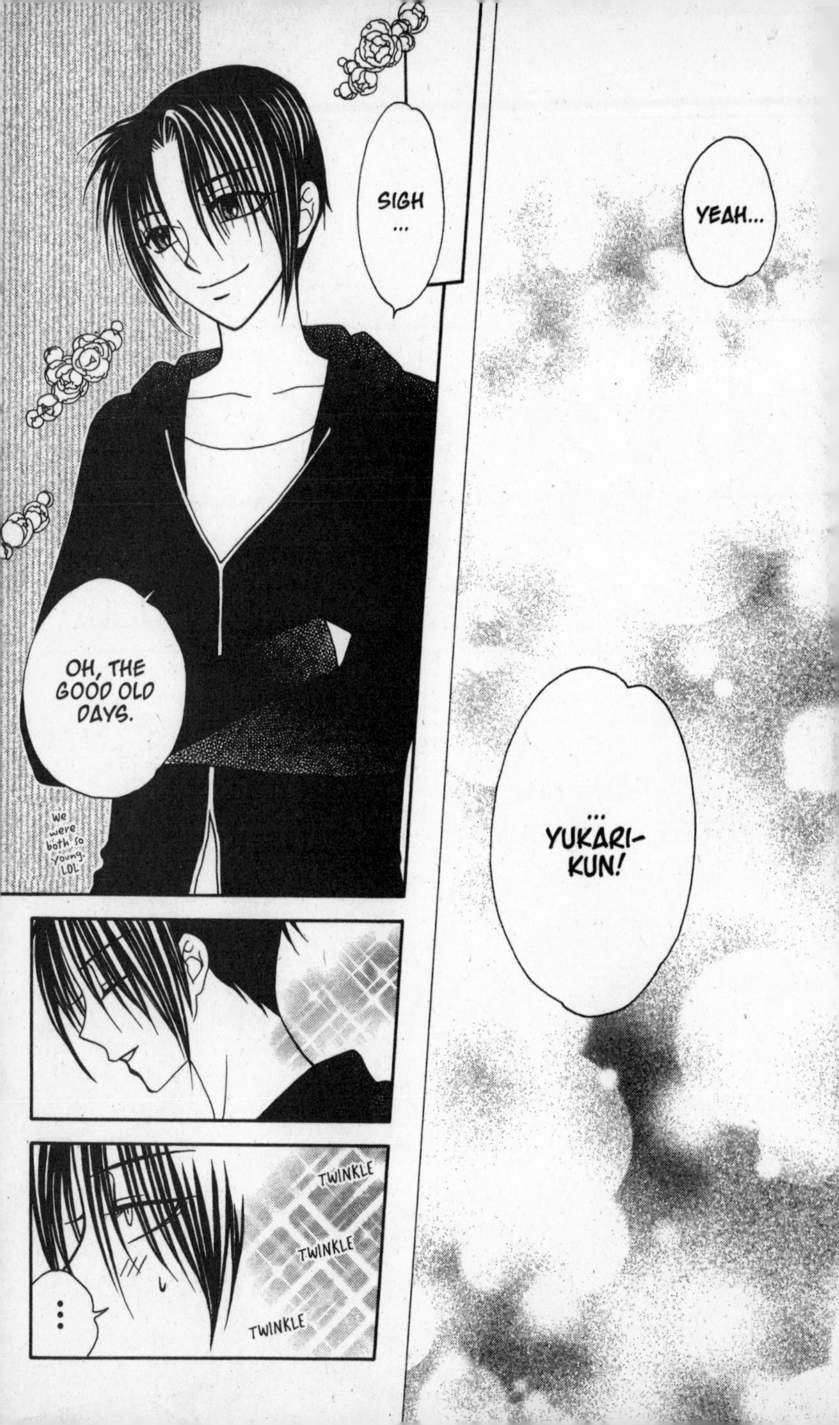
YEAH...
... YUKARI-KUN!
SIGH ...
OH, THE GOOD OLD DAYS.
We were both so young. LOL
TWINKLE
TWINKLE
TWINKLE
...

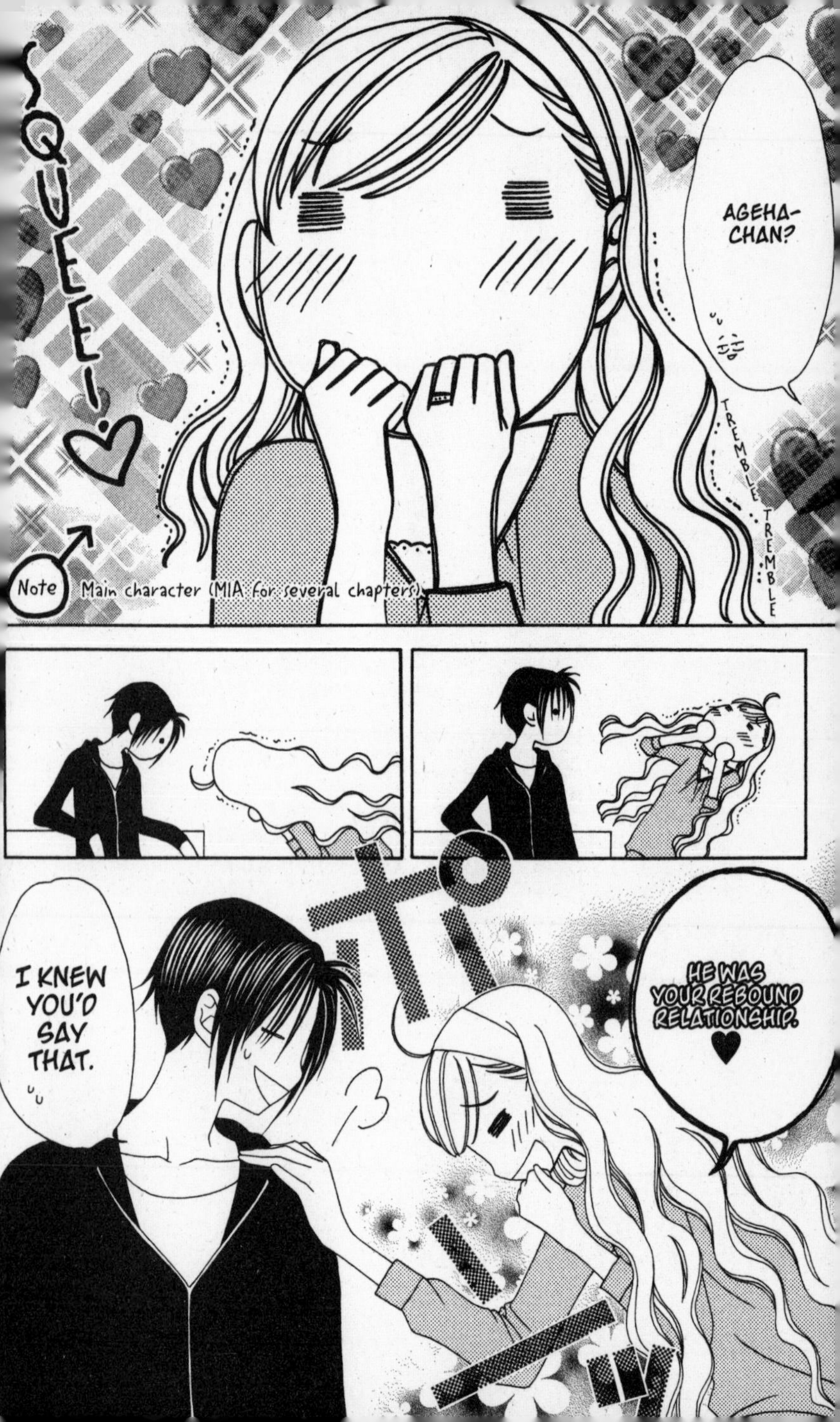
AGEHA-CHAN?
~SQUEEE~♥
TREMBLE TREMBLE
Note Main character (MIA for several chapters)
HE WAS YOUR REBOUND RELATIONSHIP. ♥
I KNEW YOU'D SAY THAT.

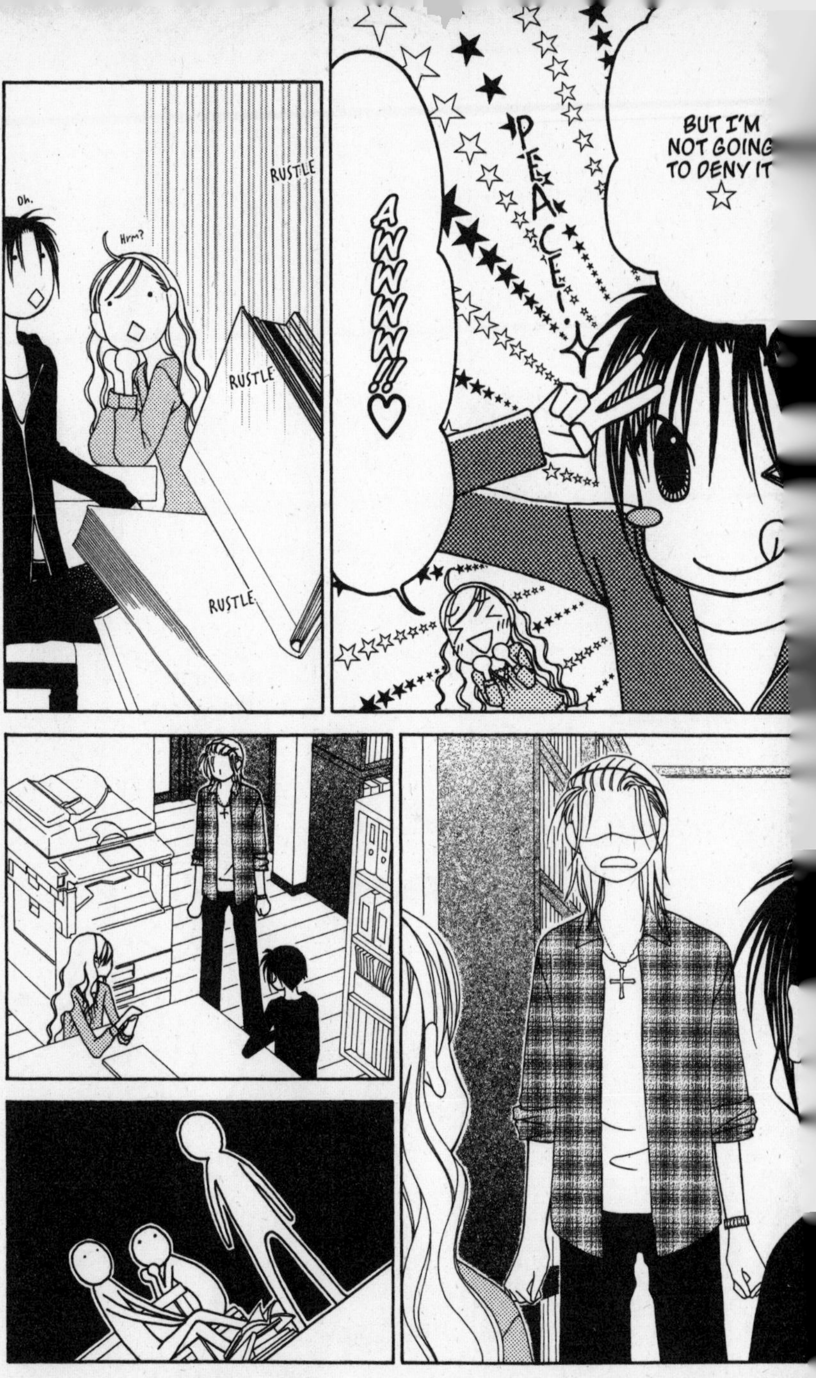
BUT I'M NOT GOING TO DENY IT ☆
PEACE!
AWWWWW!! ♥
RUSTLE
Hrm?
Oh.
RUSTLE
RUSTLE

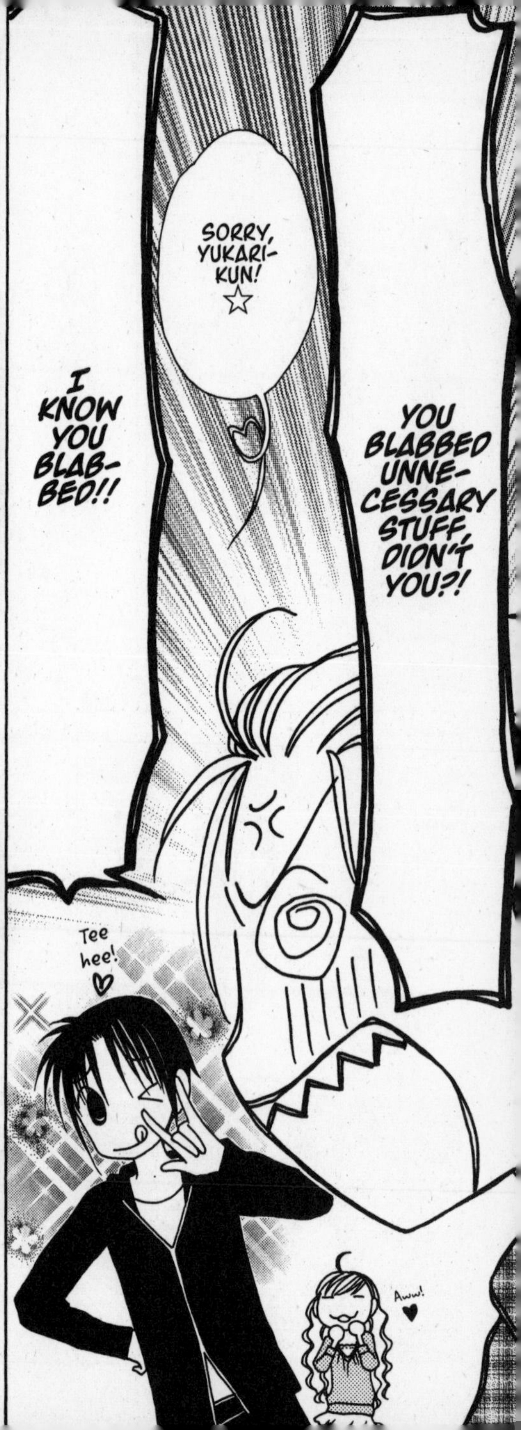
YOU BLABBED UNNE-CESSARY STUFF, DIDN'T YOU?!
SORRY, YUKARI-KUN! ☆
I KNOW YOU BLAB-BED!!
Tee hee! ♥
Aww! ♥

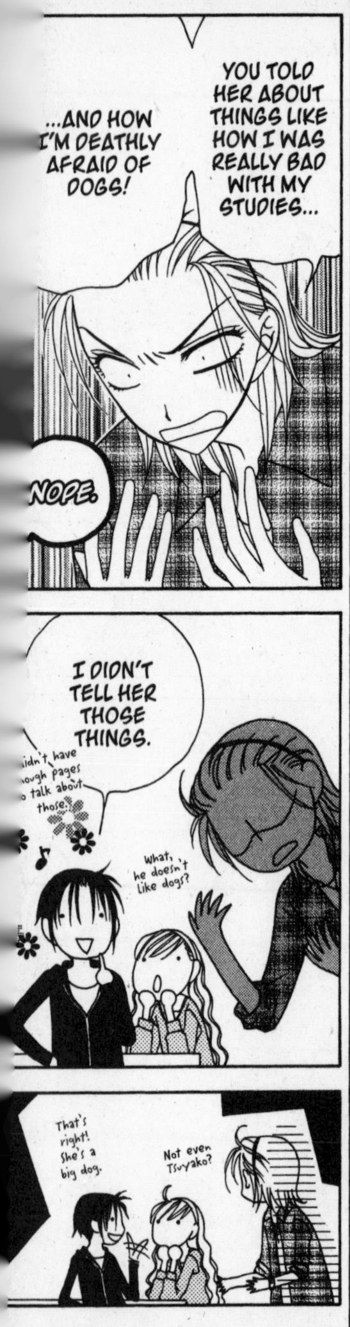
YOU TOLD HER ABOUT THINGS LIKE HOW I WAS REALLY BAD WITH MY STUDIES...
...AND HOW I'M DEATHLY AFRAID OF DOGS!
NOPE.
I DIDN'T TELL HER THOSE THINGS.
idn't have ough pages o talk about those.
What, he doesn't like dogs?
Not even Tsuyako?
That's right! She's a big dog.

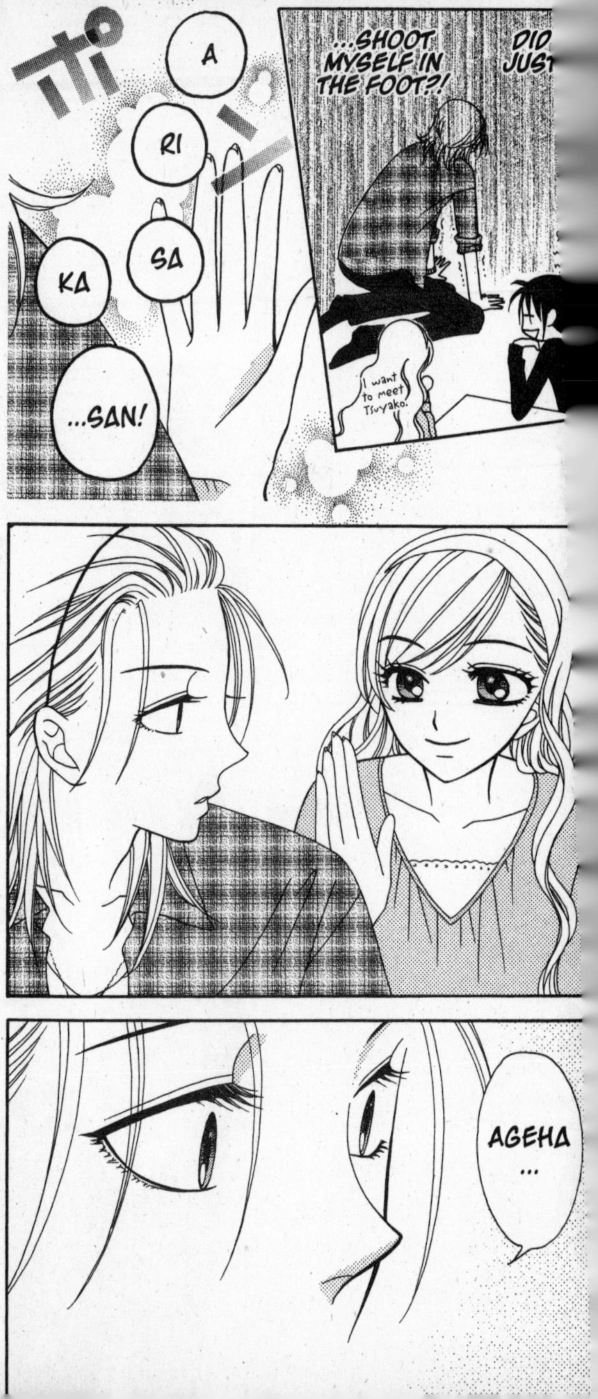
DID JUST
...SHOOT MYSELF IN THE FOOT?!
I want to meet Tsuyako.
A
RI
SA
KA
...SAN!
AGEHA ...

Fortunately, I'd been planning to take a mini vacation, so I already had a buffer from deadlines. All I did in November was sleep... because it hurt too much to look down and stuff.

After that was really crazy!!! I had to finish 90 pages for the first, second, and third issues of Hana to Yume magazine! Not to mention that the first issue was for the new year, so the deadline was way earlier than usual!!! Plus I'd been assigned the color cover of the magazine for the third issue, so 4 days were eaten up with that! Oh my gosh!! I had barely any time to finish the second and third issues! I only had 13 days to finish 30 pages. It was miserable. I usually take 4 days for the rough pencils and then the assistants take 5 days to ink, meaning the manuscript takes 9 days. But the storyboards take forever! This time, a miracle happened--it took me less than three days to finish! (Sometimes that happens).

So, I was able to maintain the quality of my work even with the pain in my neck and back. I worked really hard, even though I had to visit the hospital every day. None of this would have been possible without my assistants, Maeda-san and Hitomi-san, as well as my mom and my brother. I'm weeping tears of gratitude! Thank you so much!!!! And of course, I'm so thankful to all of you readers as well!

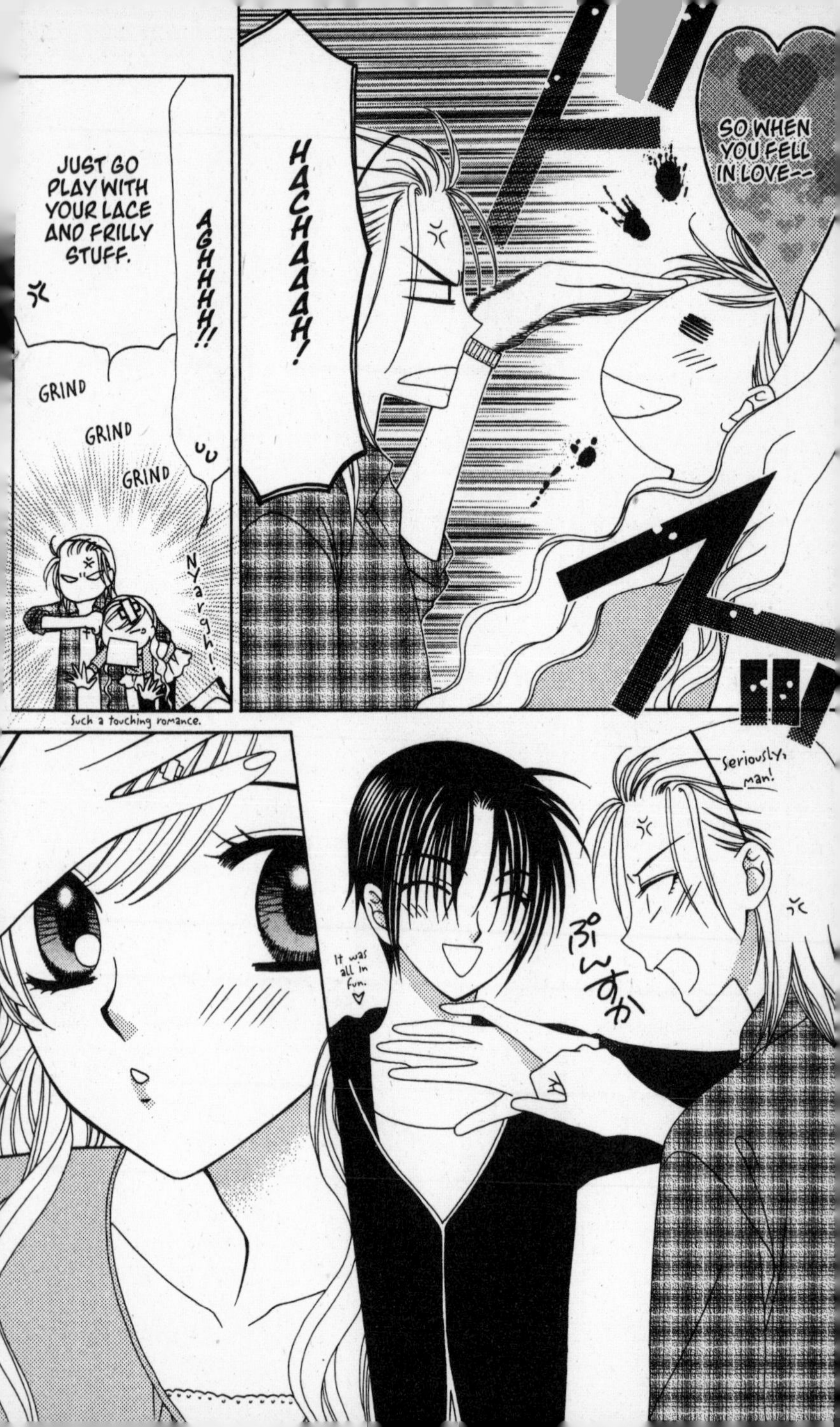

SO WHEN YOU FELL IN LOVE--
HACHAAAAH!
AGHHHH!!
uu
JUST GO PLAY WITH YOUR LACE AND FRILLY STUFF.
GRIND
GRIND
GRIND
Nyargh!..
Such a touching romance.
Seriously, man!
ぷんすか
It was all in fun.

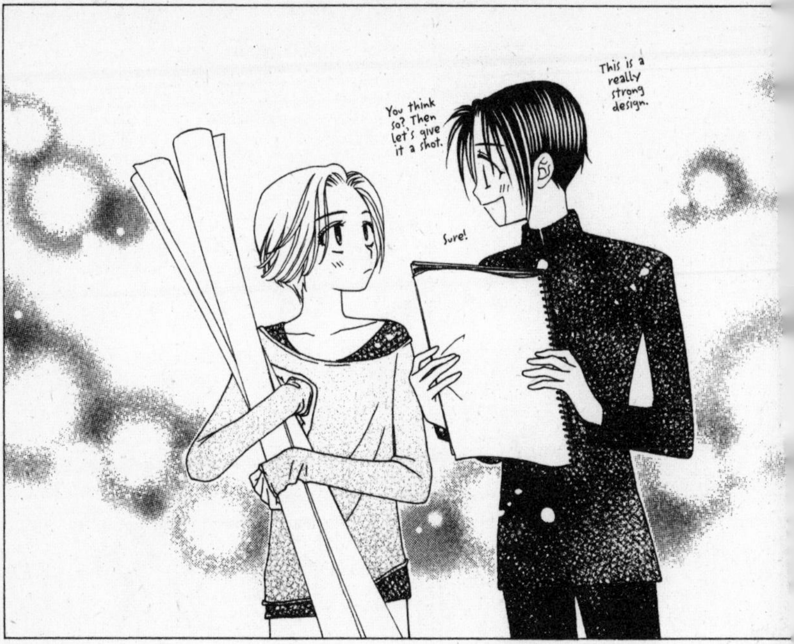
This is a really strong design.
You think so? Then let's give it a shot.
Sure!

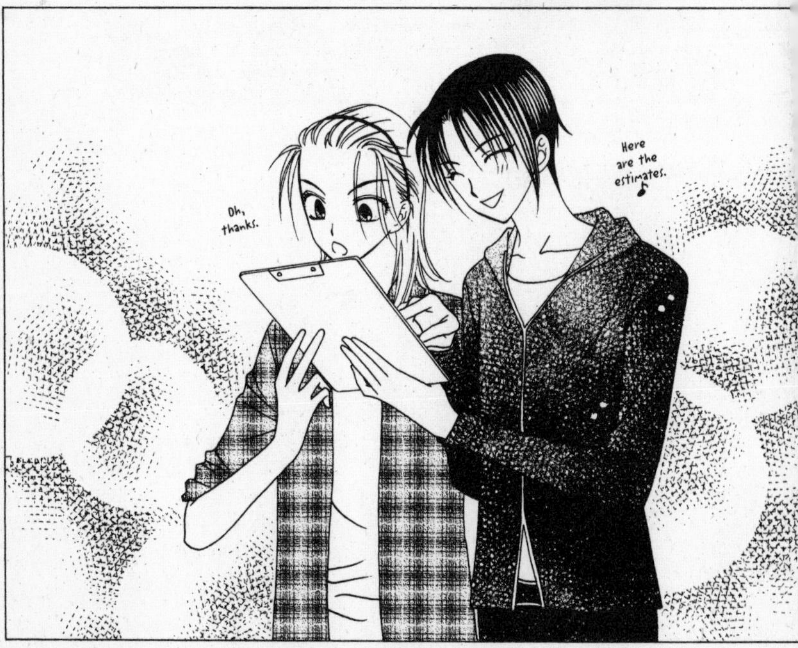
Here are the estimates.
Oh, thanks.

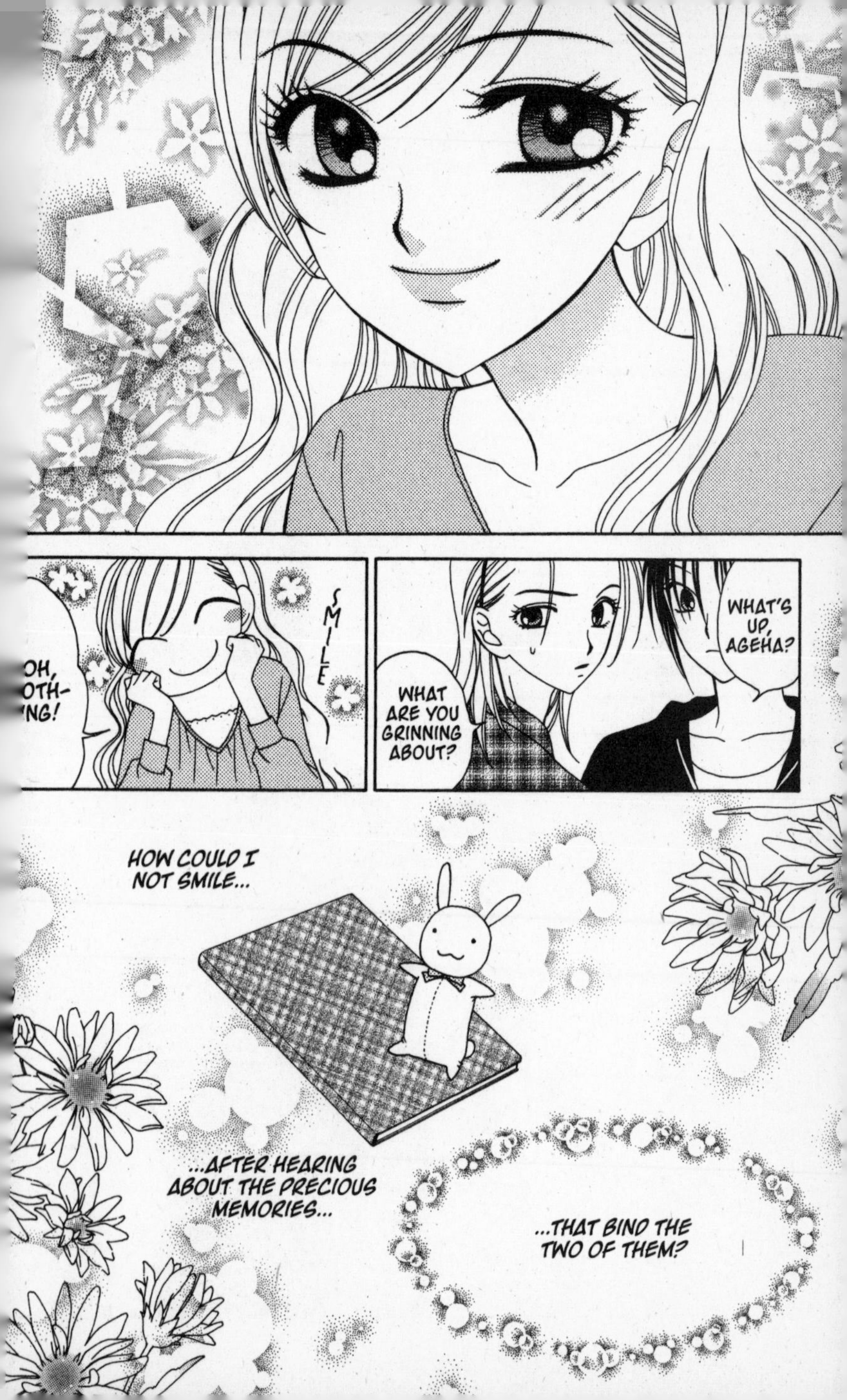
WHAT'S UP, AGEHA?
WHAT ARE YOU GRINNING ABOUT?
SMILE
OH, OTH-NG!
HOW COULD I NOT SMILE...
...AFTER HEARING ABOUT THE PRECIOUS MEMORIES...
...THAT BIND THE TWO OF THEM?

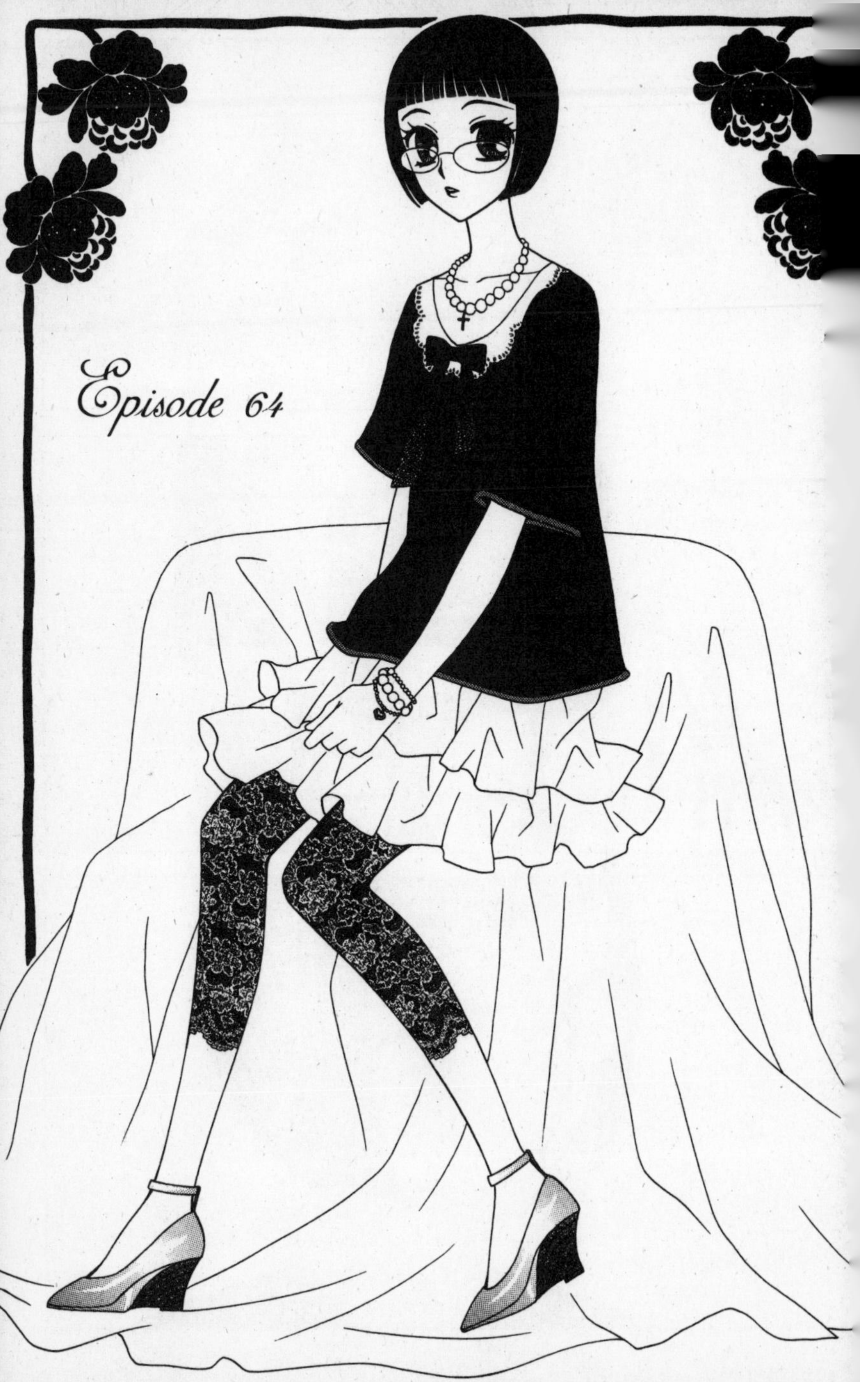
Episode 64

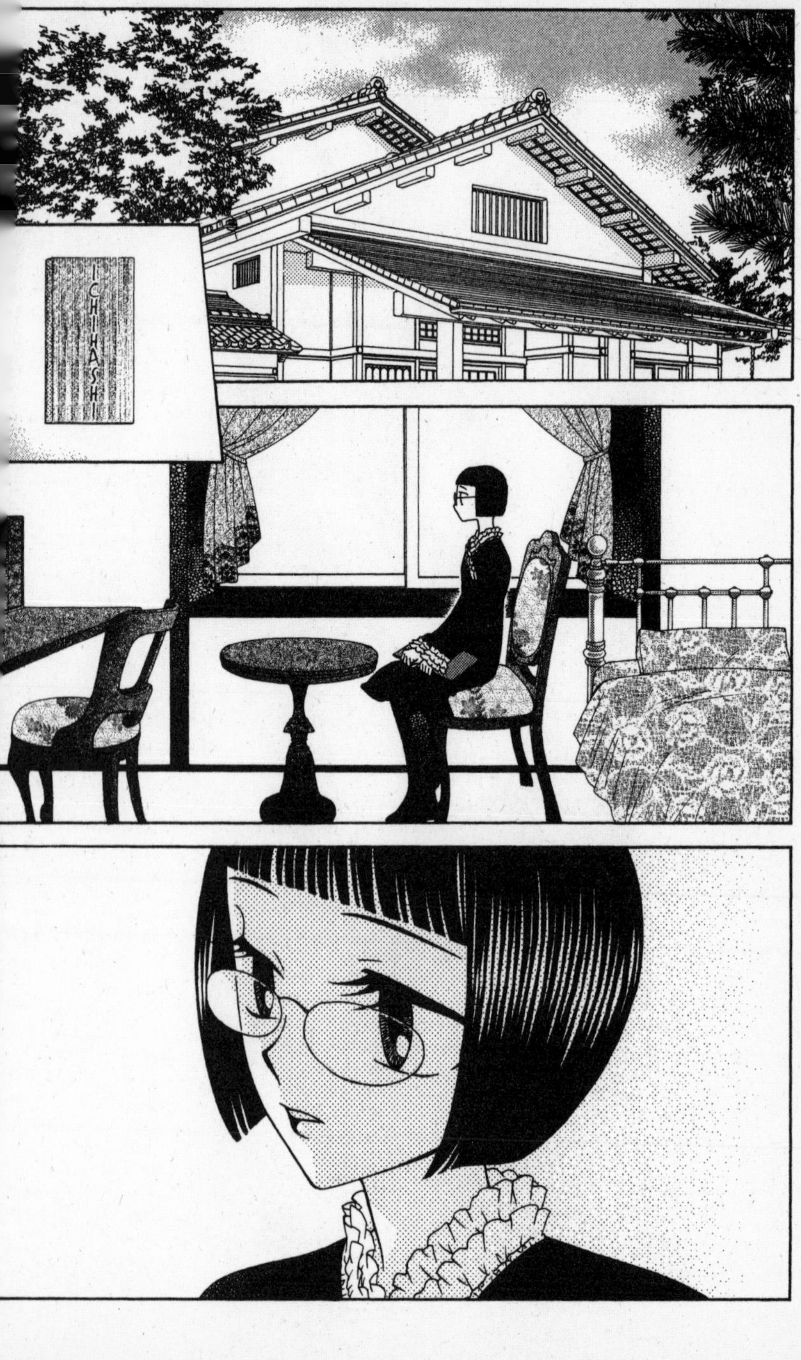
ICHIHASHI

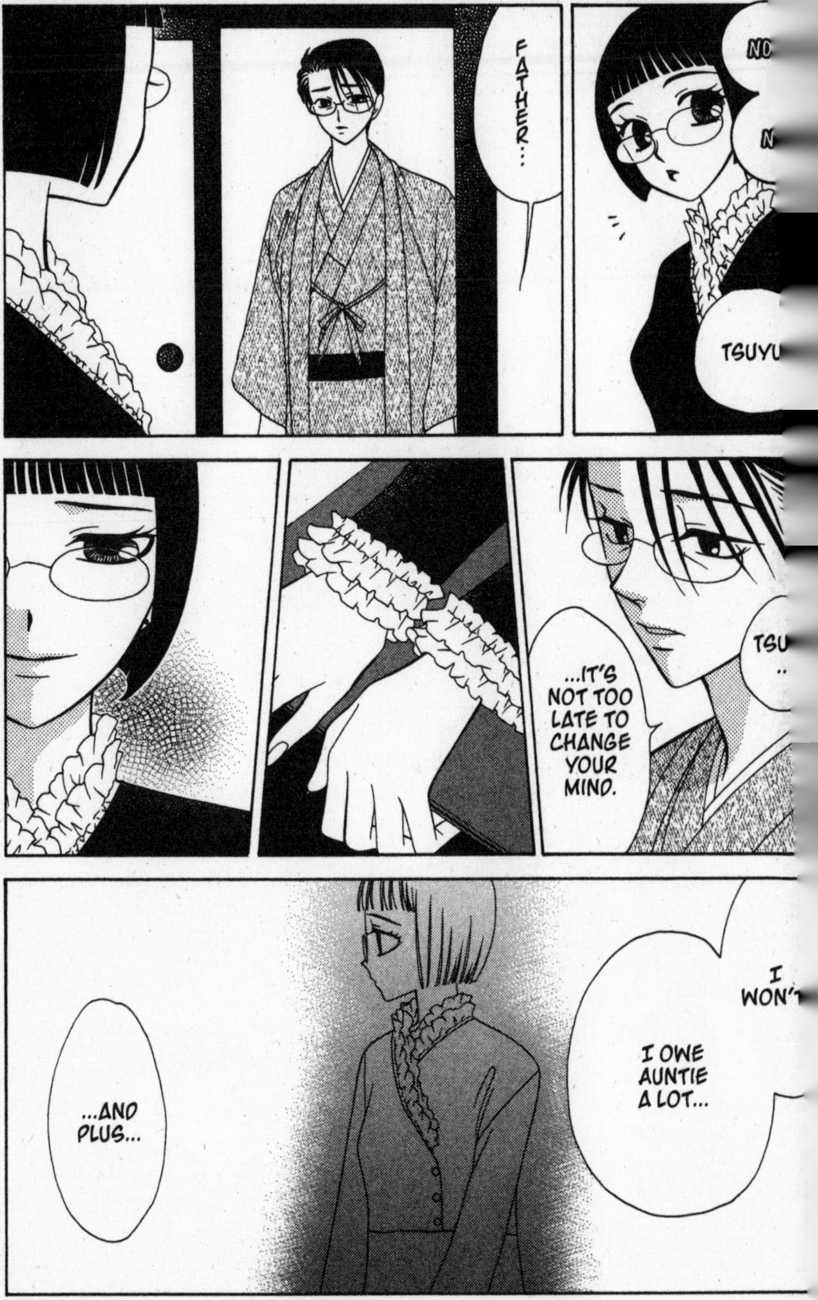
NO
TSUYU
FATHER...
TSU
...IT'S NOT TOO LATE TO CHANGE YOUR MIND.
I WON'
I OWE AUNTIE A LOT...
...AND PLUS...

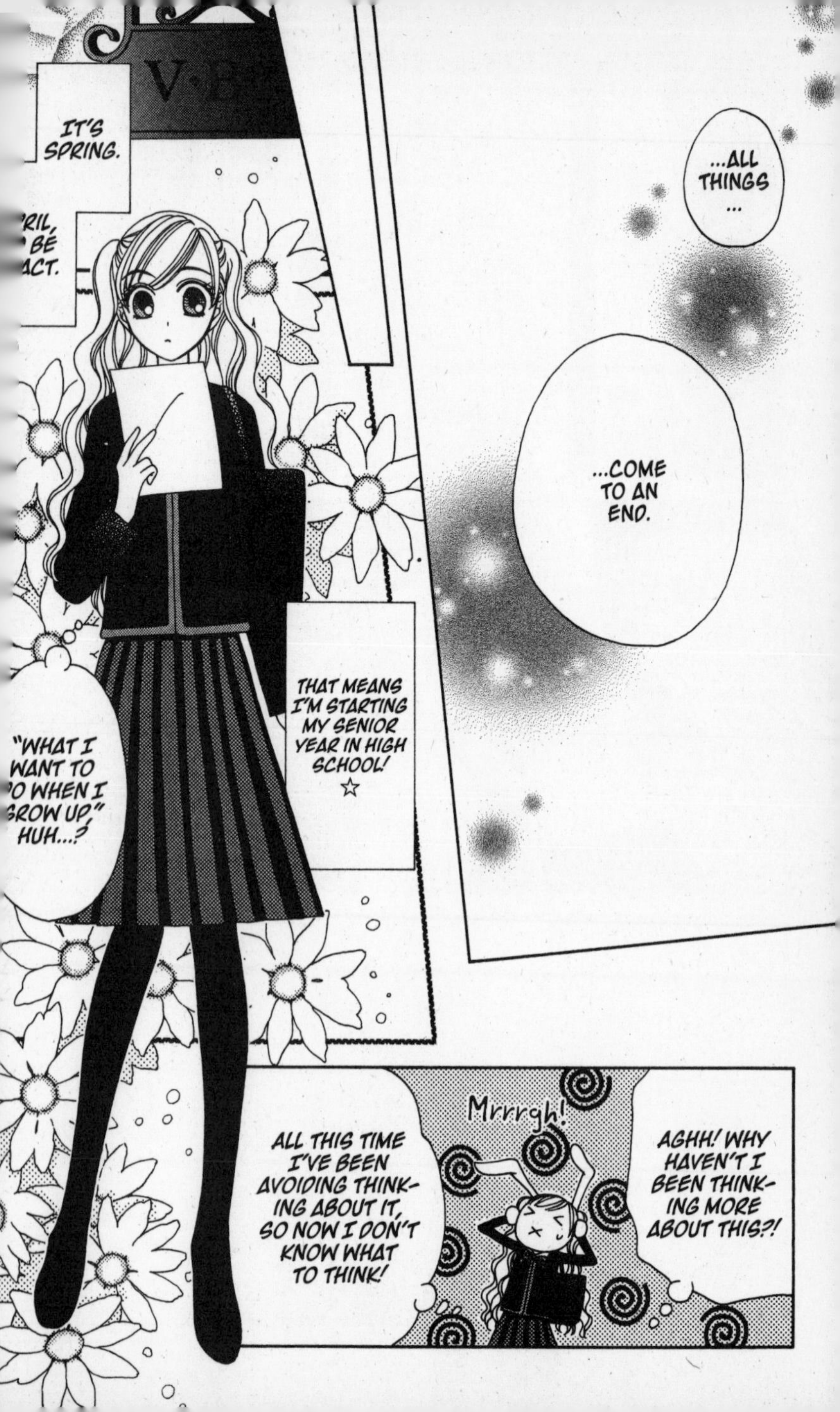
...ALL THINGS ...
...COME TO AN END.
IT'S SPRING.
RIL, BE ACT.
THAT MEANS I'M STARTING MY SENIOR YEAR IN HIGH SCHOOL! ☆
"WHAT I WANT TO O WHEN I ROW UP," HUH...?
AGHH! WHY HAVEN'T I BEEN THINKING MORE ABOUT THIS?!
Mrrrgh!
ALL THIS TIME I'VE BEEN AVOIDING THINKING ABOUT IT, SO NOW I DON'T KNOW WHAT TO THINK!

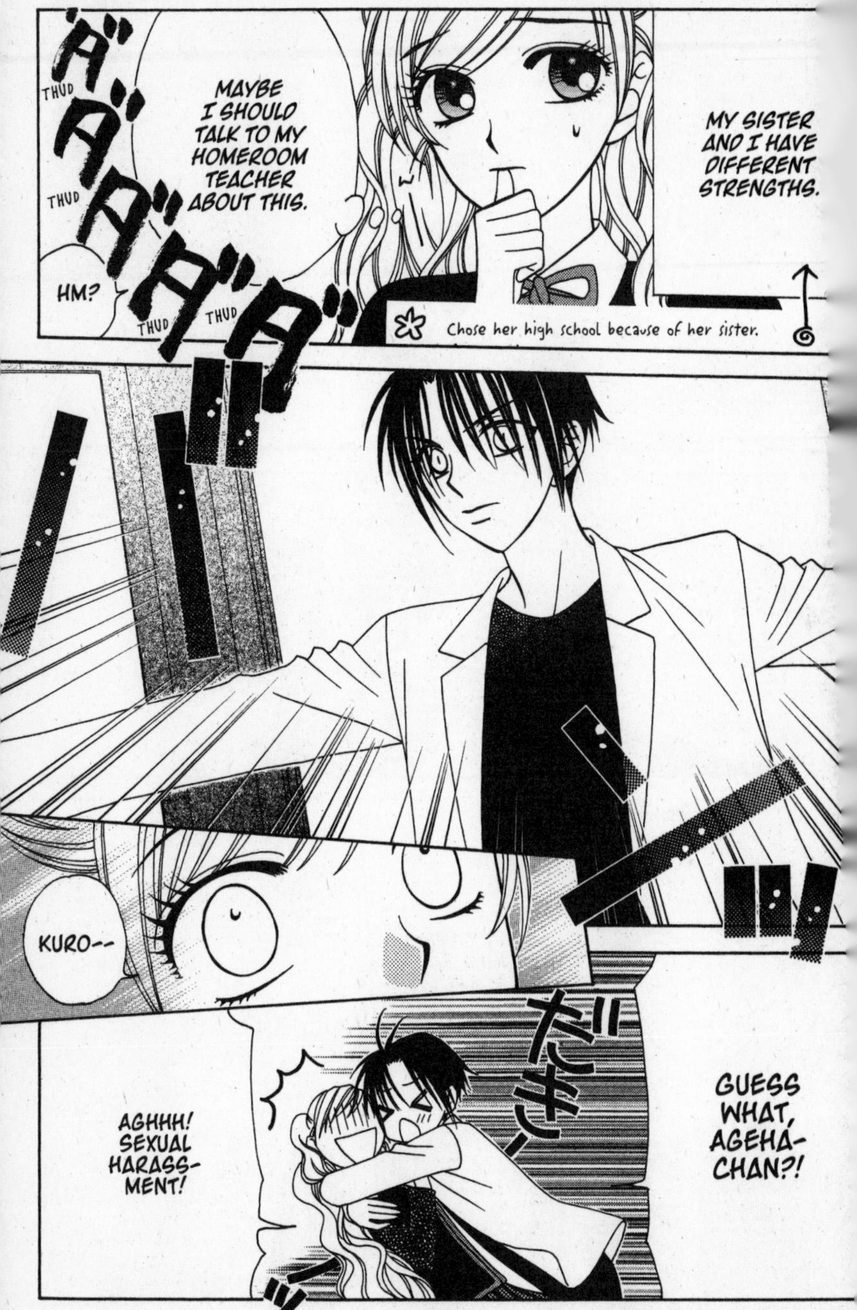
MY SISTER AND I HAVE DIFFERENT STRENGTHS.
Chose her high school because of her sister.
MAYBE I SHOULD TALK TO MY HOMEROOM TEACHER ABOUT THIS.
THUD
THUD
THUD
THUD
HM?
KURO--
GUESS WHAT, AGEHA-CHAN?!
AGHHH! SEXUAL HARASS-MENT!

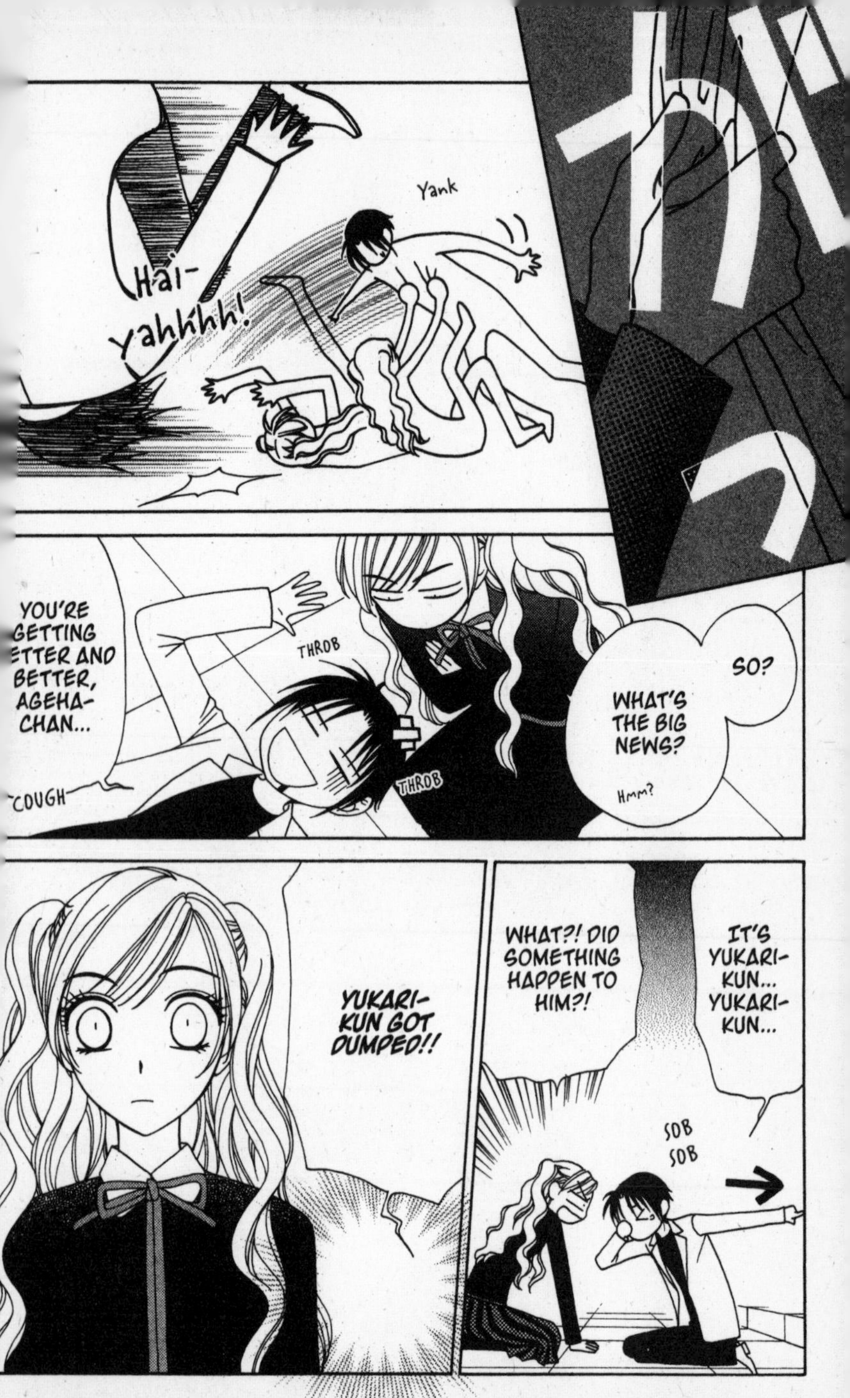
Yank
Hai-yahhhh!
SO? WHAT'S THE BIG NEWS?
Hmm?
THROB
THROB
YOU'RE GETTING ETTER AND BETTER, AGEHA-CHAN...
COUGH
IT'S YUKARI-KUN... YUKARI-KUN...
WHAT?! DID SOMETHING HAPPEN TO HIM?!
SOB SOB
YUKARI-KUN GOT DUMPED!!

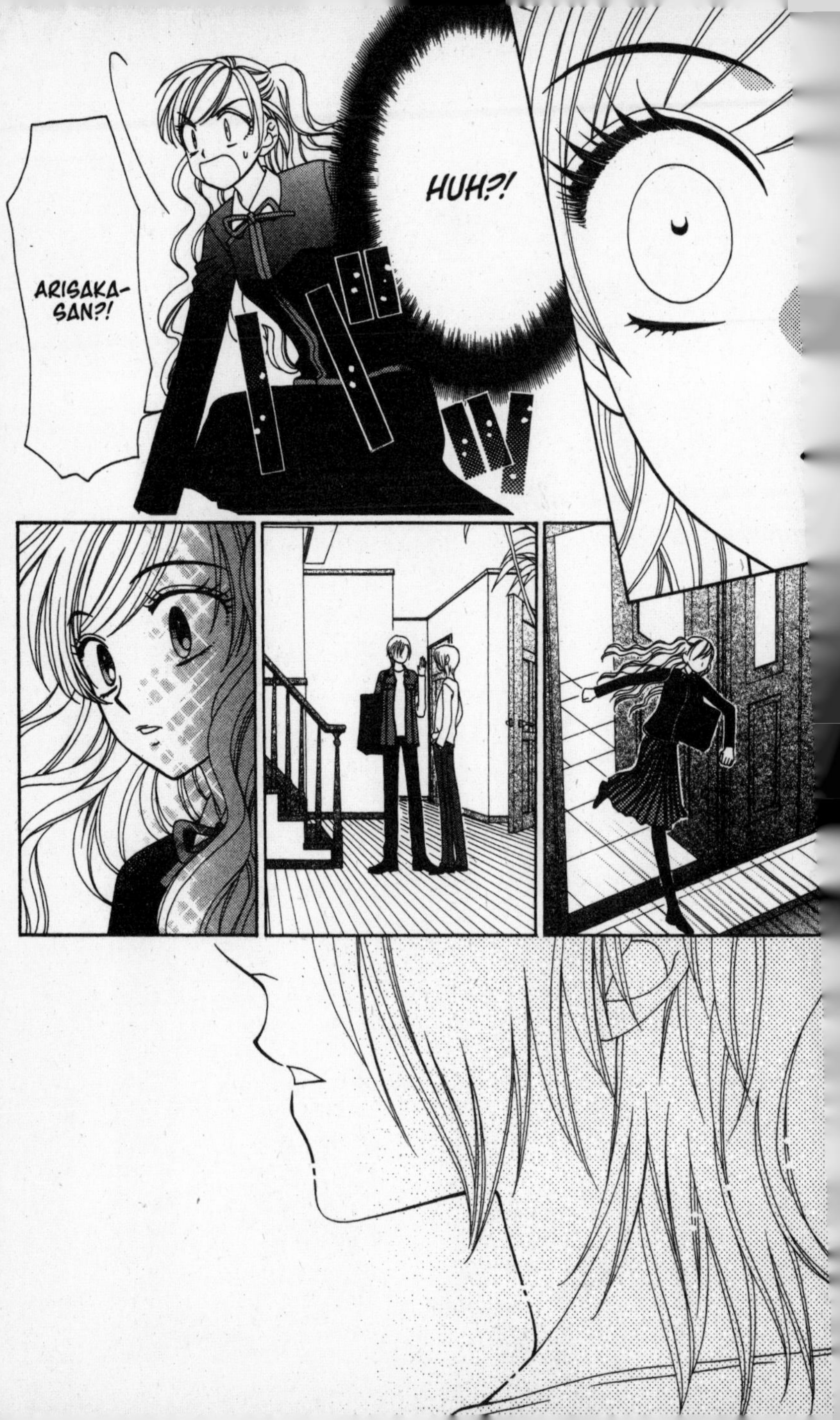
HUH?!
ARISAKA-SAN?!

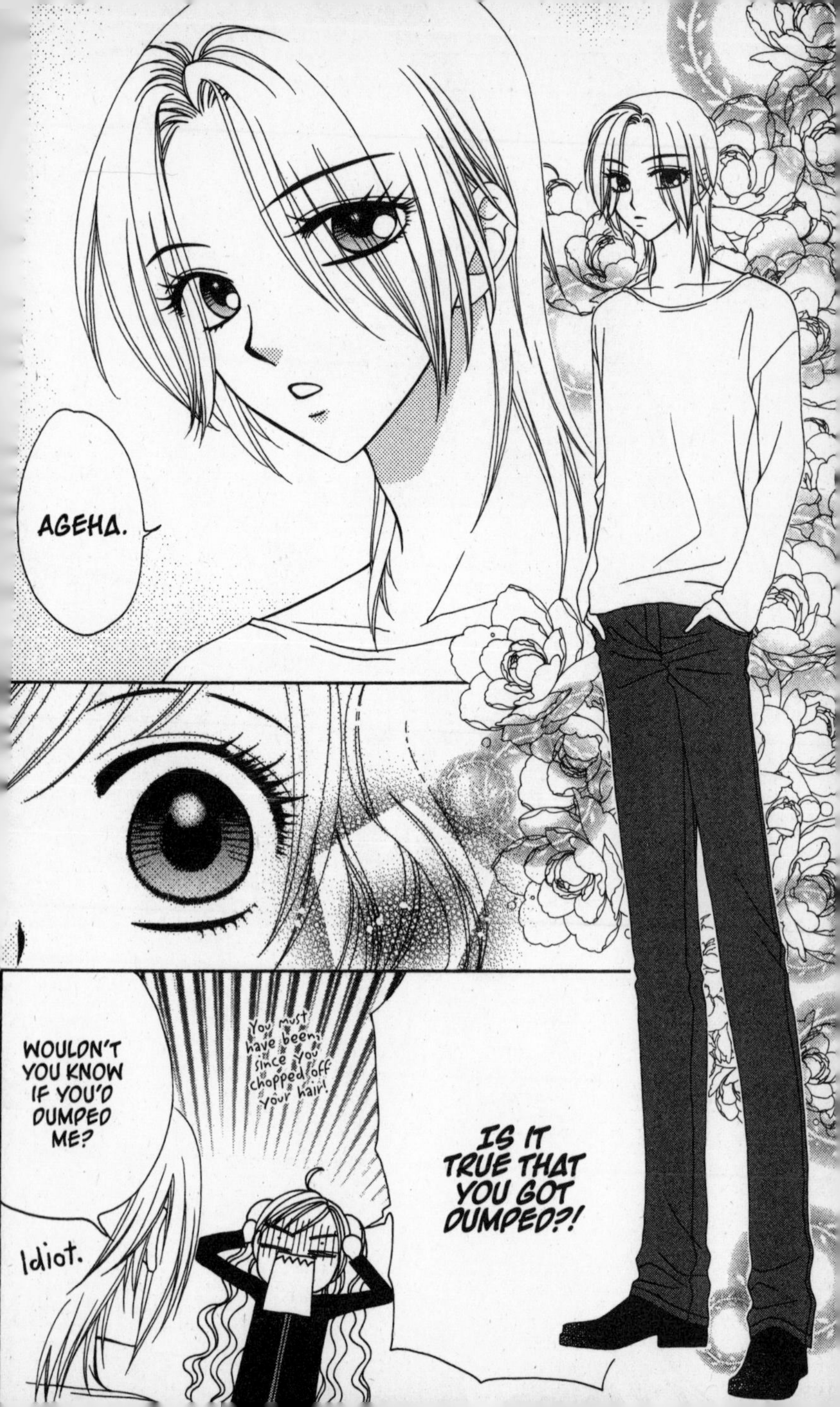
AGEHA.
IS IT TRUE THAT YOU GOT DUMPED?!
You must have been, since you chopped off your hair!
WOULDN'T YOU KNOW IF YOU'D DUMPED ME?
Idiot.

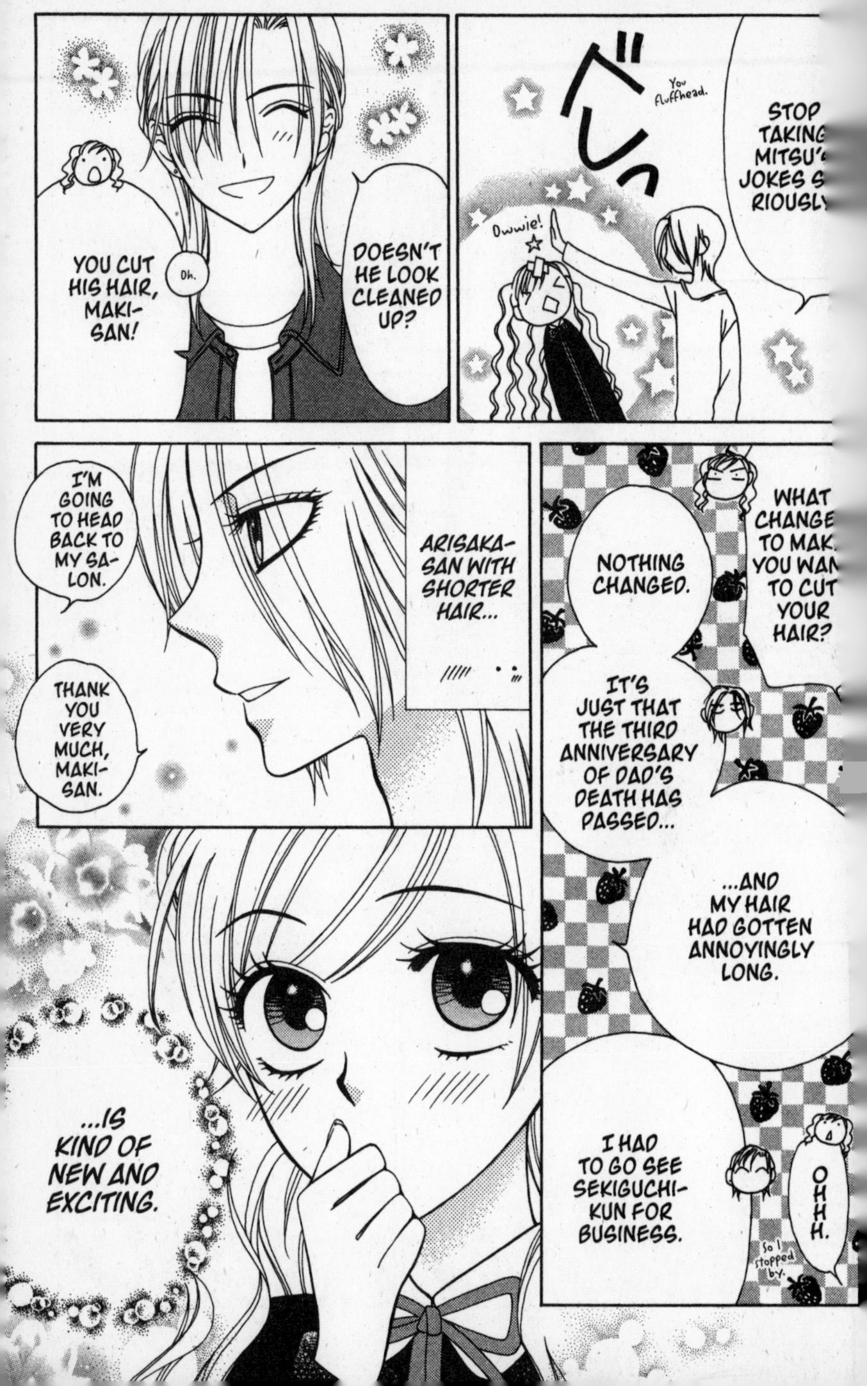
STOP TAKING MITSU' JOKES S RIOUSLY
You fluffhead.
Owwie!
DOESN'T HE LOOK CLEANED UP?
Oh.
YOU CUT HIS HAIR, MAKI-SAN!
WHAT CHANGE TO MAK YOU WAN TO CUT YOUR HAIR?
NOTHING CHANGED.
IT'S JUST THAT THE THIRD ANNIVERSARY OF DAD'S DEATH HAS PASSED...
...AND MY HAIR HAD GOTTEN ANNOYINGLY LONG.
OHHH.
I HAD TO GO SEE SEKIGUCHI-KUN FOR BUSINESS.
So I stopped by.
ARISAKA-SAN WITH SHORTER HAIR...
I'M GOING TO HEAD BACK TO MY SA-LON.
THANK YOU VERY MUCH, MAKI-SAN.
...IS KIND OF NEW AND EXCITING.

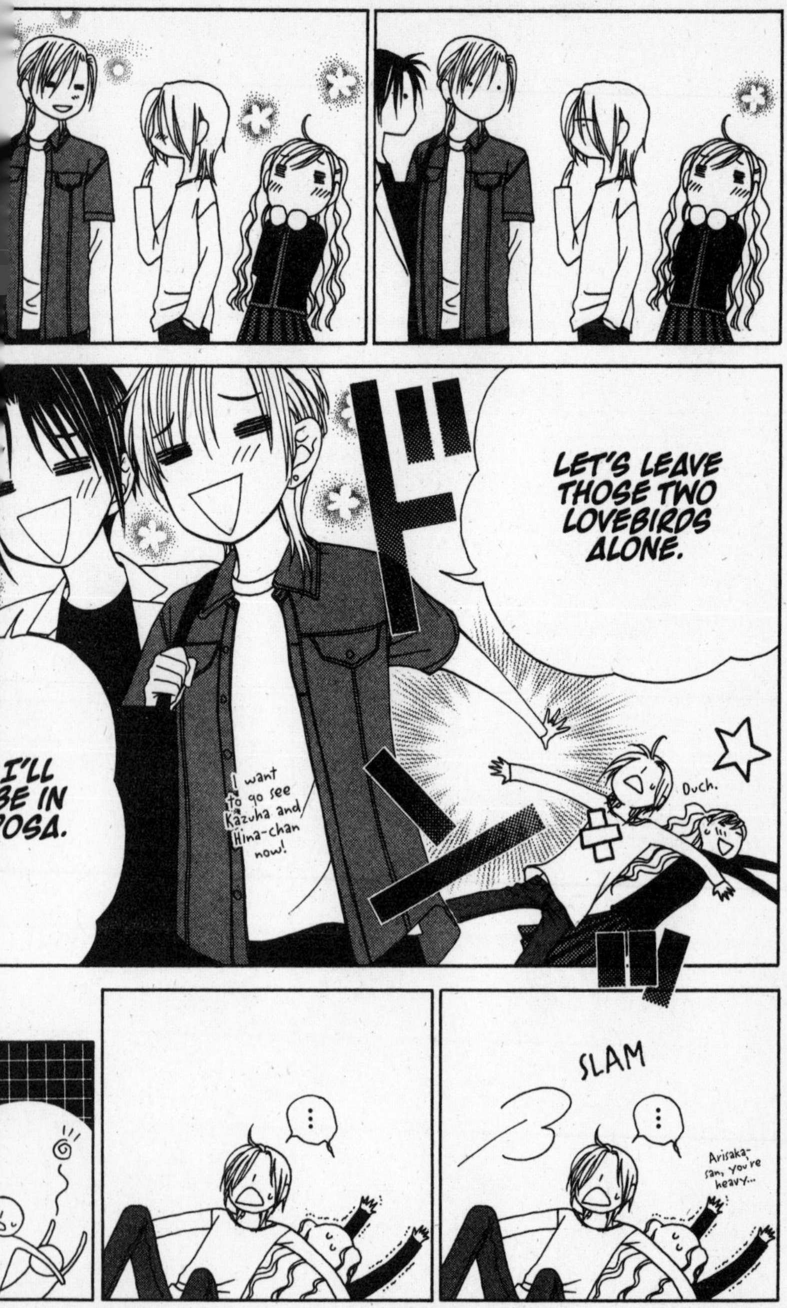
LET'S LEAVE THOSE TWO LOVEBIRDS ALONE.
Ouch.
I want to go see Kazuha and Hina-chan now!
I'LL BE IN ROSA.
SLAM
...
Arisaka-san, you're heavy...
...

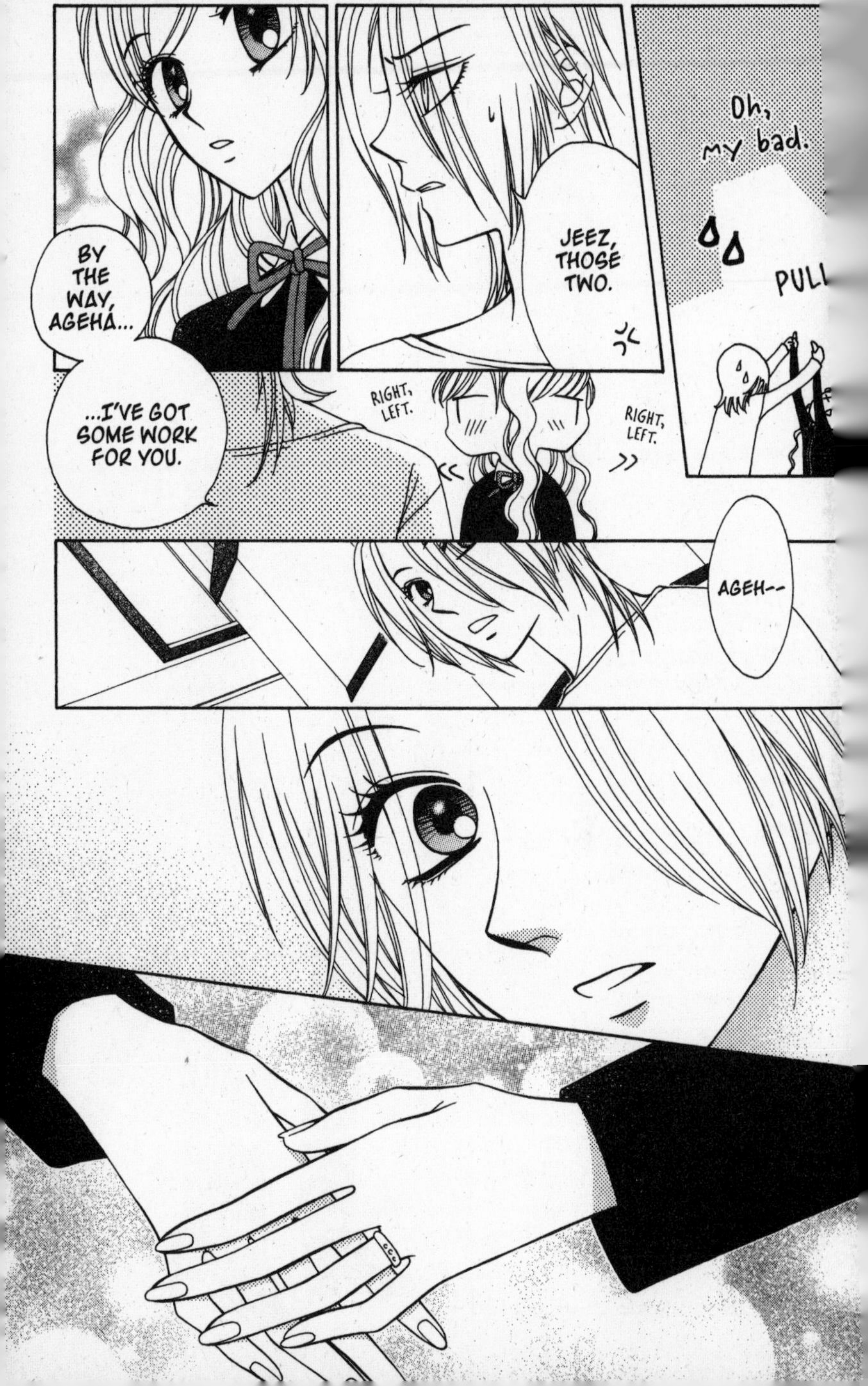
Oh, my bad.
PUL
JEEZ, THOSE TWO.
BY THE WAY, AGEHA...
RIGHT, LEFT.
RIGHT, LEFT.
...I'VE GOT SOME WORK FOR YOU.
AGEH--

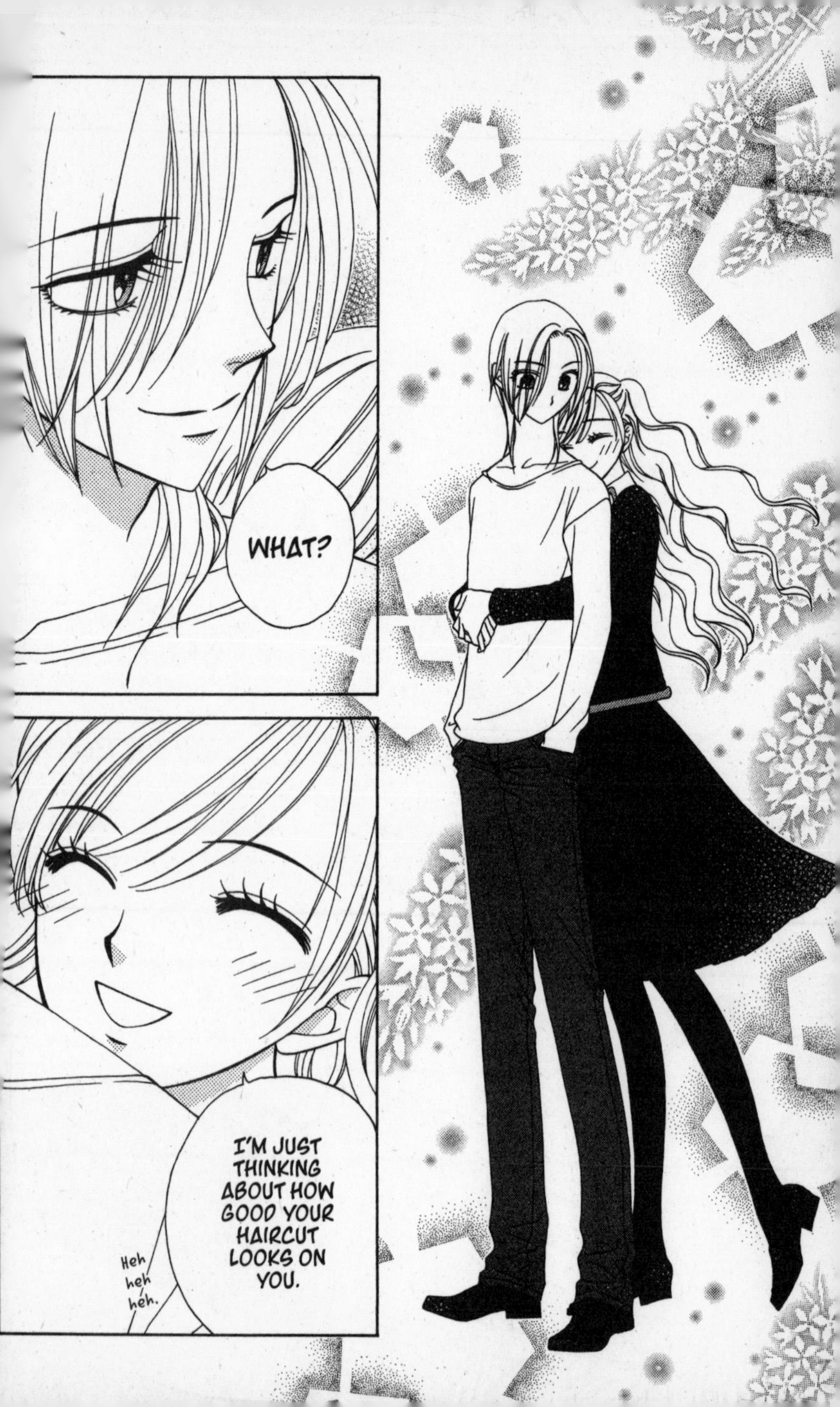
WHAT?
I'M JUST THINKING ABOUT HOW GOOD YOUR HAIRCUT LOOKS ON YOU.
Heh heh heh.

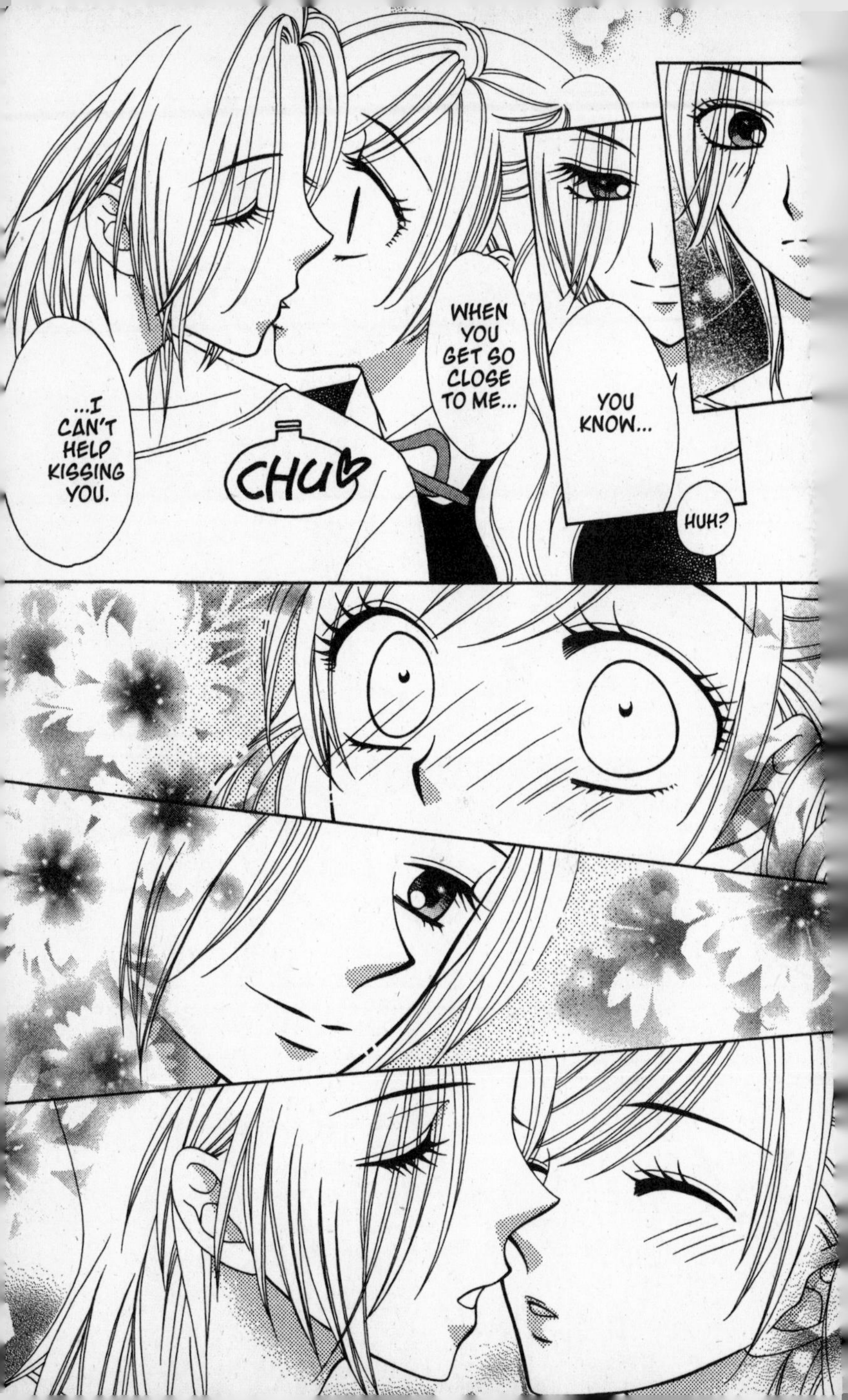
HUH?
YOU KNOW...
WHEN YOU GET SO CLOSE TO ME...
...I CAN'T HELP KISSING YOU.
CHU

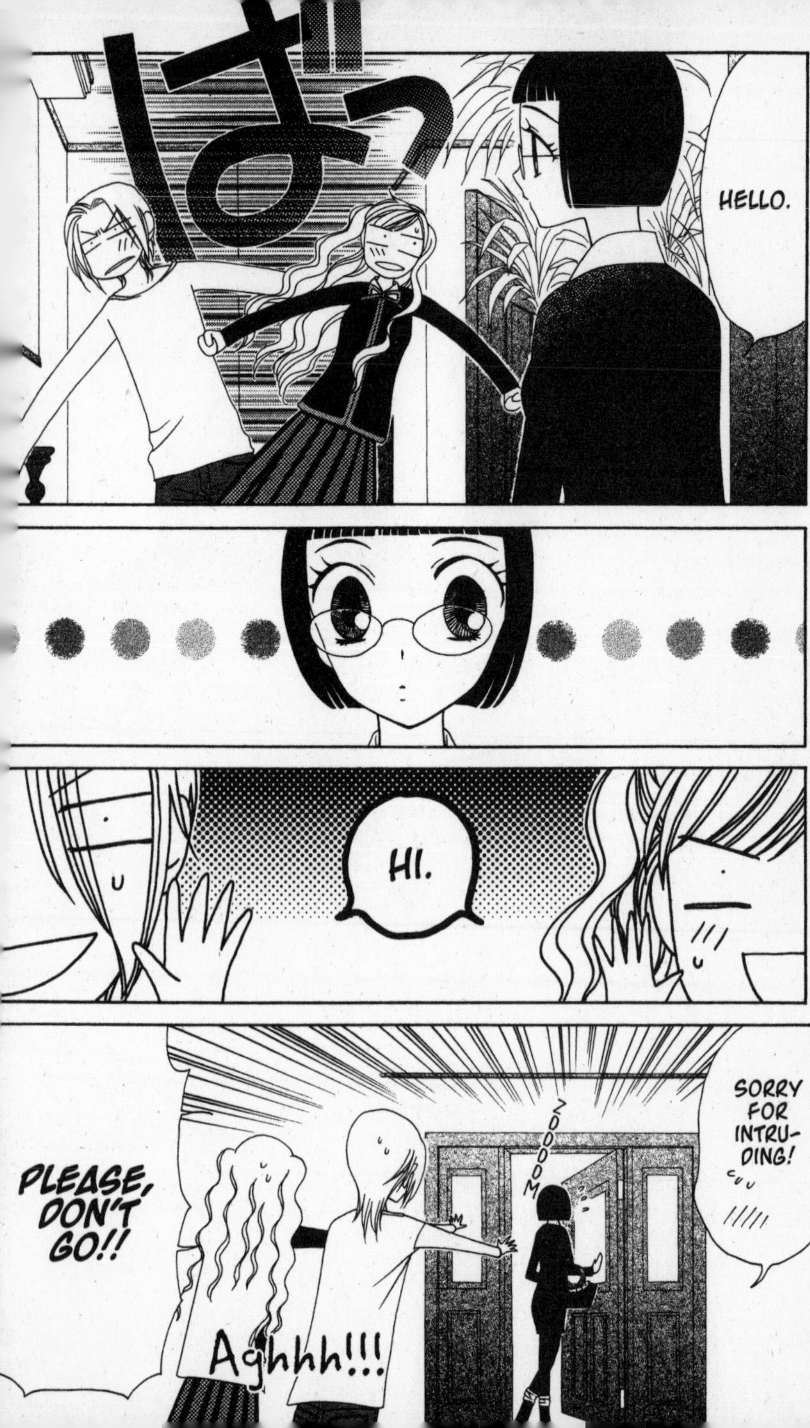
HELLO.
ばっ
HI.
SORRY FOR INTRU-DING!
ZOOOOOM
PLEASE, DON'T GO!!
Aghhh!!!

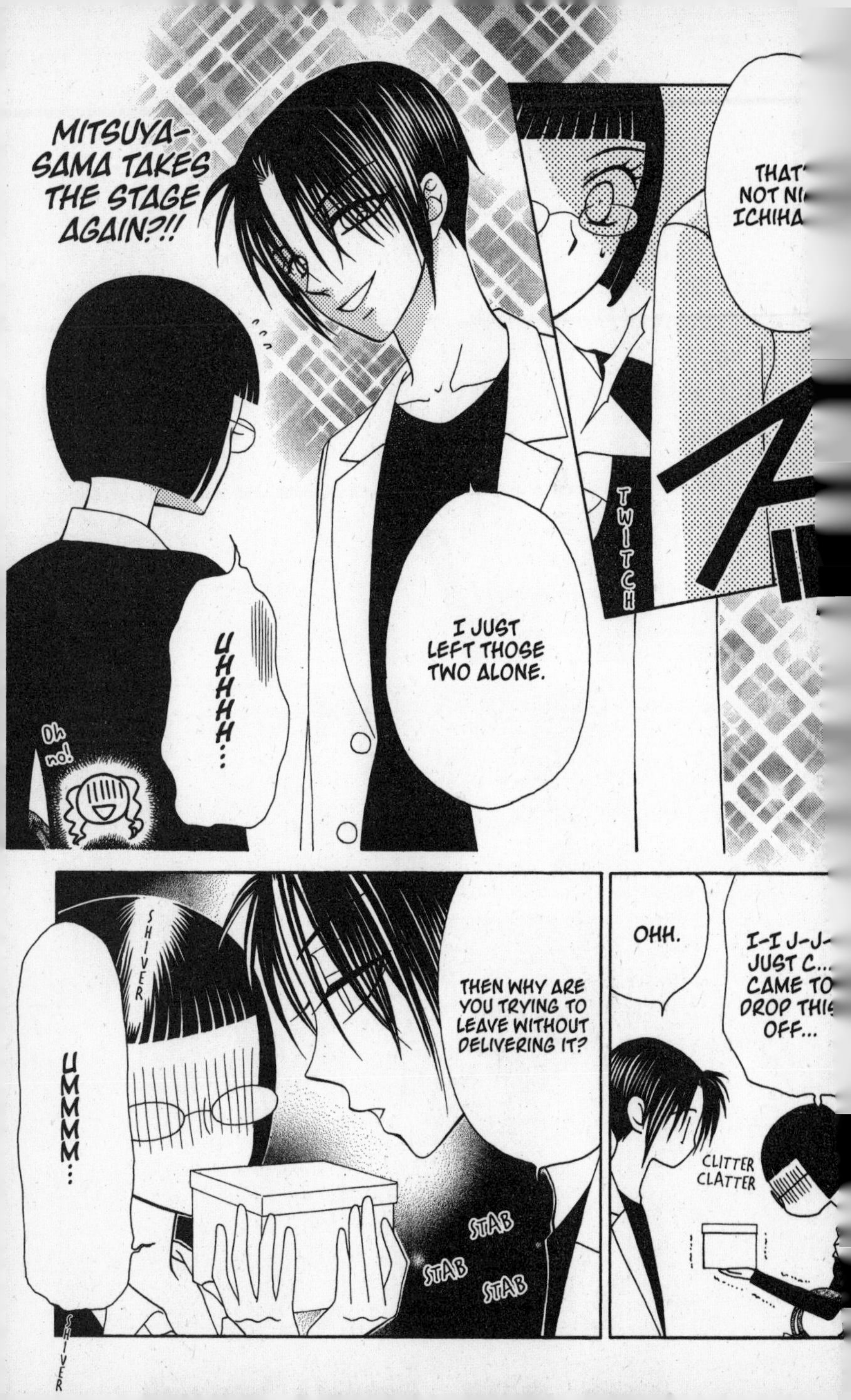
THAT' NOT NI ICHIHA
TWITCH
MITSUYA-SAMA TAKES THE STAGE AGAIN?!!
I JUST LEFT THOSE TWO ALONE.
UHHHH...
Oh no!
I-I J-J- JUST C... CAME TO DROP THI OFF...
OHH.
CLITTER CLATTER
THEN WHY ARE YOU TRYING TO LEAVE WITHOUT DELIVERING IT?
STAB
STAB
STAB
SHIVER
UMMMM...
SHIVER

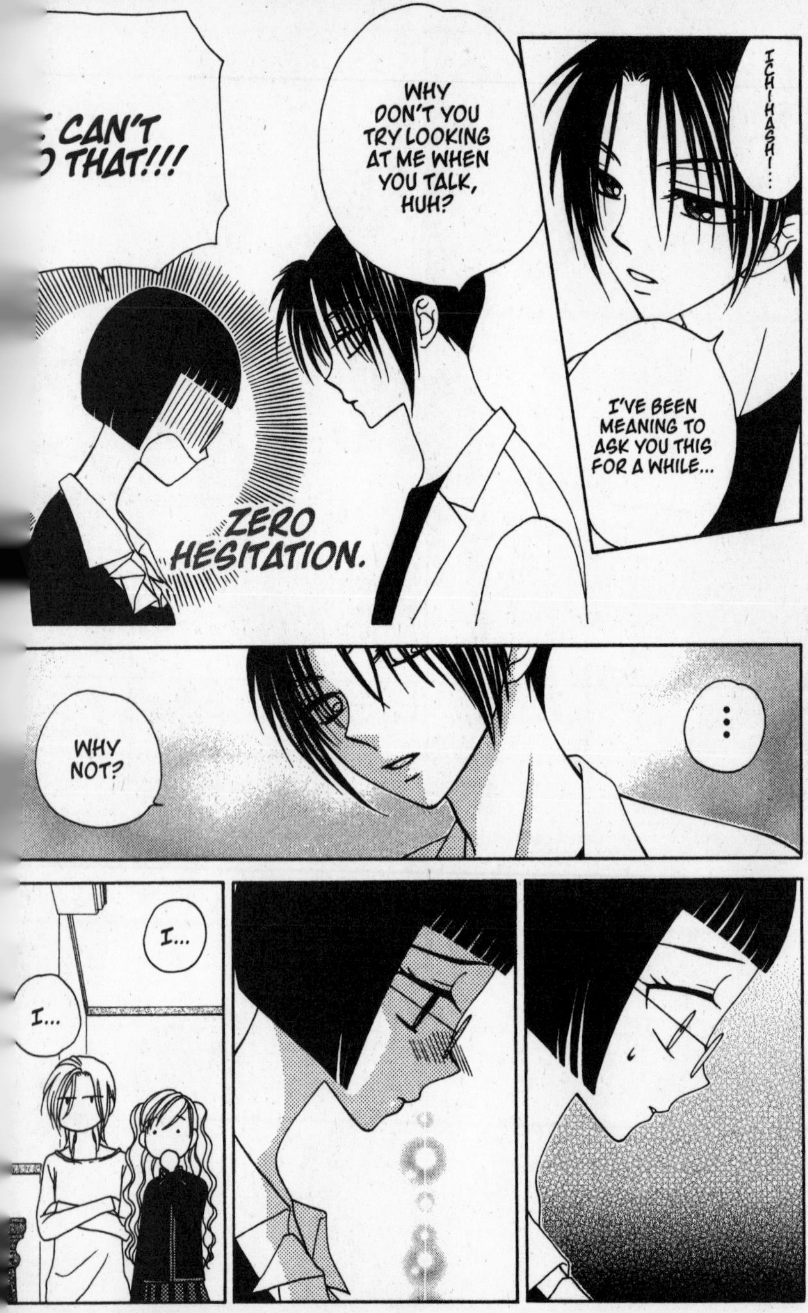
ICHIHASHI...
I'VE BEEN MEANING TO ASK YOU THIS FOR A WHILE...
WHY DON'T YOU TRY LOOKING AT ME WHEN YOU TALK, HUH?
E CAN'T
O THAT!!!
ZERO HESITATION.
...
WHY NOT?
I...
I...

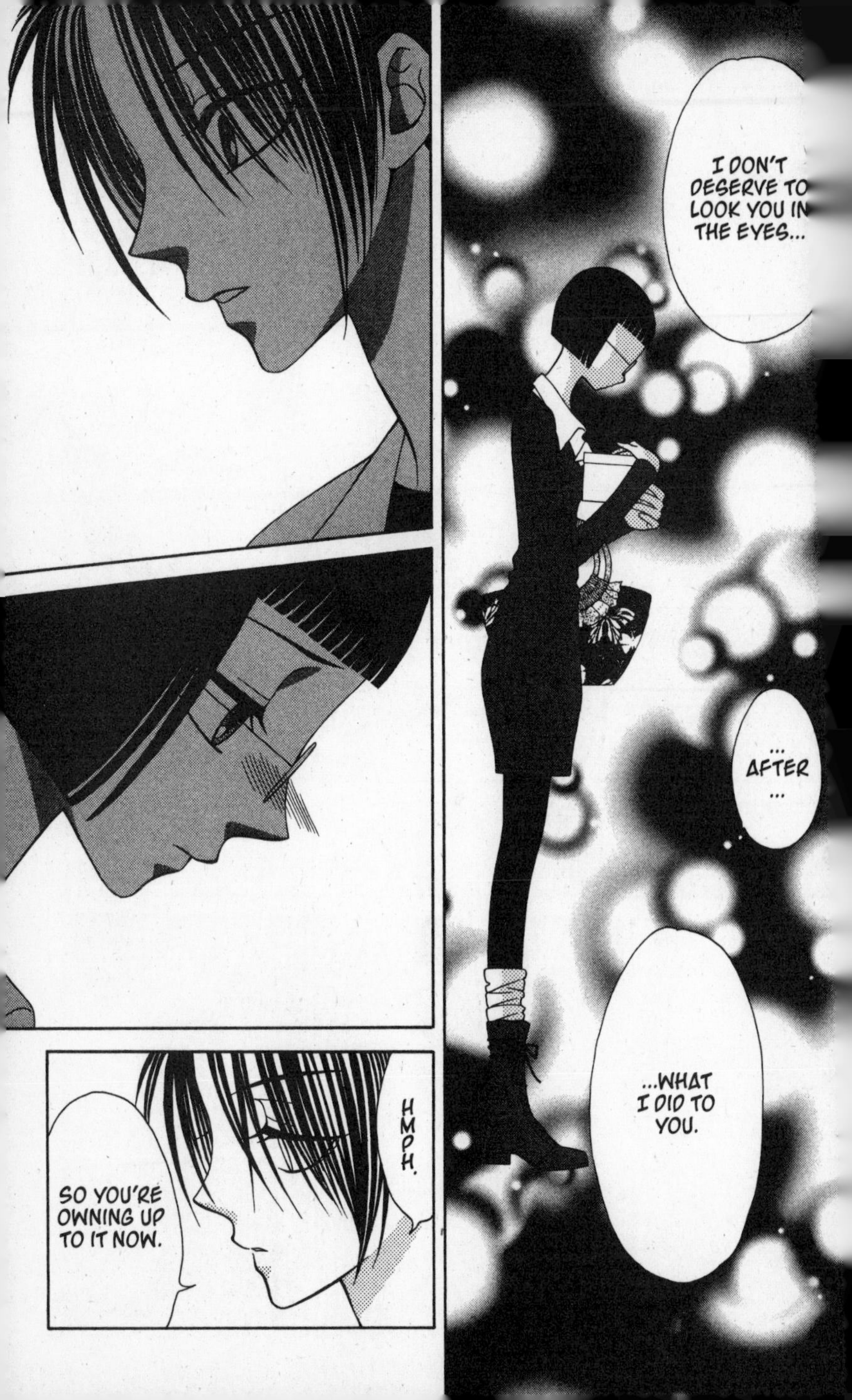
I DON'T DESERVE TO LOOK YOU IN THE EYES...
...AFTER...
...WHAT I DID TO YOU.
HMPH.
SO YOU'RE OWNING UP TO IT NOW.

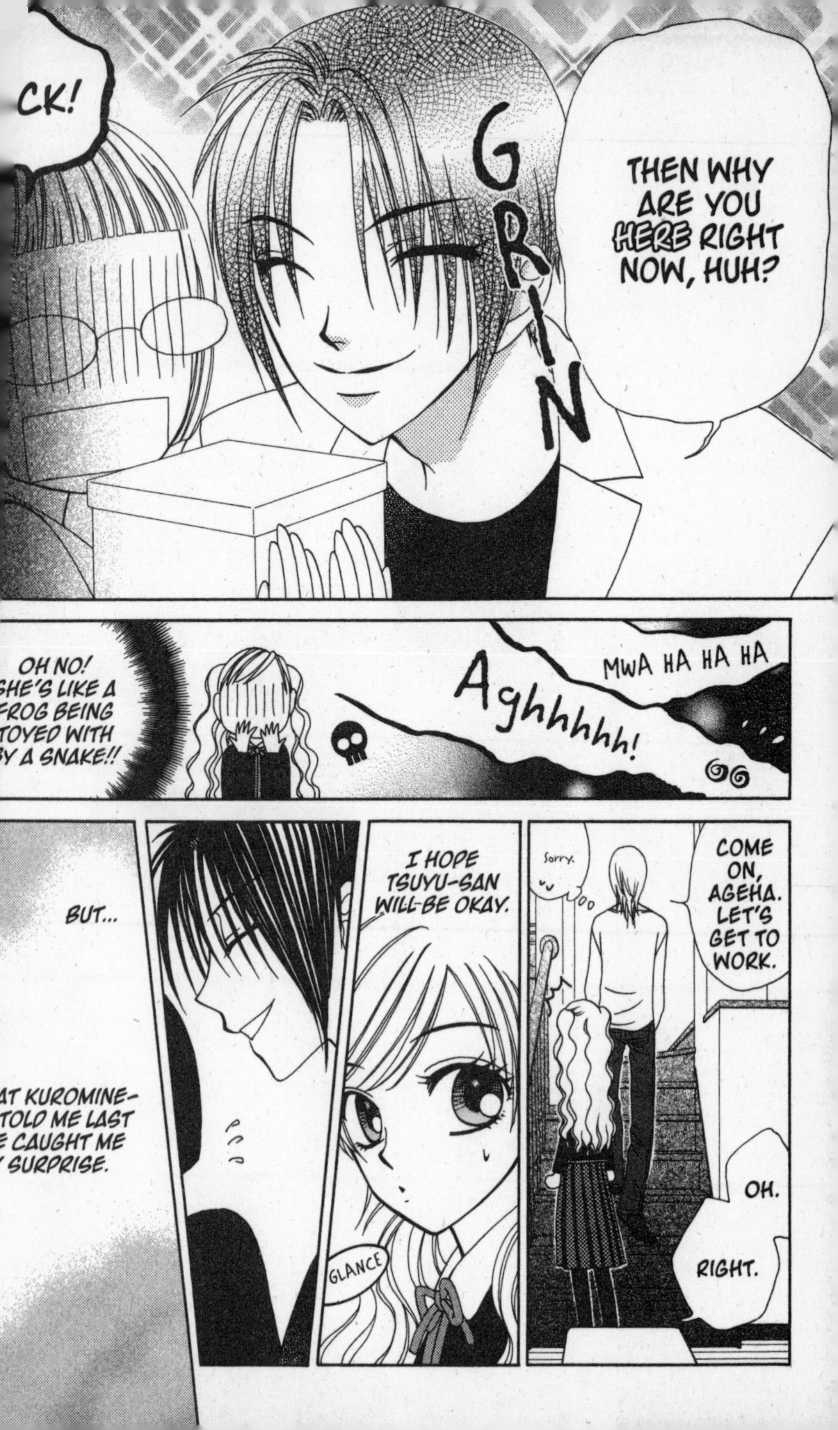
THEN WHY ARE YOU HERE RIGHT NOW, HUH?
GRIN
CK!
MWA HA HA HA
Aghhhhhh!
OH NO! SHE'S LIKE A FROG BEING TOYED WITH BY A SNAKE!!
COME ON, AGEHA. LET'S GET TO WORK.
Sorry.
OH.
RIGHT.
I HOPE TSUYU-SAN WILL BE OKAY.
GLANCE
BUT...
HAT KUROMINE-
N TOLD ME LAST
ME CAUGHT ME
BY SURPRISE.

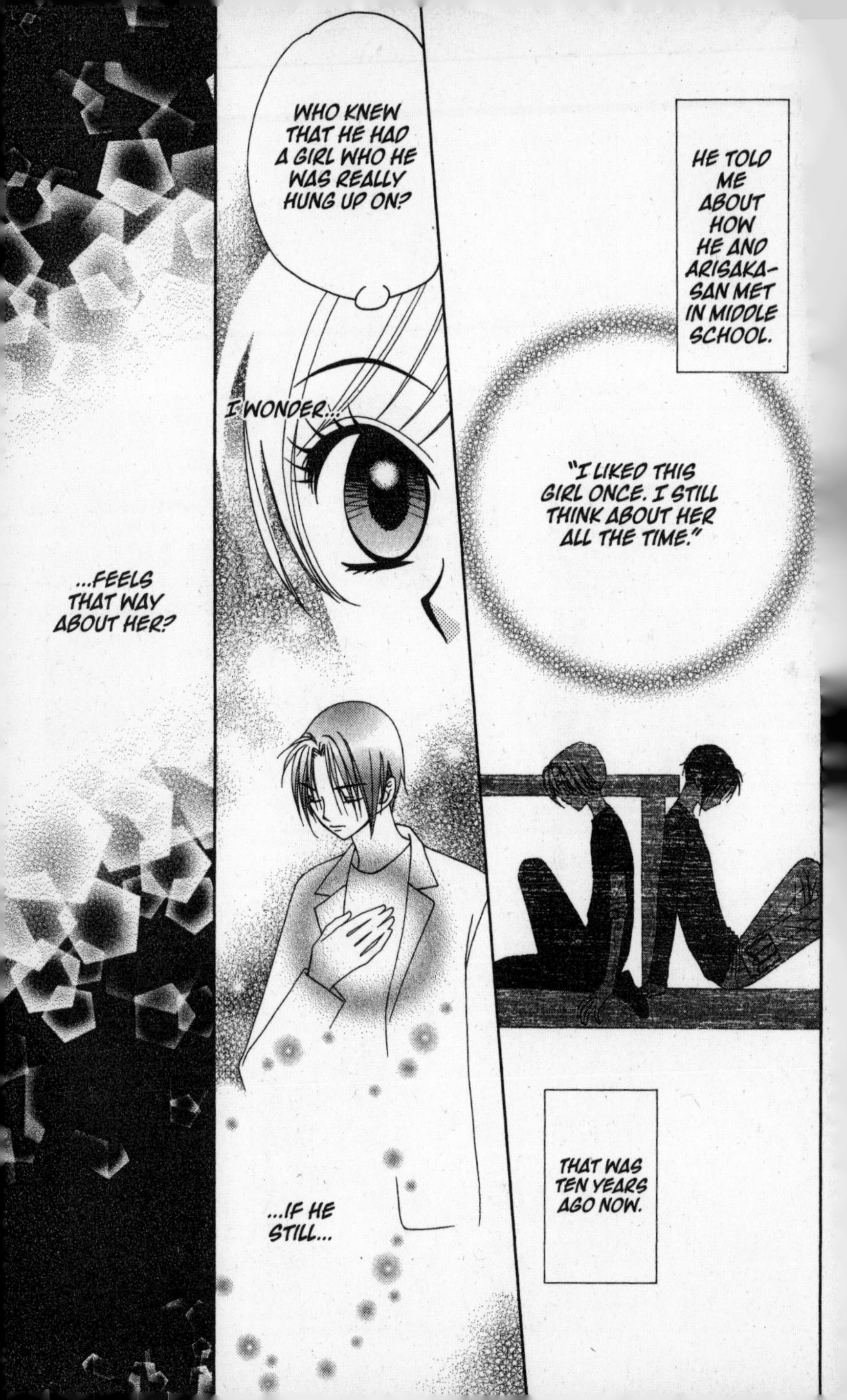
HE TOLD ME ABOUT HOW HE AND ARISAKA-SAN MET IN MIDDLE SCHOOL.
"I LIKED THIS GIRL ONCE. I STILL THINK ABOUT HER ALL THE TIME."
THAT WAS TEN YEARS AGO NOW.
WHO KNEW THAT HE HAD A GIRL WHO HE WAS REALLY HUNG UP ON?
I WONDER...
...IF HE STILL...
...FEELS THAT WAY ABOUT HER?

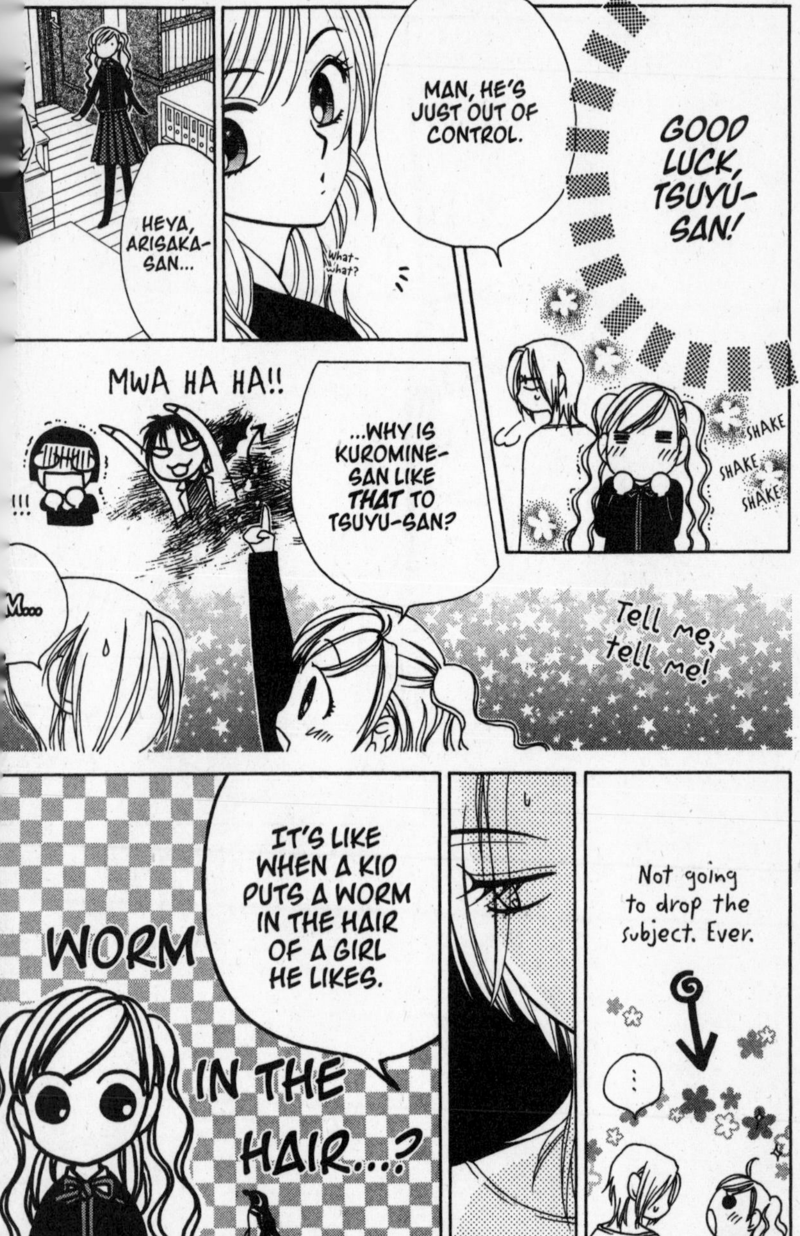
GOOD LUCK, TSUYU-SAN!
SHAKE
SHAKE
SHAKE
MAN, HE'S JUST OUT OF CONTROL.
What-what?
HEYA, ARISAKA-SAN...
...WHY IS KUROMINE-SAN LIKE THAT TO TSUYU-SAN?
Tell me, tell me!
MWA HA HA!!
!!!
M...
Not going to drop the subject. Ever.
...
IT'S LIKE WHEN A KID PUTS A WORM IN THE HAIR OF A GIRL HE LIKES.
WORM IN THE HAIR...?

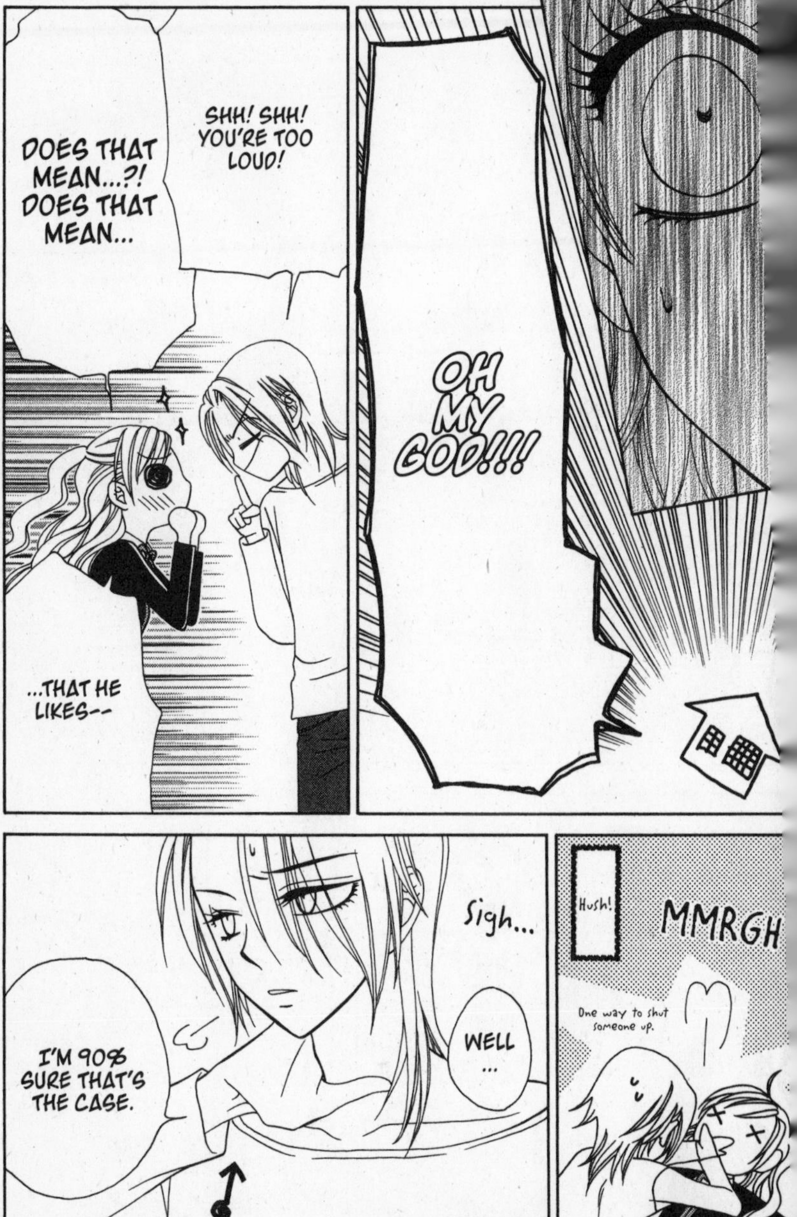
OH MY GOD!!!
DOES THAT MEAN...?! DOES THAT MEAN...
...THAT HE LIKES--
SHH! SHH! YOU'RE TOO LOUD!
Hush!
MMRGH
One way to shut someone up.
Sigh...
WELL ...
I'M 90% SURE THAT'S THE CASE.
Sometimes he's not positive either. HAH!

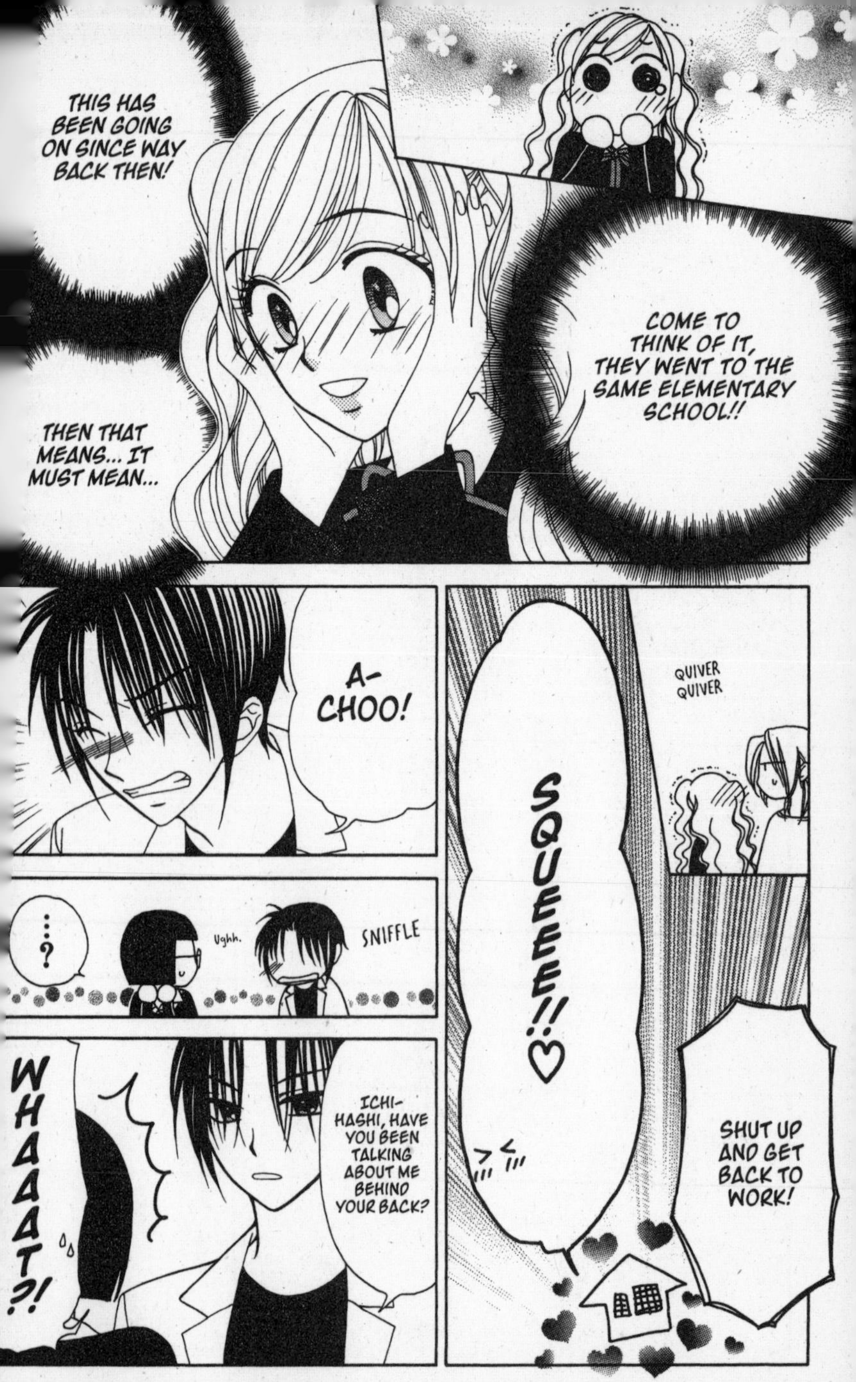
COME TO THINK OF IT, THEY WENT TO THE SAME ELEMENTARY SCHOOL!!
THIS HAS BEEN GOING ON SINCE WAY BACK THEN!
THEN THAT MEANS... IT MUST MEAN...
QUIVER QUIVER
SQUEEE!!♡
SHUT UP AND GET BACK TO WORK!
A-CHOO!
SNIFFLE
Ughh.
...?
ICHI-HASHI, HAVE YOU BEEN TALKING ABOUT ME BEHIND YOUR BACK?
WHAAAAT?!

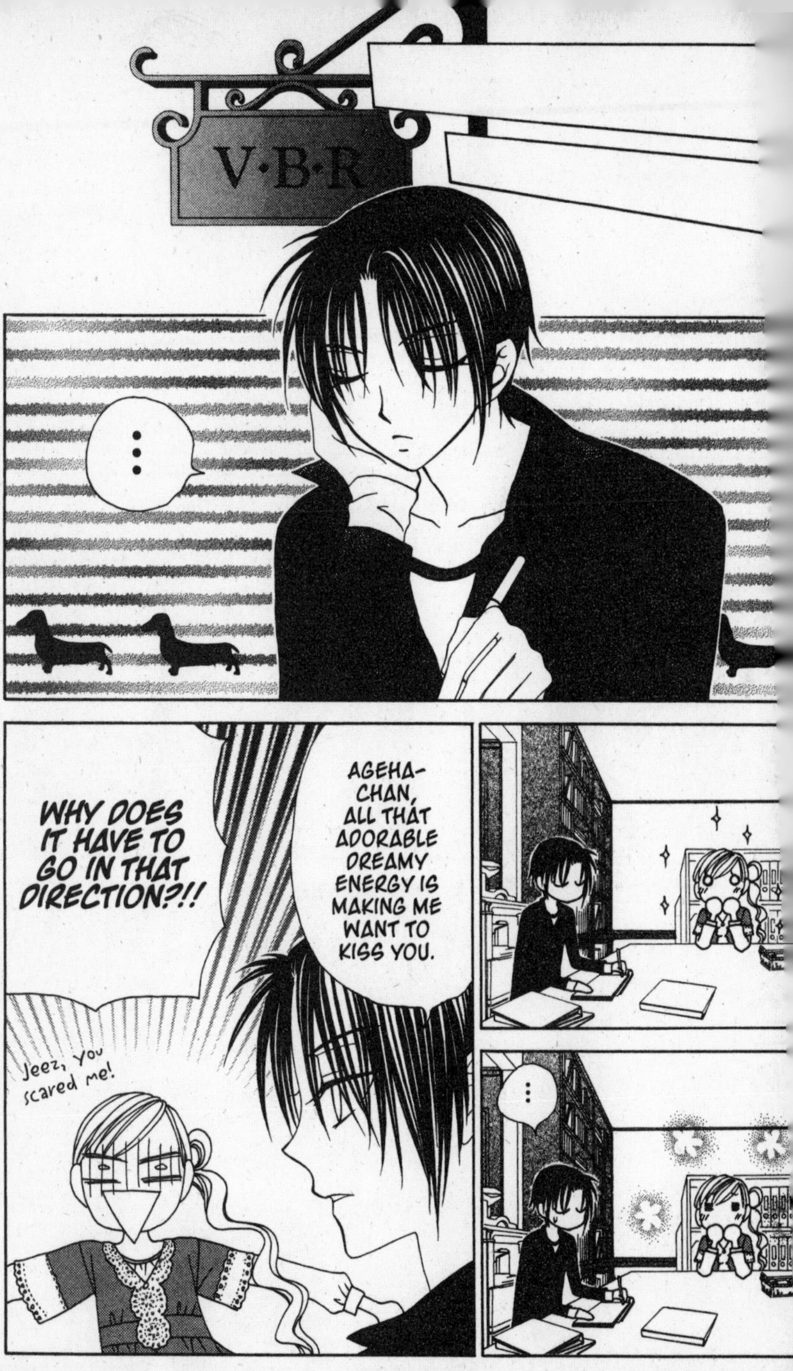
V·B·R
...
...
AGEHA-CHAN, ALL THAT ADORABLE DREAMY ENERGY IS MAKING ME WANT TO KISS YOU.
WHY DOES IT HAVE TO GO IN THAT DIRECTION?!!
Jeez, You scared me!

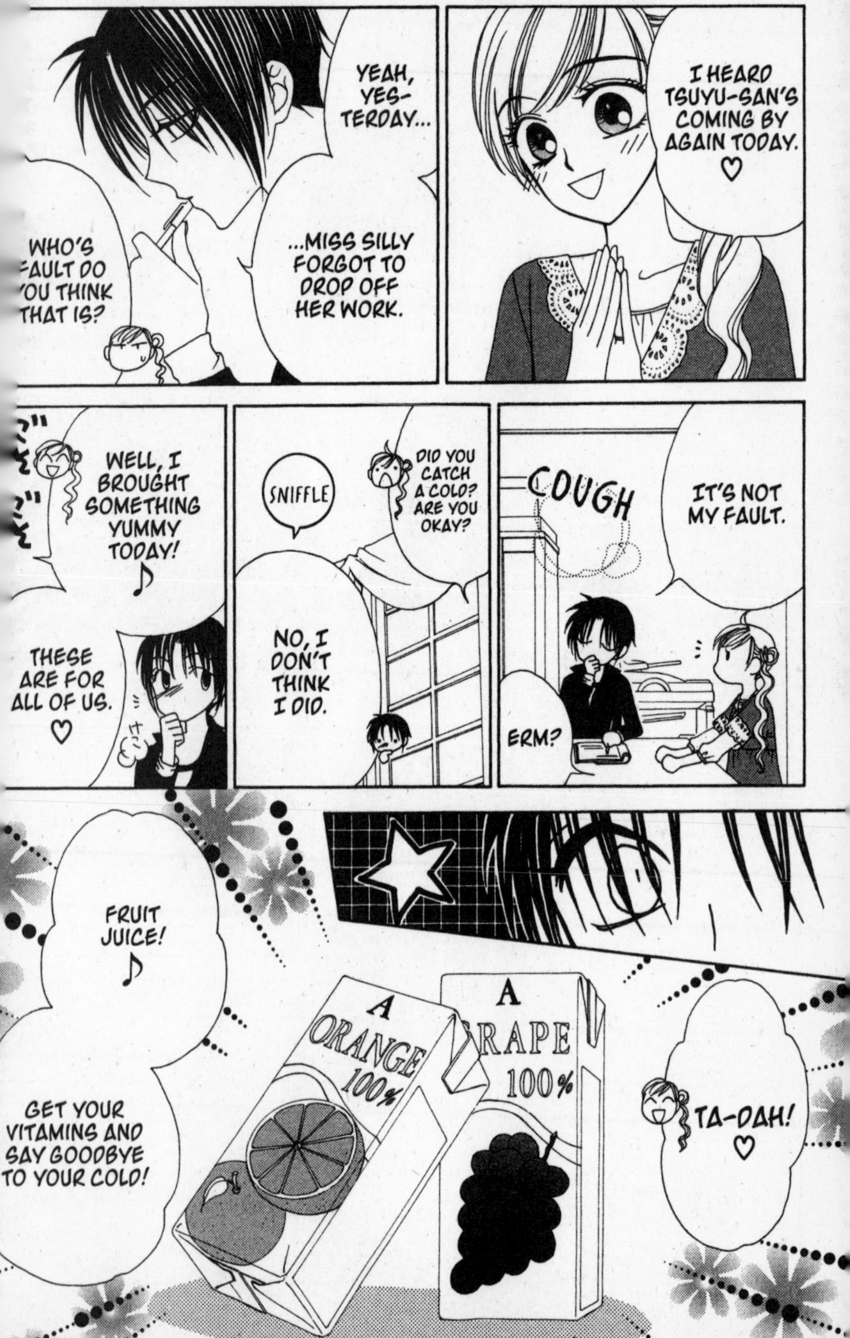
I HEARD TSUYU-SAN'S COMING BY AGAIN TODAY. ♡
YEAH, YES-TERDAY...
...MISS SILLY FORGOT TO DROP OFF HER WORK.
WHO'S FAULT DO YOU THINK THAT IS?
IT'S NOT MY FAULT.
COUGH
ERM?
DID YOU CATCH A COLD? ARE YOU OKAY?
SNIFFLE
NO, I DON'T THINK I DID.
WELL, I BROUGHT SOMETHING YUMMY TODAY! ♪
THESE ARE FOR ALL OF US. ♡
TA-DAH! ♡
A GRAPE 100%
A ORANGE 100%
FRUIT JUICE! ♪
GET YOUR VITAMINS AND SAY GOODBYE TO YOUR COLD!

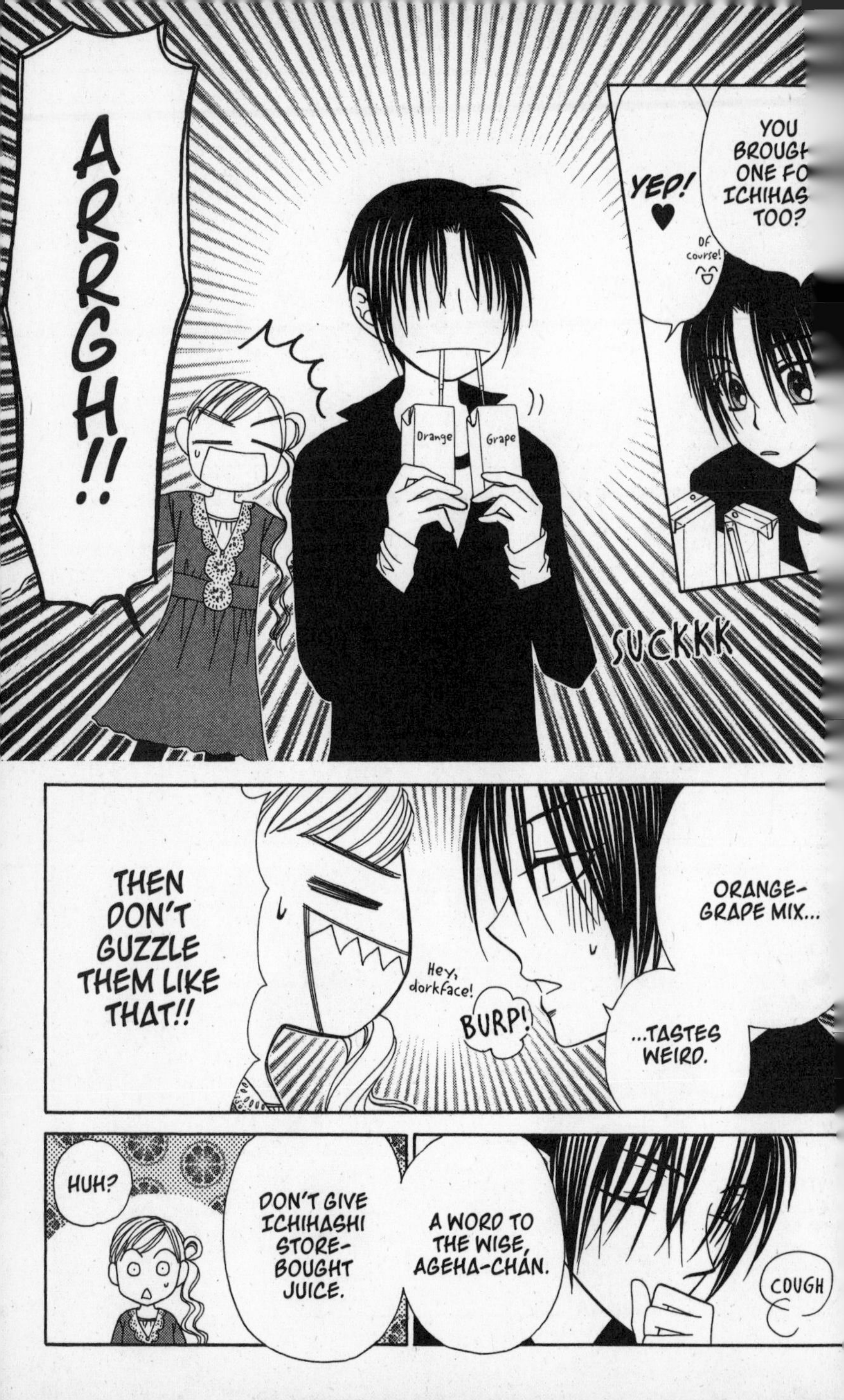
YOU BROUGH ONE FO ICHIHAS TOO?
YEP! ♥
Of course!
Orange
Grape
SUCKKK
ARRRGH!!
ORANGE-GRAPE MIX...
...TASTES WEIRD.
BURP!
Hey, dorkface!
THEN DON'T GUZZLE THEM LIKE THAT!!
COUGH
A WORD TO THE WISE, AGEHA-CHÁN.
DON'T GIVE ICHIHASHI STORE-BOUGHT JUICE.
HUH?

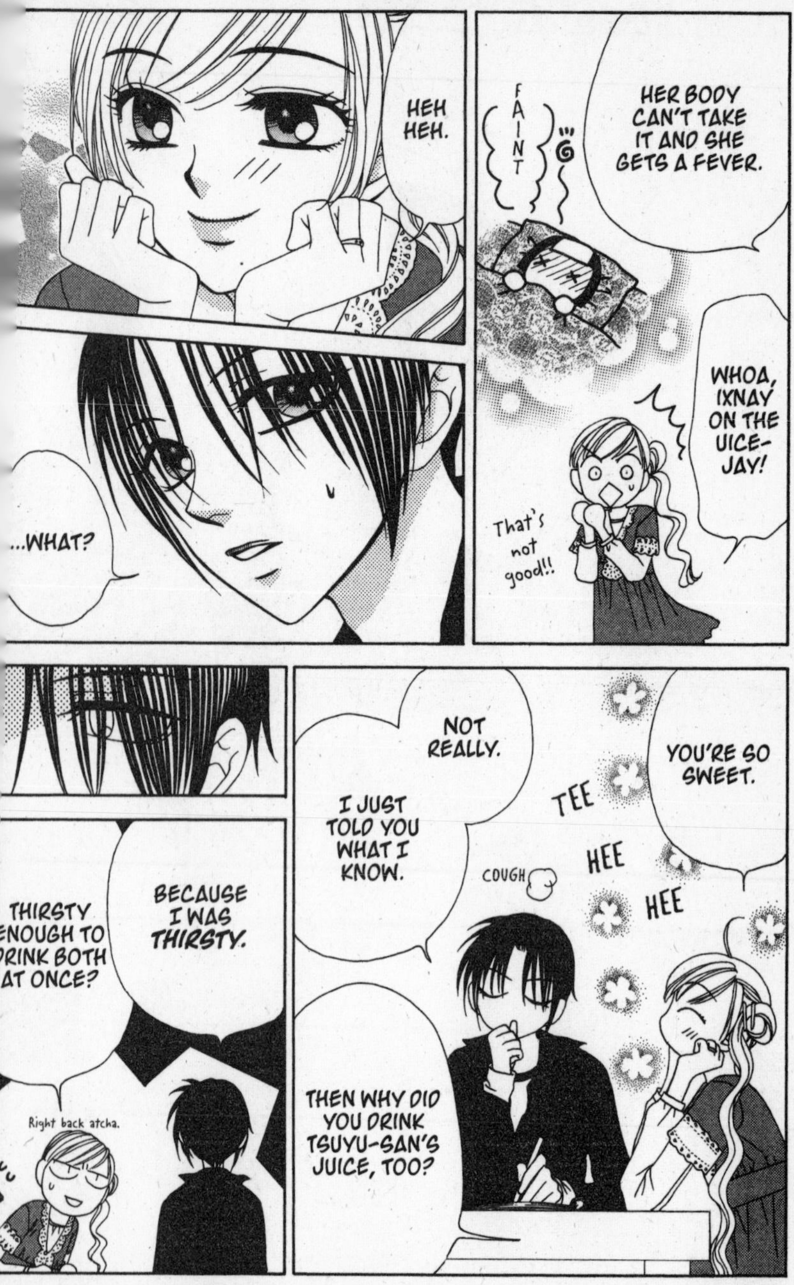
FAINT
HER BODY CAN'T TAKE IT AND SHE GETS A FEVER.
WHOA, IXNAY ON THE UICE-JAY!
That's not good!!
HEH HEH.
...WHAT?
YOU'RE SO SWEET.
TEE HEE HEE
NOT REALLY.
I JUST TOLD YOU WHAT I KNOW.
COUGH
THEN WHY DID YOU DRINK TSUYU-SAN'S JUICE, TOO?
BECAUSE I WAS THIRSTY.
THIRSTY ENOUGH TO DRINK BOTH AT ONCE?
Right back atcha.

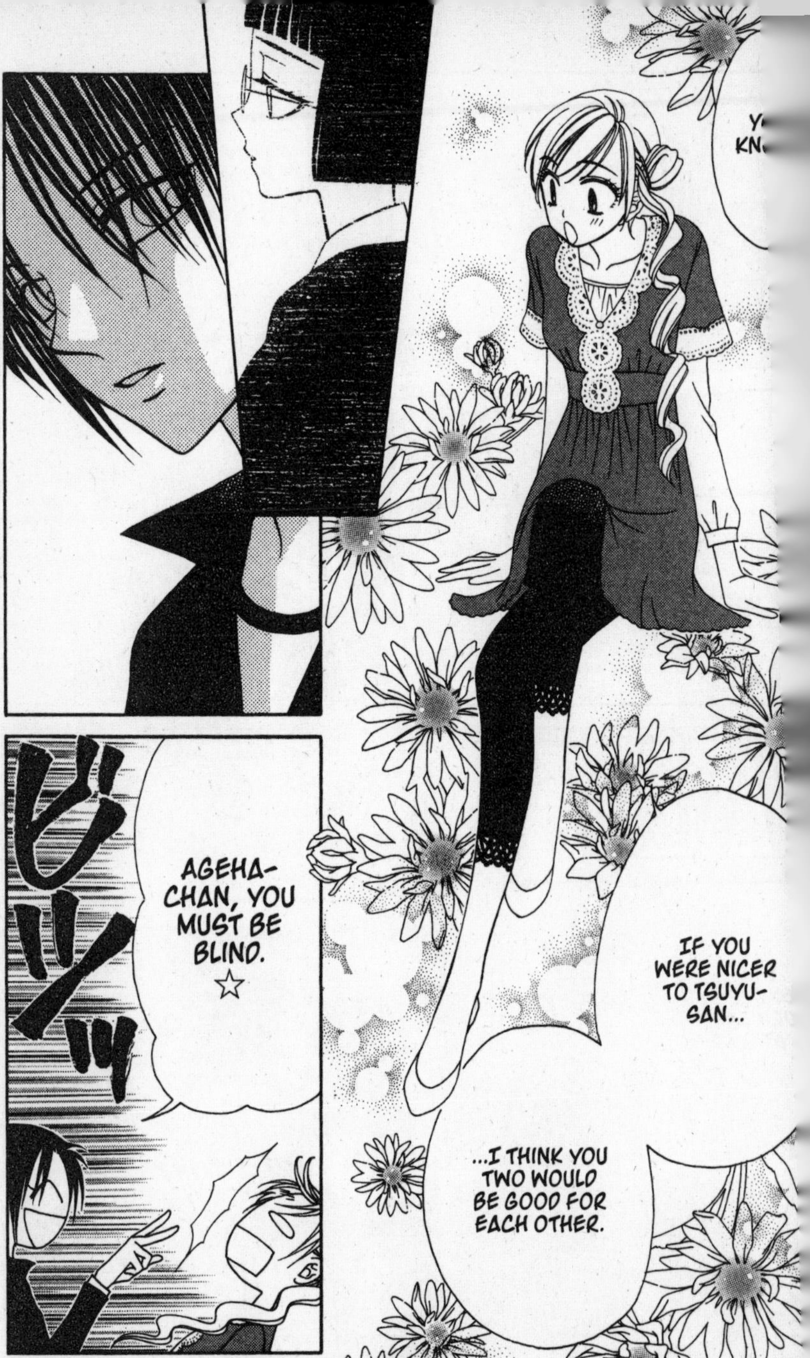
IF YOU WERE NICER TO TSUYU-SAN...
...I THINK YOU TWO WOULD BE GOOD FOR EACH OTHER.
ビシッ
AGEHA-CHAN, YOU MUST BE BLIND. ☆

The dreaded "forehead flick" offensive.

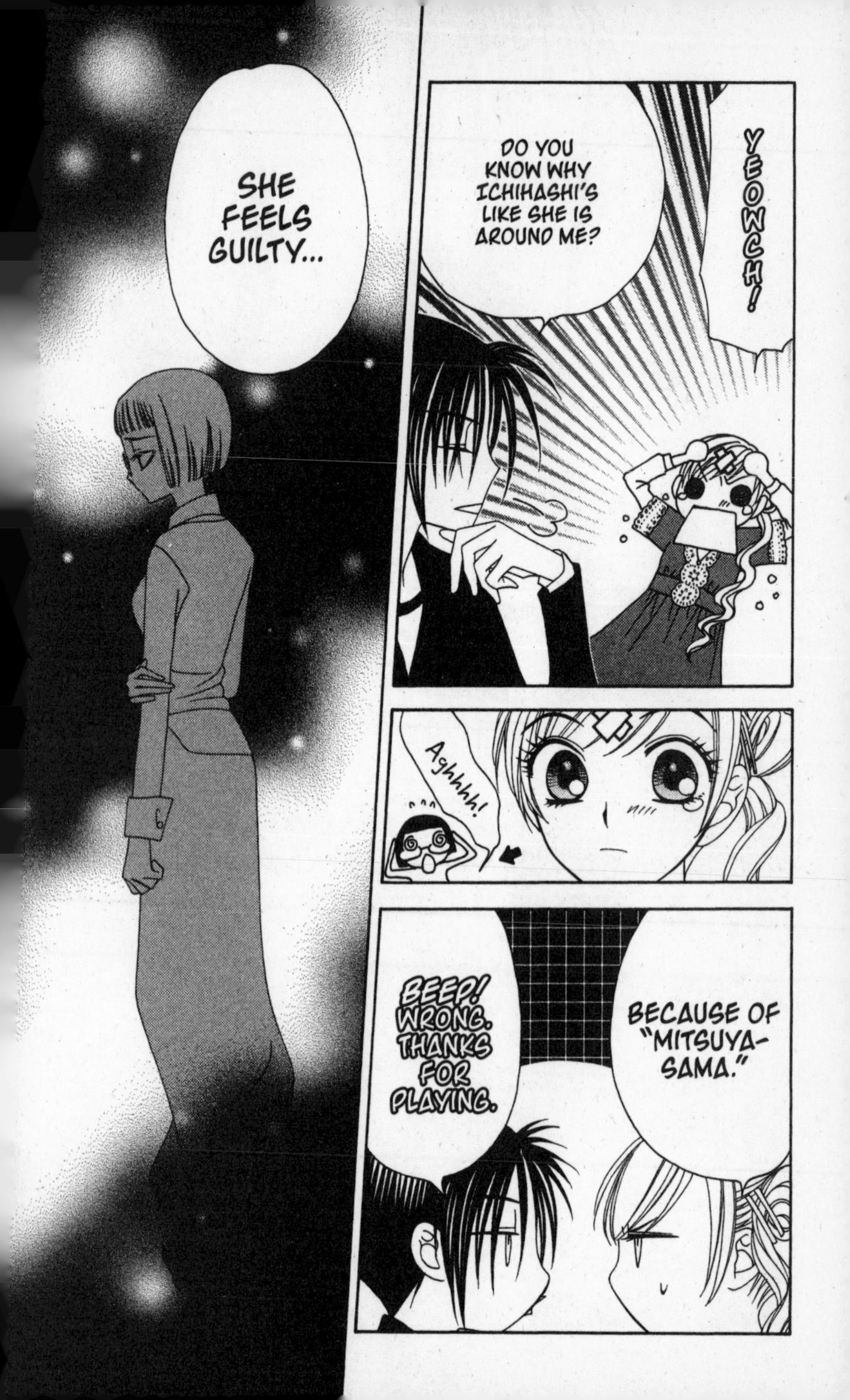
YEOWCH!
DO YOU KNOW WHY ICHIHASHI'S LIKE SHE IS AROUND ME?
Aghhhh!
BECAUSE OF "MITSUYA-SAMA."
BEEP! WRONG. THANKS FOR PLAYING.
SHE FEELS GUILTY...

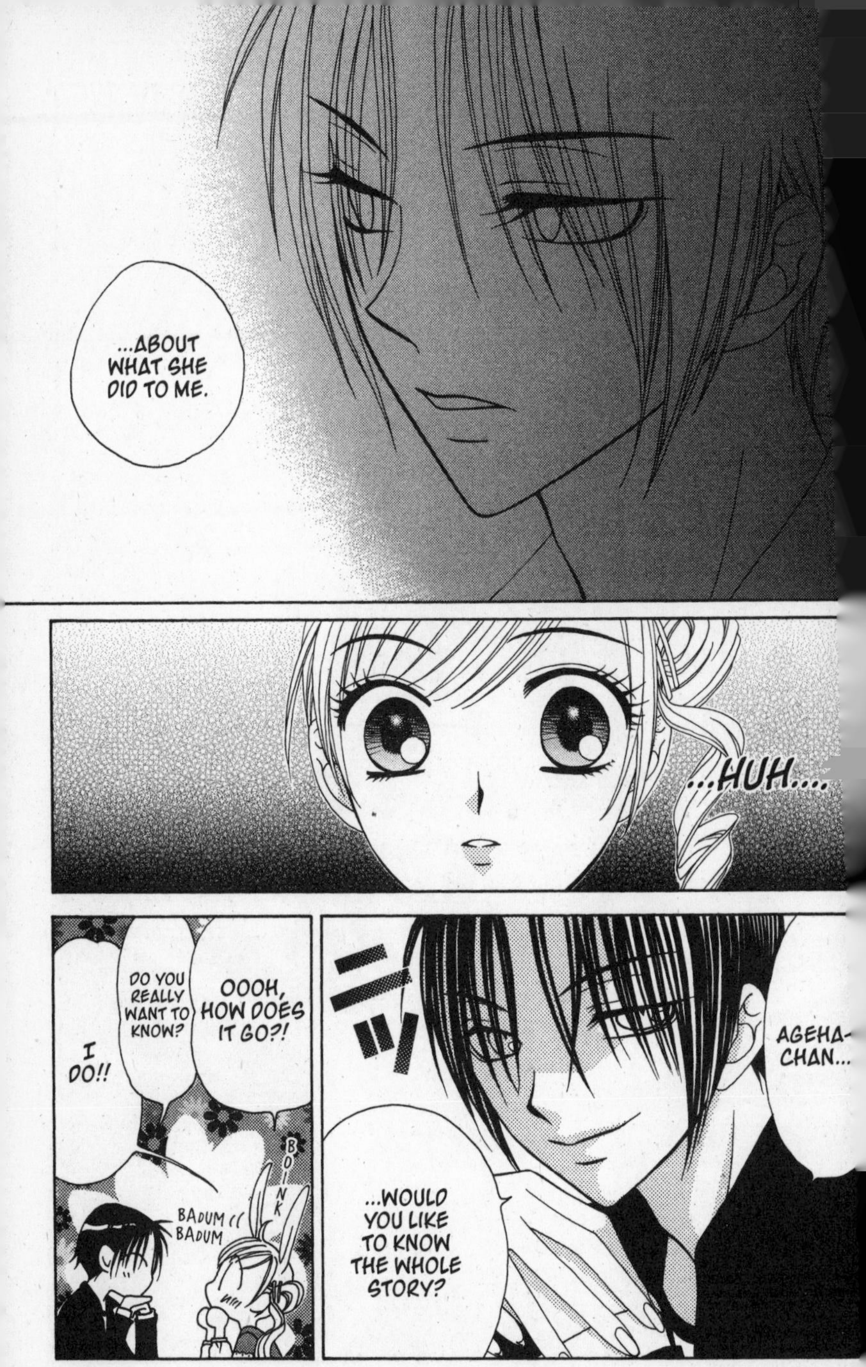
...ABOUT WHAT SHE DID TO ME.
...HUH....
AGEHA-CHAN...
...WOULD YOU LIKE TO KNOW THE WHOLE STORY?
OOOH, HOW DOES IT GO?!
DO YOU REALLY WANT TO KNOW?
I DO!!
BOINK
BADUM BADUM

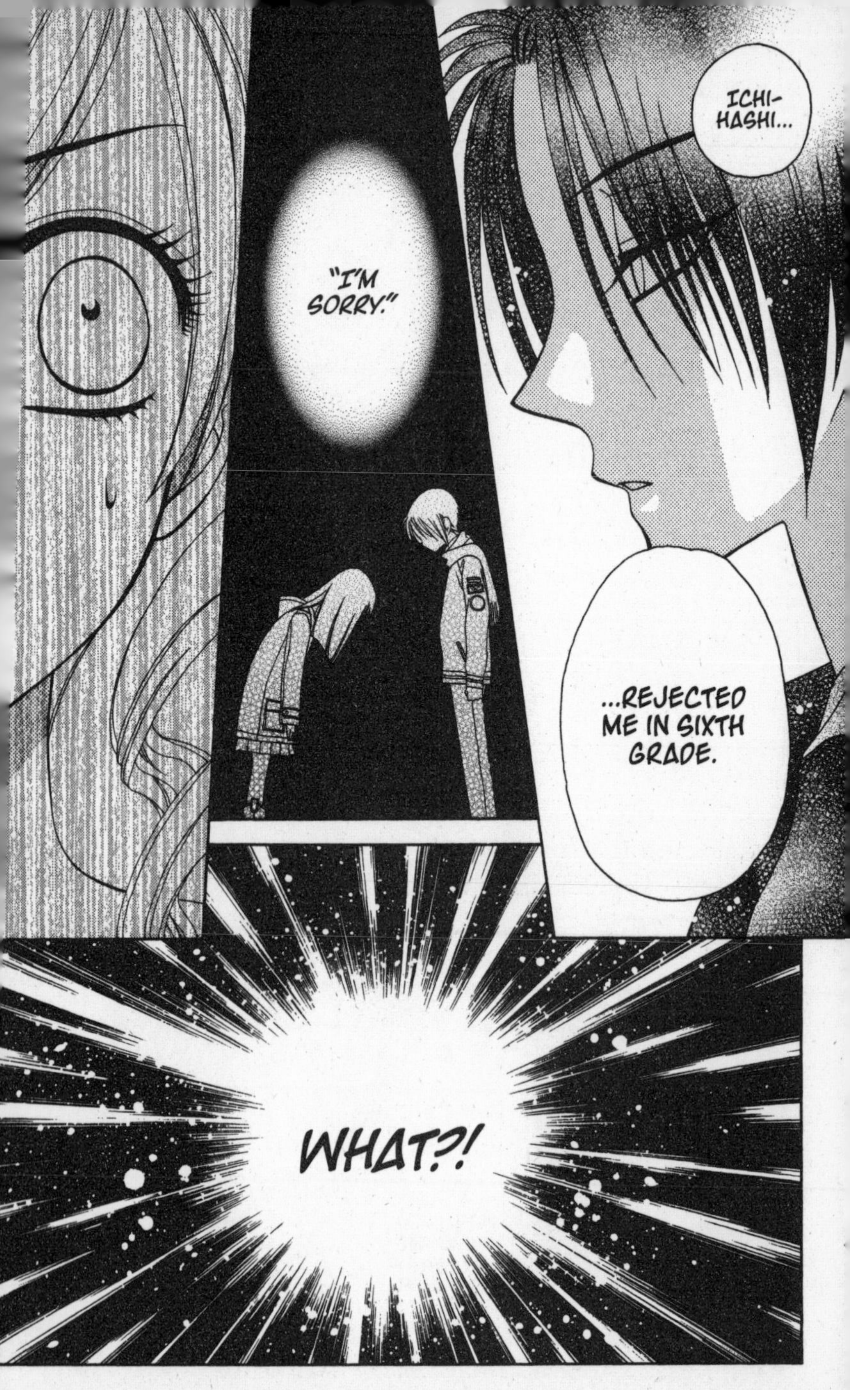
ICHI-HASHI...
...REJECTED ME IN SIXTH GRADE.
"I'M SORRY."
WHAT?!

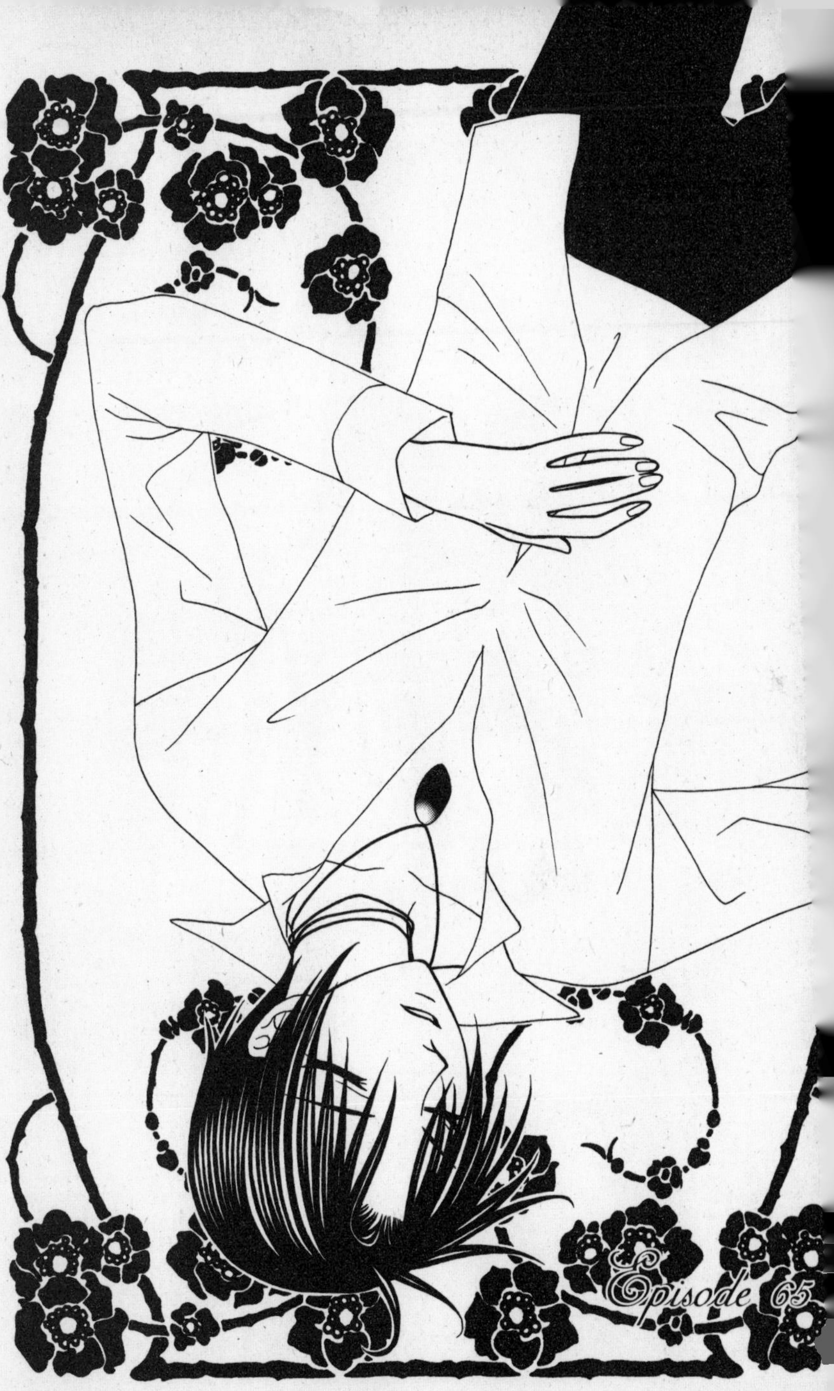
Episode 65

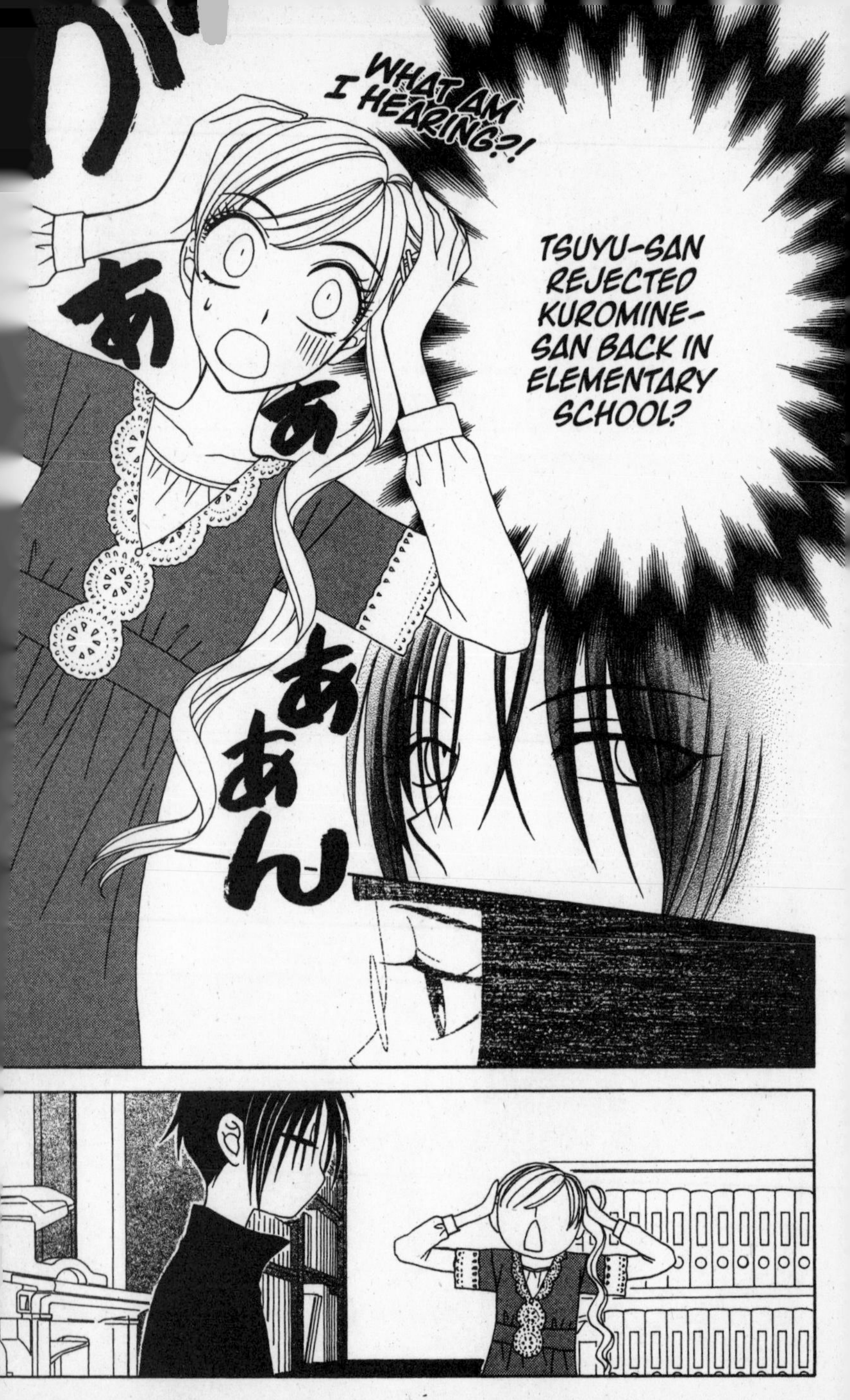
TSUYU-SAN REJECTED KUROMINE-SAN BACK IN ELEMENTARY SCHOOL?
WHAT AM I HEARING?!
ああああん

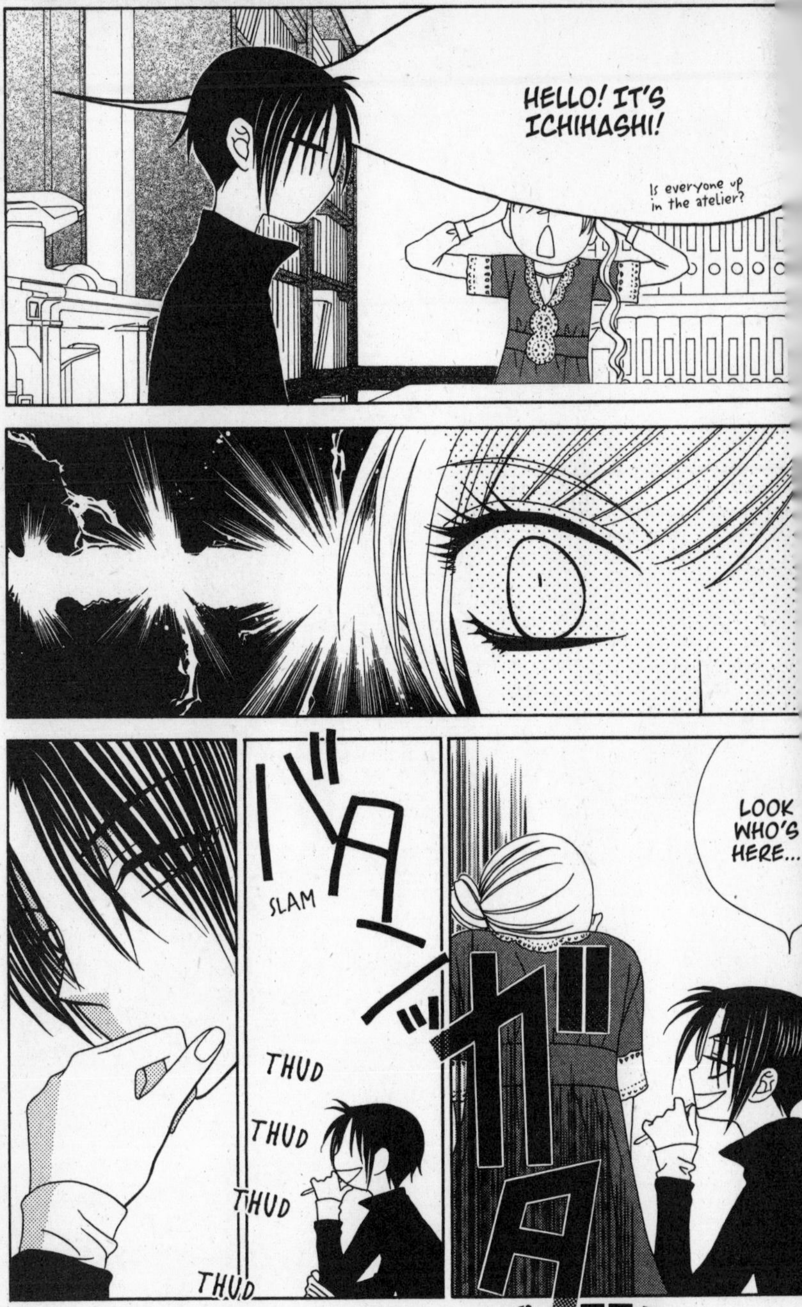
HELLO! IT'S ICHIHASHI!
Is everyone up in the atelier?
LOOK WHO'S HERE...
CLATTER
SLAM
THUD
THUD
THUD
THUD
THUD

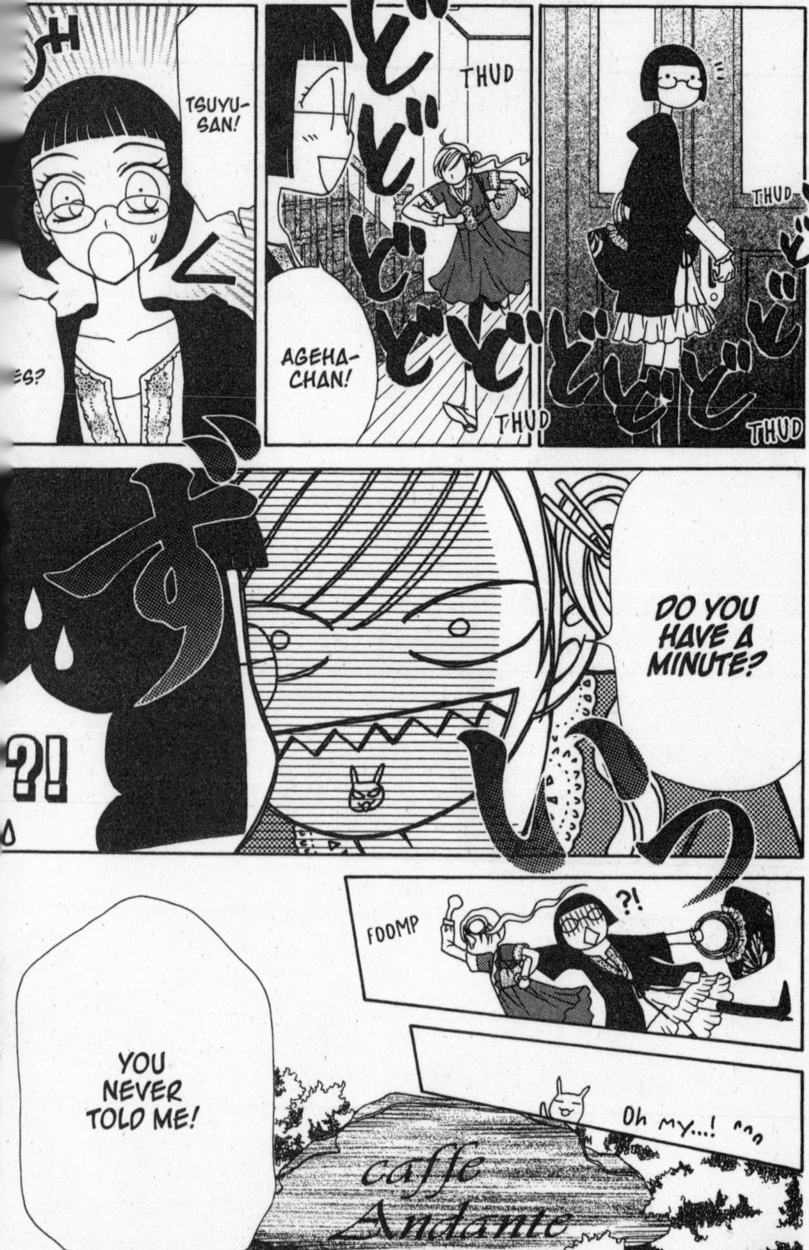
THUD
THUD
THUD
AGEHA-CHAN!
THUD
TSUYU-SAN!
DO YOU HAVE A MINUTE?
?!
?!
FOOMP
Oh my...!
caffe Andante
YOU NEVER TOLD ME!

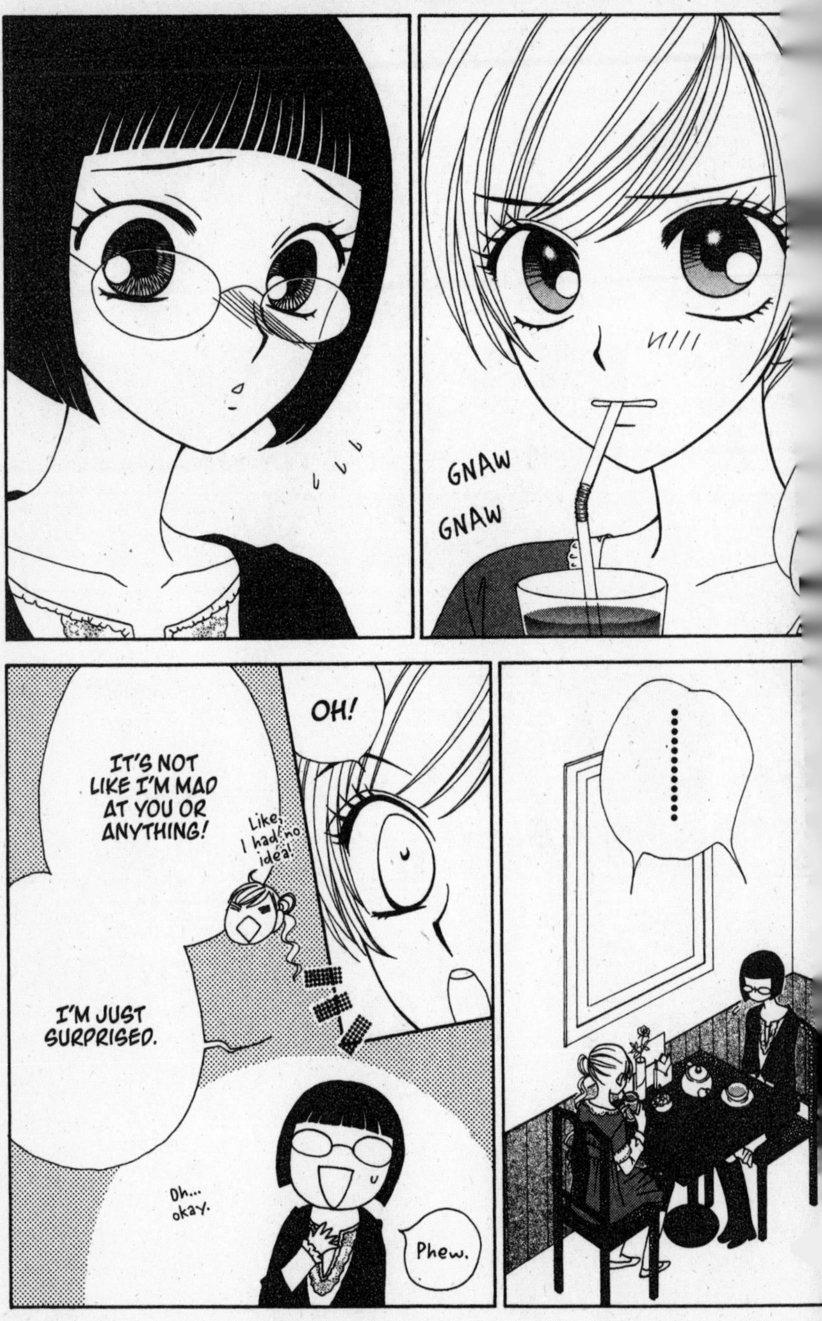
GNAW
GNAW
......
OH!
IT'S NOT LIKE I'M MAD AT YOU OR ANYTHING!
Like, I had no idea!
I'M JUST SURPRISED.
Oh... okay.
Phew.

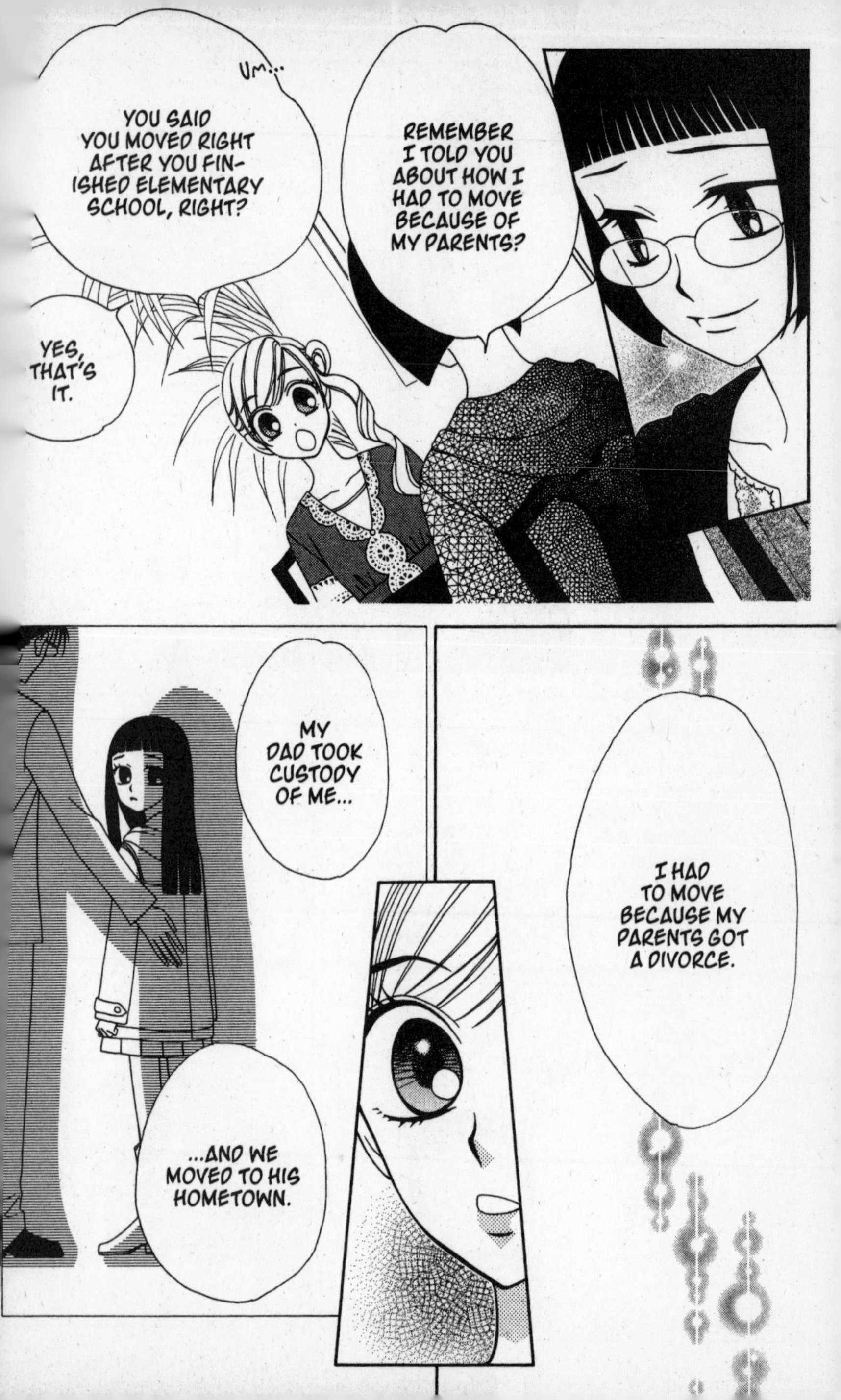
REMEMBER I TOLD YOU ABOUT HOW I HAD TO MOVE BECAUSE OF MY PARENTS?
UM...
YOU SAID YOU MOVED RIGHT AFTER YOU FIN-ISHED ELEMENTARY SCHOOL, RIGHT?
YES, THAT'S IT.
I HAD TO MOVE BECAUSE MY PARENTS GOT A DIVORCE.
MY DAD TOOK CUSTODY OF ME...
...AND WE MOVED TO HIS HOMETOWN.

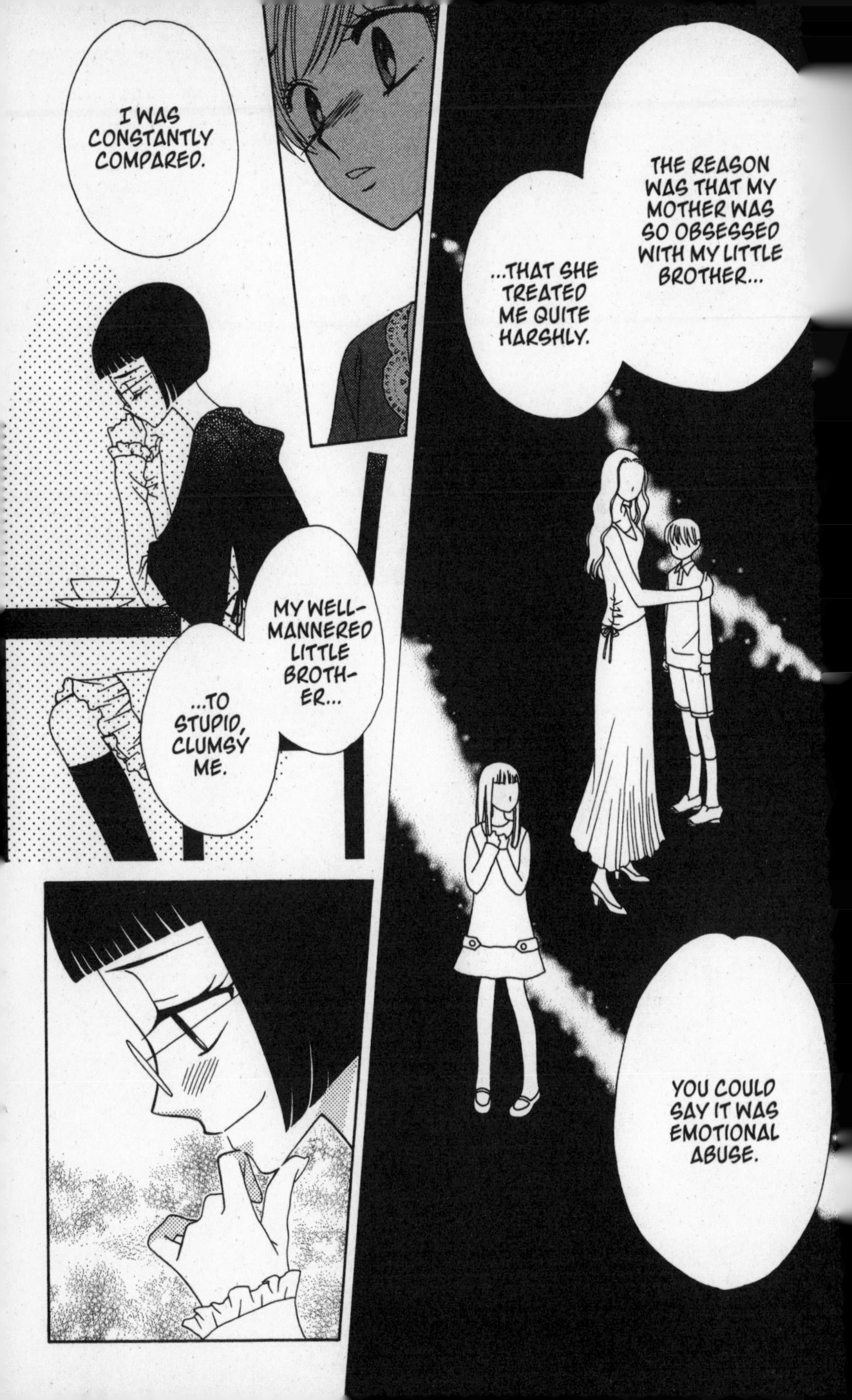
I WAS CONSTANTLY COMPARED.
MY WELL-MANNERED LITTLE BROTH-ER...
...TO STUPID, CLUMSY ME.
THE REASON WAS THAT MY MOTHER WAS SO OBSESSED WITH MY LITTLE BROTHER...
...THAT SHE TREATED ME QUITE HARSHLY.
YOU COULD SAY IT WAS EMOTIONAL ABUSE.

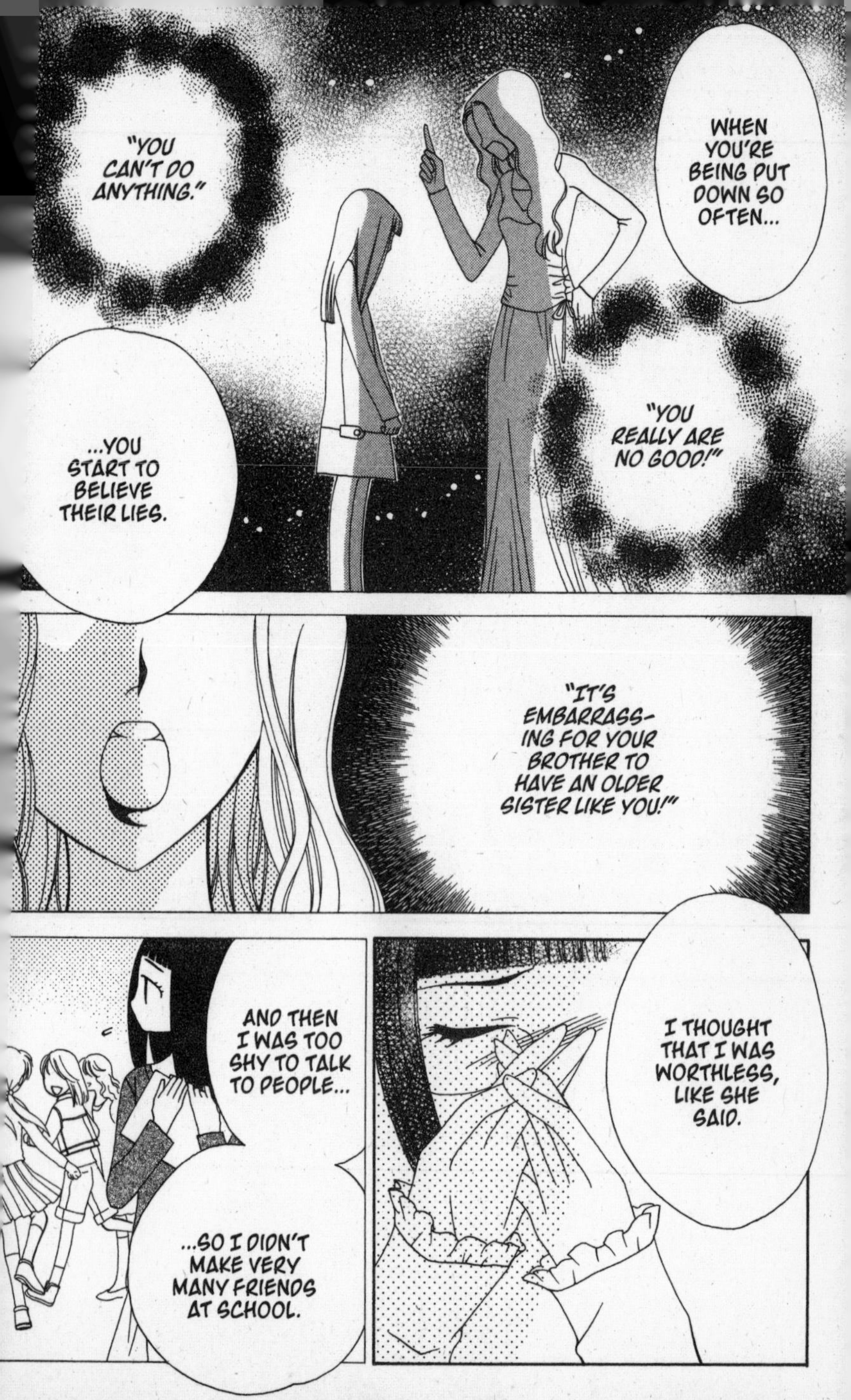
WHEN YOU'RE BEING PUT DOWN SO OFTEN...
"YOU CAN'T DO ANYTHING."
"YOU REALLY ARE NO GOOD!"
...YOU START TO BELIEVE THEIR LIES.
"IT'S EMBARRASS-ING FOR YOUR BROTHER TO HAVE AN OLDER SISTER LIKE YOU!"
I THOUGHT THAT I WAS WORTHLESS, LIKE SHE SAID.
AND THEN I WAS TOO SHY TO TALK TO PEOPLE...
...SO I DIDN'T MAKE VERY MANY FRIENDS AT SCHOOL.

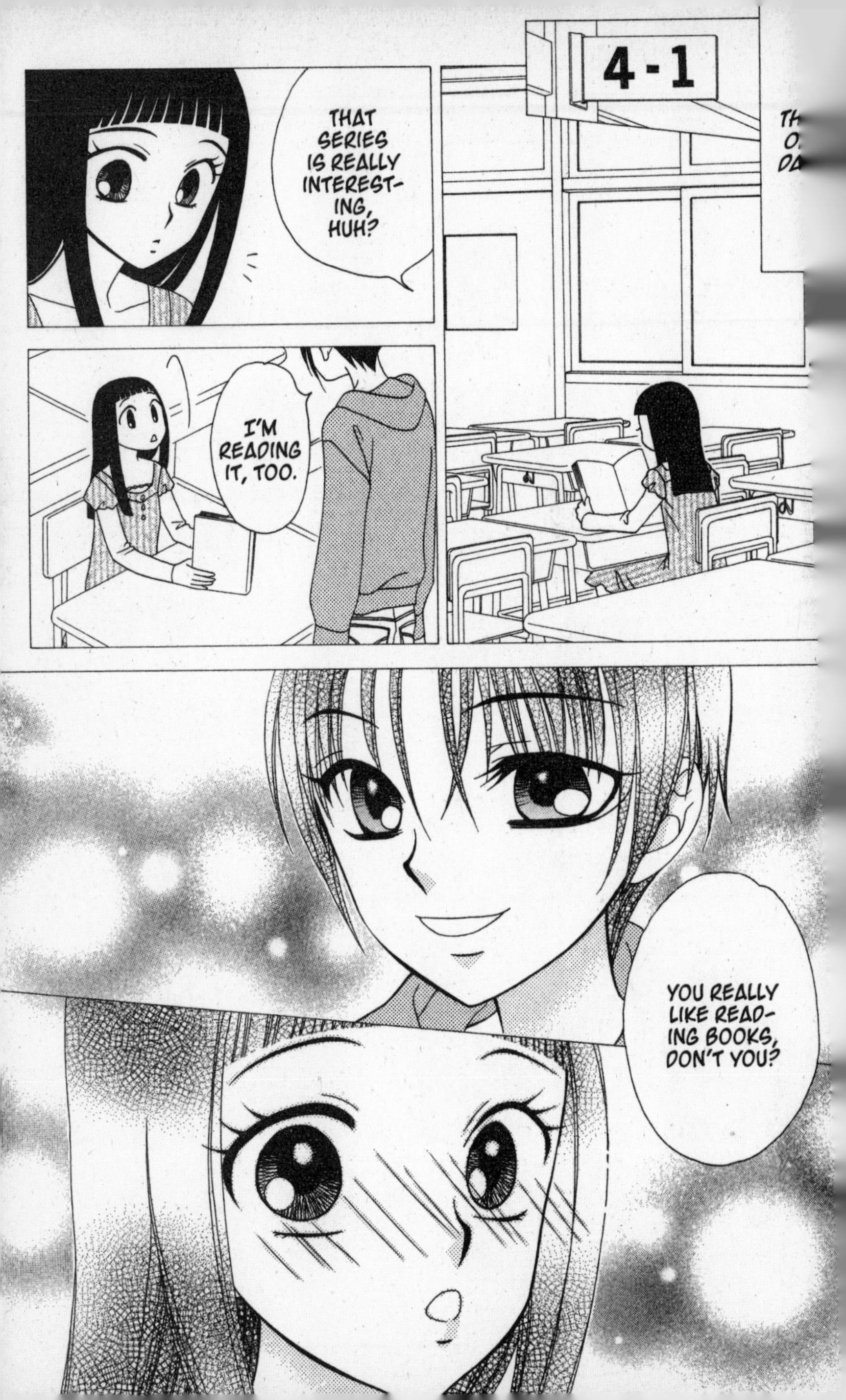
4 - 1
THAT SERIES IS REALLY INTEREST-ING, HUH?
I'M READING IT, TOO.
YOU REALLY LIKE READ-ING BOOKS, DON'T YOU?

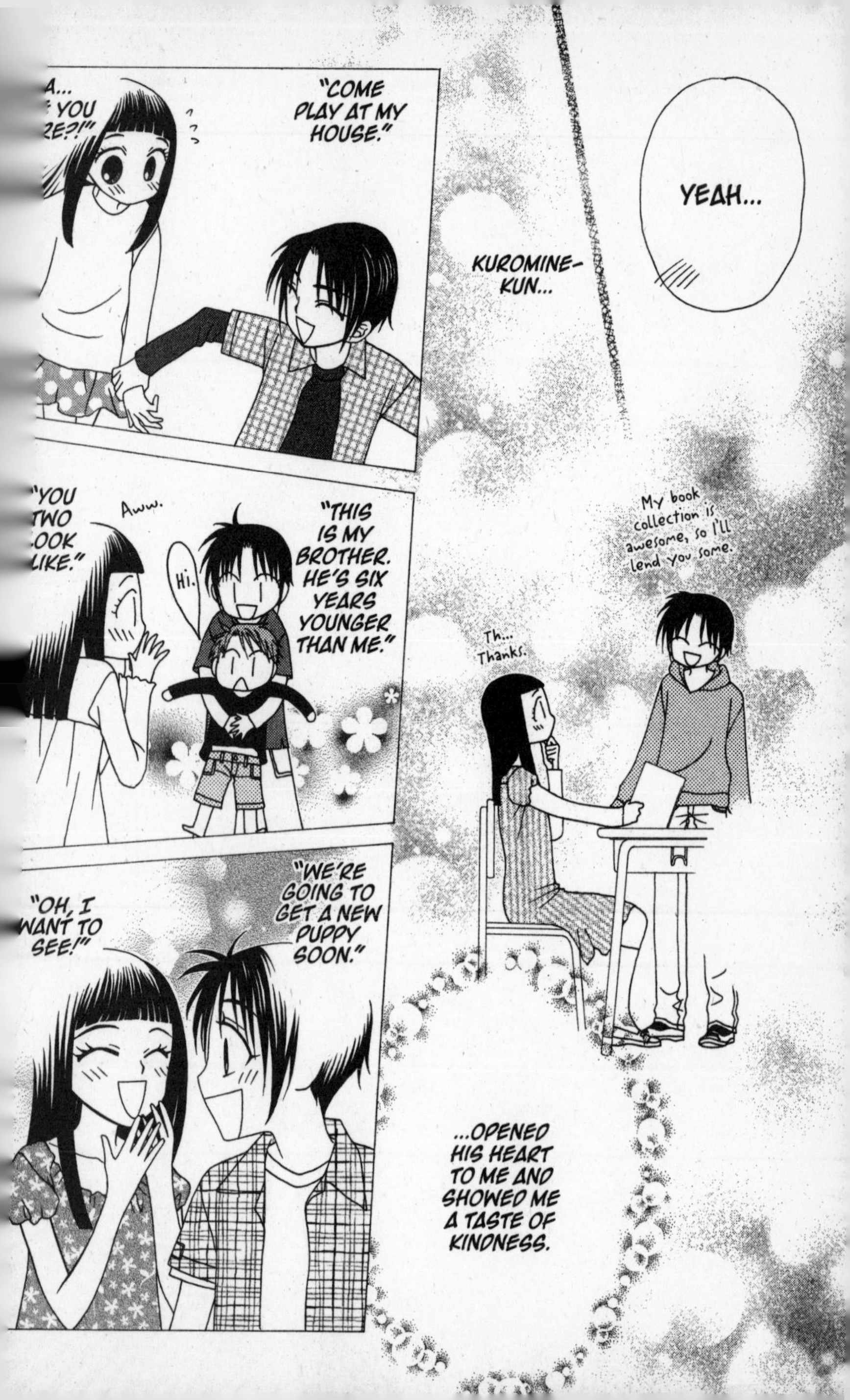
YEAH...
KUROMINE-KUN...
My book collection is awesome, so I'll lend you some.
Th... Thanks.
...OPENED HIS HEART TO ME AND SHOWED ME A TASTE OF KINDNESS.
"COME PLAY AT MY HOUSE."
A... F YOU RE?!"
"THIS IS MY BROTHER. HE'S SIX YEARS YOUNGER THAN ME."
Hi.
Aww.
"YOU TWO OOK LIKE."
"WE'RE GOING TO GET A NEW PUPPY SOON."
"OH, I WANT TO SEE!"

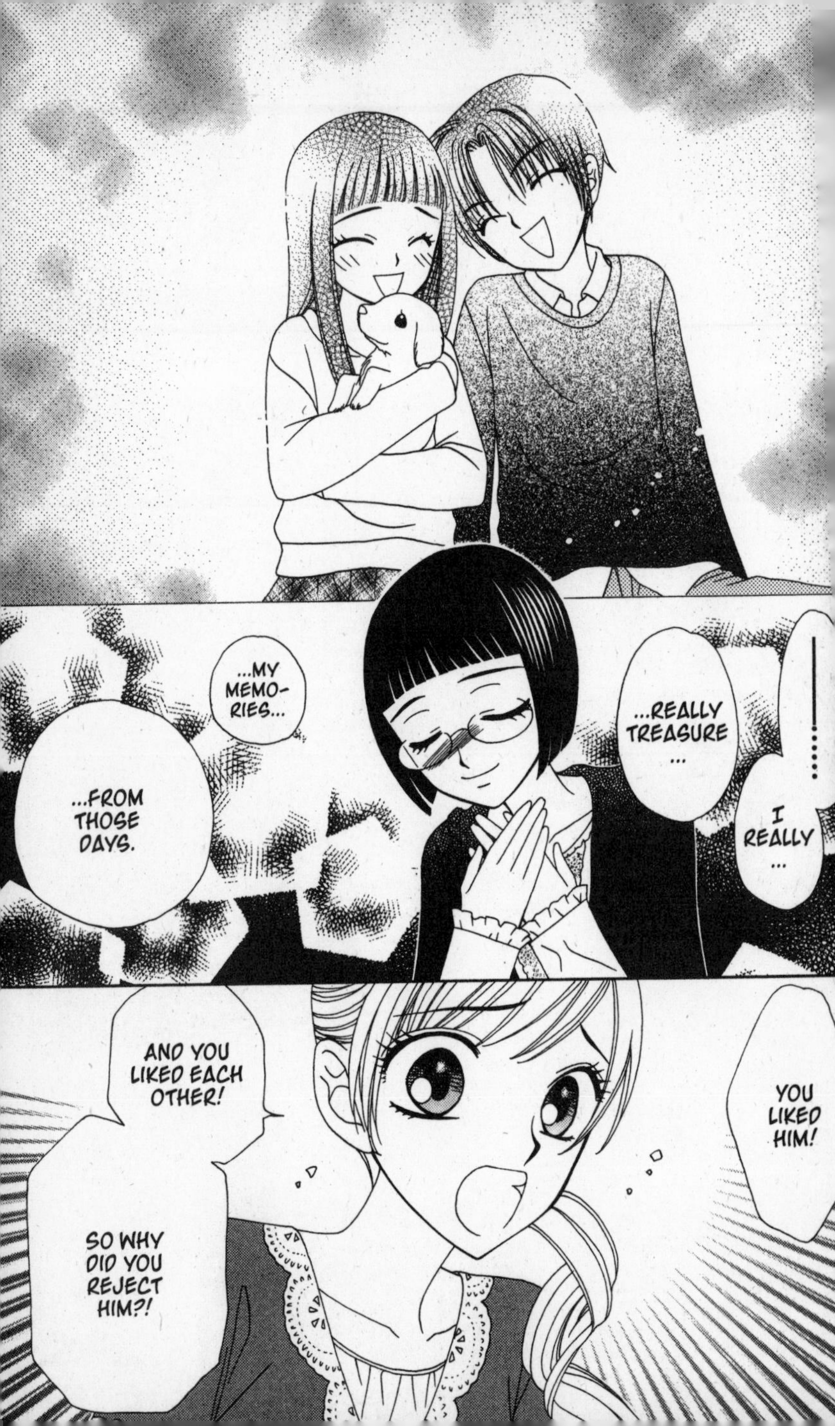
——......
I REALLY ...
...REALLY TREASURE ...
...MY MEMORIES...
...FROM THOSE DAYS.
YOU LIKED HIM!
AND YOU LIKED EACH OTHER!
SO WHY DID YOU REJECT HIM?!

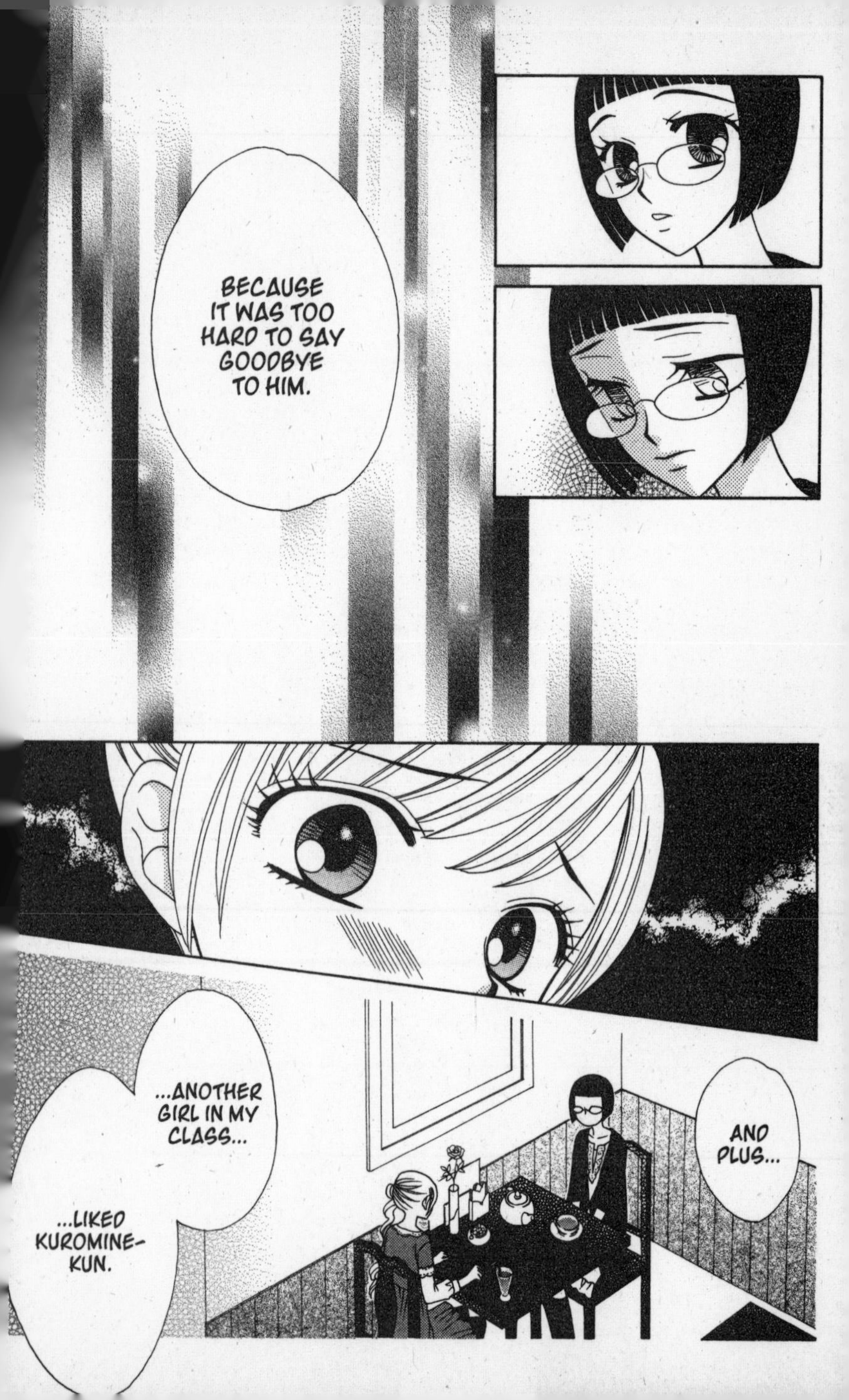
BECAUSE IT WAS TOO HARD TO SAY GOODBYE TO HIM.
AND PLUS...
...ANOTHER GIRL IN MY CLASS...
...LIKED KUROMINE-KUN.

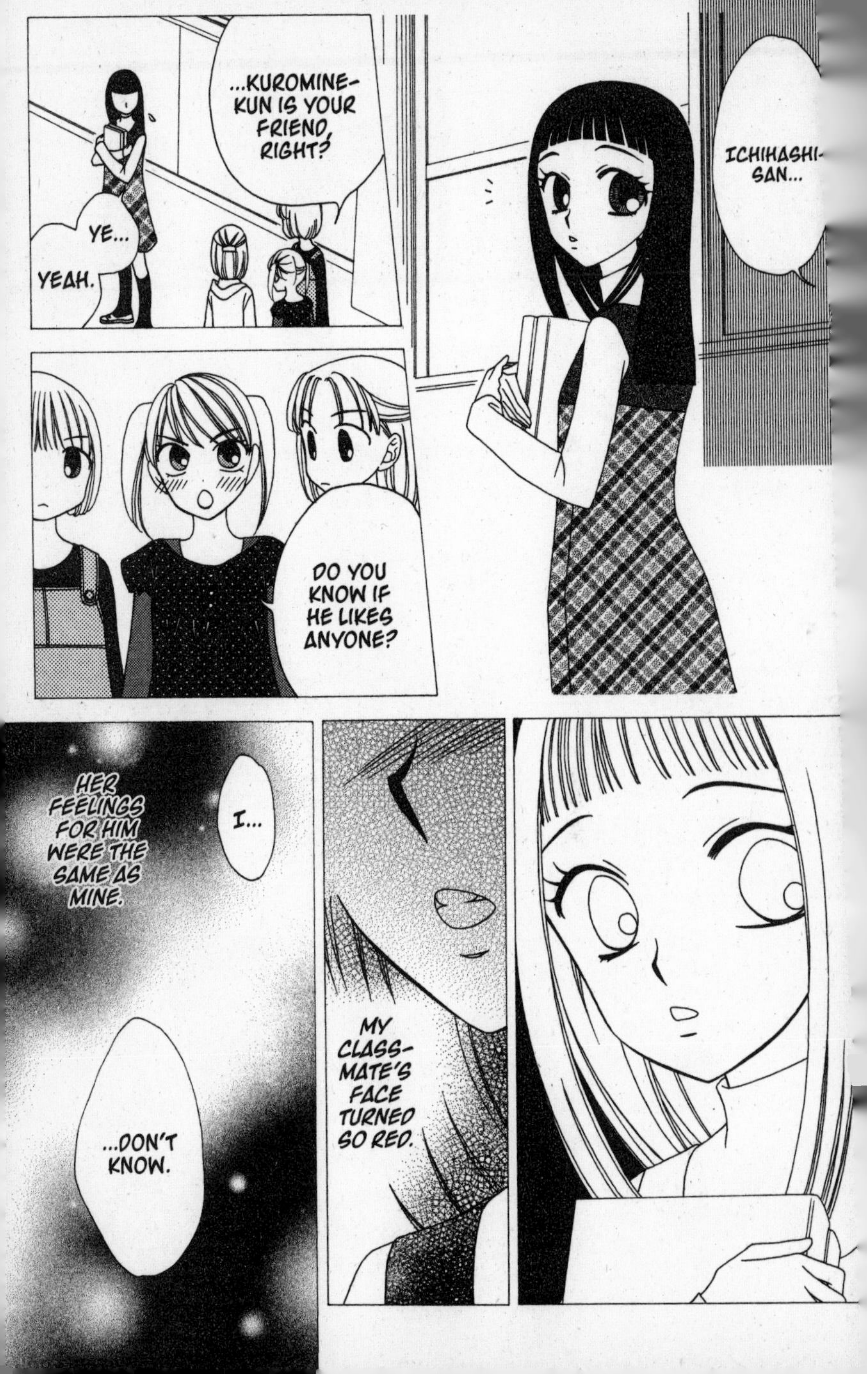
ICHIHASHI-SAN...
...KUROMINE-KUN IS YOUR FRIEND, RIGHT?
YE... YEAH.
DO YOU KNOW IF HE LIKES ANYONE?
MY CLASSMATE'S FACE TURNED SO RED.
I...
HER FEELINGS FOR HIM WERE THE SAME AS MINE.
...DON'T KNOW.

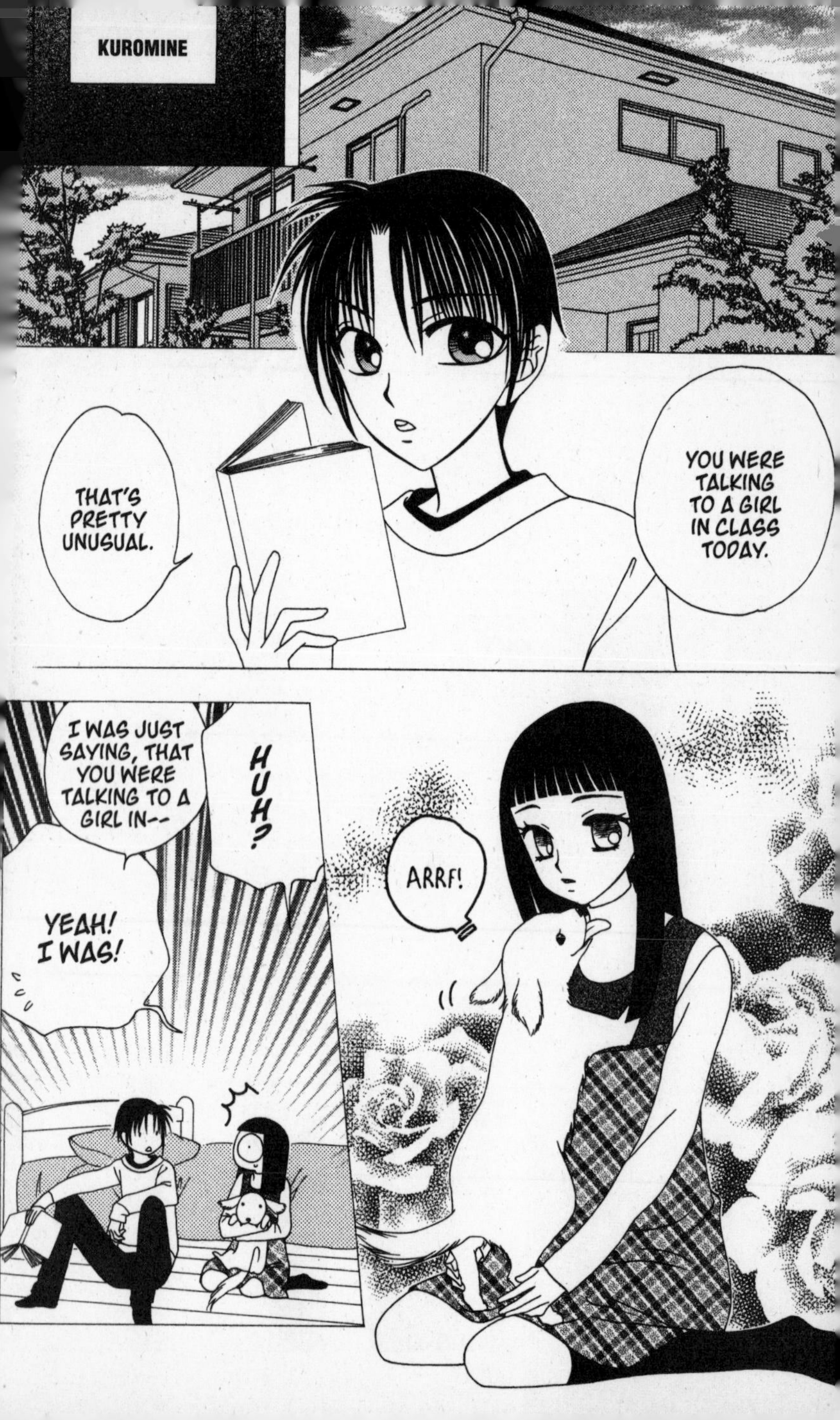
KUROMINE
YOU WERE TALKING TO A GIRL IN CLASS TODAY.
THAT'S PRETTY UNUSUAL.
ARRF!
HUH?
I WAS JUST SAYING, THAT YOU WERE TALKING TO A GIRL IN--
YEAH! I WAS!

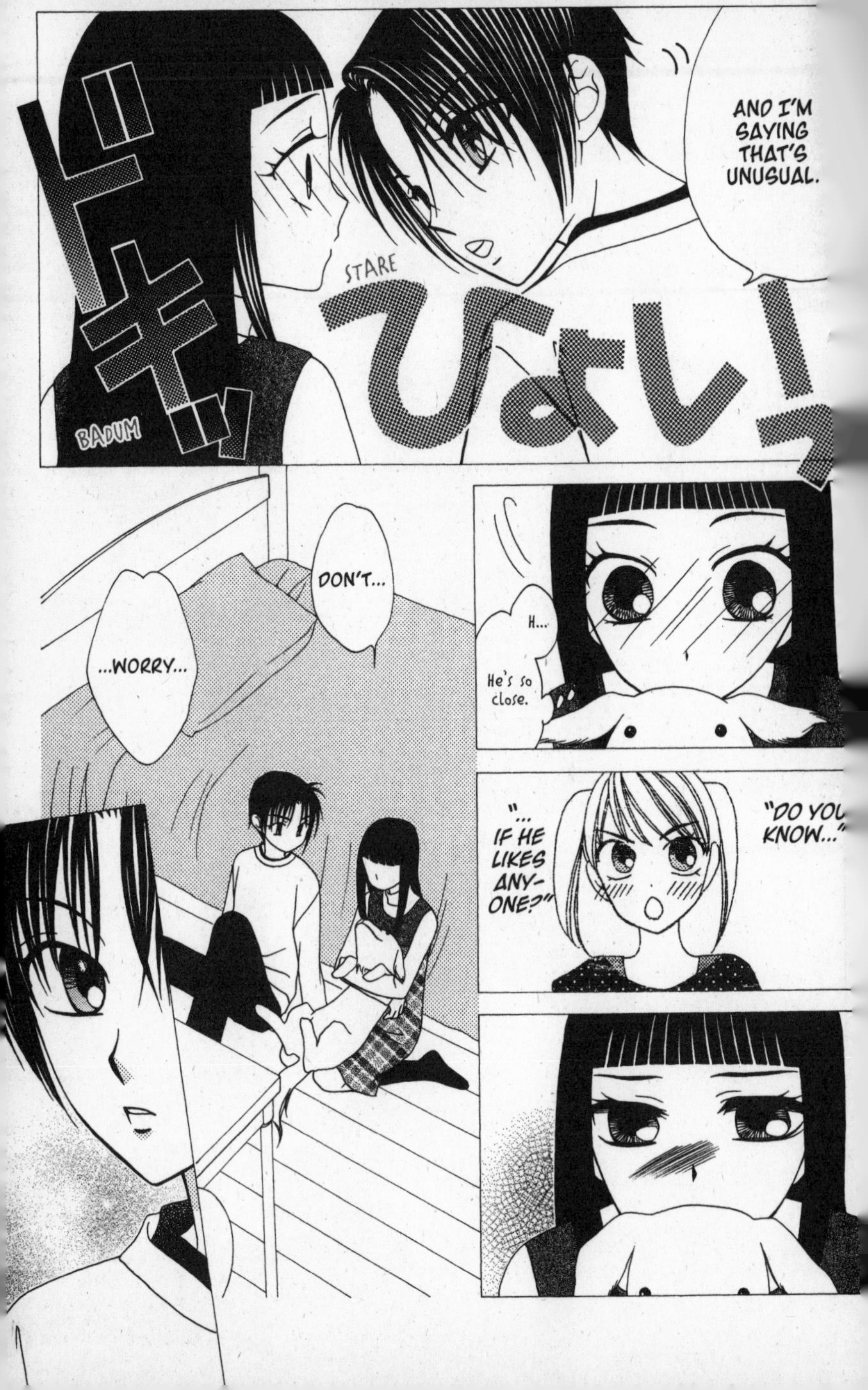
AND I'M SAYING THAT'S UNUSUAL.
STARE
BADUM
H...
He's so close.
"DO YOU KNOW..."
"...IF HE LIKES ANY-ONE?"
DON'T...
...WORRY...

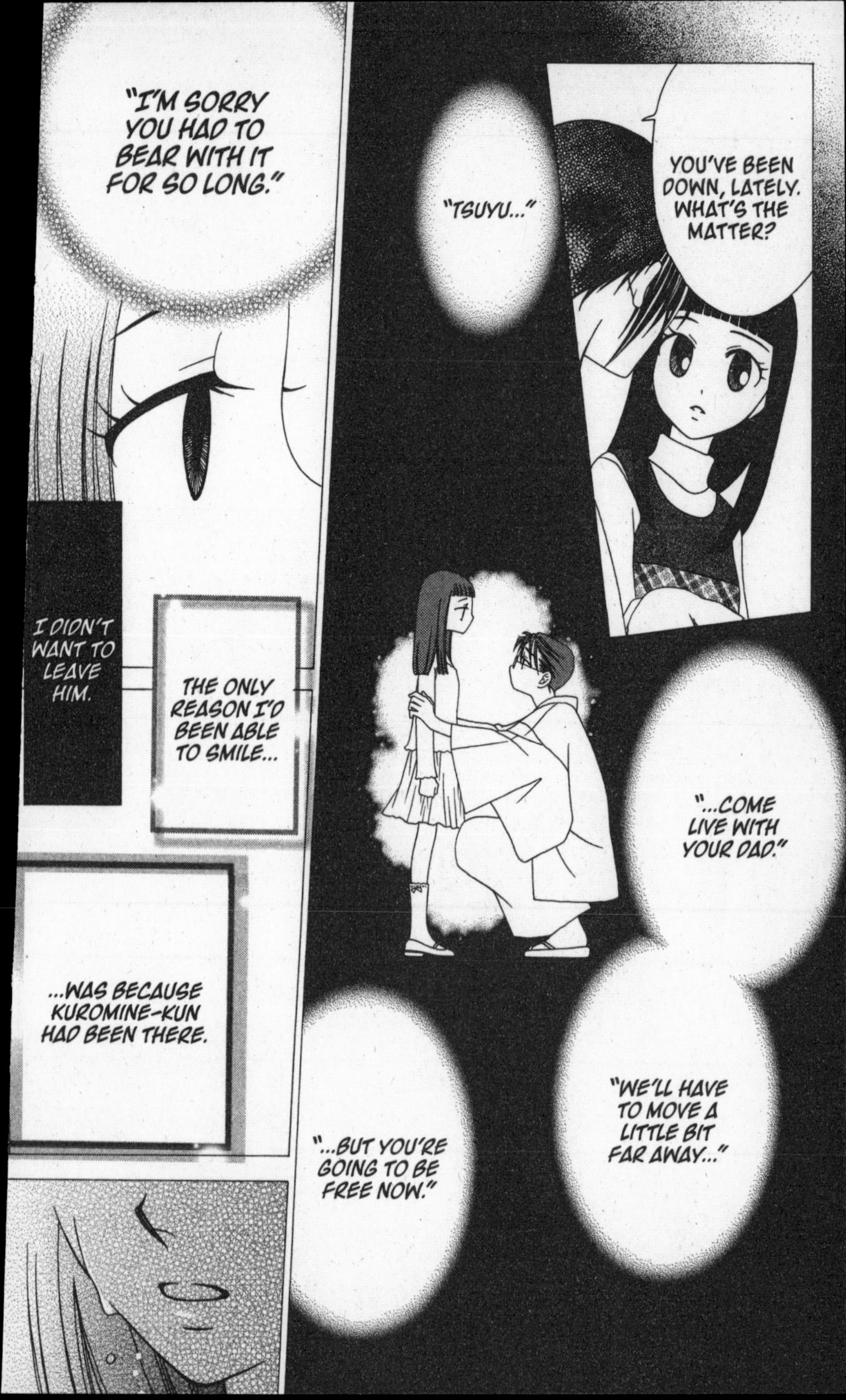
YOU'VE BEEN DOWN, LATELY. WHAT'S THE MATTER?
"TSUYU..."
"...COME LIVE WITH YOUR DAD."
"WE'LL HAVE TO MOVE A LITTLE BIT FAR AWAY..."
"...BUT YOU'RE GOING TO BE FREE NOW."
"I'M SORRY YOU HAD TO BEAR WITH IT FOR SO LONG."
THE ONLY REASON I'D BEEN ABLE TO SMILE...
I DIDN'T WANT TO LEAVE HIM.
...WAS BECAUSE KUROMINE-KUN HAD BEEN THERE.

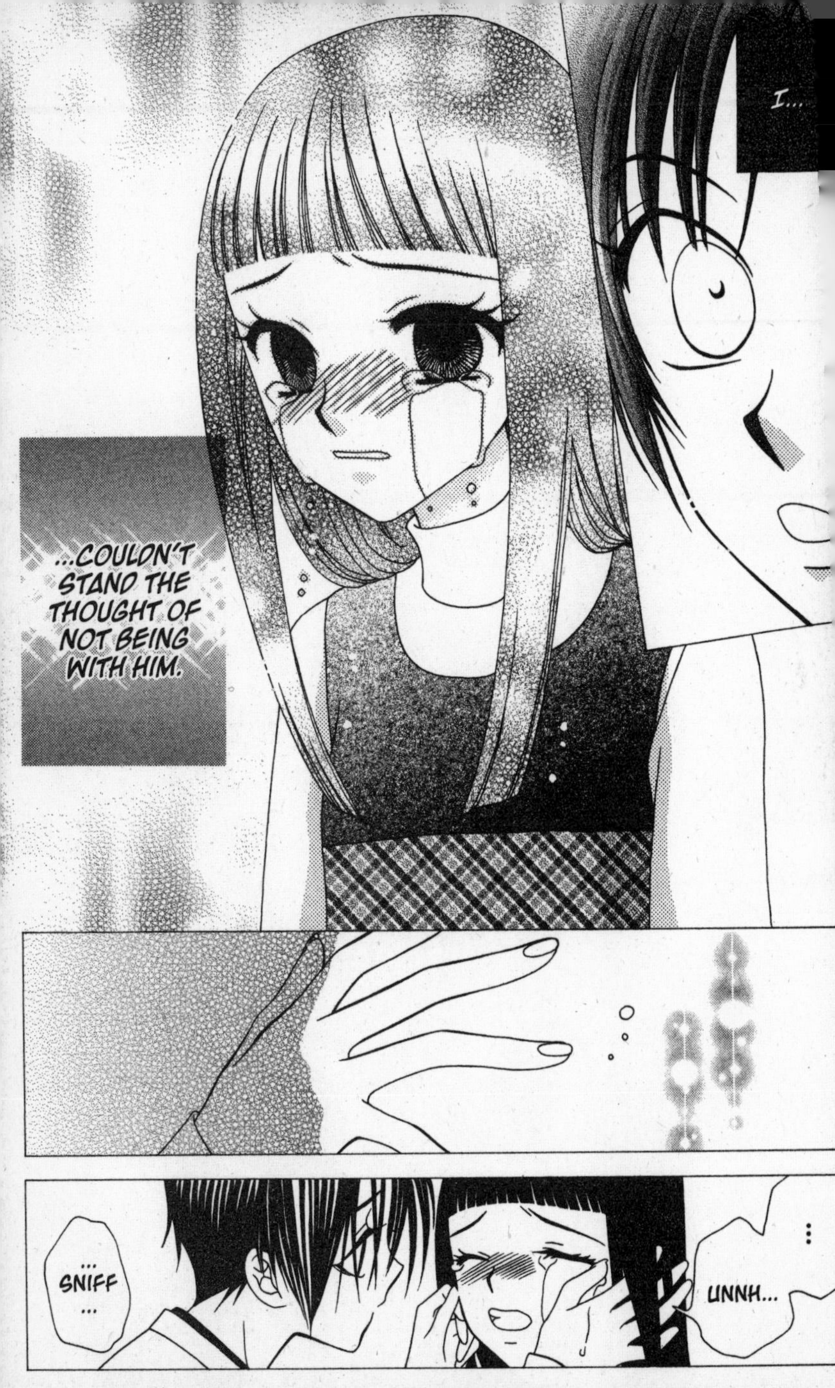
I...
...COULDN'T STAND THE THOUGHT OF NOT BEING WITH HIM.
...
UNNH...
...SNIFF...

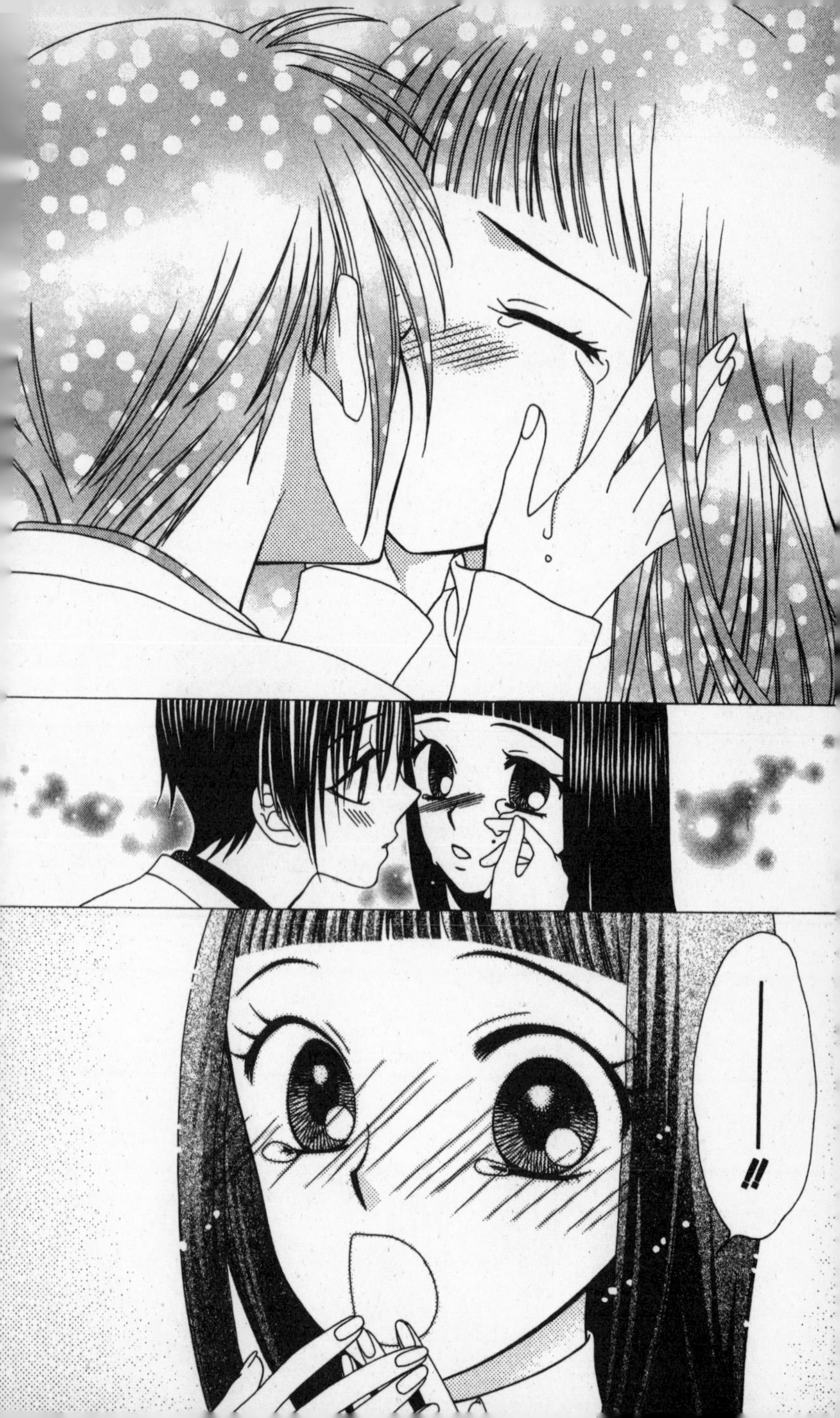
—!!

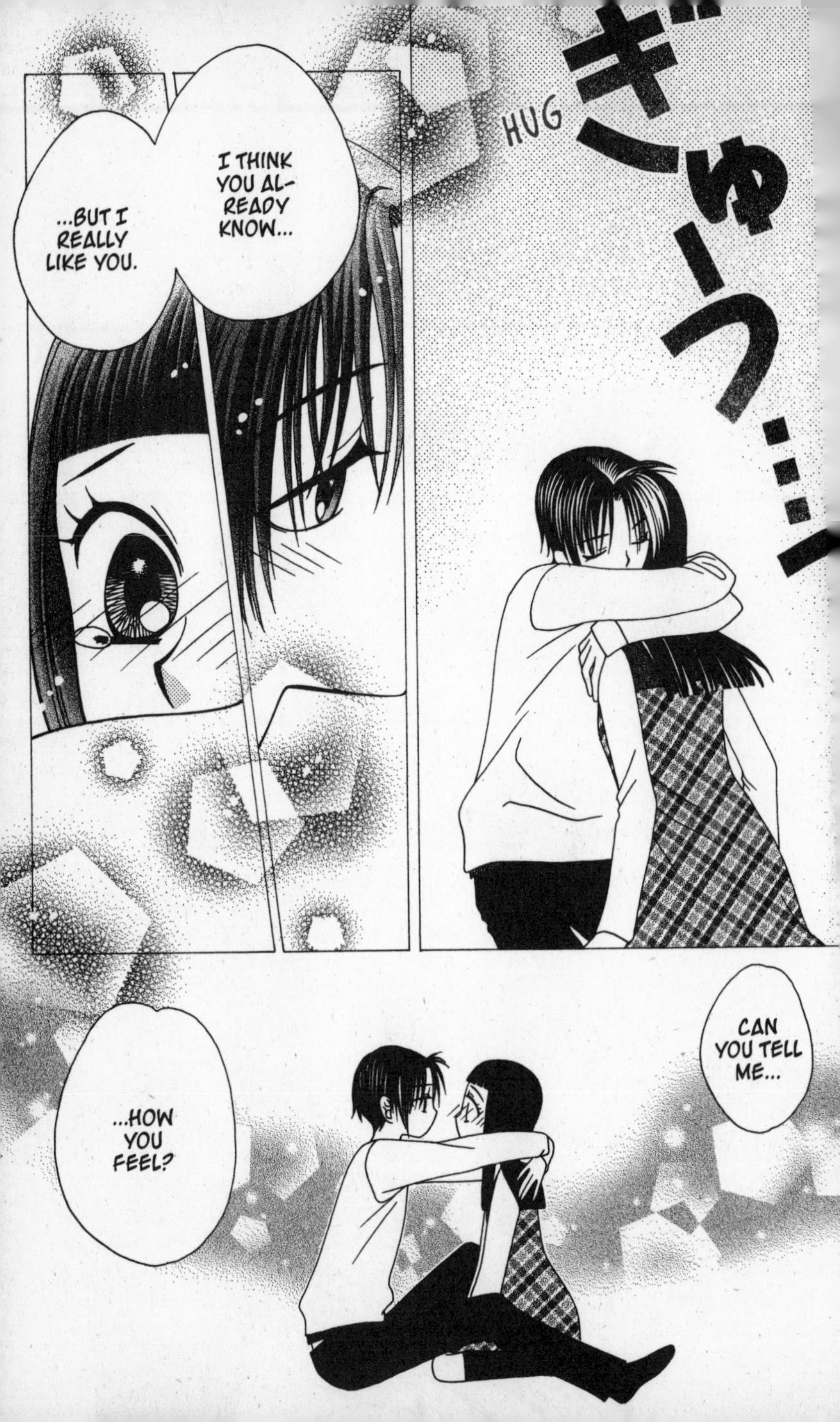
ぎゅーっ…!!
HUG
I THINK YOU AL-READY KNOW...
...BUT I REALLY LIKE YOU.
CAN YOU TELL ME...
...HOW YOU FEEL?

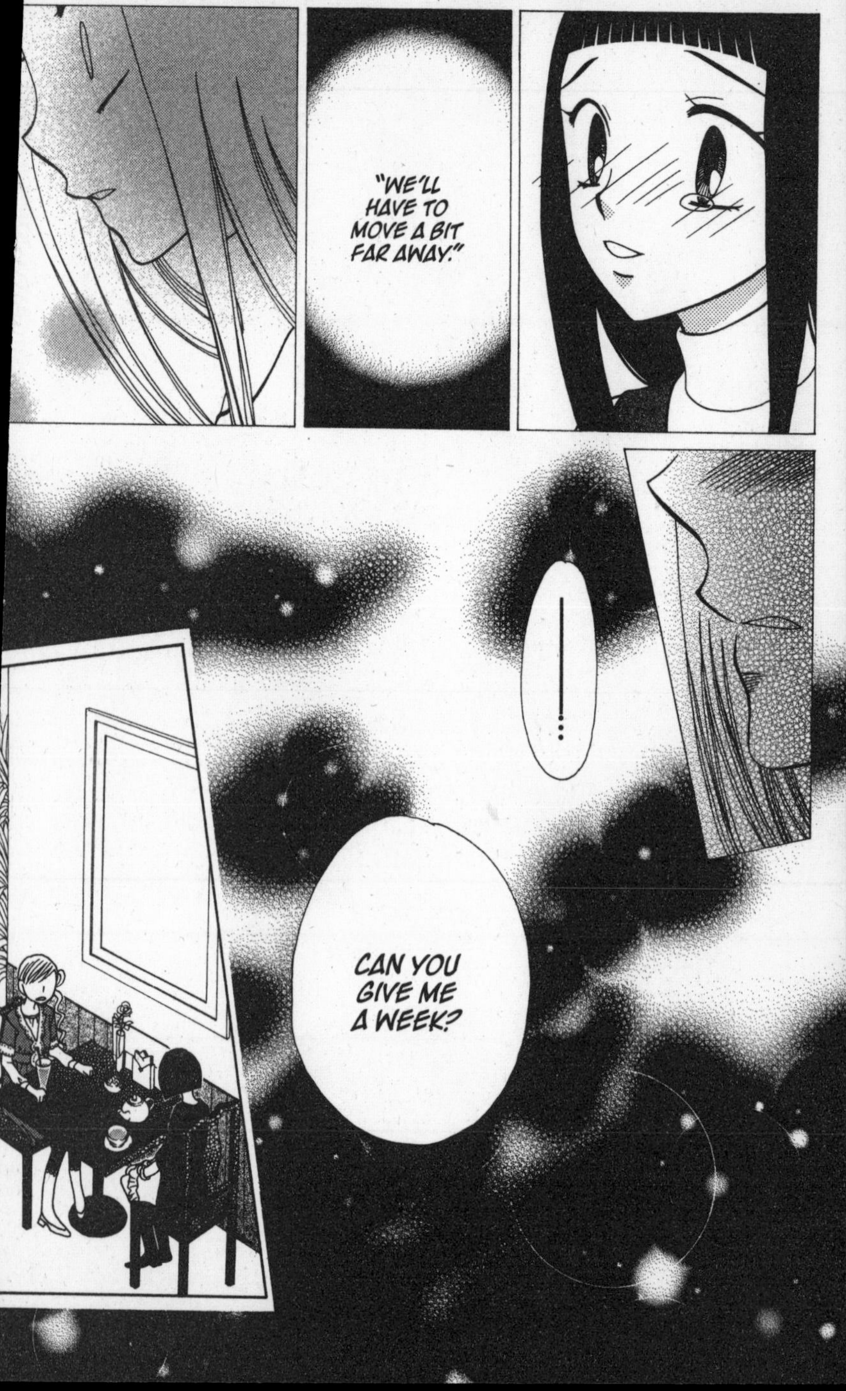
"WE'LL HAVE TO MOVE A BIT FAR AWAY."
......
CAN YOU GIVE ME A WEEK?

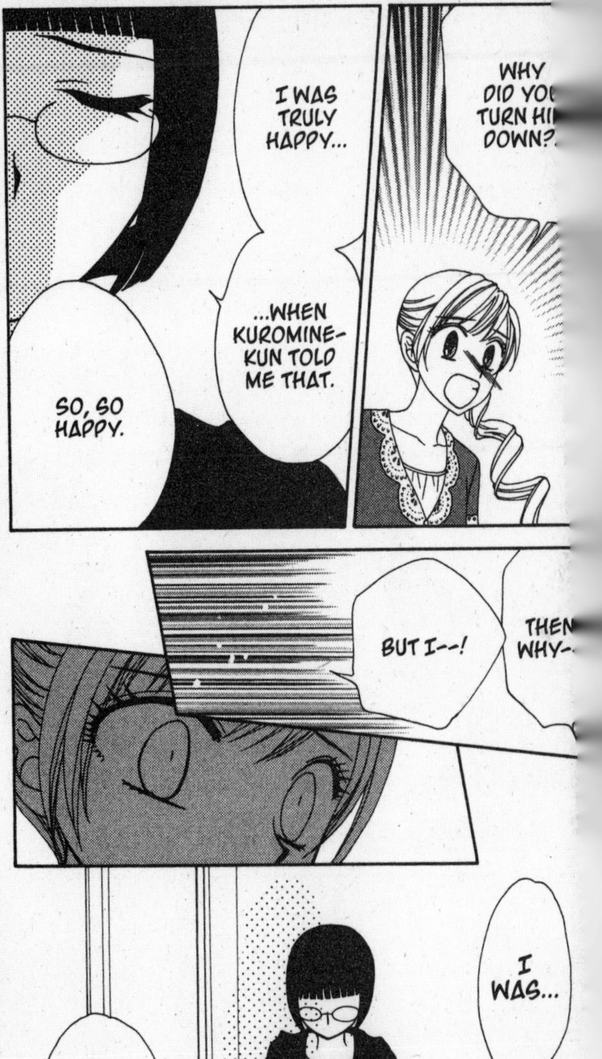
WHY DID YO TURN HI DOWN?
I WAS TRULY HAPPY...
...WHEN KUROMINE-KUN TOLD ME THAT.
SO, SO HAPPY.
THEN WHY-
BUT I--!
I WAS...
...GOING TO BE LEAVING.

I'm sorry I filled all of the columns with the story of my accident. I tried my best to make it sound non-depressing...did it not work?

I don't know how to say this...but for those of you who are reading this--!! You may run into challenging and painful situations, but you'll get through them! Yargh!!! Life is beautiful!! Thank you so much for traveling along this road with me!

Hmm... That didn't sound very professional.

Anways, everyone. ♡ Let's all drive safely and follow the rules of the road with Hidaka!! ☆

So!

The new car that I awaited with baited breath for arrived in December, and I'm still driving it like it belongs to the dealer. Yes, that cautiously. Meanwhile, my mom will scream at me from the passenger seat, "Hey! Hey! Aren't you driving too fast?! I just know it's too fast!" when I'm driving at 50~60km/hr.

It's kind of crazy.

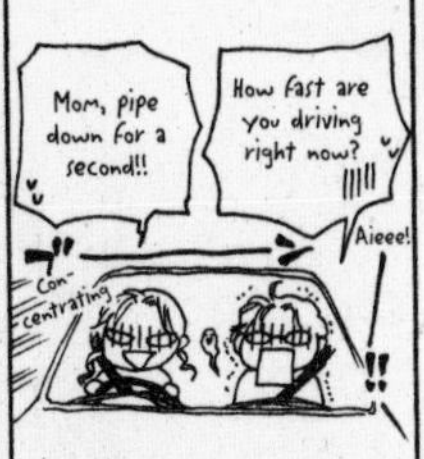
Mom, pipe down for a second!!
How fast are you driving right now?
Aieee!
Concentrating

We're both traumatized! (We're victims, after all.) So anyways, that was my 2007.

end

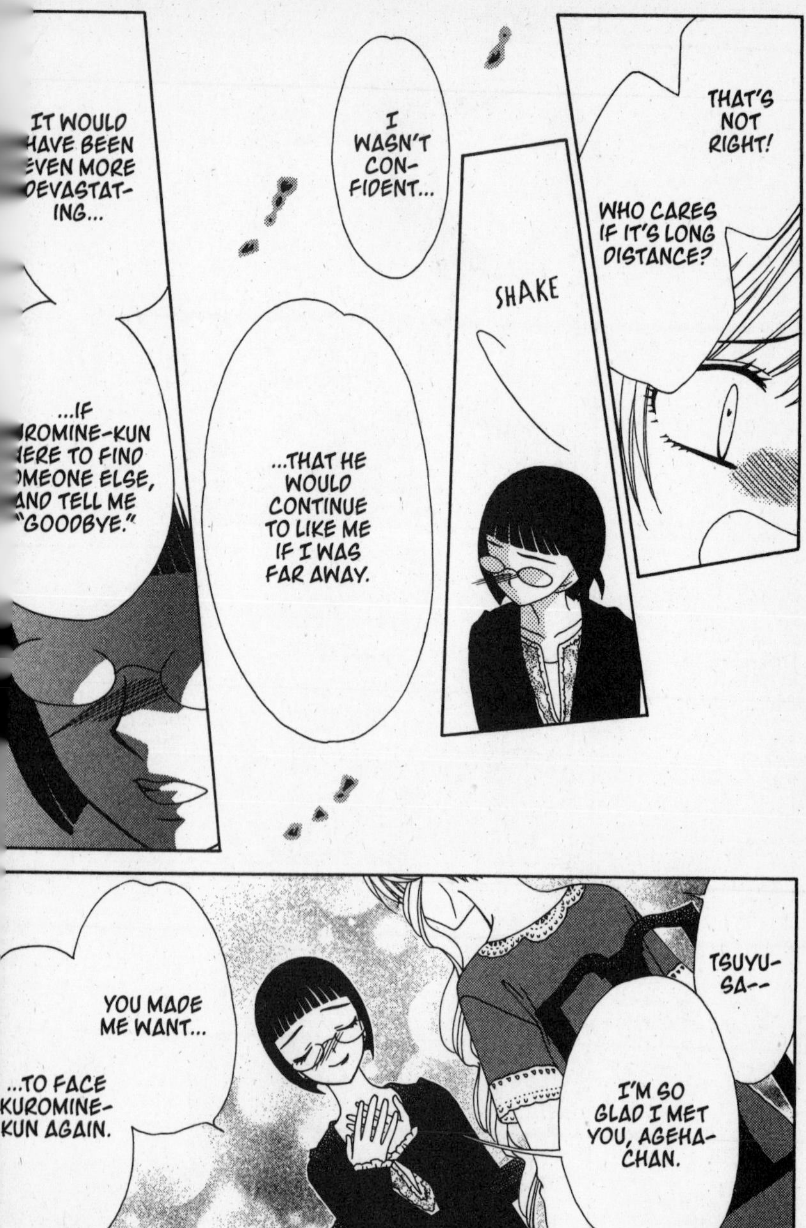
THAT'S NOT RIGHT!
WHO CARES IF IT'S LONG DISTANCE?
SHAKE
I WASN'T CONFIDENT...
...THAT HE WOULD CONTINUE TO LIKE ME IF I WAS FAR AWAY.
IT WOULD HAVE BEEN EVEN MORE DEVASTATING...
...IF KUROMINE-KUN WERE TO FIND SOMEONE ELSE, AND TELL ME "GOODBYE."
TSUYU-SA--
I'M SO GLAD I MET YOU, AGEHA-CHAN.
YOU MADE ME WANT...
...TO FACE KUROMINE-KUN AGAIN.

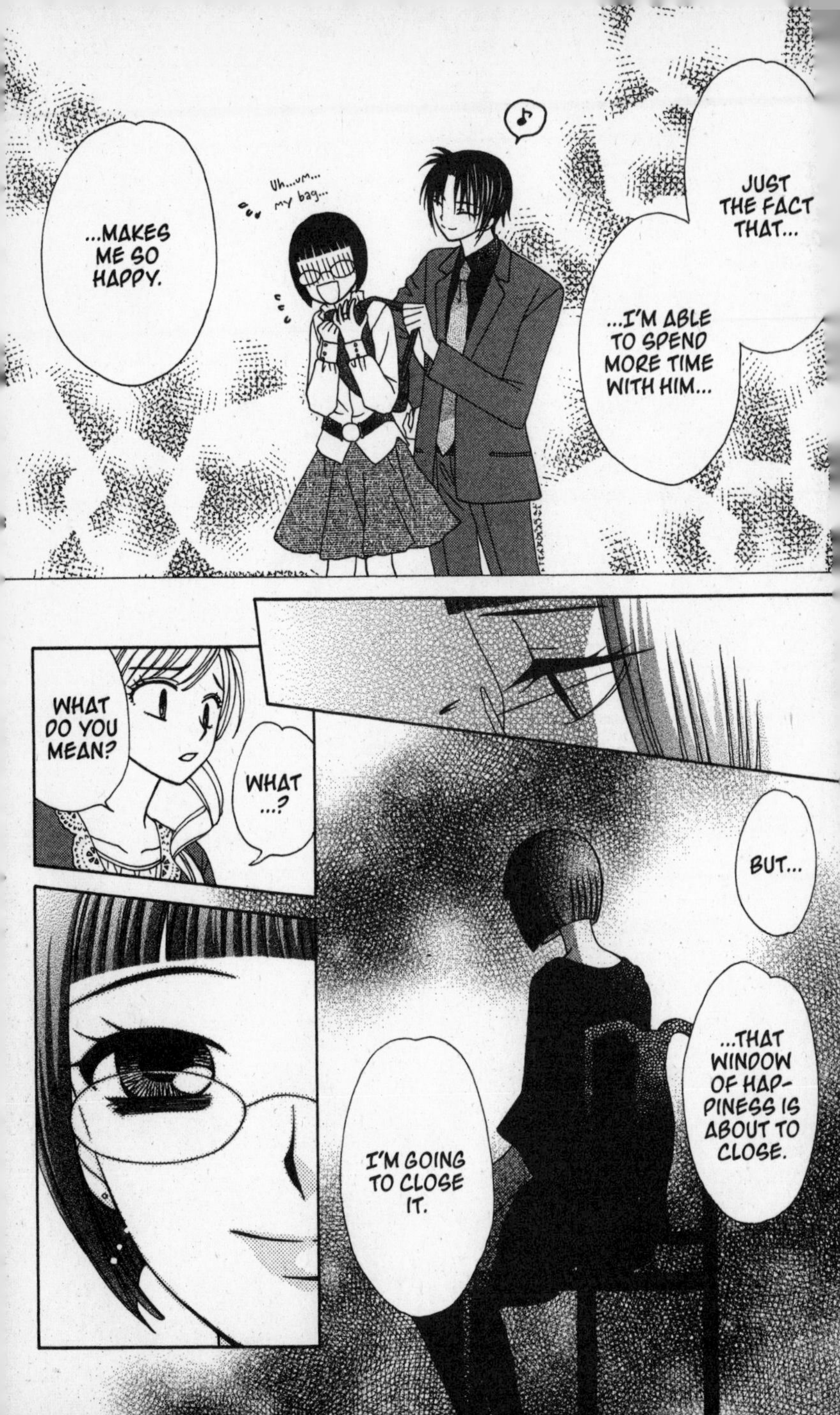
JUST THE FACT THAT...
...I'M ABLE TO SPEND MORE TIME WITH HIM...
♪
Uh...um... my bag...
...MAKES ME SO HAPPY.
WHAT ...?
WHAT DO YOU MEAN?
BUT...
...THAT WINDOW OF HAP-PINESS IS ABOUT TO CLOSE.
I'M GOING TO CLOSE IT.

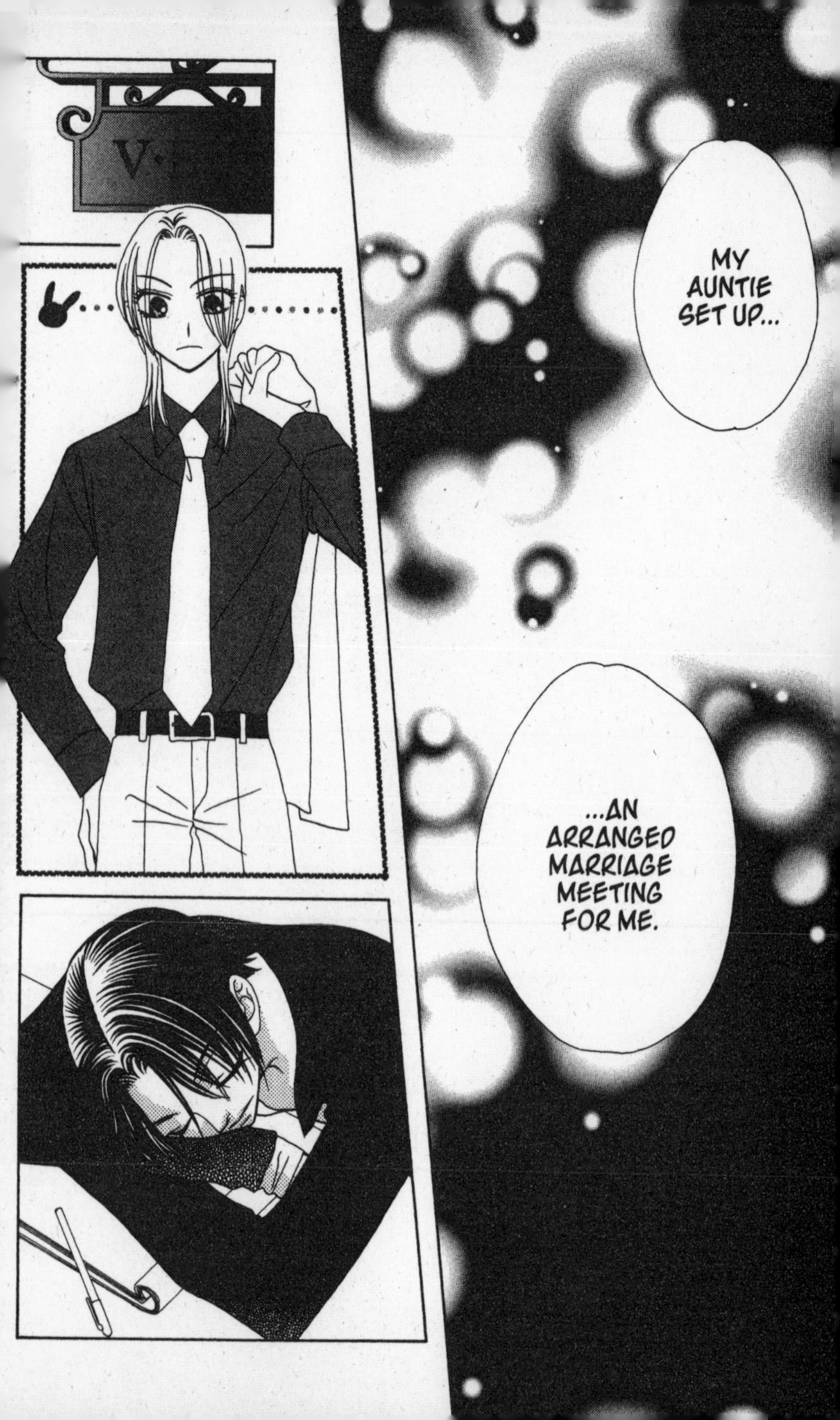
MY AUNTIE SET UP...
...AN ARRANGED MARRIAGE MEETING FOR ME.

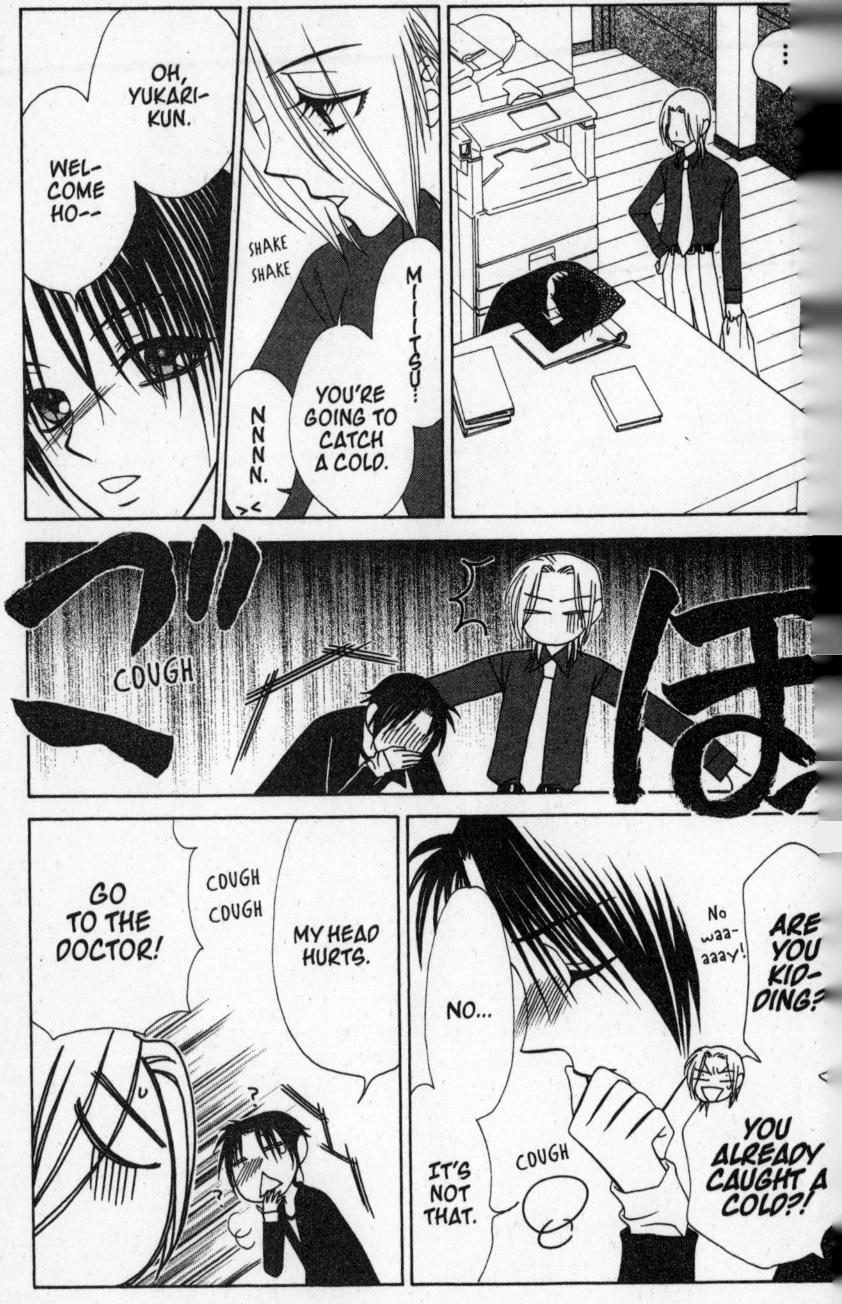
...
MIIITSU...
YOU'RE GOING TO CATCH A COLD.
NNNN.
SHAKE SHAKE
OH, YUKARI-KUN.
WELCOME HO--
COUGH
ARE YOU KIDDING?
No waaaaay!
YOU ALREADY CAUGHT A COLD?!
NO...
COUGH
IT'S NOT THAT.
MY HEAD HURTS.
COUGH COUGH
GO TO THE DOCTOR!

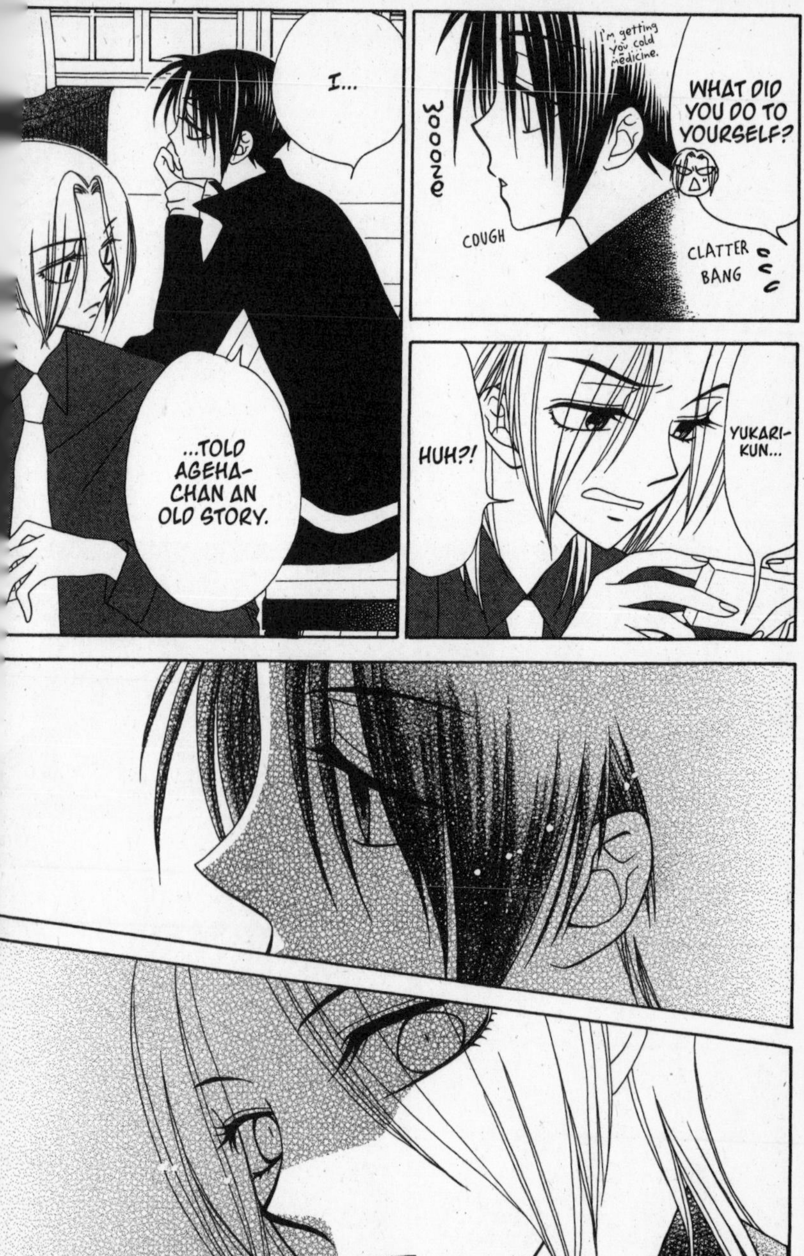
WHAT DID YOU DO TO YOURSELF?
I'm getting you cold medicine.
CLATTER BANG
COUGH
WOOOZE
YUKARI-KUN...
HUH?!
I...
...TOLD AGEHA-CHAN AN OLD STORY.

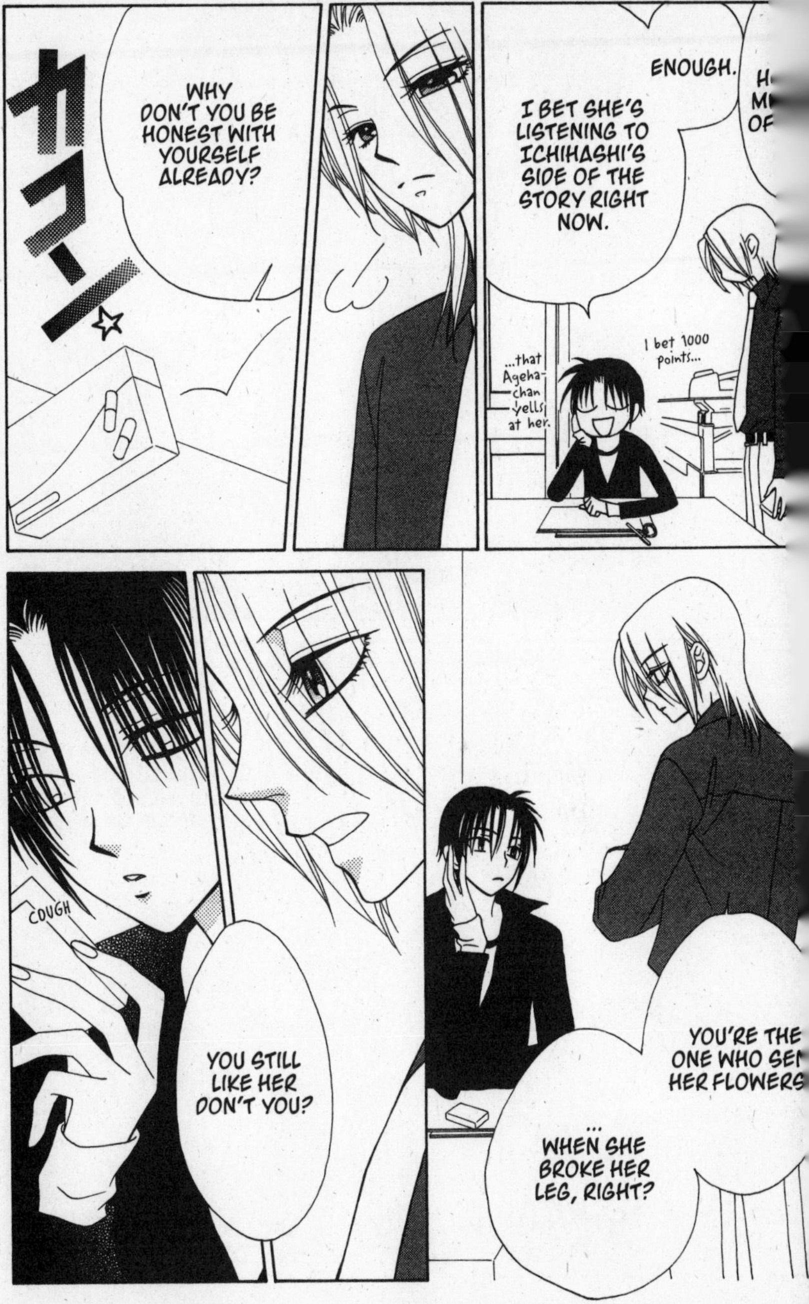
ENOUGH.
I BET SHE'S LISTENING TO ICHIHASHI'S SIDE OF THE STORY RIGHT NOW.
I bet 1000 points...
...that Ageha-chan yells at her.
WHY DON'T YOU BE HONEST WITH YOURSELF ALREADY?
カコーン☆
YOU'RE THE ONE WHO SEN HER FLOWERS
... WHEN SHE BROKE HER LEG, RIGHT?
YOU STILL LIKE HER DON'T YOU?
COUGH

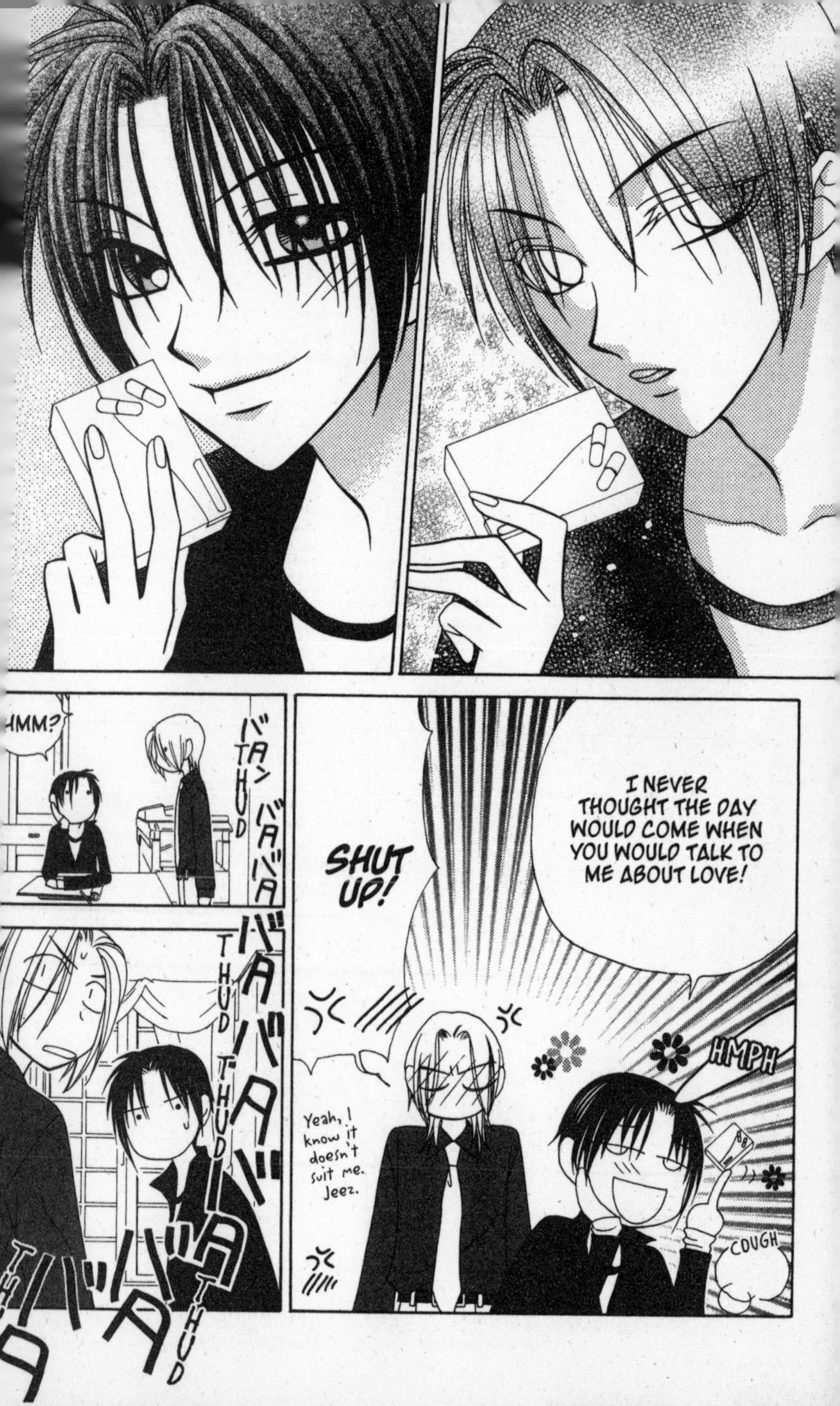
I NEVER THOUGHT THE DAY WOULD COME WHEN YOU WOULD TALK TO ME ABOUT LOVE!
SHUT UP!
HMPH
COUGH
Yeah, I know it doesn't suit me. Jeez.
HMM?
バタン
THUD
バタバタ
THUD
THUD
THUD

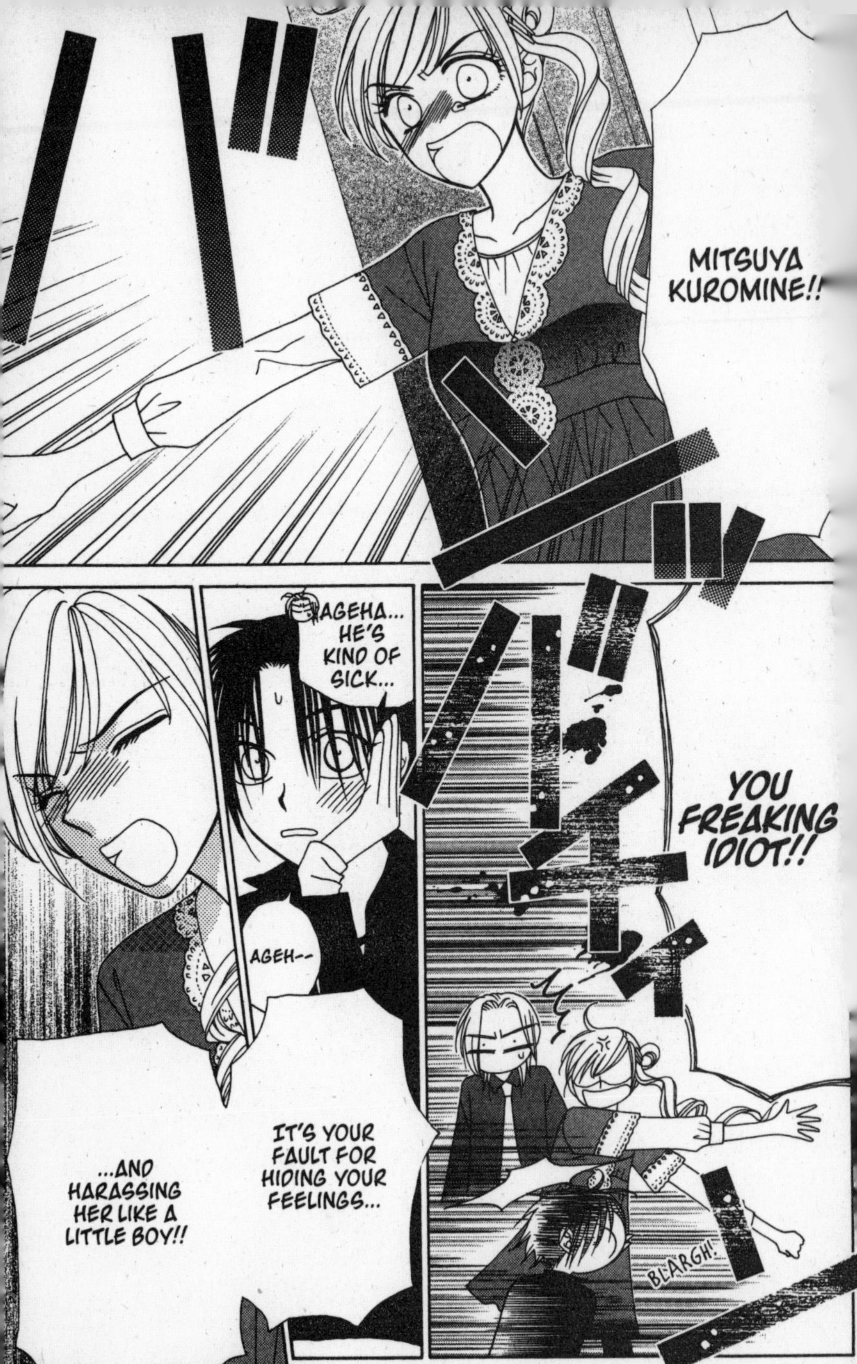
MITSUYA KUROMINE!!
YOU FREAKING IDIOT!!
BLARGH!
AGEHA... HE'S KIND OF SICK...
AGEH--
IT'S YOUR FAULT FOR HIDING YOUR FEELINGS...
...AND HARASSING HER LIKE A LITTLE BOY!!

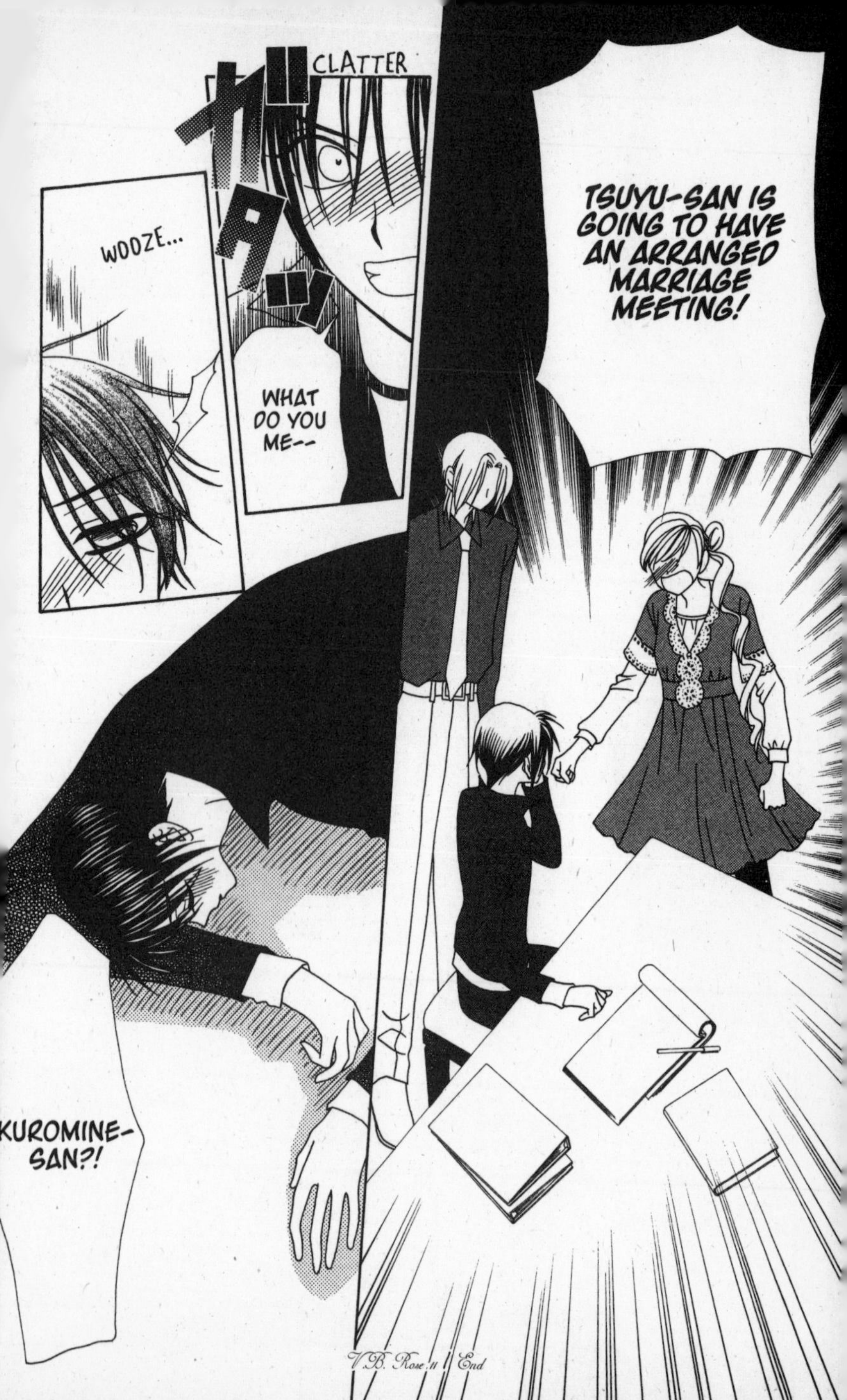
TSUYU-SAN IS GOING TO HAVE AN ARRANGED MARRIAGE MEETING!
CLATTER
WHAT DO YOU ME--
WOOZE...
KUROMINE-SAN?!

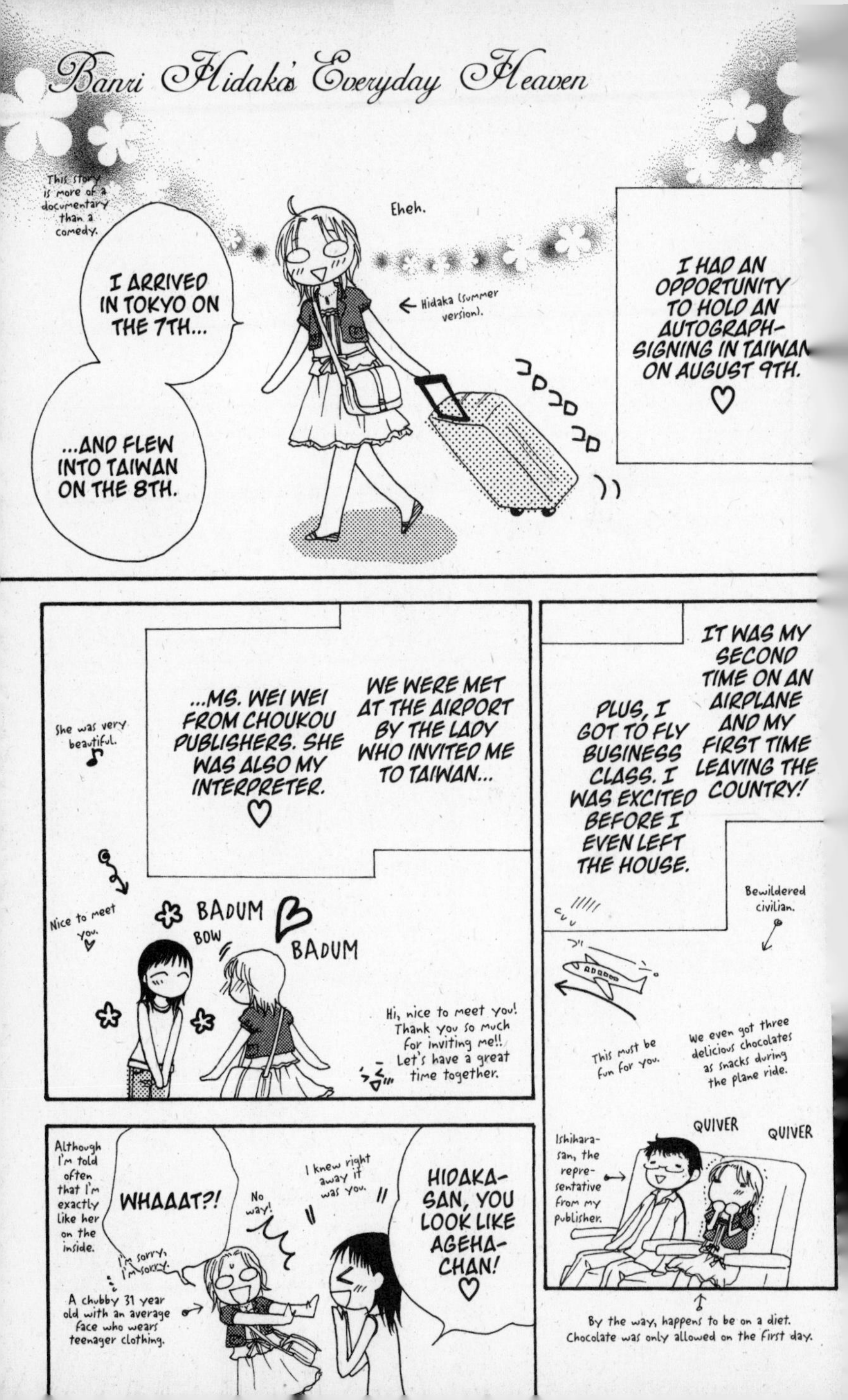
Banri Hidaka's Everyday Heaven
I HAD AN OPPORTUNITY TO HOLD AN AUTOGRAPH-SIGNING IN TAIWAN ON AUGUST 9TH. ♡
Eheh.
← Hidaka (summer version).
コロコロ
This story is more of a documentary than a comedy.
I ARRIVED IN TOKYO ON THE 7TH...
...AND FLEW INTO TAIWAN ON THE 8TH.
IT WAS MY SECOND TIME ON AN AIRPLANE AND MY FIRST TIME LEAVING THE COUNTRY!
PLUS, I GOT TO FLY BUSINESS CLASS. I WAS EXCITED BEFORE I EVEN LEFT THE HOUSE.
Bewildered civilian.
We even got three delicious chocolates as snacks during the plane ride.
This must be fun for you.
QUIVER
QUIVER
Ishihara-san, the representative from my publisher.
By the way, happens to be on a diet. Chocolate was only allowed on the first day.
WE WERE MET AT THE AIRPORT BY THE LADY WHO INVITED ME TO TAIWAN...
...MS. WEI WEI FROM CHOUKOU PUBLISHERS. SHE WAS ALSO MY INTERPRETER. ♡
She was very beautiful. ♪
BADUM
BADUM
BOW
Hi, nice to meet you! Thank you so much for inviting me!! Let's have a great time together.
Nice to meet you. ♡
HIDAKA-SAN, YOU LOOK LIKE AGEHA-CHAN! ♡
I knew right away it was you.
No way!
WHAAAT?!
I'm sorry, I'm sorry.
Although I'm told often that I'm exactly like her on the inside.
A chubby 31 year old with an average face who wears teenager clothing.

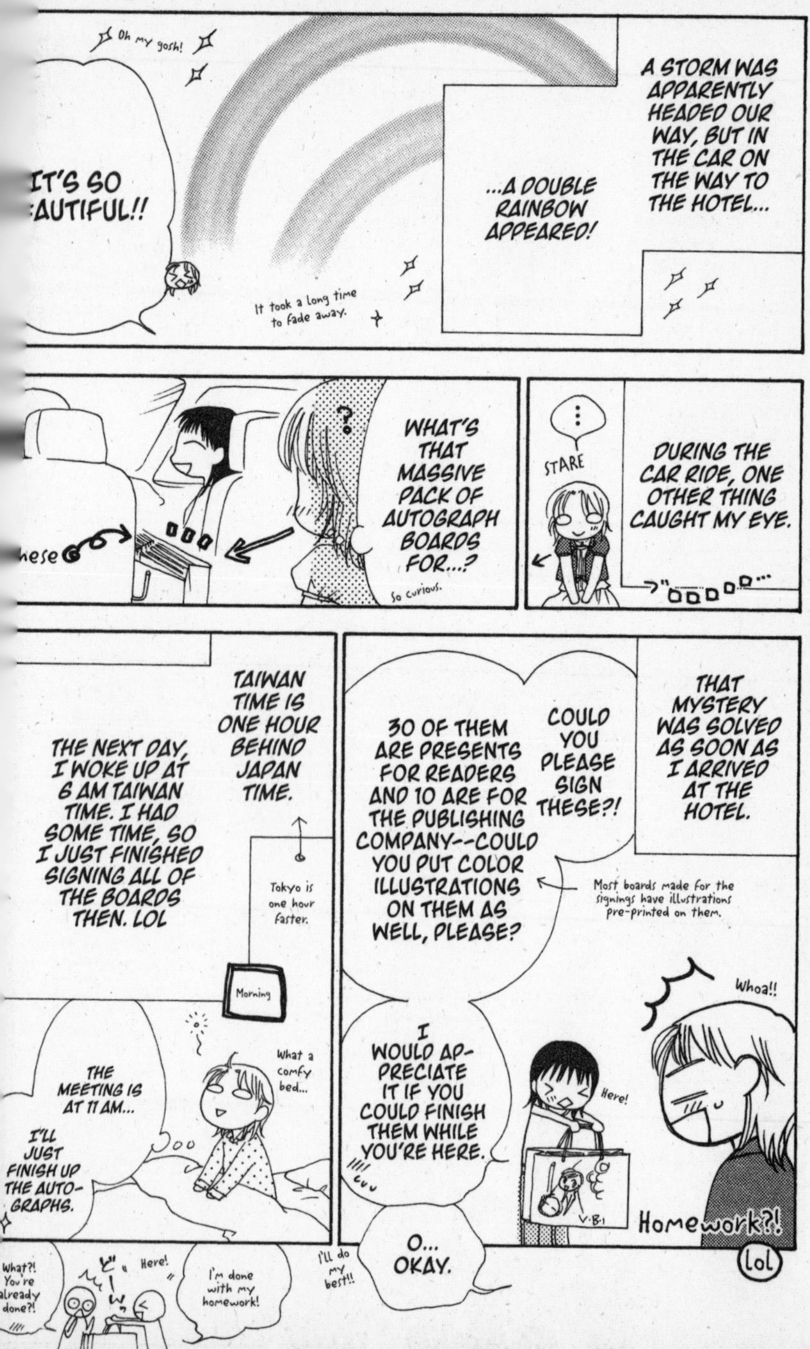
A STORM WAS APPARENTLY HEADED OUR WAY, BUT IN THE CAR ON THE WAY TO THE HOTEL...
...A DOUBLE RAINBOW APPEARED!
Oh my gosh!
IT'S SO
AUTIFUL!!
It took a long time to fade away.
DURING THE CAR RIDE, ONE OTHER THING CAUGHT MY EYE.
STARE
WHAT'S THAT MASSIVE PACK OF AUTOGRAPH BOARDS FOR...?
So curious.
hese
THAT MYSTERY WAS SOLVED AS SOON AS I ARRIVED AT THE HOTEL.
COULD YOU PLEASE SIGN THESE?!
30 OF THEM ARE PRESENTS FOR READERS AND 10 ARE FOR THE PUBLISHING COMPANY--COULD YOU PUT COLOR ILLUSTRATIONS ON THEM AS WELL, PLEASE?
Most boards made for the signings have illustrations pre-printed on them.
Whoa!!
Here!
I WOULD AP-PRECIATE IT IF YOU COULD FINISH THEM WHILE YOU'RE HERE.
O... OKAY.
I'll do my best!!
Homework?!
lol
TAIWAN TIME IS ONE HOUR BEHIND JAPAN TIME.
THE NEXT DAY, I WOKE UP AT 6 AM TAIWAN TIME. I HAD SOME TIME, SO I JUST FINISHED SIGNING ALL OF THE BOARDS THEN. LOL
Tokyo is one hour faster.
Morning
What a comfy bed...
THE MEETING IS AT 11 AM...
I'LL JUST FINISH UP THE AUTO-GRAPHS.
I'm done with my homework!
Here!
What?! You're already done?!

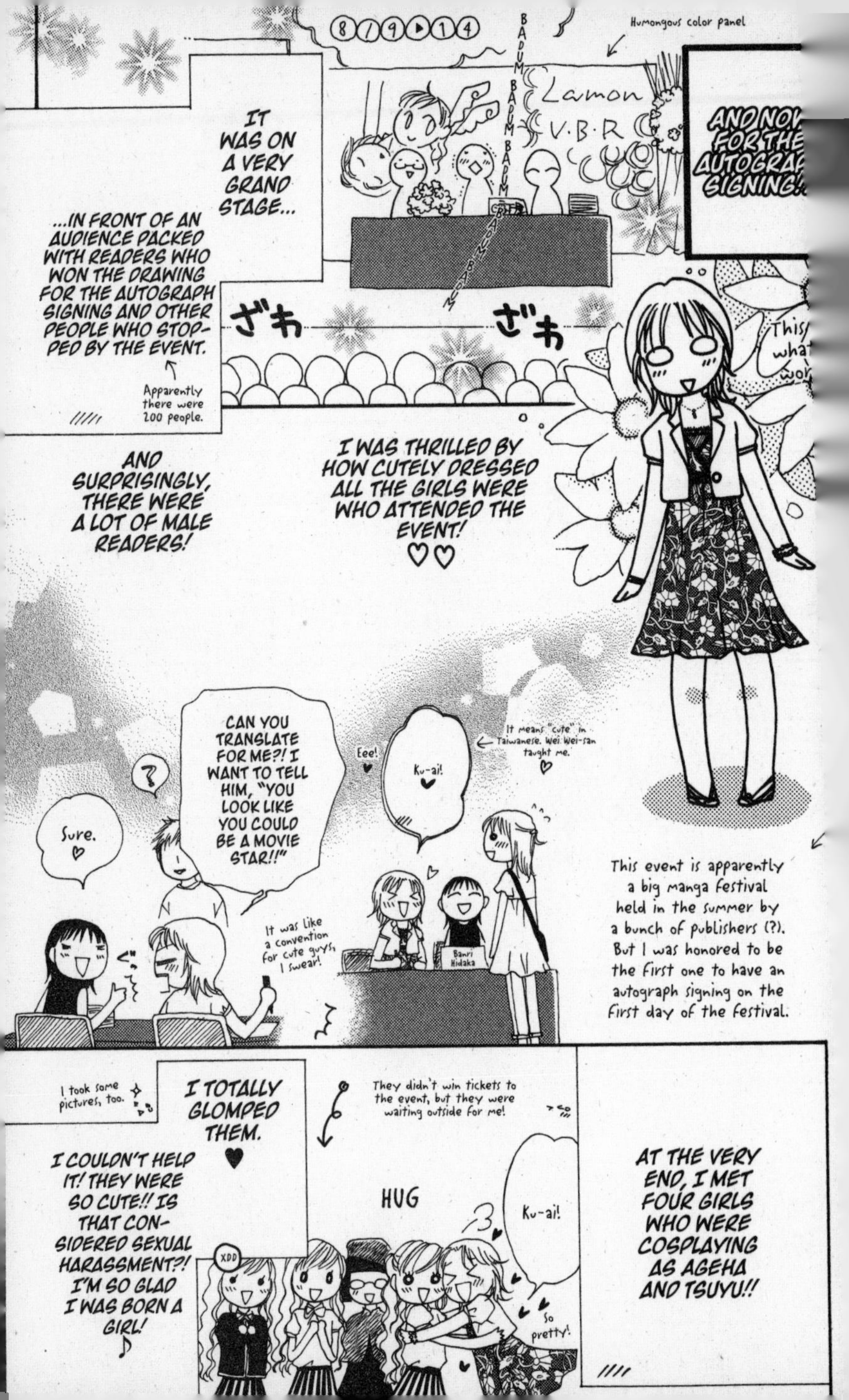

8/9▶14
Humongous color panel
AND NO FOR THE AUTOGRAP SIGNING
Lamon V.B.R
BADUM BADUM BADUM BADUM BADUM
IT WAS ON A VERY GRAND STAGE...
...IN FRONT OF AN AUDIENCE PACKED WITH READERS WHO WON THE DRAWING FOR THE AUTOGRAPH SIGNING AND OTHER PEOPLE WHO STOPPED BY THE EVENT.
Apparently there were 200 people.
ざわ ざわ
This
I WAS THRILLED BY HOW CUTELY DRESSED ALL THE GIRLS WERE WHO ATTENDED THE EVENT! ♡♡
AND SURPRISINGLY, THERE WERE A LOT OF MALE READERS!
This event is apparently a big manga festival held in the summer by a bunch of publishers (?). But I was honored to be the first one to have an autograph signing on the first day of the festival.
It means "cute" in Taiwanese. Wei Wei-san taught me.
Ku-ai!
Eee!
Banri Hidaka
It was like a convention for cute guys, I swear!
CAN YOU TRANSLATE FOR ME?! I WANT TO TELL HIM, "YOU LOOK LIKE YOU COULD BE A MOVIE STAR!!"
?
Sure.
AT THE VERY END, I MET FOUR GIRLS WHO WERE COSPLAYING AS AGEHA AND TSUYU!!
Ku-ai!
So pretty!
They didn't win tickets to the event, but they were waiting outside for me!
HUG
I TOTALLY GLOMPED THEM.
I took some pictures, too.
I COULDN'T HELP IT! THEY WERE SO CUTE!! IS THAT CONSIDERED SEXUAL HARASSMENT?! I'M SO GLAD I WAS BORN A GIRL! ♪
XDD

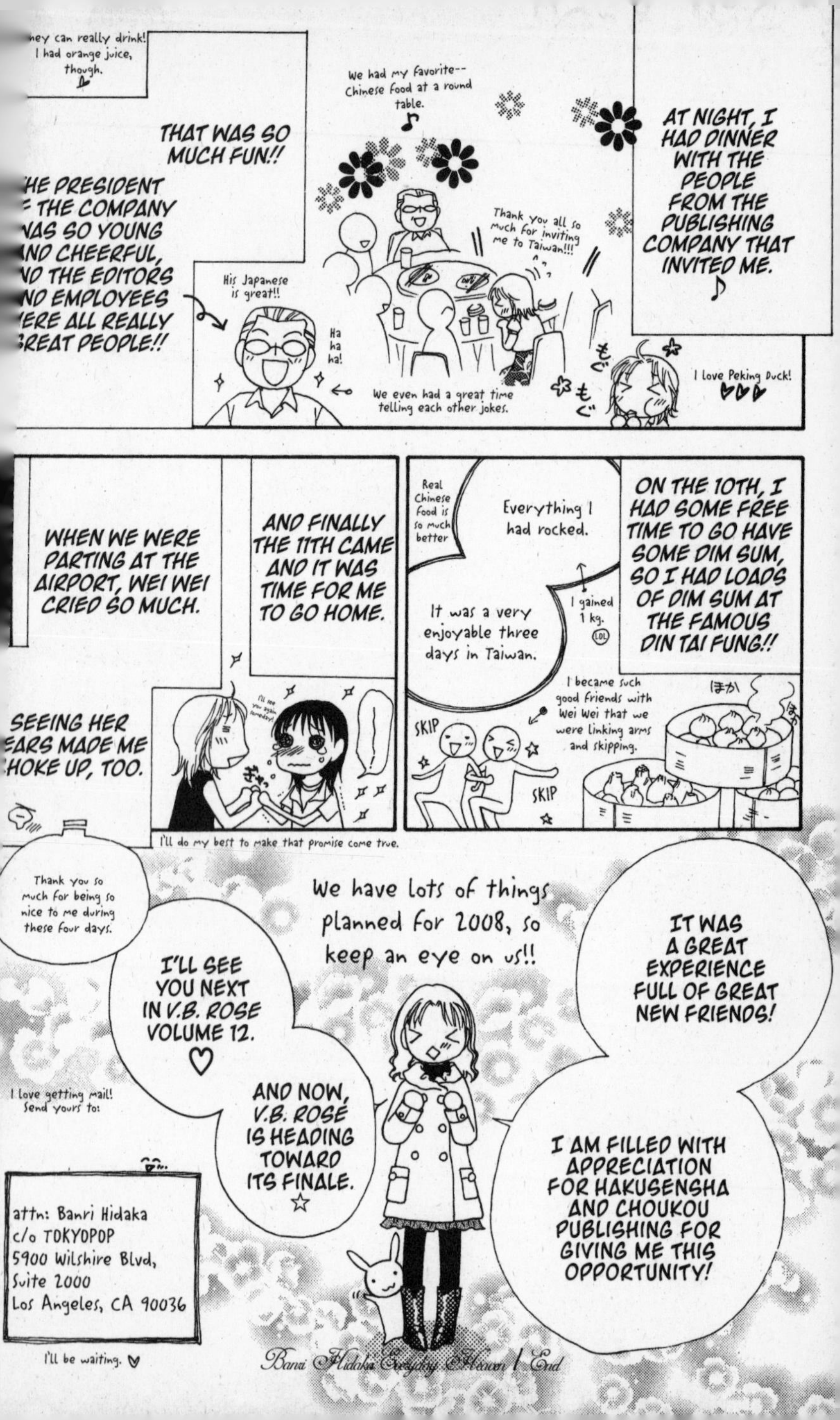
AT NIGHT, I HAD DINNER WITH THE PEOPLE FROM THE PUBLISHING COMPANY THAT INVITED ME. ♪
We had my favorite-- Chinese food at a round table. ♪
Thank you all so much for inviting me to Taiwan!!!
もぐ もぐ
I love Peking Duck!
ney can really drink! I had orange juice, though.
THAT WAS SO MUCH FUN!!
HE PRESIDENT F THE COMPANY NAS SO YOUNG AND CHEERFUL, ND THE EDITORS ND EMPLOYEES ERE ALL REALLY REAT PEOPLE!!
His Japanese is great!!
Ha ha ha!
We even had a great time telling each other jokes.
ON THE 10TH, I HAD SOME FREE TIME TO GO HAVE SOME DIM SUM, SO I HAD LOADS OF DIM SUM AT THE FAMOUS DIN TAI FUNG!!
Everything I had rocked.
Real Chinese food is so much better
I gained 1 kg. LOL
It was a very enjoyable three days in Taiwan.
I became such good friends with Wei Wei that we were linking arms and skipping.
SKIP
SKIP
ほか
AND FINALLY THE 11TH CAME AND IT WAS TIME FOR ME TO GO HOME.
WHEN WE WERE PARTING AT THE AIRPORT, WEI WEI CRIED SO MUCH.
I'll see you again someday!
SEEING HER EARS MADE ME HOKE UP, TOO.
I'll do my best to make that promise come true.
IT WAS A GREAT EXPERIENCE FULL OF GREAT NEW FRIENDS!
I AM FILLED WITH APPRECIATION FOR HAKUSENSHA AND CHOUKOU PUBLISHING FOR GIVING ME THIS OPPORTUNITY!
We have lots of things planned for 2008, so keep an eye on us!!
AND NOW, V.B. ROSE IS HEADING TOWARD ITS FINALE. ☆
I'LL SEE YOU NEXT IN V.B. ROSE VOLUME 12. ♡
Thank you so much for being so nice to me during these four days.
I love getting mail! Send yours to:
attn: Banri Hidaka
c/o TOKYOPOP
5900 Wilshire Blvd,
Suite 2000
Los Angeles, CA 90036
I'll be waiting. ♡
Banri Hidaka Everyday Heaven / End

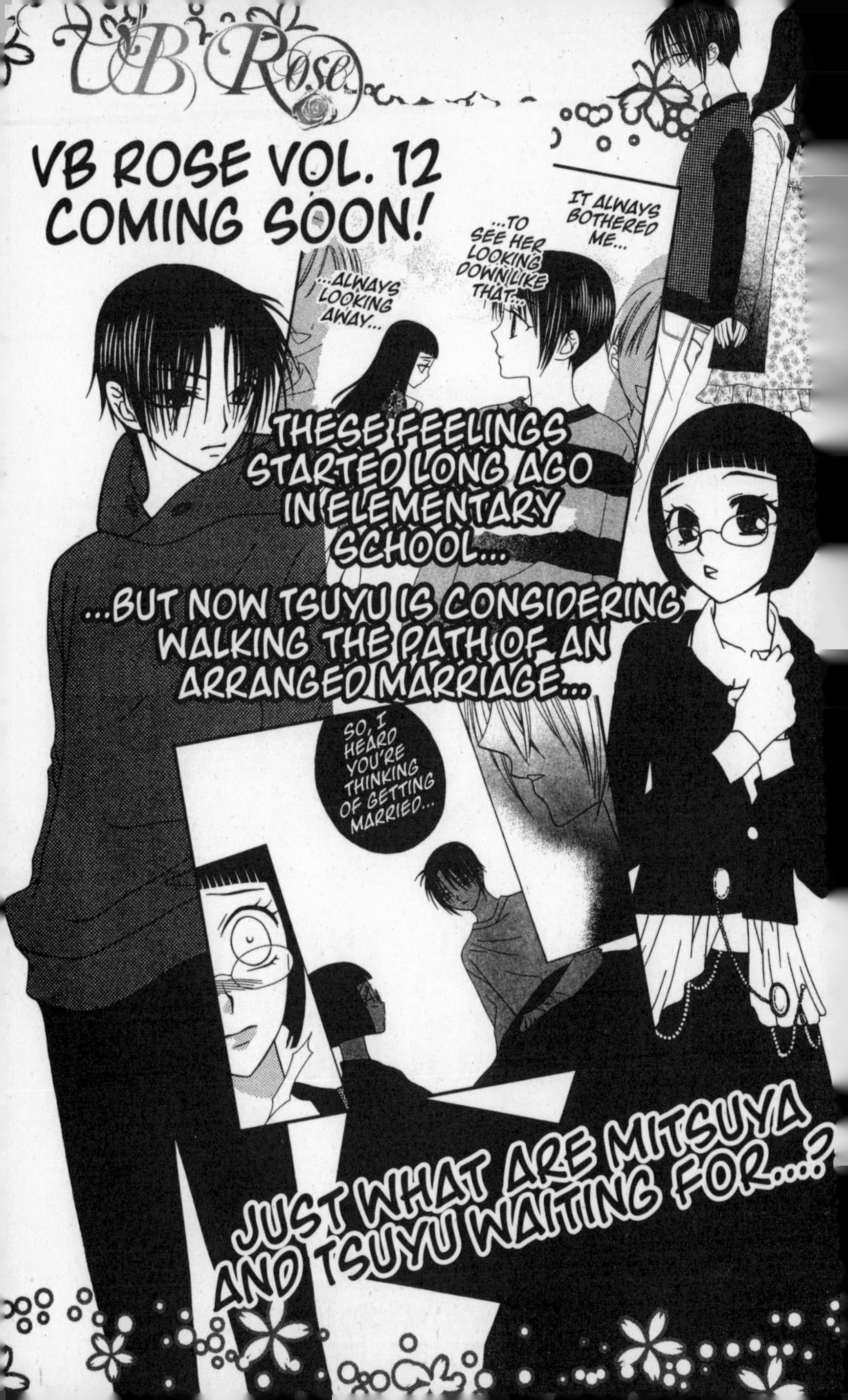
VB Rose
VB ROSE VOL. 12 COMING SOON!
IT ALWAYS BOTHERED ME...
...TO SEE HER LOOKING DOWN LIKE THAT...
...ALWAYS LOOKING AWAY...
THESE FEELINGS STARTED LONG AGO IN ELEMENTARY SCHOOL...
...BUT NOW TSUYU IS CONSIDERING WALKING THE PATH OF AN ARRANGED MARRIAGE...
SO, I HEARD YOU'RE THINKING OF GETTING MARRIED...
JUST WHAT ARE MITSUYA AND TSUYU WAITING FOR...?

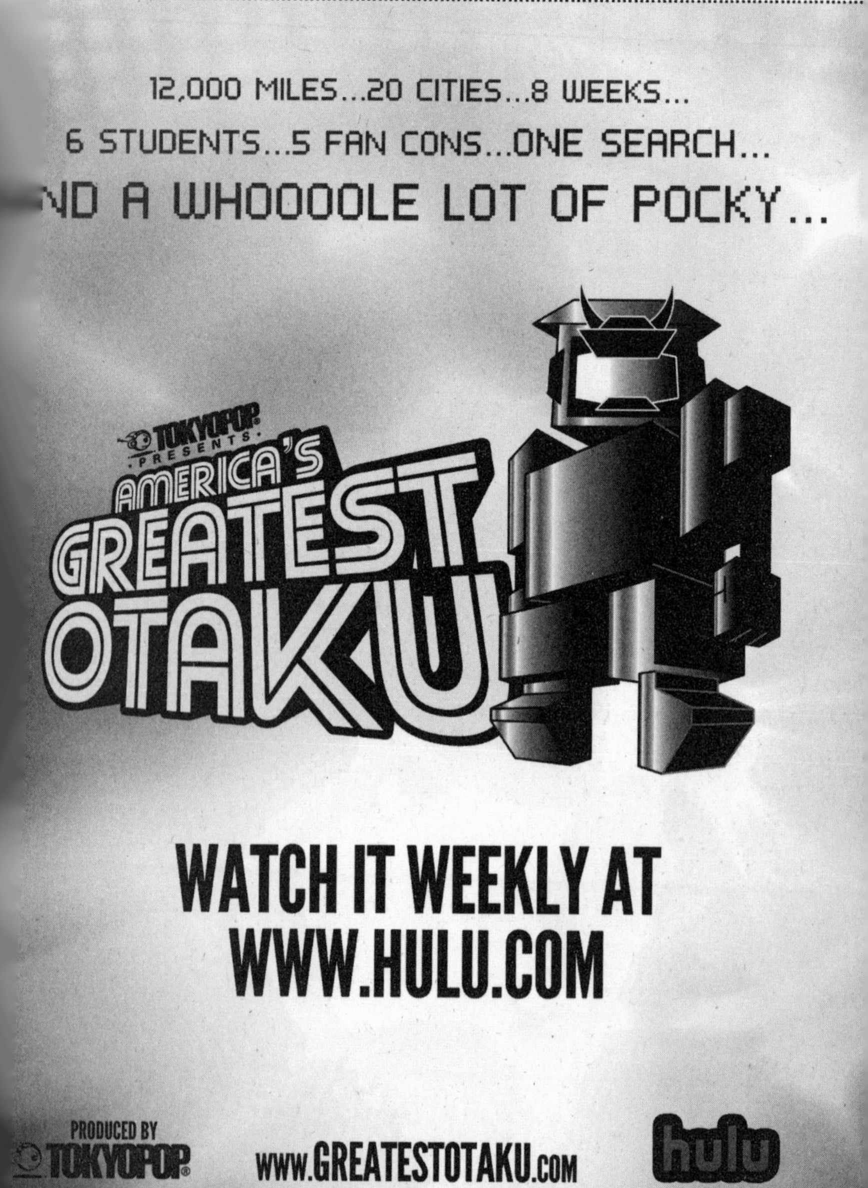
12,000 MILES...20 CITIES...8 WEEKS...
6 STUDENTS...5 FAN CONS...ONE SEARCH...
ND A WHOOOOLE LOT OF POCKY...
TOKYOPOP PRESENTS
AMERICA'S GREATEST OTAKU
WATCH IT WEEKLY AT WWW.HULU.COM
PRODUCED BY TOKYOPOP
www.GREATESTOTAKU.com
hulu

BE SURE TO VISIT WWW.TOKYOPOP.COM/SHOP FOR EVERYTHING YOU COULD EVER WANT!

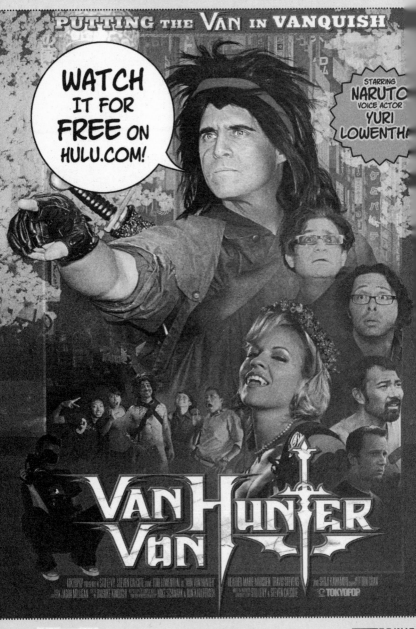

chibi Vampire
AIRMAIL
TOKYOPOP
Created By:
Yuna Kagesaki

**The wait is over, Karin Fans,
Chibi Vampire:
Airmail is here!**

A collection of manga stories that follows the continuing adventures of our favorite vampire, Karin! In these short stories, you'll find out what happened to our favorite characters and even get a glimpse of some European vampires that were never seen in the main series! Also included are some manga strips detailing creator Yuna Kagesaki's trip to Seattle's Sakura-Con!

COMEDY OT OLDER TEEN AGE 16+

BE SURE TO VISIT WWW.TOKYOPOP.COM/SHOP FOR EVERYTHING YOU COULD EVER WANT!

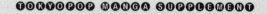

Learn From the Best!

Featuring the artists behind *Fruits Basket*, *Vampire Knight*, *Maid Sama* and many more!

SHOJO MANGA KA NI NARO! © 2006
Hana to Yume, Bessatsu Hana to Yume, LaLa, Melody / HAKUSENSHA, Inc.

Wanna draw your own sl
manga but not quite sure
where to start? The edite
Hakusensha Publishing, h
of such beloved shojo ser
Fruits Basket, *Vampire Kn*
Maid Sama and *Ouran Hig*
School Host Club, have
assembled a book jam-pac
with useful tips and practi
advice to help you develop
your skills and go from
beginner to ready for the
manga big leagues!

Join aspiring artist Ena as
strives to make her big bre
drawing manga. Aided by
editor, Sasaki, and some o
the best shojo artists in Ja
follow along as Ena create:
short story from start to
finish, and gets professiona
feedback along the way. Fr
page layout and pacing to
pencils and perspective, th
guide covers the basics, an
then challenges you to go
the next level! Does Ena (a
you!) have what it takes to
pro? Pick up this book and
learn from the best!

ROMANCE

TOKYOPOP MANGA SUPPLEMENT

Happy CAFE

Enjoy VOL 4

Our strong and sweet heroine continues to spread happiness at Café Bonheur . . .

Happy
CAFE
Enjoy
VOL 4
Kou Matsuzuki

Uru finds herself stuck in Shindo's apartment during a blackout. As the evening wears on, she accidentally falls asleep on hi shoulder, keeping him up all night and eventually getting him sick! Ca Uru help cure his ills?

If you like Me and My Brothers, you'll definitely enjoy Happy Café!

BE SURE TO VISIT WWW.TOKYOPOP.COM/SHOP FOR EVERYTHING YOU COULD EVER WANT!

STOP!

This is the back of the book.
ou wouldn't want to spoil a great ending!

ıis book is printed "manga-style," in the authentic Japanese right-to-left ɾrmat. Since none of the artwork has been flipped or altered, readers ɛt to experience the story just as the creator intended. You've been ɜking for it, so TOKYOPOP® delivered: authentic, hot-off-the-press, ıd far more fun!

1
2
3
4
5
6
7
8
9
10

DIRECTIONS

If this is your first time reading manga-style, here's a quick guide to help you understand how it works.

It's easy... just start in the top right panel and follow the numbers. Have fun, and look for more 100% authentic manga from TOKYOPOP®!

THE MANGA REVOLUTION • LEADING THE MANGA REVOLUTION • LEADING
漫画革命